On the
Edge

On the Edge

Living with an Enlightened Master

Yoga Punya

Although I have researched the events depicted in this book to the best of my knowledge, this is still a personal account, so any errors or misconceptions are all my own.
Some names have been changed to protect privacy or because I could not remember them.

ISBN: 978-1507787960 (CreateSpace)
2nd edition 2016

Cover design and photo of Fool by Shivananda Ackermann
Cover background photo from iStockphoto
Photos of author by Lollas Studio
Photo of and quotes by Osho © Osho International Foundation
Website with photos for each chapter: punya.eu

For Osho, my beloved Master

Contents

Foreword

In the past few years there has been spate of books written about Osho, by both sannyasins and non-sannyasins. This is excellent because no single book, written by any particular person, can alone encompass the complexity, the sheer enormity, the wondrous luminosity of Osho's life and legacy. It is the different points of view, written from the perspectives of widely differing people, which collectively create a tapestry that illustrates something of the extraordinary phenomenon that is the enlightened master, Osho.

In my humble opinion, Punya's book, 'On the Edge', ranks as one of the more important of all these books. Punya was not a 'close' (in physically proximity at any rate) disciple; she was not a famous person, she was not one of the acclaimed (rightly or wrongly) group leaders doing Osho's work; rather, she was a regular commune member going about the regular commune routine of work, play and meditation.

Punya first met Osho in Mumbai in 1974 (making her one of the 'older' sannyasins) and has stayed with him through all the various phases and changes of the communes in India, the United States and around the world. She now lives in Corfu, Greece, where a different kind of sannyasin community has developed, enabling her to maintain an intimate connection with sannyas and Osho.

Her book is a collection of experiences written in such picturesque detail that the reader is plunged into those hauntingly beautiful moments of the sights and sounds of early morning India, the arid vastness of the Ranch in Oregon, the magic of the music produced seemingly unrehearsed and without effort by the commune musicians, the joy of the love and friendship of thousands of seekers gathered together in one place at one time – and of course the unfathomable silence and mystery surrounding our beloved master.

But hers is also a down-to-earth factual account of the day to day functioning of the various communes in their various manifestations and, as such, provides an invaluable 'historical' record for posterity. She has a phenomenal recall of events and did a huge amount of research to be as accurate as possible about chronologies, dates, discourse series, names of places, people and politicians, specific factual data etc, etc. The book is written in a poetic, humourous, observant, devotional, reflective and highly intelligent way. I know of no other that records the times with Osho and his communes so comprehensively.

Punya was in a unique position to chronicle all these events because it is her multi-faceted character, with her huge number of differing skills, that allowed her to 'jump into' and successfully perform so many of the 'jobs' that had to be done in order for the communes to function efficiently. I had four 'jobs' in my long time in the commune – Punya must have had over twenty!

Her classical education gave her a love of and proficiency in languages. Living in Italy but with Swiss parents she spoke Italian and Swiss German from an early age and later learned High German, French and finally English. These language skills were of huge importance in an international community such as ours and enabled her to work in many departments where dealing with the people flocking in from all over the world was necessary.

To earn the money to visit and live in the various communes, she focused on well-paid office management jobs, most particularly in the fields of publishing and advertising, in both Switzerland and Italy. Again these skills were to prove invaluable in many departments in the communes; for example, putting the Ranch's PR office in order – the 'Twinkies', as the women running that department were called – were great at smiling and imparting information to all the visiting tourists and government officials, but not so good at keeping a busy office organised. Punya was also able to give tours in four different languages to the thousands visiting the Ranch. No-one else could do that!

Being physically strong and coordinated she was a valued worker on Ranch construction sites and also drove taxis and buses shepherding sannyasins and goods around the Ranch. In Pune 1 she worked for years in the commune kitchens under the eagle eye of Deeksha – a huge learning experience in itself which provides a myriad of dramatic stories! Because of her passion for music she was involved in many events as music was an intrinsic part of our commune life and meditations. And last but not least, she was focused totally on being a disciple of her beloved master. All of this adds up to a rare position from which to observe and record all that was going on.

'On the Edge' is not an obviously chronological account; rather, it is like looking through a treasured photo album and coming across this snapshot and that, sometimes looking back, sometimes looking forward, sometimes in the here-and-now. As one delves further, however, it becomes apparent that Punya is using an intriguing device: there are parallel sequences or threads of past and present interlacing throughout the text. Her stories are further enhanced by well-chosen, revealing quotes from Osho which give them further dimensions and poignancy.

While older sannyasins will greatly enjoy the memories of so many special moments triggered by Punya's words, those newer sannyasins now working on their own spiritual path, and the vast number of people around the world now fascinated by Osho, can also savour something of the ambience of being in his presence, can gain touching unknown glimpses and a deeper more comprehensive understanding of the life and work of this great master – this Buddha for our present times – and the people who came from all corners of the globe to be transformed by him.

This is a very special, very precious book.

Ma Prema Veena (Veena Schlegel), July 2013

1

Yes, This Is It!

Dynamic

For some mysterious reason I promised myself to do 21 days of Dynamic. I am now halfway through the three weeks and by now I wake up by myself, even before the clunky loud alarm clock goes off. My partner's slight snoring tells me that my getting up from bed has not woken him up. It is 5:30am and, being winter, it is pitch black outside. My clothes lie ready on the chair in the living room. I throw a maroon robe over my knickers and bra and, after a quick brushing of teeth, fling a shawl over my shoulders.
I carefully slide the inside bolt open and the flat's door closes with a just perceptible click. In order not to wake up the whole neighbourhood, I place my feet flat on the marble steps as I walk down the few flights of stairs until I reach the street where I can let my flip-flops do their happy flip-flopping while I walk.

The road is now known to me in all its details and I could walk it with closed eyes. I know exactly where that treacherous open manhole is and where the banyan trees have lowered their roots onto unsuspecting passers-by to catch them by their hair. The brisk walk keeps me warm, but I am in no hurry, so can enjoy the walk as a walk and not just as a march to a destination. I can tune into the rhythm of my legs' stride accented by the 'flupflup' of my rubber *chappals*, and listen to the birds chirping and calling the new day (they know it is coming, although it is still dark). I hear the low rumbling of lorries approaching town over the distant bridge and then, closer, the high-pitched sound of rented Kinetic Hondas being parked along the road at the back gate by other early meditators. Our destination is the Osho Meditation Resort

and we are in Pune, India. The year is 1994. We produce our
meditation passes at the gate to the guard who pretends to check
them in the dark, and slip through the gate.

The paths through the garden are lit in places by low lights
peeping from under luscious foliage. There are many opportunities to stumble and fall as the path meanders here and there
and the steps have different heights – as if it was intentionally
designed in such a way that we have to remain mindful at all
times. People in maroon robes are now also streaming in from the
well-lit front gate, with trailing shawls and blindfolds in hand.
We move through the opening in the mosquito netting which
surrounds the hall. A single bulb faintly illuminates a portrait of
Osho displayed on an easel on top of the podium, the very place
from where he used to talk to us. My favourite spot is on the right
of it, close to the netting – I like to feel the breeze and, when
I open my eyes again, I want the plants in the garden to be the
first things I see.

There is some tapping on the microphone by the meditation
leader of the day to check if it is working, and then come the
instructions. I always like to hear the instructions although I do
not need to understand anything new, but they bring my attention
to where I am and what I am going to do next, a bit like putting
on the safety belt to bring myself into 'driving mode'. This time it
is 'dynamic mode' which for me means 'totality': breathing totally,
catharting totally, jumping totally, then remaining absolutely
still like a statue – until I can dance lightly in those last fifteen
minutes, first arms then torso flowing with the music, and enjoy
the freedom of movement in the fresh air. I feel part of the new
morning, which is already being celebrated by the chirping
melodies of the birds.

The very first time I did Dynamic Meditation was on a beach; more
precisely, on Chowpatti Beach in Mumbai. It was also 6am and it was
also winter and dark. Two days earlier, two Italian girls had invited
me to attend but then I overslept and missed, so I was quite proud to

have made it this time – although I had to convince my poor Indian hosts to set up alarm clocks in my room and in theirs to assure my getting up. A dozen of us gathered around a young man who gave the instructions on how to do the meditation and then – at a signal – off we went, each one on his or her little spot on the beach. I plunged with all my youthful power and stamina into the heavy and chaotic breathing, oblivious of any passers-by who must have thought we were crazy. Then came the catharsis! What a freedom it was to scream and shout – to let out all the steam – and be allowed, even encouraged, to do it!

That moment I knew: "Yes, this is it! I have found it!"

I have tried this way and that to avoid writing about my life before this event, but I think I need to give some clues about what this discovery actually meant for me. The first time I remember looking for 'it' was in grammar school. I remember writing with green ink the words of Socrates, *Know Thyself,* in big Greek letters on the first page of our student song book. These two words must have intrigued me so much that I started, quite unconsciously and casually, to look for ways to find this 'Thyself'.

I came across Jesudian and Haich's book on Hatha Yoga which impressed me, not so much because of the illustrations of the strange postures on its glossy pages, but because of the statement that God lives within ourselves, and not somewhere outside, high up in the sky, as it was common to think in a Christian environment. It was probably the first book on Yoga available to the general, German-speaking public. The first Yoga school in Switzerland had been opened in Zurich by the authors probably just a few years earlier. So Yoga was still something exotic at the time.

The idea that God lived within ourselves made so much sense to me that it brought all my church-going to a fairly abrupt end, much to the disappointment of the Mother Superior who was running the Catholic boarding house where I was living. I managed to get fainting attacks during our early morning Thursday Masses in our little chapel, just below my room, so I was exempted from attending them for good. Mother Superior frequently asked me if I had been to church on Sundays but it was very easy for me to lie! When my father heard about it he was very disappointed because he had thought that by having me stay at the Catholic home while studying at grammar school he had done his Christian duty. On the other hand, my mother and my grandparents could not have cared less because they were Protestants.

For my final exams I chose the subject of Baroque poetry which turned out to be boring and tedious, in contrast to the music of that period which fascinated me tremendously. So it often happened that, while sitting on a bench along the river Aar and stooped over the rhymed verses almost in despair, I looked at the river for solace and dreamed of a country house in the Vosges mountains in France, where people would have gathered to work together and – at the same time – find out who they were. A bit like a monastery but without the praying, the black robes and the miserable vibe about it. That this place was in France, a country not too far from where I was living but with which I had no ties whatsoever, was the most intriguing part of the picture.

When I and my fellow students finally had our baccalaureate in hand we discussed our decisions about what we were going to study next. My fellow students knew that I was going to the Arts and Crafts School in Zurich for which I had already passed the entry test. They knew that I was good at drawing and Art History, but not so good at Mathematics or German. The other students were going to study Theology, History, German or Biology, etc.

When I once asked myself what I really wanted to make out of my life, I knew that I could tell some friends that I wanted to become a photographer, and my more intimate friends that I wanted to become a mime artist. But what I really wanted to become was something I could not tell anyone and that was to become a 'saint'. When this word popped up in my head I was astonished – it was not really a word in my vocabulary, as I had left all the Saint Theresas and Anthonys from religion class far behind.

Some people might assume that maybe a psychological imbalance was behind these ideas, but I think that I was quite a 'normal' teenager. We all felt the pressure of school, the demands of our Swiss parents for whom we were never 'good enough', the fears of not passing exams – although in my case there might have been slightly more problems than for others because I was far away from my family and was not studying in my mother tongue.

My father had not only wanted to fulfil his religious duty but also those of a Swiss expat in Italy. So when I had turned 14 he sent me to Switzerland because he wanted me to learn German properly and that was the only way, at the time. My grandparents would be living close by and I could visit them over the weekends. I knew them quite well from the many times I had spent with them as a small child and from the summer months which we always spent at their holiday cottage.

When I arrived at school I was suddenly at a disadvantage because my classmates were one to two years older than me. Also, this was the class which had Greek and Hebrew as an option, so was full of what we call 'nerds' nowadays, but I never felt I was talked down to. My German was really awful in my first year, but my fellow students and the Latin teacher enjoyed it when I read aloud from the *De Bello Gallico* in the way the Italians thought the Romans had spoken, with all the soft Cs and Gs and, of course, with an Italian accent. Slowly, slowly my German vocabulary and grammar improved whilst at the same time my native Italian, which I never spoke except during the few weeks of holidays, deteriorated drastically.

It might have been lonely for a teenager not to have a mother to confide hopes and fears to, or to talk about crushes on this boy or that, but my mother had not much say in big decisions at home. This was a patriarchal family! She was just so happy that my father had delayed the application to a boarding school until it was too late, otherwise I would have ended up in a huge forbidding Catholic school for girls only. (Whenever I ride past that school on a train, near Brunnen, I still get goose bumps!)

Aarau, the town where the grammar school was and where I

lived, was famous for its culture, with a big C. It had just opened a modern art museum which we visited on our own and with our art teacher, and there were weekly concerts, operas and theatre performances by many famous companies and soloists. I had a best friend called Bica, who stimulated me intellectually and artistically, and I was adopted by her boyfriend's family at whose home we were dinner guests once a week. I was allowed to play on their grand piano whenever I wanted. The father was a successful painter and the mother was interested in Yoga and other occult things – she was the one to whom I had confided that I wanted to become a mime artist. Her name was Eva and she reminded me of a character of the same name in Hermann Hesse's *Demian* – and in a way she was my surrogate, more intellectual, mother for those years.

My real mother, on the other hand, had left the family in Milan and escaped with a young lover to live in the South of France. Although I used to write her long letters I never received an answer and wondered why. I always felt her more like a big sister rather than a mother so, in a way, I liked the idea of her crazy adventure. Sometimes I used to go into the woods on a full moon night and 'talk' to her, just sending greetings, without crying or feeling miserable about myself. 'This is how it is and let's make the best out of it' must have been my motto.

At art school my artistic abilities were soon put into perspective by the likes of Urs Lüthi and David Weiss who were quite a few years younger than me. They painted with the power of tigers and had creative ideas which were totally out of the box, whilst my work always looked 'too harmonious', as they said, which meant good but boring. The experience of this introductory year was one of the best things that happened before my time with Osho and credit goes to our main teacher, Hansjörg Mattmüller. We learned from him to make the pencil tips 'hum' on the paper, to let the arm move the hand in big strokes, to construct a painting with rigid logic and then bring in something odd, out of the ordinary. His deep respect for each one of us and our different ways of expressing ourselves made us forgive him when he gave us the task of copying natural objects (a tedious project on which we worked at one piece for an entire year – albeit in stages). But he was clever enough, in the afternoons, to allow us to splash with wild colours and use various media like sand and scouring powder. The command was, "Put on your aprons!" and then the fun began.

I had started taking photographs at age 12 with a plastic one-click camera which was given to me as a long awaited birthday present. The subsequent upgrades had interchangeable lenses, a manual focus and aperture – and then 32mm film with lots of shots became available. Objects of my experiments were my ever compliant sisters in various poses, and later Bica, until I ventured into the streets taking snap shots *à la* Breton and Bischof who were my heroes. They took photographs in far away countries and this is where I wanted to go – and get paid for it. (I had also thought of studying medicine after reading Dr. Schweitzer's autobiography – not so much for helping people but for the travelling.)

So here I was taking my four-day exam for the very prestigious photo class in the college (Oliviero Toscani was still there, if you do not mind me dropping another famous name). There were 21 applicants and only a third would get accepted. But a few things went wrong with the camera and one day I even came late – very strange. I was also missing the necessary emotional support because our beloved teacher was away for his yearly military duties, and my mother…

A few months previously my mother had suddenly appeared at the college and I was called out of class. I can still see her standing there at the end of the long corridor in a pink outfit with a little pink hat! She had escaped from her lover in France and deeply regretted having left the family. I also came to hear that all the mail we had sent to her had been confiscated by the lover out of fear she would leave him and return to us.

It made sense that we would share the flat my father had given to me to stay in while I was studying in Zurich; it was half an hour away from town by train. Quite soon she found a job as a shop assistant which unfortunately was not the best option for her poor legs. At night she was exhausted from eight hours of standing and being nice to people. Hence she wasn't much of an emotional support to me.

Although my portfolio and the photos taken during the exams were praised, the verdict was, "Your work is good, but we only want to take one girl (they soon get married, etc.). The other girl is younger so we will take her. You already have the baccalaureate and you will have more chances." There was not much support from anywhere to digest this either. I guess I was in shock because I do not remember what came next. I just see myself back in Milan. There was no Plan B and I was too scared to discuss with father what I should do next. He was, from the very start, strongly against me choosing an artistic and 'artisan' profession like photography, when I could work in an office 'with my languages'. Even more so when I mentioned mime and work in theatre.

I had already taken mime classes in Zurich and now, back in Milan, I enrolled at the school of the Piccolo Teatro. The teacher, Marise Flach, was so impressed by my ability to create invisible objects that she allowed me to attend the evening classes as well, at no extra cost. We put on a show at the end of the year, but I did not manage to find companions to start our own company, maybe due to my tall frame which, in those days, was quite unusual for Italy. Later I was even asked to be part of a proper production at the Piccolo, but had to cancel the invitation because I was at the beginning of a pregnancy and, at the time, had decided to go through with it. I did, however, change my mind and had an abortion but then it was too late to join the rehearsals.

It was my impression that I had something to express and that I could do this through one art form or another. But my desire to make my way in the arts kept encountering one obstacle after the other. When my father finally consented to support me for a six-month period when I could be a volunteer with one of the big photographers in Milan, I visited each of them and their comments were, "We cannot ask you as a girl to help us carry our heavy equipment from place to place." Another suggested I remain nonprofessional saying, "If you start working as a professional photographer you will lose your spontaneity and expressiveness."

Eventually, after working as a layout designer for a couple of years, earning peanuts, I succumbed to the necessity of working in an office. It was going to be with a publisher, Giangiacomo Feltrinelli Editore. I had no training in typing, and they knew that, but they were keen on my knowledge of German and French and so I was quickly posted to the contract office which dealt with the translators and publishers from all over the world. Slowly my typing picked up speed and I learned many office organisational skills from the secretaries there. I left when I understood that my English needed improving and spent a six-month period as an *au pair* in London to do my Cambridge Proficiency. I lived near prestigious Baker Street, just opposite the Anthroposophical Society. I had read a few books by Steiner and was tempted a few times to push open that heavy door, but always desisted.

Upon my return to Milan I found work at a magazine publisher. And after I had learned as much as I could about printing and editing and no longer felt sufficiently challenged, I moved to an import-export company whose boss needed a secretary with fluent German. I slowly built up a proper import department – with those acquired organisational skills – and even had an assistant. My boss was so pleased with my work that he gave me a bonus on my salary out of his own pocket. In this company there was one young employee who was studying Biology at the University at night. This felt very tempting. Maybe my search for 'what life is' could be found through studying nature? From an economical point of view this change in career didn't make much sense because, as I heard later from some student friends, any salary after the degree would not have been much more than what I was getting already. But there was something pushing me to go along this route. So I enrolled and after a few months my boss allowed me to work part time so that I could dedicate more hours to my studies. With this change of contract I was also allowed to take a few weeks holiday – in the middle of winter!

At this point I have to introduce my Portuguese friend, João, with whom I had been sharing a flat for the previous few years. He had a graphic design studio together with a friend just across the landing. Life was full with friends and parties and fun: cinema, dinners and taxi rides at the beginning of the month and tram rides and dinners at home towards the end. Our flat was filled with artists, painters, and photographers every night – I am not sure if it was because of my successful culinary experiments or because of the still-natural Barbera wine we used to get from a vendor on our side street. We even had guests stay with us for months at a time in our tiny flat. João was happy with my going to Yoga classes and happy with my new studies. He was proud of being with a 'modern', independent woman.

On the same landing there was a third flat and we became friends with the couple living there. One day I saw one of their friends take leave at their door. He had long blond hair and was wearing an orange outfit; around his neck there was a long necklace made of wooden beads with a pendant. Very spontaneously I grabbed the pendant and looked at the picture on it. It showed a bearded man with a bald head and happy eyes. I turned the pendant around to see what was on the back and was surprised to see the same picture. I asked him who this man was.

"He is my master."

"Did you meet him personally? Can you actually talk to him?"

"Oh yes. He lives in India."

There was not much more to get out of him as he was in a hurry to leave and, imagining the long and expensive journey to India (a country I had always wanted to visit, even as a child), I buried this meeting in deep recesses of my unconscious, so much so that I remembered it only when I saw this man again – after an entire year of wearing orange clothes and one of those necklaces myself.

When João's business partner, who used to be a flight attendant, decided to go back to a regular job he easily found one with an airline. It was Air India and it so happened that within a few weeks he got a new manager who had just arrived from India. We liked Saeed and we soon showed him around town and took him to our favourite restaurants and bars. A few weeks later his wife, Ashrafa, and their two little daughters arrived. They were accompanied by Husena, the girls' grandmother, to help out in the household and I remember a delightful incident about her: It was already autumn and they needed to find suitable footwear for her. It took them a whole day and still they came back without any shoes – they were all either too tight, in the front or in the back, or too large. This comes from wearing sandals your whole life; feet spoiled with freedom.

Our friendship grew closer and we often got invited to their home – and we enjoyed our very first Indian meal! There were no Indian restaurants in Milan, nor was there any other foreign food available in Italy in those days. So for us, being with them was a new and exotic adventure.

One day João was asked by Saeed to make a plan for a new interior design in his office. As his plans in the end were not carried out, probably for budget reasons, he was paid, not in cash, but with a ticket to India – the equivalent of two of our monthly wages. But as India and Portugal were still squabbling over Goa, Portuguese citizens were not allowed entry – which meant that the ticket went to ME!

Because I had changed my work contract from full-time to part-time I received a good redundancy payment and, as I said before, was allowed to take a holiday in December – although holidays in Italy were usually only in August. And now there was a ticket...

Once a year, around Christmas I used to write and receive a letter from a friend in Holland; I got to know her because she was the mother of an elementary schoolmate, but our friendship developed independently. We had this beautiful ritual of writing to each other once a year, a ritual which continued for at least 10 years. That Christmas I summarised the happenings: my imminent journey to India, the unexpected cash and holidays, my good understanding with João. Everything was a gift fallen from heaven. I was scared to death. 'It was too good to be true', I wrote.

At the very moment I was struggling to close my suitcase I

received a phone call. The man at the other end had heard from his friends, my next-door neighbours, that I was leaving for India and he wanted me to have an address. I wrote it down: Bhagwan Shree Rajneesh (this is how Osho was called in those days), A-1 Woodland, Peddar Road, Bombay (now Mumbai).

"You will come back totally transformed," he added. But I had no clue what he meant by 'transformed'…

In Mumbai I was picked up at the airport by Shabbir, Ashrafa's brother, and brought to their home in downtown Colaba in a memorable taxi ride. The following morning I ventured out on my own to discover the neighbourhood. We were living close to the Gateway of India, a sandstone arch built during the British Raj, facing the port on one side and the Taj Mahal Hotel on the other. On the side streets there were many antique shops with beautiful Indian artefacts on sale. It was a world of new smells, colours, foods and sounds. Shabbir, who was still a student, often took me with some of his friends to one of the many tea shops around there and I learned how to drink the national beverage *chai*, which was served in tiny glasses, without burning my fingers.

I soon became part of the family and learned from Husena, Shabbir's mother, how to fold *samosas*; because they were Muslims they were filled with minced meat. I also watched her prepare *chapattis*, the traditional flat breads. With swift movements of her wrist she rolled little dough balls – at supersonic speed – into perfectly round flat breads with a tiny rolling pin. They were then flung onto a slightly curved metal plate filled with an already sizzling dollop of purified butter. When done, they were stacked on a plate ready for lunch.

This plate was a fatal attraction for a ubiquitous inhabitant of India: the crows. I watched one sneak through the anti-burglar bars which guarded the kitchen windows, pick up a *chapatti* and fly off with it hanging from its beak. All this behind Husena's back. When she saw what was happening it was way too late for her screaming and waving of arms to have any effect.

On that day crows became my favourite birds!

After I had visited all the museums in town as well as the handloom fabric bazaars, I thought of moving on. As a teenager I had many pen pals from all continents because this was the only way, back then, to get to know something of the world. One of them was Kirtidev. He was an Indian medical student in London during the time I attended grammar school in Aarau. One day, on his way back to India, he came to visit me and we went on an excursion into the mountains. On Mount Rigi there was a high wind and while walking he said to me, "Feel the wind on your cheeks!"

This one sentence changed the way I perceived my body from then on. The body was not something to transcend but to cherish. This was a totally new outlook for someone like me who came from a culture where the body was something to be overcome and neglected for 'higher' values, like the spirit. Many times I would then, with closed eyes, take a bath and feel the warm water around my body and not think of anything else.

I was so grateful to Kirtidev for that one sentence that a visit to him was a must. He was living in Ahmedabad, still at the same address I knew by heart, but he was now married, of course. He and his wife showed me around town; we saw the palace where he grew up and which was later confiscated by the state, we climbed the famous shaking tower, and then, back at home, his wife showed me an heirloom. A sari woven entirely of gold! But what struck me the most was a little photograph wedged into the frame of a mirror. Kirtidev told me that it was their guru who would come once or twice a year to visit them. I thought that it would be nice to have a guru who could help me in finding what I wanted to find; to have some guidance in my ever so unconscious and sporadic search. At any rate, I decided that, when back in Mumbai, I would definitely go and seek out that other guru whose address was in my travel diary.

There were many more addresses in the diary, of shops, hotels and travel agents which Saeed had given me. I visited New Delhi, Jaipur in Rajasthan (an elephant ride was part of the excursion) and of course the splendid Taj Mahal in Agra. I was almost embarrassed to be wearing blue jeans and a white top, seeing how beautifully the coloured saris of the Indian women highlighted the white marble arches from a distance.

I spent a lonely Christmas in a hotel in New Delhi with belly dancers in the main hall – and then it was time to head south to Mumbai as there were only a couple of days left before my departure. It was an almost two-day train ride but it was very comfortable. In the ladies' compartment the bunk beds were placed along the windows and I could look out the small grated windows as if from a recliner. I watched this beautiful country slide by – at a slow pace which made it even easier to absorb.

As soon as I arrived in Mumbai I took a taxi to the address in my diary. 'Woodland', or 'Woodlands' how everybody called it, turned out to be a multi-storied apartment complex in the middle of this busy city. It had a few mature trees in front of it which looked like Cedars of Lebanon to me. The taxi climbed the ramp and dropped me at House A where the uniformed watchman showed me the stairs to the first floor. The door was opened by a servant who ushered me in and introduced me to a little woman who was wearing a *kurta* and *lungi*, the traditional Indian outfit I had come to know, and hers was in orange. Later I was told she was called Laxmi and that she was Osho's secreatary. She welcomed me with a fresh smile and told me that there would be a lecture that night at 7pm and that I could come under condition that I was freshly bathed and wearing clean clothes. She asked me where I was from and when she heard I was from Italy she called for Lalita and Deeksha who were also from Italy. Lalita was hiding behind big glasses and let Deeksha do the talking. She was the perfect PR person for that. They took me down some stairs into the living room. It was quite a sight as its walls were full of shelves crammed with books. Some other people, also wearing orange clothes, were sitting on pillows on the floor, reading or softly talking to each other.

Deeksha introduced me to the various stages of a meditation with chaotic breathing. She was adamant that I try it out and explained to me where I would find their group on the beach the next morning. She also talked about how Osho accepted sex as a natural phenomenon which we should live out instead of repressing. I was a bit shocked because sex was not something people would talk about in those days. We did have *Playboy* which was, by the way, the only magazine I bought because of its intelligent articles, but the word 'orgasm' had not yet become the 'in' word in women's magazines. Before I left, Deeksha gave me a few booklets to read and I think that one of them was called *From Sex to Superconsciousness*.

I had learned how to read the numbers written in Hindi on the buses and was proud to reach home with one of them instead of using the expensive taxis. I was going to take the same bus back in the evening for the lecture. That was the plan – but it turned out that the bus, in the other direction, made an unexpected loop, causing me to arrive at Woodlands after 7pm. I ran up the flight of stairs, saw all the many sandals lined up on the landing, and the door was locked! I was late. The lecture had started. I was left out. And tomorrow I was leaving!

To my delight I learnt the next morning that my flight was booked out and that I could not fly that day. It seemed that I should have re-confirmed my return a few days before but I was still a novice traveller so hadn't done it. This meant that I could go to the lecture and do the meditation which I had also missed. When I met Deeksha a day later at breakfast after the meditation and told her the whole story, she said, "It's all the mind coming in the way. It's all the mind!" I had absolutely no clue what she meant by 'the mind'.

The lecture was held in that big living room lined with bookshelves. I sat down at the back because Deeksha had told me that the seats in front were reserved for the *sannyasins*, the disciples, which I understood were the ones wearing orange. I was a bit disappointed because I wanted to see the man from close up and wanted to be seen: I wanted this 'Bhagwan' to know that I was here, that I had arrived. Osho was talking about Yoga and I heard the name Patanjali from time to time, but could not make out much more of his lecture. His accent was very heavy and I was not yet accustomed enough to Indian English to understand it easily. Also his physical presence did not have the same impact as the 'aha' moment I had experienced during the meditation in the morning. But I would not have to wait too long for things to change.

After a few days Deeksha had an appointment to see Osho and I was invited to go along. I followed her into his room and copied her way of greeting him with folded hands in *namaste* and then sat next to her on the floor at his feet. He asked me if I had been to his lectures which I affirmed – and in the back of my mind I understood immediately that I was not going to get much recognition from this man. How could he have missed seeing that new fair-skinned woman sitting erect at the back of the audience?

Deeksha had brought with her a long letter from her lover in Italy and was reading it to Osho. In the meantime Osho was holding my right hand and swaying my arm from side to side while he was listening to her. It felt awkward at first but then I relaxed into the rhythm and the swaying became like a lullaby. It must have taken some of my apprehension away because when we left, I looked straight into his smiling eyes and saw in there something I had not seen before in any person's eyes. I had never experienced anyone look at me like that. They seemed to say, "You are accepted and loved exactly the way you are!" No hints of improvements to be made, no shoulds or buts.

And those eyes captured me forever!

Deeksha told me that the following week there was going to be a ten-day meditation gathering at a hill station in the north of India and she insisted that I should postpone my departure and come along. She was so determined that she arranged for me to see a doctor who could write a sick note – I think I had 'amoebic dysentery' – and booked the hotel for me and the train journey together with hers once I had agreed to go. I sent a wire to the office in Milan saying that I would be back in a month and re-booked my flight.

Before making my decision I wanted to ask Osho if I was 'spiritual enough', or some strange concept like this, to attend the camp (these meditation gatherings were called 'camps' because in the past people would actually sleep in tents – and the word stuck). But Osho was taken ill, all interviews were cancelled and I had to decide for myself. When interviews were again available Laxmi gave me an appointment, but I had nothing left to say. But Osho had something to ask and that was: "Do you want to take sannyas?" to which I replied with an almost scared, "Maybe after the camp."

From Deeksha I had heard the expressions 'to take *sannyas*' and '*sannyasins*', the people who have 'taken *sannyas*'. '*Sannyas*' was apparently the Hindi word for 'monk'. Unlike these traditional sannyasins, Osho's sannyasins did not have to renounce the world, but he kept the traditional orange colour of the clothes and the necklace, the *mala*. His sannyasins also received a new name.

Surrounded by these orange people, all so excited to leave for the camp, and chatting to them while drinking tea at the chai shack after the meditation, I started to feel awkward in my blue jeans and white top. I did not want to feel like an outsider; I wanted to become part of this whirlwind which was happening around me. I booked for an interview with the intention of taking sannyas, although it was not yet 'after the camp' as I had planned.

"Your name will be Ma Yoga Punya. *Ma* means mother. I call all my women sannyasins *Ma*, because all women are basically mothers. *Yoga* means union and *Punya* means virtue." This is what I remember Osho saying to me. When we used to translate from Latin, the word *virtus* (virtue) always had a tinge of morality and to be called this was not really to my liking; also that the name would start with a P (which is brown in my mind's eye) and followed by a U which is such a 'pushy' vowel did not go down well either. Moreover, to be called a 'good' person really pushed my buttons (although this expression had not entered our vocabulary yet). How did Osho know that I was always trying to be a good girl to get people's approval?

I asked Osho about the exact meaning of the word 'Punya' and if it had that sense of morality in it. His reply was, if I remember correctly, "Virtue is the opposite of sin. In Hindi we have the two words – *papi* for sin and *punya* for virtue." In the meantime I have understood that what Osho means with sin is totally different from what I knew then. His meaning of 'sin' is to go off the track, to be unaware, to act unconsciously. At times I ponder over the meaning of my name and I sense something like 'action with awareness and love', but I rarely think about the meaning of my name.

When I got up to leave, Osho said with a smile something like, "I know you will go very far." This is the first time I have said this to anyone. I did not know what he meant by it, and still do not know, but it certainly was an exquisite encouragement at the beginning of this very beautiful journey.

The next morning I found my reserved seat in a ladies' compartment on the train waiting at 'Bombay Central'. We were going to a hill station called Mt. Abu in Gujarat. Already seated on the comfortable padded seats were Greek Mukta and Karuna, a big and loud Indian lady who, as I would discover, knew at each station we stopped which were the specialities we should buy from the vendors. It was a compartment full of jolly, orange-clad women, some from India, some from abroad, all talking with various accents. I do not remember that we slept but we must have because the journey was more than thirty hours long. When Mukta told me that Osho was travelling on the same train, in a separate air-conditioned carriage, it gave me a delightful feeling.

When we finally arrived at Abu Road, the junction below the hill station, we all got off the train, hauled our luggage into the waiting taxis and drove up the hill on a winding road until we reached Mt. Abu. My taxi stopped at a small Parsee guest house and let me out, while others were driven to the Palace Hotel where Osho was staying and where the meditations were going to be held. The guest house was simple but clean and my roommate was an American sannyasin. We had a great laugh the first night when we actually had to get dressed to go to bed because the room was so cold and there was no heating in the house (we were in a hill station and it was winter!).

The next morning, at the breakfast table, we met an Indian couple, Manu and Hansa (close friends to this day); Swabhav, with his imposing voice and his quieter wife; but best of all was the meeting with Sita who was there with her son. He had come all the way from Canada to attend the camp and to be with his mother, and was happy to translate between me and her. Sita's gentle demeanour made her connect with people's hearts at their very first encounter, and it is no wonder that she became for many of us a beloved grandmother figure.

The Parsees, it was explained to me, were originally from Persia and had come to India while escaping from the invasion of the Arabs (and forceful conversion). They do not consider themselves to be Indians even after centuries of living here: they have remained Zoroastrians by religion, do not cook spicy food and have a habit of decorating the front steps of their houses with intricate designs drawn with rice powder. So now, stepping out of the guest house was really a balancing act!

While walking to the meditations I would slowly start thawing in the first morning rays, slanting in at an angle. They gave the valley a warm, rusty tinge. During my travels in the previous weeks I had never come across a scene which reminded me of anything I had seen before, but now the little pond I saw in the distance, with its lonely palm tree mirroring the fronds in the water, was exactly the picture I had in my mind when thinking of India as a teenager: the red earth, the palm tree, but mostly the mysterious feeling which came with it. I knew I had come home.

Further up the road there was a beautiful, smooth rock. It was so huge and so dark that yellow marks had to be painted on it so that cars would not drive into it at night. I was going to become very fond of it and each time I passed by I would pat its polished surface in greeting. It felt so alive.

The Palace Hotel turned out to be an imposing regal mansion. I mostly remember the big hall on the ground floor with French windows opening onto the gardens from two sides. This was where the lectures and the meditations were taking place. At one end of the hall there was a podium from where Osho spoke and led the meditations and where the drummers would sit. The floor was soft; mattresses were placed there for us to sit on.

The day started with the morning meditation which was led by Osho. He gave a detailed introduction, in Hindi and in English, and once we had started he fired us up with calls to breathe harder, be more total, go more crazy. He supported our 'hoo hoo hoo'! in one of the phases – all this over the noise of the drummers who made a hell of a racket next to him. The meditation has gone through various changes since then. Osho worked on it and adjusted the phases over the years until it reached its present form of five stages. In those days the third stage was without the jumping and the final stage was lying down. But we were not spared because at night, after the evening lecture, we had the Tratak meditation and this was quite a number!

Osho would stand on the podium with arms raised, moving them up and down in rhythm with the drums. In the hall the hundreds of us had to jump up and down – trying not to step on each other's toes – shout 'hoo' and at the same time stare into Osho's eyes without blinking. And this lasted for half an hour! At times I felt that my body was jumping up and down and shouting independently from me and that I was resting somewhere in the middle, calmly looking into his eyes.

But before getting to this final, exhausting, meditation which made us all ready for bed, there were other events on the daily programme. After the 'chaotic meditation'– as Dynamic was called then – we had breakfast and a shower at our hotel or guest house and then attended the morning lecture back in the same hall. Once I became more accustomed to understanding Osho's English I was keen to memorise everything he said. The lectures were about Yoga and he commented on Patanjali's texts. I remember with a smile how after the lectures I would make notes on a pad on what he had said and then, with the help of my Indian fellow boarders, fill in the gaps which I had not understood.

The lectures were great eye-openers. Osho said things I had always known but had never heard anyone express and had never verbalised inside myself either. It was a continuous refrain in my head, "Of course, I know it but why has nobody ever said that before?"

Sometimes in the afternoons we had a healing session with Asanga. He would stand on top of a table and move about like a wizard: rotating his torso, gesturing with his arms and looking around with wide open eyes – while the drummers drummed furiously. I had never seen anything like it but decided to participate nonetheless. The atmosphere would get thicker and thicker in the hall like a dull hum – once, at some point, I started laughing and laughing and could not stop for the rest of the hour. I was rolling on the ground, tightly holding my tummy, feeling utterly stupid, but could not stop.

I do not know what had triggered this laughing attack but it got momentum when I remembered the dream I had had the previous night. It went like this: I went to visit Osho in his room where he was lying down on a quite dirty, brown and white striped bare mattress. Then a second visitor came in and started talking but she left when she saw that Osho was asleep. He was not asleep, just pretending – and he wanted me to know this – because he imperceptibly kept stroking my hand. What a rascal! It reminded me of C.G. Jung's dream described in his autobiography where God defecated on the village church. I felt a huge relief. Osho is sacred to me and also very close. And he is a human being – with a great sense of humour.

During the day there were other meditations such as Kirtan. A band of singers, drummers and musicians on various exotic instruments played for us to dance. The music became very frantic at times and we danced as wildly as we could. The idea was to forget our bodies and to disappear totally into the music. In the end we lay down to rest in absolute silence.

Another meditation we did individually and in the open was called Gibberish. We went into the hills to find a spot where we could lie on our backs and talk nonsense to the sky. From the distance we could hear the babbling of the others who were doing the same meditation. I babbled nonsense words out loud, feeling lighter and lighter as the sky willingly received it all. After twenty minutes I would look at the blue sky with an empty mind – as far as that was possible. Then, with closed eyes, I tried to see the empty sky inside.

In the evening we walked back to the Palace for the evening lecture. This was reserved for questions the participants could send in to be answered. I wrote a question asking if the sound OM was the reverberation of the big bang. The big bang theory had just been 'invented' so I was quite proud to send in an intelligent question. But I never received an answer although Mukta thought that it was a good question. I think I did not send in another question for quite a few years – perhaps because many of my real, and not intellectual, questions were answered by Osho in other ways.

All your questions will be answered. Sometimes I answer your question in reference to somebody else's question. You have just to listen rightly [...] I will be answering them without your ever asking them. I may have answered it yesterday or I may answer it tomorrow... When the right time comes, I answer. And unless the right time is there, you will not be able to understand it. My answering is not important – your understanding is important.

Osho, *At the Feet of the Master*

After the strenuous Tratak jumping meditation we ambled back to our guesthouse with our torches – but the day was not over. My roommate and I, after getting into our jumpers and under our covers, did our last meditation together. We chanted the mantra AUM: first an in-breath, then we slowly chanted the vowels on the out-breath, pronouncing them very clearly and holding the M as long as we could. It became one of my favourite meditations and I did it for many months back in Italy. Mostly after work I would lie on my bed and do it. I remember the feelings it created in my body; sometimes I became heavier and heavier, dark blue in colour, almost falling through the mattress, each cell of my body vibrating like a musical instrument. It also created the sensation of my skin being stripped from my body from head to toe – it almost felt physically painful – but still I went on doing it.

During the camp we all had the opportunity to go and see Osho. He had a room which could be accessed from the courtyard and that was where I waited until it was my turn. It was quite dark in his room – compared to the glare outside – so I saw him only faintly sitting in his chair when I walked towards him. Then I sat at his feet and he repeated a few times what I remember as:

"I am very happy. You are doing so well."

I was quite astonished that an important man like him had any concern about how I was doing and that he was even happy that I was doing well.

Looking back, I feel a lot of compassion for the girl I was then: courageous to get involved in the meditations headlong without too much questioning. If Osho said to jump for half an hour then I would jump for half an hour. I trusted that what he asked us to do was for our own good.

That's what sannyas is: co-operation with the master. The disciple simply becomes so attuned with the master that he starts taking hints. He is no longer in an argumentative mood, he argues no more. With the master there is no argument possible; one simply listens and follows. And things are so simple that if one can listen and follow, it can happen immediately, instantly.

Osho, *At the Feet of the Master*

Soon this beautiful and intense holiday came to its end and we headed back down towards the plains to catch the train back to Mumbai. This time I travelled in a carriage with three-tier bunks together with other Indian sannyasins and I remember the hours I spent on the top bunk feeling so wonderful, as if on a cloud, my body weightless and the hard bench so soft. I lay there savouring this floating feeling – which has rarely abandoned me since. What a wondrous gift!

When it was time to leave India my body reacted to the pain of departure by developing a fever and a cough. I said goodbye to Osho standing at the door as I did not want to affect his health. I promised him, but mainly myself, to be back for my summer holidays.

Remembering... at Breakfast

The last sounds of the celebration music of the Dynamic are fading, leaving space for the song of the birds. I open my eyes and look around Buddha Hall, now in full light. I bow down with my head to the ground, feeling grateful that Osho had invented this tremendous meditation and ask myself why I don't do it more often. Too lazy to get up in the morning? I promise myself to come back tomorrow.

I collect my maroon blindfold, socks and shawl and walk to the exit of the hall as the cleaning crew is unrolling the hose ready to water down the marble floor. While walking through the hall I feel uneasy – as if I am wearing a jacket back–to–front. Much has been stirred and I need some time to feel comfortable again. I go for a long hot shower to clean off sweat, static and all sorts of ghosts.

Wearing a fresh robe I find my way to the canteen through the silent gardens. Many have gone home; others are already seated in quiet spots and are eating their breakfast in silence. Everybody needs some time alone to digest the meditation. It is not a time for socialising. I choose my favourite Indian chickpea-flower crackers, the *kakras*, a cup of chai and find an empty table under the bamboo trees. Looking over the fence I see into the garden of the master's house – luxuriant foliage spotted by the morning sun – and remember…

In August, six months after my first visit to India, when all offices in Milan shut down *en bloc* for holidays, my destination was, of course, India. Through Deeksha I had heard that Osho was now living in Pune (until recently still written with the British spelling, 'Poona').

On the same day I arrived I made an appointment to see Osho. I was shown into his garden and there he was, sitting on a recliner, already surrounded by a few sannyasins. His physical appearance had changed so much from last time I saw him that I was taken aback for a second. His black hair and beard had turned grey and his whole form – which in Mt. Abu was that of a muscular young man, he was only 43, just about ten years older than me – had become that of a frail, much older man. His outer appearance had changed but the feeling of him and the twinkle in his eyes were the same as before. Sitting close to him I felt comfortable and uncomfortable at the same time; comfortable because it felt like coming home; uncomfortable because I could sense that a long and uncomfortable journey lay ahead where many more of those banana skins would be peeled off me, illusions shed, opinions destroyed.

To be with me is to be in danger. I am unpredictable, and to be with me is to live in a wilderness. Nothing will ever be certain again; all certainties will be gone, all securities will be gone. You will have to manage from moment to moment, day to day.

But that's how the whole universe is managing: moment to moment and day to day. There is no planning in existence; it is unplanned, hence it is beautiful. An unplanned life has tremendous beauty because there is always some surprise waiting in the future. The future is not just going to be a repetition: something new is always happening and one can never take it for granted.

Osho, *Believing the Impossible Before Breakfast*, Ch. 2

Before we stepped onto the lawn, where we left our sandals, there was a sign "Do not pick the grass"! Yes, we do get nervous in front of him, our hands become fidgety and we pull out bits of the poor, innocent grass. I do not remember our conversation. Maybe Osho just asked me how long I was going to stay and maybe my reply was: "For the rest of the month." And probably his answer to this was his usual "Very good!"

Not only Osho's appearance had changed but the whole set-up had. Mukta had bought a bungalow in the most elegant residential area of Pune. She was the divorced wife of a Greek shipping magnate who was – in my imagination of course – like an Onassis and I was so pleased that with this kind of money she could buy such a beautiful place for Osho.

The entrance from the road to Osho's residence had already been blocked off, to give Osho more privacy, and the house could only be accessed from the one which had been bought soon afterwards and was already housing Laxmi's office. To identify the two houses we would call them by their postal numbers – 33 and 17 – until Osho gave them the names Lao Tzu House and Krishna House. But the number '17' is still the one in the ashram's address: 17 Koregaon Park, Pune, Maharashtra.

Koregaon Park was true to its name: quiet roads lined with banyan and decorative trees accessing some remarkable mansions initially built under the British Raj for Indian royalty and higher authorities. If you ventured a few roads outwards all you could see were fields in all directions. Pune proper, of which in the beginning I knew only the route from the railway station to my hotel and then on to the ashram, apparently had 2 million inhabitants, the same number as my home town, Milan. But Pune sprawled over such a vast area that it did not feel crowded at all.

Pune came into favour with the British because of its mild climate (it is almost 600 metres above sea level) and because it is only a four hour train ride from Mumbai. A vast section of the city, which I could see from the rickshaw when I went shopping on M.G. Road, was taken up by a military facility, an area called 'Camp', also a legacy from earlier days. Pune is an industrial city but is also famous for its technical institutions, medical facilities and universities. Pune (the name means 'City of Virtue') had previously known the presence of another master, Meher Baba, a silent Parsee, and would also become the home of the Iyengar Yoga Institute.

Osho's move from Mumbai to Pune was organised for the anniversary of his enlightenment day, on 21st March 1974.

I saw the event on a video where flower-garlanded cars moved in a procession up the winding roads of the *ghats* and many orange-clad figures were singing and dancing to welcome Osho at the gate of his new residence.

I was in Italy back then, importing electrical switches and dimmers from Germany. Sometimes I was afraid that the memories from Mt. Abu were only a dream, an illusion, and that one day I would wake up and everything would be gone – 'poof!' But then I would just lower my eyes and look at my new orange clothes and the mala to find reassurance that it had been a reality indeed. Nobody in the office noticed that I was wearing orange only. In fact, I realised that people are so much involved with themselves that they rarely looked at others. When I first saw Deeksha and Lalita's wardrobe in Mumbai, with nothing but orange clothes, I was not sure if I could follow such a 'rule', but it turned out that it was very easy. The only problem was to find ready-made clothes of that colour – so I became, out of necessity, an expert dyer (mind you, I was trained by master-dyer, Deeksha).

I loved to wear orange! To walk around in a big orange coat on a winter day in a grey city like Milan was an exhilarating feeling. How could I even think of being miserable wearing this brilliant colour? I remember once dashing around a corner in my wide orange coat when a man stepped back in awe at this apparition. He might have exaggerated his response, being an Italian, but he certainly received the effect with sincerity. So, I realised, my wearing orange affected the world as well.

Also my new name was adopted by my closer friends. In my family the first ones to use it were my nephews, the last one was my father – it took him 20 years, just a few months before he died. Soon I started to use my name in the office as well and would sign the business letters with Punya as my first name.

The moment you drop the old name and the old identity you feel unburdened. It is not just a name; it is the very nucleus of the whole past around which our whole life has been revolving.

Osho, *Dance Your Way to God*, Ch. 12

The mala had more mysterious reactions: a girl in my office hated the sight of Osho's picture on the locket of the mala. It reminded her of death. Widows in Italy used to wear a photo of their late husband on a porcelain brooch, which indeed looked very similar to the locket. It reminded her of death and she was quite right in her own way. Sannyas is a death, as Osho says:

Dropping the ego looks like death. It is possible only in a deep love affair with the master that slowly, slowly you gather courage. As your trust in the master grows, it becomes possible for you to risk. And the moment you are ready to risk the ego, bliss starts flowing from every nook and corner of existence.

Osho, *At the Feet of the Master*

I loved the mala and I felt it gave me a kind of protection from outside influences which were not good for me. I always took it off as soon as I reached home and could pop out to the grocer again without it. But if I had to cross the 'safe distance' mark then I had to put it back on. During meditations, when things were getting a bit scary, like during the Aum meditation, I could hold it in my hand and feel safe. Meditations do sometimes feel scary if we get into a space where we have never been in before. Once that space becomes familiar we can move on and cross into a new layer which, in its turn, feels frightening again, and so on. I guess that we are always afraid of anything unfamiliar and overwhelming. We hate to lose control and be at the mercy of what is happening to us. But there is also that sense of curiosity that keeps us moving on! Eventually in death we will be leaving all our friends, our belongings, our projects and our body behind and step into an altogether new space. I do not know the esoteric workings of the mala, all I know is that I took care of it, re-stringing it from time to time to avoid running after the beads escaping all over the floor when the string broke by accident. I also cherished it because it was a present from my master.

To have these exterior signs to show that one is a sannyasin was quite a clever tactic on Osho's part. It helped me remember that, in a far-away country, I had made myself the promise to walk on this path of meditation – and that I wanted to stick with it. It also helped me to stay with my decision despite the fact that friends and family would have preferred to have me the way I was before.

When someone was leaving for the West, Osho often said to them, "Help my people there." He even said it to me. In the beginning I did not understand what kind of help he meant – certainly not the Christian way of helping – but later, when Deeksha came to visit me all the way from Geneva with her American boyfriend, Krishna Bharti, and Bhakti, her delicate mother, I knew that it meant just giving each other support by being together. After a healthy vegetarian meal at my place we spent the afternoon looking at the pictures Krishna Bharti had recently taken of Osho and shared a few more useful clothes-dyeing tips. All we did was just be together, and that gave me the reassurance that I was not alone in my endeavours.

On my return to India I was up for the next adventure. Many new people had arrived, from England, Ireland, Germany, Italy and the USA and I made many new friends. We found accommodation in modest hotels, or lodges as they were called, and walked to the ashram to attend the events there. The daily programme was: Dynamic at 6am, Osho's discourse at 8am, Whirling in the late afternoon and then the *darshan*, the interview with the master – at 7pm. The discourses and the darshans (for which we could sign up with Mukta maybe once a week) were held on the porch of Osho's residence. The meditations were in the still barren garden in front of Krishna House which was now covered by a tin roof to protect us from the sun and the monsoon rains. Everybody came with their own roll-up bamboo mat as if we were going to the beach.

Now we could have intensive meditation days – they were still called 'camps' – every month without travelling anywhere. They started on the eleventh of each month and lasted for ten days. The meditations followed each other with intervals of fifteen minutes and with an hour for lunch-break. It was very intense; it felt sometimes like going from one movie to the next but, instead of getting a headache by the end of the day, we would feel lighter and brighter.

During the morning discourses Osho was commenting on a Zen

master who used to hit his disciples with a whip. Some of the disciples got hit but others would move just seeing 'the shadow of the whip'. So, for the strenuous meditations which involved jogging on the spot and the Whirling which lasted two hours I often imagined that shadow of the whip behind me to help me keep going. Nevertheless, it seemed my body had an endless resource of energy; the more I ran and danced, the more I could jump – and the feeling was always that of weightlessness.

With a smile I remember that once during the silent phase of a meditation I got so very annoyed by the heavy clatter of the manual typewriters of the girls typing on the balcony in front of Laxmi's office that I went up to the meditation leader, Teertha, and asked him if he could do something about it. He suggested I go and complain to Laxmi and, from the way he said it, I suspected that he must have told her already and that he was now happy to have me as an ally. So I went and Laxmi's wonderful answer was that nothing could be done as the letters had to be written and, moreover, the girls also had a hard time with their work because of the loud music of the meditations. After that, the typewriters were never a disturbance again...

When the camp was over I had a lot of free time between the basic meditations and the discourses to just hang out in shabby cafés. I became friends with Puja from Germany and we enjoyed telling each other our dreams and other gossip, but we never talked about what was happening to us during the meditations. We had understood that it was not good to pay too much attention to the sensations and visions of light, or whatever we had experienced while meditating.

One of the most fundamental things to remember – not only by you but by everyone – is that whatever you come across in your inner journey, you are not it.

You are the one who is witnessing it – it may be nothingness, it may be blissfulness, it may be silence. But one thing has to be remembered: however beautiful and however enchanting an experience you come by, you are not it. You are the one who is experiencing it, and if you go on and on and on, the ultimate point in the journey is the point when there is no experience left – neither silence, nor blissfulness, nor nothingness. There is nothing as an object for you but only your subjectivity.

The mirror is empty. It is not reflecting anything. It is you.

Osho, *The Hidden Splendor*, Ch. 10

Puja shared with me the same prefix, 'Yoga', which was not very common, and we thought that we must be similar in some ways. We discovered that we both loved to disappear. When we wanted to understand things, like appreciate a sunset, we would actually try to become it and disappear into it. Just to look at the sunset would not have been enough – it had to become our bone and marrow. It was good to have found a friend with whom I could share these very intimate discoveries.

When my time was up, at the end of August, I travelled back to Mumbai to catch my plane. When I arrived at the airport I was told that the flight had been cancelled but would take off the following day. A paid overnight stay at the Taj Mahal Hotel, so close to my beloved Colaba, was the best part of this inconvenience. However, the following day, at the check-in desk, it turned out that the charter flight had been over-booked by two seats, and one of them was mine. It was now a gamble between four people and we were left standing there anxiously waiting for quite some time. To my great relief I was one of the rejected ones! This meant at least another week in India, but then it turned out that I could not re-book the flight with that same ticket. The only thing I could do was to contact my father and ask him to organise a new ticket for my return and I called my bank to send me the remaining money I had on my account. Then I went straight back to Pune!

The cheapest way to spend this time, I calculated, was to go for a retreat in Lonavala. From some sannyasins who had been there I had heard of this retreat facility. Before I left Osho gave me very clear instructions: Dynamic in the morning, a walk for an hour – looking only at the ground, about two feet ahead – and the new, very energetic meditation, the Mandala, in the late afternoon. During the day I should sit silently and watch my breath, if possible using earplugs and a blindfold. Also, I should not eat too much: if one gets bored one tends to eat more, was the reason he gave.

Lonavala is a hill station about an hour's train ride from Pune – and is famous for its tasty sesame and nut bars, called *chikki*. To get to the retreat, part of the walk from the railway station was on the rail tracks which, as I quickly discovered, were commonly used by pedestrians as paths or as a shortcut. Just a vigilant ear was needed to hear the sound of any approaching train.

The hut I had been assigned was probably the same as the other half dozen in the compound. It had a little porch with a wooden bench, a door and a window. The furniture consisted of a concrete elevation which served as a bed on one side, a concrete ledge instead of a table on the other side and many shelves built into the walls. So nothing could be taken out of the hut except the cotton mattress.

With the caretaker, who luckily spoke a few words of English, I agreed that he would bring me food only once a day at lunchtime (in the hope of curbing my eating habits as Osho had suggested) and that I could make tea on the little kerosene stove. He would leave the *thali* with my lunch on the front porch and I could then put it outside when I had finished eating. One day, by mistake, I left my teaspoon with which I used to eat my food on the *thali* – and so lost it forever. From then on I was obliged to eat with my fingers as Indians do. I had seen Saeed and his wife eat this way – I found it a bit gross – but I would never have guessed that it was such a skill!

I thoroughly enjoyed the retreat, its discipline, the aloneness and playing out my 'big girl' stance: I am doing something difficult. The days passed by, one after the other, in their simple monotony, just like the breathing I was watching. Lying on my cot I noticed that my heart rate had gone very slow, down to 42 beats per minute (I had plenty of time for these kinds of experiments).

Relaxation *was* happening, but…

There was this new meditation, the Mandala, which was creating some anxiety. There was no problem with running on the spot, then the soft swaying in the lotus posture, but when it was the time of rotating the eyes I had the impression the whole room was going to fall straight over me. I tried to postpone the meditation until late at night – the candle light even helped to add to the eerie feeling – but somehow I never skipped it. Definitely one of those hold-on-to-your-mala situations!

Not talking to anyone for three weeks was quite an undertaking, because the mind talks continuously even without anyone to talk to. In the beginning the talk was inside my head, but in the last week I was even talking aloud, giving great political speeches, walking around the hut making inspirational gestures. This was quite a surprise to me as I never participated in any politics back home.

In his instructions, I remember Osho saying that if we enjoyed the meditation we could stay an extra day or two, but that we should stick to the minimum of twenty-one days. At the end of that time I looked up, straight into the eyes of my neighbour, a tall girl from the USA. She had been doing her exercises in a less regimented way – in fact she started talking to me – and we agreed that I would wait for two more days and that we would travel to Pune together. Now I had the freedom to look around and dance about, as she had done all along. We danced barefoot on the newly-grown grass after the monsoon rains, on the smooth lava rocks and on the rough concrete edges of the suspended canals built for Mumbai's drinking water.

We cleared our huts of our few belongings, paid our bills and walked towards Lonavala to catch our train. I was curious to see how the busy village would impact me after the retreat. The noises from the sweet merchants' shacks and the curious glances of the women in their bright-coloured saris just sunk into me. I did not feel crushed by the vibrant impressions, just a bit shaky.

As soon as we arrived at the ashram, Mukta, who was sitting in her customary spot on the steps of Krishna House, asked us if we wanted to see Osho. "There are not many people tonight." She promptly added our names to her list in her little spiral notebook. How could you decline such an offer? We dashed to our hotel, took a shower and changed into clean clothes to be back before 7pm and wait at the gate of Lao Tzu House.

It was twilight already and the birds in the trees overhead were reporting to each other the events of the day – or so it seemed. To go and see Osho always had something magical about it; the preparation, the waiting at the gate and then the slow approach to the lit porch where Osho, already seated, was waiting for us. After bowing down with our foreheads to the ground, in the traditional Indian manner, we sat down around him on the two wide steps. That night there were just us two and a third girl, Madhuri, to be interviewed; a few Indian visitors sat on the side listening to the conversation or just enjoying the presence of the master.

Osho enquired about our days in Lonavala. I complained about constipation and about waking up in the middle of the night with cramps in my limbs. Osho asked me to stand up and move to the side, in front of the lamp – it was a bronze statue of a young man holding up a lamp – a fairly kitschy monstrosity, maybe a present or something to shock our European idea of good taste. I stood a few yards from him, waiting for further instructions. "Now shake! The whole body!" To my stunned facial expression probably meaning "What are you talking about?", Osho moved his hands trembling like a leaf in the wind. So I did my best: shaking arms, hands, knees and head and soon enough the contraction took over my body again. "See, that's how it goes," I complained to him. "Keep shaking," and so I did while Mukta, on Osho's instructions, came over to put her hand on my belly. At that point I yelled out a scream I had never heard before – it almost appeared that the scream which had come out of my throat, had nothing to do with me at all. I felt embarrassed to have disturbed the meeting with such a noise. When I sat back in front of Osho. I heard him say, "You need more energy." How could that be? I had felt so much energy since being here that I could hardly deal with it! Osho then suggested I should shake every night for twenty minutes and then report back after two weeks.

Sitting now on the side, I was listening to the conversation between Madhuri and Osho and suddenly, out of the blue, the same way the scream had erupted, a big wave of hatred took possession of me. I had been looking at the beautifully pedicured feet of Osho peeping out from his white robe and suddenly this hatred made them look horrible and despicable. Of course I was embarrassed about these feelings and fought them back – I did not want to hate my master – and the only way out was to start crying. When Osho left, greeting us lovingly in *namaste*, Mukta put her arms around my shoulders and whispered consoling words while we walked out.

I did my shaking dutifully for the next two weeks in my hotel room and enjoyed the experiment more and more. It was not only my body which was shaken, though, it seemed my whole character structure was getting looser and falling out of frame. In the mirror of the dresser I could see my body, naked because of the heat, and for the first time accepted its shape. Because of the one meal a day I had lost weight and was finally in an 'acceptable' form. For so many years I had been reproached by my family members for those extra pounds! It was lovely to come closer to my body now that I could accept it.

When the two weeks were over I went to see Osho again in a darshan. I told him that I intended to go to Goa and was encouraged with a beautiful smile. Despite the fact that the plane ticket had arrived by now I was in no hurry to return to the West. I am ashamed to say that, very irresponsibly, I had not even contacted João about my plans or rather about me not having any plans. It was as if I was living on another planet. Next day I packed a few belongings and jumped on a bus. When we got to Mumbai, the daily bus to Goa was still there in the big and noisy bus station, as if waiting for me. The journey was as smooth as the rest of the holiday.

Goa is the Indian state just south from Maharashtra and was until 1961 part of Portugal (but became an Indian state only in 1987). This was the reason why I could talk in my broken Portuguese with some older people, and why everybody was Catholic. The local people were quite relaxed about us swimming in the ocean stark naked and walking around with just a *lungi* around our necks. Many hippies had already adopted Goa as one of their destinations, the one for the winter, when it was too cold in Manali in the Himalayas, and we mingled with them when we met in the chai shops where we used to have our vegetable *bhaji* or lime sodas. The whiff of 'grass' was ubiquitous and also tolerated by the locals. But that was not my cup of tea.

Since the night of that scream I had the impression that I was seeing things the way they actually were – without the constant film of thought and judgement between me and the world. I had done art classes, but I had never seen colours with the subtlety and harmony as I could see them now. And while meditating, when looking inside, I felt as if nobody was there – just an empty space. It made me laugh, because Osho kept saying that we should go inside to find ourselves, and when we did that, what happens? Nothing is found. He is such a trickster!

Meditation is looking into your emptiness, welcoming it, enjoying it, being one with it, with no desire to fill it – there is no need, because it is already full! It looks empty because you don't have the right way of seeing it. You see it through the mind; that is the wrong way. If you put the mind aside and look into your emptiness, it has tremendous beauty, it is divine, it is overflowing with joy. Nothing else is needed.

Osho, *The Book of Wisdom*, Vol. 2

Instead of 'doing' things it felt rather that things were 'happening' to me. I did not have a fixed place to sleep; I would leave in the morning with my little bundle and then settle at night wherever my feet had taken me that day, sometimes sleeping on the beach around a fire or as a guest at a friend's place. Such a different life from what I had had until recently as a responsible multilingual secretary! I knew that this was going to end sometime, but while it lasted it was worth enjoying.

One day tall German Sagar asked me if I wanted to join him on a trip to Hampi. I had no idea where this was and how far it was from Goa but I immediately said yes and packed my few belonging. It turned out that it was quite a few miles away, even in another state! and that it would take too long to get there if we did not take the occasional bus. It was like living out a dream of being a *sadhu*, a wondering monk. People on the road always asked the same questions, "Which country do you belong? What is your name? How many sisters and brothers you have?" but were always very friendly and helpful.

Sometimes we slept in lodges, but not sharing the same bed because we were not lovers, and sometimes in claustrophobic concrete water pipes. Hampi was an amazing place with huge rocks spread over the countryside as if giants had played with pebbles. Yogis and other saints lived in surrounding caves.

We settled outside a temple to spend the night. Maybe because I had got sunstroke I came down with diarrhoea, but was not much worried about it. In the morning, however, a yogi came up to us and told us that he had a dream or a vision that a foreigner somewhere needed his help so he started searching from temple to cave to find where I could be. That's why his first words were, "Here you are!" He then walked with us to his house in the nearby village where we stayed for a few days until I recovered. He gave me some drugs which helped me get better quite quickly but also gave me some interesting hallucinations when we went to a guru celebration that night. I wonder what they were…

Morning Discourse

After a leisurely breakfast, sunk in images of the past I have never remembered so vividly, I drop my dirty dishes at the bussing station. The marble path encircling Buddha Hall leads me past the swans' pond. Orchids hanging in clusters from the branch of a tree seem almost unreal. Caressed with my fingers, the stiff pink petals reveal their freshness and their delicate scent. Just underneath, in the middle of a big spiky palm leaf, I discover a microcosm made up of mosses and seedlings from the pods which had fallen from the tree above, lit up by precious dew drops trembling in the morning light. A mongoose family, accustomed to the international gathering in this place, makes its way to its den under the heart-shaped leaves of creepers. With them around we are safe from all sorts of snakes.

At the entrance to the hall we are greeted by a seated Buddha, a marble statue offered to us as a present from Osho after we returned from the States. Since then it has always been somewhere around the hall, inspiring the meditators sitting with closed eyes in front of it or – after it was moved to the main entrance – as a reminder to those entering the hall. At times somebody would pick up a red flower fallen from a tree and place it on the open hand. The few steps lead me to the vast expanse of shiny white marble; on my left, on the north side of the ellipse, rises the podium with its pagoda-like roof. Greeting the photo of Osho with my eyes, I sit down on the cushion I have brought with me. Others, in their maroon robes, have also gathered, waiting for the audio discourse to start.

Indian classical music is composed for specific hours of the day. This means that a song composed for a certain time will never be performed at another hour. Over the centuries Indian musicians have discovered that every hour has its own mood, and at different times of the day we are sensitive to certain scales and melodies. In the same way we are receptive to Osho's discourses in the morning in a particular way. Not yet fully awake and not yet engaged in worldly affairs, we hear his words with an innocent heart, open and fresh, in harmony with the soft light filtering through the leaves, the slowly dissipating mists in the undergrowth. His voice intermingles with the chirping of the birds; their song and the cuckoo's accents deepen the silence between his words.

There are many ways to receive Osho's words: we can read his books which are the transcribed discourses, listen to his voice on a CD, or watch him on video. Each way is different. In the books we can go back and read the paragraphs time and time again; the tapes reveal the melody and power of his voice; the videos give us a close look at the vibrant expressions on his face and the elegant gestures of his hands.

For years, maybe because of my weak eyesight, I used to keep my eyes closed while listening to Osho, as I am doing right now. In a way, while listening to a discourse, I do not feel the difference if Osho is in the body or not.

Osho is reading a question, not forgetting the addressee's 'Beloved Osho' as he starts. While hearing the question I tune into it, trying to sense in which way he might answer. Is it a question just coming from the head or a real, existential one? Is the questioner involved in it, or is he just showing off his knowledge? Is he prejudiced against the subject of his question? Where is he coming from? A long gap of silence, a gap also in my mind, not knowing what the first sentence will be... The question is not so much answered, but revealed from different angles, using at times relaxing anecdotes from Osho's own life or from other masters. The questioner is exposed, then encouraged to pursue his enquiry.

While listening to Osho's harmonious voice the sound penetrates my body, not only my ears. It creates a vast space inside me as if there are no bones, no organs. At times I grab a sentence, thinking it important to remember with my logical mind; then his words become sounds of exquisite music and the silences in between shower over me – millions of pink petals, soundless, just touching my skin.

Listening from the heart, there is no argument, there is no judgement. One listens just as one listens to the song of the birds or to music or to the wind passing through the pine trees. One is not questioning it, there is no why, one is simply enjoying it. The master has to be enjoyed!

Remember: the master has to be, in Jesus' words, eaten. The disciple has to be a cannibal. Don't be worried… to be a cannibal is perfect with me! To be with a master simply means to digest his being, to let him come into you, to allow him to the innermost shrine of your being where you have never allowed anybody, where you yourself have never entered, to open all your doors and windows. And then one understands not only the words, one starts understanding the silences too.

Osho, *At the Feet of the Master*

A joke is on its way! Osho changes his tone of voice. I immediately become alert. He is reading the joke from a pad, slowly and jerkily. Some jokes are sent in by us, using words we like him to say, like 'Aha!' or 'Really!' I laugh to my heart's content at the twist of the joke I had not foreseen. The joke is about a Polack, or Giovanni the Italian, but we all know well that the joke is about us.

The next question touches a sore spot in my present life. I am listening attentively to each single word trying to catch every nuance and possible meaning. It is not time to space out now. I want to understand. Relaxing into his words, unexpectedly the understanding sinks into me like a stone in a lake. With a few simple and pragmatic sentences, light has been shed on a once obscured issue. This time it is about the wrong assumption that there is a soul mate out there waiting for me to find him. It is sad, but it is better to know the truth than to have illusions.

Osho's "Enough for today" or "OK, Maneesha" – used as a full-stop to his discourse – cuts the magic between us. We open our eyes and leave the hall. The hour gone by feels like eternity and five minutes at the same time. If you ask me what Osho has been talking about, I do not remember a word. I have learned just to listen, to open my ears to the sounds, open the heart to the melody of his sentences, open the soul to the lovingness of his voice. Just for accuracy I want to add here that whenever I hear this same discourse again, I will mysteriously remember all the answers to the questions and, without mistakes, all the punch lines of the jokes, word for word.

I stretch my body and lean back to look up at the roof of the hall. The shadows of the trees and birds play on it soundlessly. The roof is actually a giant canvas and plastic tent supported by a steel arch across the narrower side of the ellipse. The canvas is stretched with steel rods attached to concrete structures in the ground. Because of planning permissions a permanent roof is not allowed and this is a brilliant solution. The mosquito netting covering the sides, from roof to floor, keeps mosquitoes, flies, birds and leaves out, while still allowing a cooling breeze to air the hall.

When the porch became too small because many more people had arrived, Osho gave his morning lectures on a large upstairs veranda of his house. It was roofed and had a marble mosaic floor and trees nudged up against the ceiling. We had to walk up a flight of steps to the first floor – and I liked the cool, silent feel inside his house. But the veranda also became crowded only after a few months. We sat cramped with our knees under our chins, touching each other front and back. The discomfort was soon forgotten when we saw Osho enter the door, almost floating, in his white robe. With folded hands he greeted us, letting his eyes wander over the gathering and then sat down in his chair. I always enjoyed watching the way he slipped his left foot out of his sandal and lifted his left leg to cross it over his right leg. It was the same movement every day but it had such a beautiful quality to it. It was not automatic, but carefully done. I came back to myself when he addressed us through the microphone with "The first question…"

Fortunately a new auditorium was already in the process of being built. We could see it while walking past the house on our way out. Twisted poles at funny angles held up (in Indian fashion) the planks for the concrete roof to come. One afternoon the roof collapsed and Osho commented, according to what my friends told me, that it happened because of our negative minds. "Each time when you walked past you thought that the roof would collapse and so it did." The debris was cleared and the roof rebuilt. I could not believe that thoughts could be as strong as that – but maybe they are.

Back from Goa I was surprised to see that the shaking meditation which I had been practising on my own had now become a standard meditation and had replaced the Whirling in the afternoon. To the shaking stage of fifteen minutes Osho had added dancing, listening to music with stillness, to finish with the silent stage. There was now also a music track to help us get into the feel of the stages (some brilliant snake charmer's flute) and to make it clear when the stages change. It was called Kundalini, after the snake-shaped energy which uncoils from the bottom of our spine to reach the top of our heads. My days on the beach had taught me that I could let things happen, rather than actively do them, so I let the Kundalini meditation happen by itself. I used to just stand there and wait until the shaking would start by itself and let the meditation take its course. Nowadays Dynamic and Kundalini are the most popular meditations created by Osho.

Here, in my meditations, do them, but not wilfully. Don't force them – rather, let them happen. Float in them, abandon yourself in them – be absorbed, but not wilfully. Don't manipulate because when you manipulate you are divided, you become two: the manipulator and the manipulated. Once you are two, heaven and hell are created immediately; then there is a vast distance between you and the truth. Don't manipulate, allow things to happen. If you are doing the Kundalini Meditation, then allow the shaking, don't do it. Stand silently, feel it coming and when your body starts a little trembling, help it but don't do it. Enjoy it, feel blissful about it, allow it, receive it, welcome it, but don't will it.

If you force it, it will become an exercise. Then the shaking will be there but just on the surface, it will not penetrate you. You will remain solid, stone-like, rock-like within; you will remain the manipulator, the doer, and the body will just be following. The body is not the question.

When I say shake I mean your solidity, your rock-like being should shake to the very foundations so that it becomes liquid, fluid, melts, flows. And when the rock-like being becomes liquid, your body will follow. Then there is no shake, only shaking. Then nobody is doing it, it is simply happening. Then the doer is not.

Osho, *Hsin Hsin Ming: The Book of Nothing*, Ch. 2

On 11th December we celebrated Osho's birthday on the lawn of his garden. Many little multi-coloured lights were hanging from tree to tree as is traditional here for weddings and parties. The gates were decorated with strings of marigolds. Indian sannyasins had arrived from their villages to pay their respects and the western sannyasins had also increased in number. Osho, sitting in his armchair on the lit porch, received one by one the visitors who, in the traditional Indian way, prostrated themselves before him and touched his feet. A group of singers lead by Taru were accompanied by a harmonium, drums and bells. They sang Kirtan songs in honour of Krishna.

The long, slowly advancing queue, which was winding itself through the people sitting on the grass and the porch, became shorter and shorter in front of me. Suddenly it was my turn to greet Osho. I did not want to touch his feet as I respected his fragile body, so I placed my hands next to them and, miscalculating the distance between my head and the step, banged my forehead with a big bonk. Stretching up, I found radiant eyes gazing into me; we both laughed, enjoying the joke. Later I found this fitting quote which reminded me of this incident:

Banging of the head won't do, but dropping of the head can do. Banging ... the head always wants to do it. That's what you are doing your whole life – banging heads, fighting. Don't try to bang. Just drop it, be headless.

Osho, *Come Follow To You*, Vol. 2, Ch. 10

On my way back to my seat on the lawn I saw a young man – he must have just arrived judging from his multi-coloured clothes – his hands trembling in front of his face, talking to himself in German. I heard an "Oh no, that is too much," so I gave him an encouraging nudge and he joined the queue. Yes, it was all a bit too much for us westerners.

During my last days in Pune I lived in the Green Hotel, a simple but clean lodge near the Railway Station. One afternoon, instead of going to Kundalini Meditation I felt that something was holding me back, so I remained sitting on my bed on the balcony and started writing in my exercise book with its blue Krishna cover. Like poems the words kept flowing, in four-liners, rhythmically following each other to form a whole. When the writing stopped I jumped up, drove to the city with a rickshaw and bought five little cards and an envelope. I neatly copied each poem on a card, stuck them in the envelope and dressed-up in my best robe to see Osho for the last time.

Sannyasins used to sometimes give presents to Osho during darshan (it is customary in India to give presents to the guru). Presents were watches and expensive jewellery, but mine were just these little poems which I slipped under his chair. I felt a little embarrassed and walked away from the darshan not even sure if he had noticed the envelope. I remember that one of the poems ended with 'your red hands', because I had started to feel Osho's energy coming from his hands, even from a distance. Maybe it was my imagination, but I thought that I had heard Osho mentioning 'my red hands' in the first discourse on my next visit. Whatever the truth, for me it was like a "Welcome back" and "I read your poems."

2

East, West and Back Again

Devavani

The tapping on the microphone brings me back to the present and
to Buddha Hall. With a distinguished French accent a black-robed
girl explains the four stages of the next meditation – Devavani –
and starts the CD. I get up to leave but the piano music is so
delicious, irresistible, that I have to sit down again and participate
in the meditation. The very first notes transport me into that world
where thoughts merge disconnectedly as in dreams. Undefined
images and sensations float by. I savour the blurred space that
I won't allow myself to get into in day-to-day life. When the music
stops I start talking like a child, with no meaning yet, experiment-
ing with the sounds, discovering new possible variations. I watch
myself sinking more and more into this blurred space and I feel
comfortable in it. At the ringing gong I stand up and allow the
body to move slowly the way it wants to, bending and turning as
if commanded by an interior force – the body has its own
language and expression separate from the mind we know. I keep
talking softly and, as if a spectator, watch the movements and the
talk. For the last fifteen minutes I lie still, feeling the cool marble
under my body, not knowing what to expect.

I had taught this gentle meditation to a very gentle girl, Kavya. We
were sitting on the bare parquet floor of one of the rooms in my old
flat in Milan. It used to be my bedroom, but was now empty of all
furniture and served as the meditation room. We were almost talking
to each other, gesticulating, as if explaining with gestures our non-

sense words. I remember her long frizzy hair which almost touched the ground. To be with her helped me to go even deeper into the innocent, child-like space of this meditation.

When Osho heard in my last darshan that I was leaving he presented me with a towel, one of those towels he used to hold over his arm and, when in discourse, place on his lap. I remember watching Nirvano get up and enter the house and when she came back she was holding in her hands a light blue chenille towel, sparkling under the lights. It was for me, a gift to take home.

There was another gift. Osho asked me to start a meditation centre in my home-town. He wrote the name of the centre on a sheet of his stationary, the same paper he used for the names of new sannyasins and, bending down towards me, showed me the name on it and said what I remember as, "The name will be Arihant. Arihant means a warrior who fights with evil. If Christ had been born in the East he would have been called Arihant."

There were already well-known and well organised centres in London and New York, but with my humble means I could hardly compete with them. The only thing I could do was to empty my old flat and make it available for people to come. I first emptied my bedroom and turned it into the meditation room and started sleeping on the guest-bed in the living room. I cleared the wardrobe of all clothes which could definitely not be dyed orange and all those fashionable shoes which were too uncomfortable to wear. During the cleaning I had to part with boxes full of rocks I had collected on holidays and Sunday outings and boxes of pieces of paper which I had collected for some future collage or just because the paper was so pretty. The unfinished knitting projects went to my mother. At the same time, João, my boyfriend, also moved out.

I had lost interest in cooking dinners so all our old friends, who used to visit for the delicious food and wine I served up, stopped coming. This left space for these new friends who were interested in meditation. I had no idea where they all came from and I do not remember who had introduced me to Kavya. And many new worlds started opening up for me: once Kavya brought a macrobiotic strawberry cake, a totally mind-boggling concept!

People used to drop in, mostly after work and we decided on the spot which meditation to do. But for Dynamic it was different because of the noise (the silent version had not been 'invented' yet). We opted to do it on Sunday mornings in the open, on the outskirts of town. We had a list of people who were interested, with their addresses and phone numbers. We first figured out the best route to take in order to pick people up on our way there and then called them – one by one according to our invisible map – and told them of the approximate time we would be at their door. At a later stage we had a few cars which came via their own routes, but we would all meet in our favourite spot. It was a poplar plantation – trees planted in rows – which was distant enough from any villages and farms that no one would be disturbed by our noise. It did not have the ideal surface for our 'hoo-hoo' jumping because between each row of trees were ruts, but then privacy was the main issue. Just the occasional hunter with his dog would walk past with an astonished expression on his face. By the time we had finished the meditation it was lunchtime and we enjoyed a meal together at a *trattoria*.

The last paragraph started with a 'we', because I had a helper now in the centre. It was Ananda Veda. One day he turned up at my door and moved in, then and there. He had just returned from India. I was the bread winner and his contribution to the centre was meditation. (He always made sure that when I came home from work I would find him in 'deep meditation'…) But he was also a good cook, a good piano player and a good lover. Through him I became aware that there was something like 'awareness'. So far in my sannyas life I had been more into catharting, dancing, and enjoying Osho's discourses and had not paid much attention to that other part of the story. So maybe this was the time for me to get acquainted with 'awareness', and I started practising it while washing the dishes.

One day we came up with the idea of organising a meditation camp. João's photographer, who became interested in what I was doing with my new life, helped us find an old country house in

Tuscany which we could rent for a few days. Before people arrived at the place we deep-cleaned it and smoked it out with incense sticks. That was one of my tasks. I had never done this before, but it felt very natural and I enjoyed waving my stick into all the corners of the rooms to prepare it for our meditation weekend.

The living room turned out to be big enough for us to do Dynamic, Whirling and Mandala. And the lectures (as we used to call them – the English way – back then) were replaced by Veda translating Osho's words into Italian directly from a book. We sat down around him on the warm carpet as if we were listening to an ancient storyteller at a campfire. Silent, attentive and grateful for every word we heard.

For the Whirling meditation we rolled up the carpet and spun around on the uneven terracotta tiles. Osho had adopted this meditation from the Sufi tradition and he told us the story of how one of the Sufi masters, Rumi, became enlightened after he had whirled for 36 hours. Our meditation lasted 'only' two hours and it was one of my favourites. What I liked about it was the moment when my feet started moving by themselves, when I started feeling like a motionless vertical thread and, above all, when my unfocussed eyes saw the surrounding blurred colours and shapes move past like in a quickly rotating kaleidoscope – the red and white tiles, the white walls and the small open windows with the green landscape all whooshing past in tranquil streaks of colours.

When tired or too dizzy we were allowed to let ourselves fall. I was always afraid to hurt myself when falling down so kept spinning – but then I also enjoyed it so much that I was happy that it would last two full hours. (After a year or two Osho changed the meditation and he had us whirl in the other direction, anticlockwise, but then it lasted only one hour.) When on the tapes the inspiring *darabuka* drums stopped, it was time to lie down and roll over so that our belly touched the floor. Time to sink into the earth and disappear into a space very close to the one we experience just before falling asleep.

On the second morning my sleep was disturbed by a loud banging on the door. It echoed through the vast and empty spaces in the house and certainly woke up everybody else in the house as well. I opened the front door and found four or five *carabinieri* standing there. I had just woken up from a dream where I was successfully fighting against soldiers, so their very impressive black uniforms and the sniffer dog at their heels did not scare me a bit. Quite naive in such things I let them in without a warrant and it turned out that about 15 of them had come for this raid. I knew that we had nothing to hide anyway. Someone must have seen us the previous day when we danced in the garden – in those days 'young people in one place' just meant 'drugs' – and called the police. The men stalked around in their shiny black boots and inspected all nooks and crannies of the house (even the toilet flushers) and once they were convinced that we were not into that kind of thing, they started asking questions about meditation and about the man with the long beard whose photo was hanging in the living room.

The visit we received on the following day was all the more appreciated. Krishna Radha had arrived by train from the south. Although she was a new acquaintance for all of us – we must have arranged the meeting over the phone – she soon became part of the group. I remember how I marvelled over her accent, a quite broad Neapolitan one, which was quite unusual for us *Milanesi*. She had just returned from Pune and brought with her a present from Osho for the centre. It was a beautifully carved teak box. We were not meant to open it, Radha said, so nobody knew if it contained Osho's hair, as she had suggested, or if it was empty.

Back in Milan work continued, Dynamic meditations in the fields, and new people coming to the centre to meditate. One night Veda had the idea for us to go back to Pune and this he planned we should do the following weekend, without telling anyone beforehand. Making some excuse I went to see my mother, and invited myself for dinner at my father's to secretly say good-bye to them. And in the office I did not say that I would not be back on Monday. This was a strange thing for me to do. Whenever I resisted the idea, Veda said that I was too attached to my belongings, unable to let go! And I certainly wanted to show him that he was wrong.

The flat was going to be taken care of by a girl who was willing to look after it until I came back. She was not a sannyasin so I suspected that she might not go on with the meditations as she promised she would. It was obvious that I was the one to get the funds together for this trip to Pune. There was my monthly salary which I had just received and we sold some of the art books I had collected over the years, but that was about it. This meant that the only way to get to Pune was to travel overland – much cheaper than by air.

The Orient Express, originating in Paris, went through Milan and, after Venice, through some of the states of the Eastern Bloc towards its destination of Istanbul. After a night's sleep in a *couchette* we were woken up at dawn by grumbling customs officials who wanted money from us for visas, even if we did not get off the train. I looked out the window and saw on the platform a stooped, shabbily dressed worker who was smoking his first cigarette of the day. Everything was soaked in the greyness of the morning. Such a desolate place!

I would have been interested to visit Istanbul where one of my sisters' godmother had lived for many years, but we had made a rule that our aim was to get to Pune as quickly as we could and we would not be distracted by sightseeing. Veda found a travel agent who offered a passage in a bus straight to Teheran which was leaving that day. I soon fell into my 'travelling mode'; I could fall asleep on a bumpy road, sitting upright in a tight seat any time I wanted to. Even the sight of buses and trucks at the bottom of rocky valleys, the 'racing driver' techniques of the bus driver when steering around a bend, or the discovery that the tires showed only vague memories of a profile did not affect that 'mode'. All this was to the total incomprehension of Veda who seemed to have absorbed into himself all the anxieties and fears a traveller would naturally have. After almost being jailed in Iran because I had over-stayed my 3-day visa (Veda had received 10 days on his Italian passport and he was fine) we finally reached Afghanistan.

Our hotel room in Herat overlooked a roundabout with some planted flowers in the middle. Horse-drawn carriages would circle around them, their small horses jingling their high-pitched bells which were attached to elaborate gear with happy red tassels. On the small balcony we ate the sweetest apricots we ever had in our lives and revelled in the relaxed, welcoming and graceful atmosphere of the place. In the evening we were invited by a local boy to attend a traditional, historical play at a theatre and later he brought us to his home where we even met his mother, unveiled. I remember, as we sat on the carpeted floor, the many pillows along the wall which, our host explained, would become beds at night.

The only route to the east was via Kandahar in the south. We travelled on buses and hitched rides on trucks until we reached Kabul back up north. Veda became ill and we spent a few days there waiting for him to recover. Over the Khyber pass we reached Pakistan. Same people, same dress, same food and same smells as the ones I knew from my previous visits in India. We were in such a rush to reach Pune that we did not even stop to visit the Golden Temple in Amritsar! From Delhi we went by train to Mumbai and then up to Pune – I remember happily sleeping in the trains, stretched out on the filthy floors. We must have arrived so dusty, unkempt and dirty.

At the arrival darshan the first thing Osho asked me was what had happened to the centre – and only then did I realise what I had done. I felt terribly embarrassed that I had been less concerned that someone should look after the centre than to show to Veda that I was not attached to career, family and belongings – and to travel with him to Pune. Moreover, at the darshan Veda did not sit next to me, as couples used to do, but chose a seat far away from me. Osho finally spoke to him, remarking that he looked tired after the journey. He suggested to start translating his books while in Pune and find a publisher when Veda was back home in Italy. He also gave specific instructions that the publishers should get a contract from Laxmi's office before going ahead with the printing – something which Veda judged as Osho having an ego!

The magic of the previous year, where I felt that everything was in a flow, where I was always in the right place at the right time, had vanished. I was plagued by jealousies, fears and indecisions. Sometimes I would ask Osho in my letters – almost reproachingly –

what had happened to my blissful state, where it had gone, but he never answered directly.

The first surrender that one feels is almost a kind of excitement of the new; it is like a honeymoon. Soon you settle down, mmm? Then the honeymoon and the euphoria disappear; then the real work starts. And one day, if one continues to work, the real surrender happens. Then it is not a honeymoon.

But it is natural: first it has to be like a honeymoon. It is a kind of falling in love. But when you are excited and the euphoria is there, you feel that the surrender has happened. Soon you will have to take note of the reality and the hard facts of life, and there will be a thousand and one situations when you will say, "The yes is not coming; the no comes, the doubt comes. The trust is not total." And it is natural – nothing special about you, it happens to everybody.

This is how one grows: hesitating, doubting, saying yes, saying no, wavering – this is how one grows. But if one persists, if one remains patient enough, then one day all those no's disappear. The ultimate victory is always of yes. But one has to wait. The impatient ones miss – the patient ones win. So just be patient.

Osho, Hallelujah!, Ch. 20

The meditations which had been a source of bliss and enjoyment in the past brought out an army of ghosts. Had these shady characters had a voice they would have spoken with words like, "I hate to feel alive. It makes me uncomfortable. I'd rather remain a little bit dead. It feels more secure. What is going to happen next? Everything is so unpredictable. I want to remain in the old, comfortable, dark hole and hide under the blankets."

But there was something pushing me from behind, or pulling me from the front, which made me stick to the meditations and to the path I had chosen. It was not time to give up now! I guess this is the miracle of being with a master. Not that Osho would have objected to my going back home, but there was no 'going back home' or any 'going back' as such. Maybe there is some warrior streak in us sannyasins for which the only possibility is to go forward. All I did was to stick to the meditations and remain open to receive whatever was to come. It could well be that the *satori* with which I was graced the previous year was testimony enough that the bad was just a passing phase. And then, just to look into Osho's smiling face, was enough not to lose heart.

I later found these beautiful paragraphs, where Osho is addressing a participant of a therapy group at a darshan. Yet it seems he was also talking straight to me so that I might understand what had happened.

Sometimes it happens that on the one hand we try to go into a thing and on the other hand we try to avoid it. That creates a conflict, a contradiction. Then your own energy starts fighting with your own energy – that is dissipation. That's how many people destroy their life. When you are going into something, go totally, go wholeheartedly, don't hold back, and great will be the benefit from it.

In fact the benefit does not depend on the group process; it depends on your wholeness. The group process is just an excuse, a situation. The real thing does not happen through the group process, it happens through your co-operation. And that is not only so in the group; that is so with me too. I am just an excuse. If you can go with me the whole way, God is bound to happen to you. It always happens when you go the whole way.

But people go very reluctantly – they go on resisting and fighting. That fight and that resistance are almost unconscious. It is not that they are deliberately doing it, otherwise why should they be here? They are here because consciously they want to cooperate with me, to go with me, to explore the unknown with me, but some unconscious fear, some unconscious habit pulls them back. The conscious is only one tenth, the unconscious is nine tenths; you cannot win against it. It has to be persuaded, seduced, so that you can go wholeheartedly – both consciously and unconsciously.

Osho, *The 99 Names of Nothingness*, Ch. 19

Between meditation camps we organised our lives around the two daily meditations – Dynamic and Kundalini – and a lot of gossip and a lot of doing nothing. I remember once seeing a girl I knew doing some sewing and I thought, "What? She is *doing* something!" which made me realise how much I had changed from the busybody I had been all my life.

And then there were Osho's discourses, one month in English and one month in Hindi. The change-over was at the start of the meditation camps, on the 11th of each month. I loved listening to the Hindi discourses, although I hardly understood a word, except for a few, like my name and the names of others of which I knew the meaning. As with listening to music, my rational mind could go to sleep while my aesthetic mind could enjoy the range from the high tones to the low ones, from the soft words to the intense ones. Asked about it, Osho suggested that it was not necessary for us to learn the language to understand his discourses – all the more reason to enjoy the music of his voice.

But sometimes my friend, Yoga Pratap, would tell me, with rolling eyes and sweeping gestures, how poetic the morning discourse had been – and that the way Osho had expressed himself would be very difficult to translate into English. He was one of the Hindi editors at the time and in later years became one of the translators of the Hindi books.

Once I went to discourse, unaware that it was the 11th of the month, and suddenly the *sutra* was read out in English. My mind gave a jolt. "What? English? Now I have to make the effort to understand?" I guess that sometimes it was time for listening to music and sometimes it was time to understand things. On uneven days we had the *sutras*. These were sections from Hindi sacred scriptures Osho was commenting upon. The *sutras* were written in a poetic form and would be sung by our wonderful singer Taru. Then came the translation read in Queen's English by Teertha, the meditation leader, who later became one of the main therapists. On even days Osho replied to our questions. They were typed and attached to a clipboard which Laxmi handed him once he had greeted the audience and sat down.

The morning discourses were now in the new auditorium which was rebuilt after the roof had collapsed. Osho named it after Chuang Tzu – Lao Tzu's most well-known disciple. We would wait at the Lao Tzu gate for our turn to enter. There were two lines: the one on the right was for the workers and residents of the ashram who would enter first and take the first rows in front of Osho. The line on the left was for common folks like me. Tall American Bhakti used to get up really early to be the first in line. It must have been part of her meditation because she was there year after year. But there were also the sneaky ones who would jump the queue, like Neerja. But she was so charming about it that no German or Swiss ever busted her for it!

When the gates opened we took the path to the right, along the construction site of the new library for Osho's books (about 16,000 at the time), around its corner between the house and Mukta's beautiful, ever growing garden. We left our shoes along the path and memorized the spot where we left them. The auditorium was attached to the back of Osho's house, a semicircle built into the garden covered by a flat roof supported by round black marble columns. The floor was a mosaic of marble pieces of different colours laid in green grouting. During the discourse I would let my eyes wander over their patterns as I did as a child on our bathroom floor. Two doors opened from the house into the auditorium: the one on the left I saw being used by Haridas, Osho's electrician, when he dashed into the hall just before discourse after an urgent repair; the one on the right was the door Osho would come out followed at a distance by his secretary, Laxmi, and Nirvano, his caretaker.

When sitting on the right hand side of the auditorium I could look through the door into the house and watch Osho come round the corner in the dark corridor. As soon as he saw us, he folded his hands in *namaste* and his figure became clearer as he approached the brightness of the hall. He walked neither slow nor fast, just at a beautiful pace. Many of us had the impression that his feet never really touched the ground – probably because of the grace and fluidity of his body movements. He then walked towards his chair, still in greeting, sat down, crossed one leg over the other and gently adjusted the towel on his lap. While looking over to Laxmi he extended his left hand towards her to get the clipboard. Bowing her upper body and holding her mala to prevent it from dangling, she handed Osho the pad with our questions or the *sutras*. These movements were the same every day, and there was something relaxing about them being the same every day, but they were never mechanical. They had the glow of presence, as if they had been discovered that very moment for the first time.

The garden which surrounded us on two sides was part of the discourse: the rustling of the trees, the shadows of the leaves dancing on the floor and the gusts of wind playing with our hair. From afar you could hear the calling of the cuckoos during mating time and the hooting of the trains – sounds you can also hear in the recordings! In spring a family of sparrows nested in the window behind Osho's chair. They would fly over our heads, missing Osho's face by just an inch, but they never interfered with the flow of his words. Every day it was a special gift – and I was aware of it – to sit there and hear his words, imbibing the air around him, his presence filling the hall and the garden behind. We did try to resist his charm but soon we opened up and let him into our hearts and souls.

Just sitting by the side of the master, doing nothing, one starts imbibing the spirit. Nothing is said, nothing is heard, but a flame is transferred.

The true religion is always a transmission beyond scriptures, beyond words; hence the true religion can only be experienced with an enlightened, awakened master. With a Buddha, with a Lao Tzu, you can experience it, but not through words. The moment something is said – something which cannot be said – it becomes false.

Words are like pictures. A picture of a Buddha or a Jesus is not the Buddha or Jesus. You have to come in communion with an authentic, alive master.

Osho, *At the Feet of the Master*

Whenever I think of the evening darshans I always get the picture of a campfire, a reunion of one's tribe, a feeling of preciousness, of being totally accepted and of being in *the* place we most wanted to be. A campfire comes to mind because of the warmth and cosiness I felt and has nothing to do with meteorological conditions. In fact, I remember one evening in particular, it must have been winter or during monsoon time, when I felt physically extremely cold, but the warm 'campfire feeling' persisted despite my shivering.

Mukta was always sitting to the right of Osho and, while glancing at her notepad from time to time, called up the interviewees one after the other. When they had seated themselves a few feet in front of Osho, she leaned forward towards him and whispered, I believe, snippets of information like: "He is leaving." "She wants to take sannyas" or "He has come back after a year."

Osho would give us more homework to do, new meditations to try at home and report back about after a period of time. He gave me this peculiar meditation which was divided into four stages of fifteen minutes each: in a sitting position, slowly sway like a metronome from side to side, shouting 'hoo' at the lowest point, followed by (if I remember rightly) sitting silently, standing and lying down. Osho demonstrated the meditation to me, leaning over the arm of his chair.

During this meditation I rediscovered sensations which I had experienced before. As a child, just before falling asleep I often had the sensation that my body was turned into a rock and that I could no longer move. The jaws were locked, hands stiff, as if my whole body was put into a cast. I would then just say to myself: "Oh, the rock man is here!" Another sensation: my body seemed to become smaller and smaller, or the duvet grew bigger and bigger. I was definitely in Alice's Wonderland and welcomed these sensations playfully, without fear. But now as an adult I was terrified because I was losing control of what was happening to me and that was scary. But slowly slowly I learned to relax, to let go and welcome the sensations the way I did as a child – and also to start to enjoy the meditations.

One evening at a darshan, Osho told me another meditation to do at home: sing 'aaaaah…' for twenty minutes, changing heights and depths and creating new tunes, then sit silently and then lie down. After the beginning trials the melodies formed themselves on their own accord without my interference and I listened to my own voice flying high, in half and quarter tones as in Indian music, arabesques dancing in red and orange wriggles like my hennaed hair. The deep notes vibrated in my chest, affecting each cell; I felt powerful and limitless.

At another darshan I mentioned the pain in my back I had had for some time and which occurred only during the meditations. I told Osho that I thought it had something to do with a fearful image I had from my childhood, but Osho waved my thoughts away suggesting that I start taking saunas. There happened to be a sauna in downtown M.G. Road so I started the 'treatment' that same week and later in Geneva I visited one on a weekly basis. I had heard of people taking drugs and going on 'trips', about their colourful visions and strange sensations, but that the heat of the sauna could create such hallucinations – and some were quite uncomfortable to go through – was quite unexpected. I religiously stuck to my weekly routine until the sensations vanished and the pain in my back disappeared. I am sure that if it hadn't been Osho who had suggested the saunas, I would have walked out of this purification process long before...

I was living in the quite elegant Guru Prasad apartments, about 20 minutes' walking distance from the ashram, and our next door neighbour was Prageet, a handsome, strong and healthy-looking American. He was giving sessions in his flat using a massage technique I had never heard of before: Rolfing. The price he asked for his sessions was exorbitant – something like a month's rent and paid in advance, of course – and rumour was that it was Osho's idea to keep the prices high. The sessions were extremely painful and I reasoned that only a high price would keep the patients from jumping up from the treatment table and running away. With Prageet, bodywork had now arrived in Pune. It was summer 1975.

If life had gone according to my wishes, I would never have left the ashram or Osho, but when the money ran out and the visa had expired it was time to leave again. Go back to the West, make money as quickly as possible to come back to Pune, was the routine – for years on end. Also our stay in the West was time and time again a test of whether or not what we had learned from Osho would survive in the heaviest of traffic jams!

So, just like the previous year, there I was standing yet again with my red suitcase at the phone booth inside the coffee bar of Piazza Cinque Giornate. Hardly a penny in my pocket, and no panic either. Out of the blue I felt like calling Saeed, the manager of Air India, just to say hello. It turned out that because many of my friends had bought their tickets to Pune from his company, I had earned two free tickets as a commission. He asked me to come over to his office right then and there. One of the tickets would go to Veda so that he could also return and the second one I could sell to Deeksha's mom who was about to leave for Pune. This meant that I immediately had some cash to start my next stay in the West.

I looked in my suitcase to see if I had something I could give to Saeed as a gift. Apart from my few clothes there was only a book: *My Way: The Way of the White Clouds* by Osho. It was the first bound and illustrated English book which had been published – a real treasure. Despite the fact that Saeed had always been quite suspicious about my orange-wearing fashion – the concept of a guru was not in the mind field of someone brought up as a Muslim – I still took it with me. The moment I put the book on his desk he started reading it without giving me any further attention. He became so absorbed in the book that I had to show myself out of his office without saying good-bye. After a month, his whole family went to see Osho and took sannyas and, after two years, he was transferred to Pune and became the manager of the Air India office there. It was a much less prestigious position but he was happy to be close to Osho all the time.

Nadabrahma

This long word means 'the sound of Brahma', of the divine. Osho named one of his meditations 'Nadabrahma'. We seat ourselves in a semicircle in front of Osho's podium, spaced close enough to hear each other. We hum relaxed, slowly breathing in and out, each one in their own rhythm. The sound of bells, big Tibetan singing bowls and small tingling bells, fills the hall with their overtones. They touch all parts of the body with their vibrations. The humming sound on the inside vibrates not only the vocal cords, but the head, the chest and even the belly. After a while it feels as if somebody else is humming with my body. I curiously watch it all happening. Thoughts try to grip my attention, decisions want to be taken, 'what if I… and if he…'. Soon my mind gets bored with the arguments, leaving me alone with the humming and the bells. The half hour seems unending but, when the bells stop, also very short. The harmonium leads me into the next phase: I stop the humming and rotate the arms, palms up, forming outward circles, and then palms down forming inward circles for the second part, in such a slow motion that my attention has to be constantly with the hands. The moment I start thinking, the movements stop. The last quarter of an hour I enjoy seated in silence.

Gayatri told me that when she first met Osho he had asked her what meditations she had done and she mentioned this technique she had learned from a Buddhist teacher. Osho suggested she pick it up again and after a few weeks it was introduced as Nadabrahma and became part of the camp programme. Gayatri, a chubby and lively economist from the States, worked for the UN in Geneva and we shared the duties and pleasures of running Osho's Meditation Centre there.

I had arranged with Deeksha that I would come to Geneva and take over her centre in order to give her the chance to be with Osho.

Lalita, who used to baby-sit the centre every six months, was now in Pune 'forever' and did not want to return. The centre was a one-bedroom flat in Onex, on the outskirts of Geneva. Deeksha introduced me to the communal washing machines, the hotel manager from whom we rented a soundproof conference room, the awkward stick shift of the Citroën 2CV and the strict rules in Switzerland: no vacuuming on Sundays, no showers and no music after ten and no loud talking in the hall. She exiled Veda to Santosh's chalet in the Jura hills, which was painful for me but also a relief. Relationships just never worked out for me, it seemed, and I felt quite jealous of Deeksha who even had a boyfriend *assigned* to her by Osho.

After this introductory month, Deeksha left with Krishna Bharti, two enormous aluminium suitcases full of Swiss goodies and a whole family in tow who wanted to take sannyas in Pune. This family was Neerja with her Italian husband, Vedant, and their little boy, Siddhartha. Also included was a Chinese straw hat that Deeksha carried on her back with its string around her neck. Osho had started wearing hats for photography sessions and as soon as the news spread, people started bringing him hats from all over the world. Deeksha's was one of the first in this trend.

I knew Switzerland from my years in grammar school, but still got a culture shock when I arrived after so many years of living in Italy – and India. Geneva, for centuries ruled by Protestants – Calvinists to be exact – was drenched in an atmosphere of strictness and tightness. Even the traffic was confining and I infuriated many a Genevan with my Italian driving. My sister Kätti, who had also lived there, compared Geneva to a rich old lady. This image applies in particular to the Quays along the Rhône with their stately, imposingly-decorated stone buildings. Sitting on a bench along the river during lunch-break I could see them across the water bathing in the sun with their Paris inspired *mansardes.* Further to the right, at the end of the lake, was Geneva's famous landmark: the *Jet d'Eau,* the tall spouting fountain. Sailing boats belonging to those lucky ones who were not confined to an office during a sunny day like this, dotted the light blue waters of the lake. Closer to me, mallards, coots and seagulls contended for the biggest bits of whole-wheat bread from my sandwich. After half an hour the lunch-break was over.

The elevators to my office were, oddly, hidden in a shopping passage which I could reach through a department store, the Grand Passage. My job was that of an assistant in the media department of McCann Erickson, a large American advertising agency. The salary was so low that it just covered the rent of the flat and that of the meditation hall, plus gas and food. My boss was Urs Hug and he was quite a few years younger than me. Because we kept in touch over the years, I learned that he later became the director of an international agency in Zurich, until he was so burnt out (aged 38) that he had to retire to the countryside. But in those days he was still on the climb – not driving a 'car' to the office but 'my Porsche'. The following year he replaced it with a stunning dark blue Ferrari Dino (I once got a ride in it!).

Every day before work I drove my little red 'duck' (that's how the Citroën 2CVs were affectionately called) to an Aikido dojo which we now used as a meditation hall to set up for Dynamic: tape-recorder, Osho's picture, a big plastic bag full of orange robes and blindfolds. The Aikido dojo was in a totally different area than the conference centre so I had to find a new route to avoid the morning traffic. But it was so much nicer for us. The floor was covered in light green *tatami* mats and a row of windows on one side let in the morning sun. The dojo was above a Migros shopping centre, which opened only after Dynamic was over, so we could do the meditation full blast without disturbing anyone.

About half a dozen people would show up each morning. Some were Gayatri's colleagues, some came out of thin air, it seemed, and some came from a psychiatrist and a physiotherapist. The latter two had a practice together on the other side of town and whenever they were stuck with a case and did not know how to go on with a treatment, they just told their clients to come up to the dojo and do the Dynamic. The almost miraculous changes in their clients were proof enough that there was something behind that meditation and in no time they packed their suitcases and off they went to Pune. This did not happen only to them: most of our 'clientele' dropped out of our classes, not because they stopped meditating, but because they also went to see Osho. So, in order to keep the classes running we had to continuously find new people.

There is a fine line between being missionaries and letting people know there is such a thing as Dynamic Meditation in town. We thought that being available was the way to go: on Tuesdays Gayatri invited her colleagues from the UN to her home to listen to a discourse by Osho and on Wednesdays we had Nadabrahma at the centre in Onex. Both Gayatri and I are Tauruses and it was obvious that food had its importance in whatever we did. There was always food after the evening get-togethers and on Sundays, after Dynamic, we brunched to our hearts' (and bellies') content on delicious buttered *délices*, fruit muesli, croissants and Danish pastries in a tea-room near the dojo.

As we are talking about food I am reminded of the Hare Krishna centre where we used to go when we were longing for some good vegetarian food, something which was not available anywhere else in town. I was quite jealous of their centre. It was a little castle situated along the lake which had previously been the seat of the German Consulate – just to give an idea of the prestigiousness of the place! They could afford the rent of such a beautiful place because they were able to draw on funds from their headquarters in India.

This was not our case; we were self-sufficient. Osho's centres relied on individual sannyasins, on their creativity in running them according to their own understanding. We were free to organise them the way it fitted with our spare time and money. Over the years I saw how different people were attracted to Osho through different centres and how each place and personality attracted their own people.

Another way to let people know about Osho was to place his books in bookshops. At the time they were available only in India, so we brought them over in our suitcases or shipped them overland. Deeksha had made an agreement with a shop where we could have a shelf of Osho's books and they would pay us after they were sold. So once in a while I visited the shop to stock up. I am reading now in a book by Devika, a woman from Geneva whom I did not meet at the time, that she became a sannyasin because she found a book by Osho in that very shop!

We also attended lectures by other spiritual people with the idea that those attending such an event could also be interested in our meditations. Wearing orange would have been enough of an advertisement; if someone was interested they could ask us questions. Nobody ever approached me, but one interesting thing happened during one of these events – a spiritual Indian woman commented at the start of her lecture, "I am so pleased to talk in this beautiful room," while looking around the room. Only I knew what she was talking about – it was the room we did Dynamic in every morning.

Today I found the following question answered by Osho: "Osho, is every disciple a medium to spread the vision of the master?"

Certainly. I am against any kind of organisation because every organisation has proved an enemy of truth, a murder of love. I trust in the individual. Each and every sannyasin, alone, is my medium. Each and every sannyasin is connected to me directly.

There is no organisation between me and you. There is no priesthood between me and you. So the more empty you become, the more you will be able to receive my vibrations, my heartbeat, my song, the more you will be able to dance in tune with me – and that is the only right way to spread the message. Because the message is not of language; the message is of being, of experience.

We cannot create catechisms, principles, ten commandments – we cannot do that. I can only do one thing: to help you to be empty so that you can radiate me as totally as possible.

Osho, *The Osho Upanishad*, Ch. 43

The person who benefitted from the centre the most was probably me, more than the participants of the meditations. It gave me a focus outside my 9-5 job. It helped me stay connected with Osho and – in this unfamiliar town – meet many interesting people. I remember when a girl from Romania called me up and asked for help the morning after another girl in her hostel had killed herself. Then there were a French housewife, a tall Swiss German technician, a clever city idiot always on roller skates, a young black jazz dancer and a bar pianist...

I never started talking about Osho unless I was specifically asked. It was interesting to see how my replies to questions always differed according to whom I was talking with and I heard myself explaining the meditations or my connection with Osho always in new ways. Quite often I was puzzled by my own words, the way they popped out of my mouth, sometimes revealing very intimate feelings. But from the intent eyes of the listener I knew that what I was saying was the right thing for them to hear.

If Gayatri had answered the same question she would have said something totally different, something which came out of *her* experience – and I often marvelled at her answers as they opened a new perspective for me. Each one of us had a different approach and understanding and we expressed that – there was no party line! And whatever I write here is absolutely my own personal experience. Somebody else has other stories to tell and will tell them differently. Osho encompasses so many aspects and has thousands of birds to sing his song.

When I heard that Deeksha also wanted to remain in Pune 'forever' and was only going to come back to Geneva to collect her belongings, I organised a three months' leave of absence at work, made sure that some friends would help Gayatri with the Dynamic and found a sannyasin couple to live in the centre while I was gone. I would not have much of a chance to go for a longer time anymore, I feared.

Returning to Pune was never a 'going back'. The ashram was always different after each absence and I always had butterflies in my stomach before the journey. "What will it be like?" I asked myself as if I were going on an uncharted trip to an unknown country. This time I found a new development in the ashram: therapy groups.

Many trained therapists and psychologists who were practising in the West realised that their work had reached a limit, that there were many questions unanswered. The most courageous ones came to Osho and he gave them the opportunity to continue their work, but under his supervision. The sannyasins would profit from the workshops and the group leaders, the facilitators, learned to integrate their work with meditation.

> *My emphasis here is on therapies which don't go on for years and years; just a few days of therapy to clear the ground for meditation.*
>
> *We are running here almost one hundred therapy groups, for every possible human being. But this therapy is not the end; therapy is a preparation, clearing the ground for meditation.*
>
> *This is the only place in the world where therapy is being used as a clearing of the ground for a tremendous transformation from mind to no-mind.*
>
> Osho, *Zen: The Mystery and Poetry of the Beyond*, Ch. 1

Now those who took sannyas not only received a mala and a new name but also a list of groups to attend. Osho chose the workshops very meticulously from a list in his hand as if it were a medical prescription (it probably was!). At the end of each workshop there was a darshan the whole group was invited to attend and where the participants, as well as the therapists, could share their experiences and ask questions. In this way the therapy groups followed pretty much Osho's vision.

For two months I helped out in the kitchen, but then I thought I should be doing something for my 'spiritual growth' and booked for Satori and Enlightenment Intensive workshops. Satori was held in a conference room of the nearby Blue Diamond Hotel and lasted for about ten days. It was a run-through of many techniques, including Encounter, Tantra, Past Lives and no technique at all. I was given permission to express anger and rage, scratching a big man's face (he did not even defend himself!) in front of the other twenty participants. Instead of being condemned for doing such a horrible thing I was considered brave for exposing myself! To cool off we could jump into the blue waters of the swimming pool during the breaks.

Enlightenment Intensive was held on the roof of Krishna House and lasted for three days. I remember a Japanese boy who replied to my question "Who are you?" that he was the son of a rich man. The next time we were partners again, he talked about himself alone. Slowly, slowly, going through the layers of our personality, we all found a spark of our authentic being.

Returning to Geneva was not a 'going back' either because many things had changed there too. Those who had left Geneva before I had arrived were now back home – as sannyasins. And I finally started to speak French! A group of them took me to the working-class neighbourhood of Carouge. In one of the brasseries, the one with the upright piano in the corner, we ordered *panaché* – beer with lemonade – and *une portion de frites*, which was a heaped plate of French fries. It could be ordered at any hour of the day and was so perfectly fried that to add mayonnaise or ketchup would have been sacrilege. Around the wooden table was a beautiful gathering of happy orange-clad friends: Praveena and Premabhakta, Marga and Bhatoi, Keerti.

The two therapists who used to send us their difficult patients had, in the meantime, also come back – in orange and with new names: Satyana and Rohit – and immediately turned their clinic into a Meditation Centre. It was odd that there would be two centres in the same town and, to my knowledge, none in any other Swiss city, but it worked out perfectly: we kept running Dynamic in the dojo while Kundalini was held in their spacious room with the French windows opening onto the front garden.

So much was happening for me in Geneva that I no longer had to drive five hours to my hometown Milan just to socialise, like I had often done the previous year. We had a meditation retreat at Santosh's chalet (she was the mother of Neerja who had remained in Pune), a Tai Chi weekend in a French castle with Malika, parties in the gardens of Satyana's house on the lake. At the chalet I showed slides of Osho that Krishna Bharti had left behind and Mukul, a New

Zealand girl working in Geneva as a secretary, fell in love with one of the photos and decided to go to Pune and see Osho in person. A few weeks later she helped Deeksha and Krishna Bharti carry more Swiss goodies to Pune: kitchen knives, dusters, spices, mixers, steam irons – in those days all luxuries in India. Mukul's link with Osho was not Dynamic, or a book, but his physical appearance. She was herself a pretty girl and beauty was possibly her way of connecting.

Then we went to listen to J. Krishnamurti, an enlightened mystic from India. He used to visit Saarnen in the Bernese Mountains every summer. My little red 'duck', filled to the brim with my friends from Carouge, just made it – except for the steepest roads where everybody had to get out of the car and help push it. There was a loving enmity between Osho and Krishnamurti. Whilst Krishnamurti taught that each one had to find their own way and that he did not want any followers, Osho argued that we needed techniques and a master. He also joked about Krishnamurti because – despite his teachings – he had gathered around him a group of people who followed him from place to place, and they were mostly old ladies... Osho also said that if we were in Krishnamurti's proximity we should absolutely attend a lecture and sit in the front row just to annoy him.

The only seats left were at the edge of the tent but we sat square in front of Krishnamurti and he could not have missed us dressed in our bright orange clothes. I noticed that he got very irritated by the noise of the local train when it drove by because he had to stop speaking. Very often I heard him asking the audience "Do you understand?" with frustration in his voice because, of course, we never *do* understand. I felt sorry for him but I enjoyed looking at his face – it had a wonderful glow.

It was the time when new therapies kept being invented every day and therapists travelled all over the world. And Geneva was not spared: Leonard Orr and a group of his disciples arrived to give Rebirthing groups and sessions and we sannyasins also participated. I remember that during a breathing session I went far back into a silent space where I could decide whether to cry or not, a point way behind emotions. It was a place I had never been before – the reason I remember it so clearly. Orr had invented a great technique, but I felt that it had become a religion for his disciples, all hooked into this one device. When I eventually met Leonard personally I was a bit disappointed. I guessed he was as much on the search as we all were. For the first time I heard about a flotation tank filled with lukewarm salty water because they were using one for the breathing session back in the States. That sounded intriguing.

It was clear to me that all these therapies were good for us to clean up traumas which had happened in our life, before birth and in past lives but that, in the end, what mattered was meditation. I heard Osho say that what he was offering was just a 'glass of water'. So simple. After a few years we also had our flotation tank in Pune and I could not resist booking a session. The cosmic space I moved into I will also remember to the end of my life: me, just a small entity floating in space between the stars.

In the centre in Onex I had a room mate for a while, Bhavana, who was working as a pharmacist. Late one evening we had a lively discussion – I wanted to have the centre clean and tidy, ready to receive guests at any time of the day and she argued that I was obsessive with my cleaning and that it was too late anyway for anyone to visit. That moment the doorbell rang and a blonde girl stood at the door. She said she had received our address from a meditation centre in Germany. Behind her was a young man, an American student from Paris, as we found out later. They had met each other hitch-hiking – so here they were looking for a place to stay.

The girl came with us to do Dynamic for three mornings until she left to continue her journey. The young man stayed on. He was observing Ramadan (i.e. fasting during the day and eating the fridge empty during the night!). I was not quite sure what this Ramadan was all about. And he was not even a Muslim! He was a kind of political guy, like my friends in Milan, so meditation was never part of our conversation. When Ramadan was over I was surprised when he started to come to the meditations. After Dynamic he drove my car back home saving me some heavy parking fees in town and in the evening we met for Kundalini. Driving back home together in the car we shared moments of friendship I cherish to this day.

A few months later he wrote to me from Paris that he had applied for an Indian visa but had been denied it. The reason was that he had mentioned on his application form that he intended to visit Osho in Pune. It took him a whole year to get a visa and finally see Osho. In Pune he took sannyas, received the name Pashupatti, and when he returned to the States he also introduced his mother and sister into Osho's world.

Another visit was that of Manju and her beautiful daughter, Videh – an inexplicable visit because neither of us knew why they had come. On their way to Pune they had made a stop-over from Nairobi where they lived in a big Indian community. They spent a few nights in a hotel in town and we met in the evenings after my work in the office. Many years later, while chopping vegetables in the kitchen, Manju told me the whole story. Osho had asked her "to visit the centre in Switzerland" but not understanding why she should do that, she kept postponing the visit time after time. But Osho kept asking her each time she arrived in Pune. So this time at least she would be able to tell him that she had indeed stopped over in Switzerland. Osho then asked her about the centre and she told him that they had felt welcomed. To which, if I remember her account, Osho replied, "Punya loves me a lot. And my message will spread like wildfire in Europe." I was so touched to hear this that I had to fight back my tears. Their visit was a beautiful gift to my little centre, as visits from sannyasins always are.

One Saturday morning I left for a week-end drive with Saroj, an Italian sannyasin, and visited Rani and Avinash, old friends from grammar school who had also found their way to Osho. They had a therapy centre near Zurich where they lived with their patients in a commune style situation. Saroj lived in Viareggio, on the Italian Riviera, so we drove south – totally blanking out that on Monday I had to go back to work. Apparently I needed space to breathe, to move, to travel, to discover. After dropping off Saroj I kept driving south and stopped at Assisi, St. Francis' birthplace. I was very fond of his poem about the sun, the moon and the water – the 'Song of the Creatures' – and I had had a particular liking for this saint since I was a child. It had helped that every day on my way to school I had to pass near a fountain with a life-size brass statue of him looking into the water, surrounded by birds.

The three churches dedicated to St. Francis were built almost on top of each other, on a steep barren slope outside Assisi. They were beautifully decorated with frescos by Giotto and other famous Italian artists. I had visited many churches and always looked at them with an artistic eye as if they were museums. But something changed in my perception the moment I entered the crypt where his body was kept. It was warm, mysterious, alive, full of prayer. At the entrance of the crypt I then discovered a cabinet displaying a tunic he had worn and other objects he had used. I suddenly started sobbing like a child, totally overwhelmed with emotion, and was glad I could find a dark corner where I could hide from all the other tourists. Back in the hotel I opened the wooden box Osho had given to me: it contained five grey hairs, relics of an alive saint. On my way back I visited sannyasins in Rimini and the beautiful mosaics in the churches of Ravenna. But these churches did not feel so alive; they rather felt like objects of pleasure for art lovers.

On Monday morning I was sitting at my desk, ready to calculate the millions of francs Rothmans cigarettes were going to invest in their next year's advertising campaign, as if there had been only a weekend – instead of a whole week – since the last time I had been sitting there. Urs Hug walked in, so pleased to see me that he almost gave me a hug. Only when I heard that they had been looking for me in all the hospitals in Geneva did I become aware of the implications of my disappearance. Although I consider myself to be a fairly responsible person I did not feel I had done anything wrong or that I should feel guilty about it.

In autumn 1977 there were rumours that the ashram was going to move to Kutch in Gujarat where Laxmi had found a property. I heard the train would leave Pune on 7th November and I wanted to be on it. So I gave in my notice at McCann. The move then got postponed (and later cancelled) which allowed me to gain an extra month to get ready.

I had invented a system for the media department to keep the deadlines and payments in order but the custom-printed cards had not arrived yet and nobody had shown up to take over my job. The only way to pass on the concept was to write a manual. It came to fifty odd pages which I typed in overtime, alone in the office at night, smoking the Rothmans which were lying around as freebies. Years later I heard from Urs that the *Punya Book* had leaked out to other big agencies who all adopted the system before computers took over the painstaking job.

Despite my orange-wearing, non-alcohol and vegetarian habits I must have been loved by some of the creative folks in the agency judging from the big farewell card they had prepared for me. It showed me riding on the back of an elephant flying towards the Taj Mahal. I was depicted with long wind-swept hair wearing my Indian orange puff trousers with strings at the ankles and a *kurta*.

Although I had lived in Italy for so many years I had never been a *fashionista*. I followed some of the most rudimentary 'laws' like that of wearing shoes and handbag of the same colour and nail polish matching my lipstick (a law which is now long out of fashion, I am told), but since I have been a sannyasin things have got worse. Just imagine, my favourite outfit was an ankle-length Tibetan hand-loom robe which I wore with a pair of white, yes white, sailing shoes with rubber soles. My excuse was that they were sooo comfortable!

After my faux-pas when I left Milan without taking care of the meditation centre, I made sure that the change-over was perfect this time. Gayatri was happy to take on the task. I closed the centre in Onex and moved the book and tape library, and the portable cassette player to her place, as well as the robes which we lent to people for Dynamic. To make space for all this, with Gayatri's permission, I started to clean out her flat, in the same way I had done with my flat in Milan: all gadgets which were not absolutely necessary were collected in boxes for the charity shop Caritas. In the evening, when Gayatri returned from her job, she went through the boxes and said goodbye to her old treasures, "Oh, that's a present from Sharon who went back to the States. This one is a Xmas present from my boss. And this one... maybe I keep it for a while, may I?"

On the last evening before my departure I counted my money: what I had received for overtime, holidays not taken and the car I sold, amounted exactly to the sum that, according to what I had heard from Deeksha, was required for a donation to be part of the ashram. In the middle of the night I woke up Gayatri and told her the good news. I could become an ashramite and live in Pune 'forever'!

3

Surrender

Heart Dance

My friend Yatro wants to participate in Meera's painting group
and asks me if I would run the Heart Dance for her this week.
('Heart Dance' is the mid-nineties' name of the circle dancing
which in earlier days was called 'Sufi Dance'.) It is a chance I
couldn't possibly turn down. Just imagine me singing in Buddha
Hall! It would be my first time, a dream come true! And what a
gift – tomorrow is my 50th birthday!

I still cannot believe the good fortune of being here setting it all
up: we lay a carpet in the middle of Buddha Hall to prevent the
drums and amps from marking the marble; then prepare the
microphones for the singers and musicians. After a quick sound
check we are ready to go. The dancers gather around us, curious
to find out what songs we have in store for them today. Visitors
from India, Japan, Switzerland, South Korea, Africa, Germany are
gathered, new faces and the old aficionados, all in maroon robes,
nationalities mingling. There are a few tasks for them: the mind
has to remember the words – are they in English, Hindi or
Swahili? The legs must remember the steps, and the melody
should be in the right pitch as well. And for many it is the first
time that they hear the song. Intense, not much space for thoughts.
Their faces start to glow.

We have over a hundred songs collected during the years in
Pune One (1974 to 1981) and the period we call Pune Two (1987
onwards), but the juicy songs, which include interaction with a
partner and are fun to dance and sing, have been repeated so

many times that we cringe just hearing the first line. So I thought of making up a new one to celebrate my debut, and this is what came out:

I have two beautiful feet
a right one and a left one
I can stomp, I can jump.
Oh, how lucky I am
to dance on this earth.

The lyrics go on, inviting the dancers to bend their knees, shake their arms and roll their eyes. It is a very childish and simple song but the dancers dive totally into it and we all have fun. The following day I think of writing another song but am unable to come up with anything interesting. I soon realise that one of Osho's messages which has firmly landed in me is encapsulated in this one song: to accept and enjoy the body. And how amazing it is that in Osho's world dancing, something which I love so much, can be used as a meditation.

I remember, as a teenager, dancing in our living room in Milan to the first rock and roll single I had bought after 'borrowing' some money from my mother's purse. I learned from her the cha cha cha moves and practised them holding onto the rim of the bathtub. A little older, I danced after school in my tiny room in Aarau to classical music. Later, dance and mime almost became my profession…

In most of his meditations Osho includes a dancing section – starting with Dynamic, then Kundalini, then Nataraj, which is a full forty minutes of dancing, and finally Whirling and Heart Dance.

Many times I have felt thankful to Osho that he made dance the main theme of a meditation and that, to meditate, we do not have to merely sit silent and unmoving. Osho must have understood us women very well because sitting is not something we are very good at. (I guess that if there had been more female masters, meditation would not be associated only with sitting silently but also with dancing.)

I almost forgot to mention the now sporadic Music Group which in Pune One was happening every night for as many years as I can remember. This involved dancing and singing until we flew out of the hall or ended up flat on the floor.

It was held in Buddha Hall and started at 7 in the evening, at the same time as Osho was giving darshan in Chuang Tzu. Like moths attracted to a bright light we were drawn to the centre of the hall where the musicians were ready to start. The first arpeggios on the guitar were an irresistible call even for those walking past the hall who might have decided to go home early. Running the show was Anubhava, a charismatic, good looking Bavarian with long black hair – our idol and friend. He was backed by a bass, an electric guitar and percussions.

I remember a song which goes:

He's the sun behind the sun, he's the moon
He's the moon behind the moon, he's the sun

Just now looking up the lyrics online I fathom the meaning of the words. I had been singing them totally wrong, for all these years! But it did not matter at all. What mattered was that I could feel an opening in my chest when singing the bright word 'sun' and then fall into a dark velvety depth with the mysterious word 'moon'. Like two opposites, male and female. The song could last for up to fifteen minutes, the same words repeated hundreds of times. On top of this almost hypnotic sea of sounds, Anubhava's tenor voice improvised, high up like a seagull in the sky. He often divided us into groups, forming a pattern like a pie chart: here the sopranos, there the tenors, over here the altos and the bass over there. We learned the harmonies if we didn't remember them from the day before. We sang with closed eyes, holding each other around the waist and swinging from side to side to the soft rhythm of the song.

Then he would introduce a fiery song for us to dance:

Oh my lord, you are the fire, burning like a thousand suns
Give me courage to go higher, fly with you towards the one
Towards the one, towards the one, towards the one…

These were not empty words we were singing. They described what was happening to us: our hearts flew off into the skies as did the solo of the electric guitar. It was so exciting to be alive! On the edges of the hall, in the darkness, I had the space and freedom to experiment with twists and turns, making up my own choreography as I went along. I was dancing, or rather flying, weaving my path around the wooden pillars of the hall with long leaps from pole to pole. This feeling was the best I had ever known. If I recalled a night spent with a man, if it had been very beautiful, I would say to myself: *'almost* as nice as dancing'. Dancing was the criterion, the best, the most fulfilling.

Have you observed yourself sometimes dancing? What happens? Dance seems to be one of the most penetrating things, in which one falls into a harmony. Your body, your mind, your soul, all fall into a harmony in dancing.

Dancing is one of the most spiritual things there is. If you really dance, you cannot think. If you really dance, the body is used so deeply that the whole energy becomes fluid. A dancer loses shape, fixity. A dancer becomes a movement, a process. A dancer is not an entity: he's movement, he's energy. He melts. Great dancers, by and by, melt. And a dancer cannot retain his ego because if he retains his ego, that will be a jarring note in his dance. A real dancer loses his ego in it. He forgets that he is. The dancer is lost; only the dance remains. Then the door opens because you are one unity. Now the soul is not separate, the mind is not separate, the body is not separate. All have fallen in one line. All have become one, melting into each other, merging into each other.

Osho, *The Beloved*, Vol. 1, Ch. 1

If you were working in the kitchen you were probably working in shifts which meant that you could either go to discourse in the morning or to music group in the evening (unless you were invited to a darshan). It was unfair to have to miss every other discourse, but if I had been asked which shift I preferred, I could honestly not decide which of the two I would rather miss. Despite the eight hours of hard physical work I was never too tired to dance and every other day you could find me there, dancing in Buddha Hall. I might have become addicted to something which had started happening during the whirling meditation: at a certain point I became so light that the dancing became effortless, the jumps and leaps became higher and longer than my body weight and effort could have possibly taken me. It took just a few moments of a little effort and then suddenly the body would take over and do the dancing. I could almost hear a click when it happened, the same click one hears the moment one falls asleep. I was no longer sure where my body started and where it ended. And very rarely did I bump into somebody else or into a pole, even while dancing with closed eyes; it was as if we were interconnected, moving like fish in a shoal, one breath, one rhythm.

I loved it when Osho talked about the great Russian dancer, Nijinsky, because I could relate to the story out of my own experience:

One of the greatest dancers of this century was Nijinsky. People were puzzled by his dance. Never before and never after has such a miracle been seen on the stage. There were some moments when Nijinsky would get so lost in his dance that everybody in the audience would feel that the dancer had disappeared. And a miracle would happen: he would start jumping so high that it is not possible, the gravitation does not allow that much height. And not only that – when he would start descending he would come so slowly, as if he had no weight, as if he was just a feather or a dry leaf falling slowly, slowly from the tree – in no hurry.

He was asked again and again 'What happens?' And he would say 'If I want it to happen it does not happen. I have tried and I have failed. Whenever I try I fail; my failure is absolutely certain. But when I am lost in my dance, when I disappear, suddenly weight also disappears from me. And I am also surprised just as you are surprised, because it looks so illogical. I don't feel the gravitation any more. It is not that I manage falling slowly; it simply happens. When I am not there, that miracle happens.'

Osho, *The Revolution*, Ch. 7

At the end of each song we moved back to the centre around the musicians. Holding each other around our waists we intoned the vowel 'aaaaah' and allowed the sound to vibrate our bodies and to expand to the floor of the hall and the walls of the houses next door. Like a magician, the solo guitar added more depth and height with a dissonant melody as a contrast to the uniform sound.

The 'aaaaah' was sometimes as long as a song, a bit like a 'song on one note and one vowel'. A continuous sound intermingling with the sound of our neighbours. 'Aaaaah' was more than just a vowel: it was an alchemical tool. The heart could not remain cold, the mind not calculate, the thoughts not hold a long conversation. We felt united within the circle, one sound, one soul; celebrating our being with the master. If during the working day some difficulties had popped up, they were washed away in these moments where only this sound existed.

Today the dancers are singing the last lines of my song:

I have a wonderful body
to sing and dance with you
a step forward and one back.
Oh, how lucky I am
to stand on this earth.

Part of me never wanted to belong to this earth. I always preferred to be light, to leave my body, to fly high and leave the earth behind.

But Osho reminds us again and again to be here in the body and, while commenting on Nietzsche's Zarathustra, he says:

Stay loyal to the earth…

That is one of the fundamentals of Zarathustra, he is against all religions. They say, "Remain loyal to heaven; remain loyal to God, who is far away beyond the clouds." Zarathustra's insistence is:

Stay loyal to the earth, my brothers, with the power of your virtue!

– with your love. Be loving to the earth. Sow the seeds of love on the earth. The question is not for you to enter into some paradise in the skies. [...]

May your bestowing love and your knowledge serve towards the meaning of the earth!

The earth is searching through you for its own meaning. You are the highest evolved part of the earth. Have you ever considered? – your body is earth, your brain is earth. You are the highest flowering, a great metamorphosis. There seems to be no connection between the earth and your eyes, but your eyes are nothing but the eyes of the earth. It is an effort of the earth to see. Your ears are an effort of the earth to hear the music.

Osho, *Zarathustra: A God that Can Dance*, Ch. 18

After each song, the dancers close their eyes and stand still so that all the energy and excitement gathers inside. I look into their faces: they look empty yet full of something. The silence is physically present in the hall – you can almost touch it. This was the last song. Those of us in the middle gently put our instruments aside and, like everybody else around us, kneel down to touch our forehead to the ground. I hear myself saying, 'Osho, thank you for letting me play in this beautiful hall.' It is a privilege to play for Osho and his people!

When I lift my head I see a maroon carpet of bodies, all bent towards the centre, the silence deepened by the chirping birds and the small noises from outside the hall. Some are slowly getting up and walking light-footedly towards the exit, others remain seated with closed eyes. The musicians always know when they did well, telling from how long the silence in the hall remains unbroken.

We come together in a hug, share if there is something to say – perhaps apologising for a mistake or a misunderstanding, expressing an appreciation – and then start dismantling our set-up.

Lunch

Feeling the cool marble under my naked feet I walk towards the side exit of the hall with my notes under my arm. Almost everybody has gone now and the Japanese girl is back after her lunch-break, again on the ladder deep-cleaning the crystal wall-lights of the podium. I look up and watch the shadows of the trees playing on the canvas roof and – what I love most – the fast-moving shadows of passing birds. I have to hurry if I still want to get something for lunch.

In summer 1974, just after the ashram had opened, food was pre-pared Indian style (that is, on the floor) in the servants' quarters behind Krishna House. During the meditation camps I would often go there, have a look and a sniff. I knew that to meditate on a full stomach was not a good idea, even less on a hungry one. But having discovered that just looking at food between the meditations would dispel my hunger, I used this device to stay light until the evening meal.

Two years later when I visited Pune during my holidays from Geneva I helped out in a more Western, but still improvised kitchen in Krishna House. Osho had given it the name Vrindavan – the name of the garden where Lord Krishna played his flute and met his girlfriends. One room was used for the preparation and cooking of the food – that was Danish Pratibha and Sangeet's domain. A few steps down into the garden was the table, covered by an awning, where I served the food directly from the pots. I vividly remember being involved in heated discussions about how full a 'full bowl' was meant to be. Sannyasins are a difficult lot sometimes!

This kitchen set-up seemed to me quite modern, in particular after a holiday in Goa where you would cook your food on a dirt floor, but things were soon to change. One morning Deeksha stormed in the back door with a few of her aides. She had probably just finished setting up Mariam Canteen, the worker's kitchen in the new property, Jesus House, and was now ready to take on a new project. The fact that everybody who followed her was wearing a blue, yes blue, apron was the scariest part of this invasion. Apparently no red aprons were available on the market! First thing the Swiss cleaning tornado did was to throw out all the Nescafé tins we used as containers for spices and dry goods and replace them with new glass jars with plastic lids and proper labels. Things became organised and the fun was over; it was time to escape, do some therapy groups and return to Geneva.

Priya is already dismantling the serving lines. From the stainless steel *bain marie*, I dish out yellow *dhal* and white rice, still warm, and the last (green) ladies' fingers, my favourite vegetable, into black rhombus-shaped bowls. A biscuit and a cup of tea for dessert also fit on the tray. I pay with my voucher card and continue the conversation with the cashier that we started last night. Now that I am through, he can leave his post, I say to him. Already brushes, powdered soap and squeegees are waiting on the railing for the big clean up. Just the empty serving trays need to be returned, via the funny-looking electric trolley, to Zorba the Buddha kitchen where they will be washed.

After all my years working in the kitchen I am so happy that now all I need to do is go to the serving line, make my choices, sit down and munch! At the bottom of the concrete steps I get fork and spoon, a small sachet of salt and one of pepper. At the end of the vast open-air dining hall, on the slightly elevated part near the bamboo trees, is my favourite table. My Swiss friends who always dine here must have gone back to work or to their workshops. Happy to sit alone I take the time to remember things again.

From Switzerland I arrived with rolls of high quality nylon fabric for the silk-screen department. For a few years we have been printing the titles on the full-colour jackets of Osho's books by ourselves – on a rooftop for extra ventilation – and fabric is what the department needed. I also brought a big roll of colour enlargements of Osho's photos which were quite cheap if ordered from Migros. All these goods I proudly laid on Laxmi's desk; they were the main part of my donation. There was also an envelope with the remaining money which I left in my pocket. Deeksha had put it there before I went to see Laxmi. "Keep it for yourself. You might need it," she had said.

If I wanted to move into the ashram immediately, Deeksha had a space for me: in a brick hut behind Buddha Hall. That is, if I was willing to share it with four men. The fifth bed had remained empty because the fifth man, Asutosh, was still not sure if he wanted to take part in the commune experiment or not. (A year later he moved into a bamboo hut he had built by himself in the garden close to ours.) I was willing and I did move in!

One of the walls of the hut was part of the fence toward the street which resonated from early morning till late at night with the engine noises of rickshaws arriving and leaving the ashram, interspersed with the typical loud and open-vowelled Marathi chatter of the drivers. But, as if to compensate, it was just a few yards away from the new Buddha Hall and only a few steps from the gravelled path where Osho drove home after discourse. He would have seen our white-washed brick hut and, along the fence, a few more bamboo huts. Some of them had beautiful gardens in front of them, created by talented night-guards who had spare time during the day. When from inside the hall I saw Osho drive along the path, I always felt he was also giving his blessings to the huts lining the edge of the property.

My roommates were, at one end and close to the door, Paritosh and Shantam. Both usually spent the night with their girlfriends, so they mostly came to the room just to get a change of clothes or a quick rest in the afternoon. Across from my bed was Veda and, behind my head, Nigama. They were both lean, tall and handsome men and, of course, had many stories to tell each other about girls. Having grown up without brothers this was a new world for me, so different from knowing men as colleagues or as lovers. What amazed me the most was to hear about their insecurities and their heart-breaks, because men had always come across to me as rather macho, untouched by sentiments and fear of rejection. Sometimes the whispers became too dim for me to hear but, while falling asleep, I kept bathing in the feeling of acceptance, friendship and brotherhood – something I will always treasure.

It was inevitable that one of us would bring a lover at night while others were in the room. Instead of fighting the intrusion I learned to relax and remain silent, while lying with closed eyes on my bed, and accept what was happening in the room. Sometimes their orgasm overwhelmed even me and filled me with blissful energy. In summer, when the nights became warmer, we slept on the roof of Jesus House. Nigama and I had special mattresses made, from coconut fibre, which were light enough to carry up the stairs. The flat roof, tiled in white mosaic, was open to the sky and I enjoyed falling asleep in the company of the full moon and my friends.

Next day was work and, as expected, I would be in Deeksha's kitchen. Nigama and Veda were already out when I woke up. Nigama was working in the bakery in town and Veda was off buying vegetables in the market. One of my first jobs was in the storeroom. It was a small room, about eleven by twelve feet, in the back of the kitchen. It had a pass-through window into the kitchen and a door at the back where deliveries came in. I shared the shifts with an English sannyasin, Vadan. The stock keeping was the easy part of the job; what was difficult was to be constantly confronted with the wishes and complaints of the cooks – and with our own likes and dislikes.

After a short time we became the two tough guards watching over the kingdom's treasures, so much so that the cooks became afraid to poke their heads through the window. They really had to be sure that they needed that very amount of icing sugar! I remember when Maneesh from Mariam Canteen came over and asked us for a litre of (imported) olive oil. To give out such an expensive item and, on top of that, for the workers' canteen, I should have asked Deeksha for permission. I liked him and decided to give him the oil without asking. When Deeksha found out... you can imagine the pandemonium! I was not allowed to use my job for my private interests and, moreover, I had to learn to say no and not to care what other people thought of me. No wonder Vadan and I rarely had a hot date between the two of us!

Another thing I had to learn was to enjoy cleaning. Maybe it was because my mother hated to do the daily cleaning for her whole family in a polluted city, and with an exacting husband, that 'cleaning' became such a dirty word to me (pun intended). But in Osho's ashram many things changed and I started to enjoy getting up from my chair, to move my body and engage in the joys of cleaning. And this was real Swiss cleaning! Down on our knees with brushes and rags! Vadan and I had sorted out our daily routine in this way: the metal and plastic bins with grains and beans were wheeled from one side of the room to the other. When the first half of the floor was clean, all the bins were pushed to the clean side and when the second part was dry, we arranged them again in alphabetical order, along the walls under the shelves and in the middle of the storeroom.

And here comes some ego-bashing from Osho:

It is very easy to do something which you like because it does not create any challenges, but something that you don't like creates challenges, and if you can make it a worship, you will grow immensely out of it.

And the thing that doesn't fit with you, that you don't like sometimes – the reason may not be in the work itself, the reason may be somewhere else. For example, cleaning – cleaning seems to be a third-rate thing. In the world that is what it is thought to be. It may be hurting your ego that Somendra is a therapist, and Teertha is a therapist, and Divya is a therapist and you are just a cleaner! It may not be exactly cleaning that you dislike; maybe the hurt comes to the ego. And you have to see that. Because you are living in a commune where every opportunity has to be used to grow.

See what it is that hurts. How can cleaning hurt you? Cleaning is such a clean job – how can it hurt you? [...] I am putting you into things and sometimes I would like you to be in a thing which you don't like really, because only that will create the friction necessary to create energy.

Osho, *Let Go!* Ch. 27

The vegetables had their own, custom-made shelves. They were placed along one wall and were about two feet deep. Mid-morning we would see Veda's silhouette appear in the back door, carrying a wide basket on his head like a *coolie*. He knew exactly how deep he had to bend his knees not to touch the top frame of the door! While he brought in the remaining crates, we started to free the papayas from the protecting straw and stack them leaning against each other, the hard ones at the back, the softer ones in front. The bananas we carefully arranged in patterns like hands lying over more hands. It had taken some bashing from Deeksha for us to learn to respect the fruits and vegetables and to appreciate them as beings rather than mere objects!

In the evenings there was enough spare time to clean the now empty shelves, to wash behind the tins of baking soda and packets of garam masala, turmeric and other spices. There were no corners we did not clean daily. It was like learning to look into each corner of our psyche, leaving no stones unturned where something might hide from conscious inspection.

In front of important people and in particular in front of Osho, I always behaved in a clumsy way, like a 'potato' as we say in Italian. If I think of it, I could have been a photographer for Osho or I could have helped with the translations from Italian, German and French into English during darshan, but... Lalita, the one who did not come back to the Geneva centre to release Deeksha, used to translate in darshan for the Italian and French speakers.

When one day she fell sick I was asked to do her job. It was going to be in French, which was the language I was least fluent in, but I would certainly give it a try.

At the gate someone introduced me to the girl I was going to translate for and, whispering into my ear, warned me to watch out that this girl was a bit 'funny'. I soon forgot the remark and when she was called up I sat next to her to translate between her and Osho. If I remember well, Osho asked her if she was doing Dynamic Meditation in the morning. Instead of replying with a yes or a no, she started telling a long story about her past which I dutifully translated into English. Osho, understandably, made big eyes at me and through my facial expression I tried to explain that I was translating verbally what she had said. The conversation became wilder and wilder as it went on and my head got more and more muddled up. At one point I had to ask Osho to repeat the sentence he had just said. It felt like standing on stage and forgetting my line!

It was immediately clear that this would be my first and last time translating for Osho. But interestingly, sitting in front of him I did not feel like a failure; there was no blame, not even towards the 'funny' girl. There were no punishing words from parents or teachers inside my head. This is how it went and there was nothing I could have done differently!

How Deeksha came to oversee a whole empire can be understood if you see how things evolved. When the cooks' aprons needed mending (they were red by now) she opened a sewing department. And as the aprons also needed to be washed and ironed she opened a laundry and an ironing department. When she wanted the cooks to have long wooden ladles to stir the milk – and was unwilling to wait for the slower pace at which the carpenters worked – cooks became handymen and a big tool-shop was opened. Her handymen finally built Osho's marble podium, but this quite a few years later... We had a bakery in town, a tofu factory on one of the roofs and a Frenchman to prepare cheese. So, as a kitchen worker you could be a handyman today and a baker tomorrow, at the whim of the boss.

So it was that one morning I found myself standing at an ironing board with a spray bottle in my left hand and a heavy iron in my right. I always thought ironing was the biggest nightmare – even worse than cleaning (even today I usually iron a dress just before wearing it). But now that ironing was my job and I was going to do it the whole day, I tried my best to start enjoying it – which I did.

There was no logic as to why we should also have to work in shifts; the only reason I could see was that we were not meant to be more privileged than the other kitchen workers. It was a shame to have to miss Osho's discourse, but the mornings were also beautiful up there. The ironing terrace was on top of the kitchen overlooking Osho's garden and I could watch how the first rays of the morning sun filtered through the big trees of his garden. The moisture in the air turned them into a blue-grey haze. Then suddenly the rays touched my forehead, my body and the ironing board and I continued to sway rhythmically back and forth while working down through the pile of red-checked and flower-patterned aprons.

Slowly the morning filled with the sounds of people walking on the path below, getting ready for the discourse and finding their way to Buddha Hall. Then occurred a long deep silence in the whole ashram, and then a crunching sound on the gravel as Osho was driven from Lao Tzu House to Buddha Hall. Now he must be greeting the gathering – and now came his first words over the loudspeakers. I could not hear the words distinctly as they were bouncing off the walls of the buildings, but the melody and harmony of his voice were soothing and turned the ashram into a fairyland.

The few cooks on shift and the beverage maker – the *chai wallah* – worked quietly without making a noise that would disturb the discourse and I silently ironed the next basket of aprons which had dried in the sun the previous day. More than ironing it was outlining the edges and the pockets, almost like making a drawing. The distant sounds from the loudspeakers were entering my heart. If I couldn't sit in front of Osho then this was an acceptable alternative.

My tea is getting cold over so much pondering. I dip the hard half moon cookie into it and in two bites it is gone. I lean back in my black plastic chair, move the black plastic tray to the other end of the black metal table and look over to the black house in front of me. Why everything black? I heard that Osho had seen a picture in a Japanese architectural book which showed a dark house with windows reflecting the sky and that after that he had given the instruction to have our houses painted black and the windows covered in blue film. Of course there were many discussions among us sannyasins, as there always is. We thought that the black colour would attract too much heat from the sun, but then the esoteric circles thought the colour would keep negative energy away (Osho was still not a favourite in the media and in political circles). And we did not quite understand why the blue windows, but apparently with all the pollution in the air we do not get enough blue light. Once the job was done I felt that it was a tremendous aesthetic improvement, mostly because the Indian whitewash could never be kept clean and pristine. The colours in the commune were now the black of the buildings, the green of the plants and the maroon of the people.

So now to sit in front of Jesus House is a real aesthetic experience. Its black walls highlight the green of the garden and the white of the peacock that, as I have just discovered, has landed on the ledge which was once the roof of the entrance porch. This is the house I had lived in for three years, on the first floor. That one window to the right of the porch was our room. I rarely think of the past even while spending time in the same place – as part of the discipline to live as much as possible in the present – but today I want to write about the time when I lived there. Many images pop up, all at the same time, fighting over which one should come first. But in the nature of writing, one thing has to come after the other…

When we arrived from the West, Osho used to ask us in darshan if we were now here 'forever'. Many of us had closed our flats, sold our houses and split from our unhappy marriages to come and stay forever with our master. Time showed that 'forever' was just a few years, but 'forever' also meant 'totality'. And in order to be with Osho totally it was important that nothing in our home country had remained unresolved.

Some wealthy sannyasins had donated all their money to the ashram, and I suspect that this gesture, apart from expressing gratitude, was for them also a way of saying, "All I want is to be here and I do not need this money any longer." After having spent the money in that hidden envelope I now existed with zero capital –

which I was happy about because sometimes, when my ego was getting a bit too uncomfortable, I would have loved to buy an air ticket and escape!

There was no need for money really – at the most some for sweets or cigarettes – because the ashram took care of all my needs. I had food and lodging and received clothes from the kitchen if I needed any. I got so used to living this way that when somebody, out of the blue, gave me fifteen rupees they felt so uncomfortable in my pocket that I had to quickly spend them. So, to get rid of them, I immediately invited some friends to eat cake for afternoon tea with me.

Jesus House, where I had just moved from the men's room, was a beautifully built house with many features. I always liked the smooth round handrail along the spiral staircase up to my room. On the landing of the first floor, Padma, my next-door neighbour, had started painting a fresco of the Buddha. So this was my address: left of the Buddha, first door to the right. We were three girls living in that room: myself, Mukul from New Zealand (the one who had decided to come to Pune after seeing a photo of Osho and who helped Deeksha leave Geneva with her many suitcases) and Sagara, a gardener from Australia.

My bed was in the loft next to the door. The space under the loft served as a wardrobe for our clothes. The room also had a spacious white tiled en-suite bathroom. Down the corridor lived Pankaja who had been a successful writer (I was so impressed by that). The last room was Chaitanya Hari's studio-cum-bedroom. We never had an opportunity to have a conversation with each other but I remember a time, a few years later, when he used to give concerts for us residents in his room.

Finally I saw the synthesiser I had heard of – and discovered that it was just a black box with lots of knobs – and the many exotic instruments he had hanging on the walls. We brought our own pillows and sat in a circle around him to listen to his music. I do not remember anything about the music, except that – at the end – we could hardly get up and leave. I was lucky that I lived just two doors down the hall, but most of the others had to negotiate the stairs. They were staggering, leaning on each other for support and holding onto the railing, taking one step at the time. I am not quite sure what kind of music this was!

My next job in the kitchen was working at the serving counter. My boss was a fair-skinned and ginger-bearded Italian, Rajendra. He later wrote, together with Prembodhi, a book about Tarot reading. He was short, quite shy, but surprisingly strong in body and mind. In the hectic minutes just before the serving lines opened he showed a tremendous, infectious drive which spilled over onto me. Together we collected the heavy pots of soup, rice and vegetables from the cooking area and dished out, at supersonic speed, trays upon trays of stainless steel bowls. We were practically working from one deadline to the next. First there was the early morning breakfast deadline at 7. It was dangerous to let the meditators from Dynamic wait in front of closed doors! Already stirred up from the energy, they were never too shy to openly voice their frustration.

The next deadline was breakfast, after Osho's discourse. For this there was no set time. Osho could be quite unpredictable and obviously he could talk as long as he pleased. If the chai was not ready or we were behind with buttering the bread, we crossed our fingers that he would keep talking for a while longer. But when the discourse was over, a hush ran through the kitchen: "Lecture is over." A guard on the path had brought us the message. This would still leave us with a few minutes because Osho was still in the hall. He would get up from his chair, greet his disciples and slowly drive around the outside of the hall, before vanishing beyond the gates of Lao Tzu House. This time people streamed to the kitchen in a more relaxed fashion, but as soon as they saw the food all those beautiful qualities like grace, compassion, love, and understanding which we embody when we are sitting at the feet of the master, mysteriously disappeared! They were pushing and shoving and fighting over the biggest croissants – very embarrassing. One day I was so overwhelmed by the greed and the uncivilised behaviour of this horde of barbarians that I burst into tears and had to hide in the back of the kitchen.

Lunch was at 12:30, tea time at 3:30 and dinner at 6. All these deadlines meant rush, rush, rush: serve, price and make everything look pretty. One day I asked Rajendra why on earth we had to go through this nerve-wracking exercise so many times a day. He rolled his eyes and rubbed his hands like a merchant who had just closed a good deal and said, "I love it. It's the best."

This was during the time that Deeksha ignored me. When she walked past, with her secretaries in tow, she made sure our eyes would never meet. If by chance I came around a corner and we happened to be in front of each other she immediately looked to the other side or up to the ceiling. She didn't care if it looked very obvious. After some time – this game lasted about a year – I had to laugh about it. I had no idea why she did it. Maybe she sensed that I wanted her approval or her attention – and she did not want to give it to me.

Osho said this to a kitchen worker in a darshan:

So just surrender to Deeksha. Deeksha is the dragon master! When I don't succeed with somebody, I send them to Deeksha!

Simply surrender and then you will find that there is no problem. Simply surrender to Deeksha. Just tell her, 'I am surrendered to you, Deeksha. Whatsoever you say I will do!' Don't make any conflict with her. This is one of the things that has to be learned in the community, otherwise the community cannot grow a soul, it will remain a crowd.

And now I will insist more and more on surrender because now the community will grow and we will have to make a solid base for it. So everybody has to surrender to the community. When you surrender to Deeksha, it is just through Deeksha that you are surrendering to the community. It is not Deeksha – Deeksha is not the point – but she is there and she has to manage everything there, so everybody who works under her surrenders to her.

And you will enjoy surrendering once you learn how to surrender. It is very easy to surrender to me – difficult to surrender to Deeksha. So I will insist that you surrender to Deeksha – that is the way to surrender to me. Deeksha will be a harder thing to surrender to – to me you can surrender easily because I don't come in your day-to-day, moment-to-moment work. So this has to be learned by everybody. Sooner or later I would like to create a collective community soul. Many more things that you cannot imagine have to be done. I cannot talk about them because if I do it will be more difficult to do them, so I will simply go on doing them.

Now this will happen more and more – everybody will have to surrender to whosoever is concerned close by. Let it be total, then there is no misery left and you enjoy things. Then Deeksha and you are not separate – whatsoever she says, it is yours!

Just do this, mm? After darshan, go to Deeksha and just surrender to her and tell her that you are utterly surrendered, now whatsoever she wants you to do… If she says to you to jump and die, you will go and do it!

Osho, The Zero Experience, Ch. 13

The last paragraph refers to a Zen story we have heard Osho tell a few times; it is the story where a Zen master asks his disciple to jump out of the window. Osho talked a lot about surrender, not as a defeat, but as a letting go – letting life take its course, rather than us deciding how life should be.

Surrender, in fact, is not the right word – in English there is no right word for it. In Sanskrit we have the right word – it is **samarpan**. *It means offering oneself in deep love and trust. The English word surrender is ugly. It is used in reference to war. Adolf Hitler surrendered, Germany surrendered, Japan surrendered. It is a sort of defeat.*

In Sanskrit, **samarpan** *is not a defeat. It's a great moment of rejoicing – that one has offered oneself. It is a dedication. If you have had a small glimpse of somebody further ahead than you, you offer yourself, you say, 'Hold my hand,' that's all. And all else will come by and by.*

And it is not just lying down under a tree and not doing anything – you will remain the same. No. Only one thing will be missing, that one thing is the ego concept. And by dropping the ego your individuality is not effaced. In fact by dropping it you will become more of an individual.

Osho, The Buddha Disease, Ch. 21

Sex, Love and Friendship

I am waiting for Amiten to finish his morning shift at the dish-washing machines. He is rinsing off the food trays and the floor; his shoes and part of his robe are soaking wet. He runs up to his locker to change into dry street clothes while I wait downstairs. Hand-in-hand we walk home along the empty back streets. And after a cool shower we rest on the bed, curtains drawn, feeling the presence of each other, feeling the soft skin, the earthiness of the muscles, the cosiness of the embrace. Resting.

After one of my first Dynamics on the beach in Mumbai Deeksha invited me to the little flat she was sharing with Lalita. She took a shower and came out to dry herself in the living room where I was sipping my tea. I was amazed that she would expose her body to a stranger, especially because she was quite overweight. This is when she talked about Osho's views on sex: that we should accept our bodies and experience sex with joy and awareness. So, in a way, I was prepared that this issue would come up in a discourse, but not in the very first interview with Osho. When he asked me if I had anything to say, I complained that I had a hard time waking up in time for the Dynamic on the beach. Osho then started asking me very personal questions: which part of my body I liked my boyfriend to touch the most, and which parts of his body I liked to touch and kiss. He enquired in particular about one part! Only years later I came to know that I had been sexually abused as a child. Maybe Osho, with these questions, wanted to see what damage this had done and if I consciously recalled that particular incident.

The following year, when I visited Pune with Veda, I sent Osho a letter where I explained that Veda was now more interested in Tantric sex and that I was missing the old ways of making love where I had a physical orgasm. At my next darshan Osho said what I remember as, "I have read your letter. Go into celibacy for two to three months. No sex of any sort. In the morning for twenty minutes fantasise about food, in the evening before sleep for twenty minutes fantasise about sex. If you don't have sex you will feel like eating more and you will dream about sex. The fantasies will be helpful." My mind was puzzled. On the one hand I was proud that Osho gave me a 'difficult' meditation – Krishna Radha had also been asked to go into celibacy – on the other hand I panicked because I thought Veda would certainly leave me now. We had already planned to go for a holiday together to Goa; we still went there but rented two separate huts.

In my morning fantasy I saw boiled spinach leaves with pine nuts fried in butter and my mother's sweet dumplings. Sometimes, when father was out for dinner, she fried them for us girls as a special treat. We ate them in the kitchen and gulped them down, still piping hot, almost straight from the pan. They were soft inside and had a crunchy crust covered in icing sugar. We even kept count of how many each one of us could eat. I love food and this food meditation resulted in catharsis. In my little hut I could shout and cry as much as I wanted without disturbing anyone. I still remember watching the shadows of the palm leaves dancing on the dried cow dung floor. Then in the evening came the sex meditation. These fantasies brought me, quite unexpectedly, much peace and calmness; after the most unimaginable fantasies, with no hindrances, morality or taboos, I was soothed into a deep sleep.

Osho had spoken about sex to big crowds in Indian cities and in the meditation camps, explaining that by repressing sex we deny a big part of our vital energy, essential for meditation. Quite a courageous thing to do considering that India's attitude towards sex was so much more conservative and repressive than what I had experienced in Italy.

Some of those talks were published in the book, *From Sex to Superconsciousness*. So from very early on Osho was referred to as the 'The Sex Guru' and when later journalists started coming from the West they already had a title ready by which to call him.

I remember Osho commenting on it. He said something like,"'Sex' is one of the words in the title, 'Superconsciousness' is the other, but nobody talks about superconsciousness."

After my father died I found in his drawers all the letters I had written to him plus carbon copies of the letters he had written to me: to Geneva, to India, to Zurich, to America and back to India again. The following is a translation of a passage from one of my letters to him from that time:

"The German Press has gone totally berserk about the ashram. A German actress gave an awful interview to the press. The newspapers take everything she says as the absolute truth; they are so eager to write a scandalous article about us. I was told that even the *Tages-Anzeiger* from Zurich has published a negative article. These stories don't disturb us here in India, because we know what is really happening."

But I could well imagine that our parents back home would not be pleased if a neighbour asked, "Is your daughter with that sect all the newspapers are talking about?"

Already it was difficult for our parents to come to terms with the fact that we had left our promising careers or posts at universities (about 50% of sannyasins have at least a BA), had gone abroad, and were engaging in something called 'meditation'. Now this German actress, Eva Renzi, who had been at the ashram for barely a week and participated in a therapy group she was not ready for, was creating this big hoo-ha which was making things worse.

In my letters to my father I tried to address his rational mind, explaining that Pune was an experiment in expanding consciousness with the help of a man who had understood our soul, psyche, heart and mind. The ashram I compared to a lab which, instead of being in a white sterile hall, was in a big garden with jungle-like vegetation, and where people were not wearing white coats but long orange robes. I have no idea if he understood what I meant because we never spoke openly about me as a sannyasin or about Osho.

I also found a clipping of a Swiss tabloid – *Blick* – which came out with a series of articles about the ashram which they called 'the sex-monastery'. In one of the articles there was a cute picture of my Swiss friends Namra, Tushita and me leaning against a table in Vrindavan's garden. I still had my hair pulled back in a bun and was wearing my kitchen apron. The headline was 'I gave up everything for the guru' and Namra was described as a former Swiss lawyer who had given up her husband and career. It is true that she gave up her job as a lawyer, but how could a lawyer's career compare with what we were living here? She had given up peanuts for gold!

In a separate box there was a quote entitled 'Bhagwan on Sex'. It sounded awful because it was taken out of context. They used just the last paragraph of this quote:

The body has a desire for sex because the body has come out of sex. The body has a desire for sex because every cell of the body is sexual. Your mother and your father, in a deep sexual activity, have created your body. The first cells of your body came out of deep sexual passion; they carry the quality of it. And those cells have been multiplying themselves; that's how your whole body is created.

Your whole body is sex passion. The desire arises. It is natural for the body, nothing is wrong in it. The body is sexual energy and nothing else.

Osho, *Yoga: The Alpha and the Omega*, Vol. 3, Ch. 2

From the questions other sannyasins asked Osho in the darshans I understood that I was not the only one who had disappointed my family. On the other hand, there were lucky sannyasins who had other members of the family join them in their adventure. I am now thinking of Kavya whose sister came to Pune and became Anasha, and their parents who also took sannyas while continuing their professional lives in Milan.

After my shifts I often visited a friend called Giri at his place. In the mornings he was at the school where he enjoyed working with the kids' theatre group. Whenever I arrived at his flat without an appointment, he would say, "I thought you might come." We were good friends but he was not my boyfriend. Sometimes he had a girlfriend and then we did not see each other for weeks. If by chance we met on the street we did not really know what to talk about. But our bodies had their own way of meeting. We played and experimented, trying to fathom what Osho had said about sex. Like when dancing I let my body move the way it wanted to move, without constraint, and at times it felt like dying, like disappearing into an endless abyss. While the bodies were merging, it was difficult to know where his body started and mine ended or if the ceiling was above or below – we were floating in a space filled with psychedelic colours. I understood now why Chagall had painted his lovers floating over the roofs of their Russian village.

The sun shines with its full strength through the curtains of my bedroom. It is time to get up, brew a cup of tea and move to the cool porch. When Upadhi from the Mystery School left Pune to go back to Italy for the summer, she left me her little flat to look after. The upstairs flats are now empty during the low season and I can enjoy the house all for myself. The shady path to the back porch and the lovely garden are all mine. I squeeze a bamboo armchair onto the tiny porch, legs on a stool and biscuits on my lap, and enjoy the breeze through the banana leaves and flowering hibiscus bushes. A little privacy in crowded India.

Nandano, my musician friend from Japan, is practising new rhythms on his electric guitar. I hear him through his open window. He lives in the house next door, on the first floor. His playing inspires me to prepare the songs for the next Heart Dance. Looking through the song book I find:

Looking for love
Everywhere I go
Looking for love
In everyone I know
I try to keep it all together
And wonder what went wrong
Till I understand
Let it all go, let it all go
And love starts chasing me

I make notes for myself on where the dancers and singers will walk around the hall, hands over their brows, pretending to look everywhere for their love. 'Till I understand' has a pointed index finger in the air. The song ends with a big muddle, everybody pretending to chase each other. Children's games. I read through the lyrics attentively and try to learn them by heart.

I *was* looking for love; for years I was yearning to have a boyfriend, not only a lover. I was so desperate that I wrote a letter to Osho. I explained the reasons I wanted a boyfriend, but also my fears of getting entangled in a relationship. There must have been a lot of back and forth in my mind because the letter grew to be five pages long. While trying to condense the letter to two paragraphs I finally found the courage to say it in one sentence: "Osho, I want a boy-friend." Fully aware of how ridiculous it was, I posted the letter in the appropriate 'Letters for Osho' box. A few days later I found Osho's even more laconic answer: "Ma Yoga Punya, Search."

Search? I knew that this could not be right; it was like catching God by the tail. This is not the way love happens. Love happens out of the blue. Deep down I had wished that he would assign a boyfriend to me as he had done with Deeksha. At least this way the man would not run away from me immediately. But, as Osho had suggested, I started to search.

This Dutch guy, maybe – soft, with a beautiful Jewish nose, cold blue eyes and a question mark in his face? He is playing with his spoon and looking at me. I considered if he could be my future boyfriend. Or what about that sturdy Australian at the table over there? I looked around at the entrance of the canteen, at the men coming up the stairs. Is this maybe the way men look at girls in a bar? Suddenly I became aware of how ugly it all felt. Men were no longer human beings. They had turned into objects of pleasure and desire, things to be had and purchased. It was like shopping for shoes. Osho had tricked me with his answer – I should have known better – but he had pushed me to the very edge from where I could see the ugliness of greed and desire.

I quickly forgot all about my question and Osho's answer and, of course, a few days later I met a beautiful Italian friend, Nello, with whom I spent many weeks.

Since I was a child I knew that if I wanted something very badly I was not meant to think about it. This was the case with the piano. On my way home from school I used to come across a pharmacist's clock at the corner of Via San Marco. Many chemists in Milan had clocks like that to advertise their shop. For some reason this clock always reminded me of my secret wish. My dream was to come home after school and find a piano in our living room. I imagined it standing in the corner where Mother had her house plants; it would be shiny, in red polished wood. But the condition for this wish to come true was that I would need to forget it. I usually managed most of the way – until I got to that clock! But one day – I must have missed the clock – I came home and a beautiful piano in red wood was standing in our living room, in the very corner where the plants used to be.

My whole family was amazed at the sudden appearance of this huge object and was standing around it in awe. My father was the kind of person who would take decisions on his own, without previous consultation, not even with Mother, and then surprise us. The same happened when he bought the new Giulietta. One evening he asked us to put on our coats and come downstairs. Neatly parked in front of our house was his latest acquisition: a new light blue Alpha Romeo.

The arrival of the piano was like Christmas for me. I'm not recounting the dramatic beginning of a musician's career. I would never become a musician, but music has always played a big part in my life. I caressed the white and black keys and, standing on tip-toe, opened the lid to inspect the strings, impressed by the size of some of them. By evening I had learned to play – with my right index finger – a simple children's song; then later my piano teacher introduced me to Cesi Marciano, Mozart and Bach. Great melodies pinned down to black dots to learn by heart.

I knew that for a wish to come true we need to want something with great intensity but at the same time relax about it; but later I understood that it was best not to have any wishes at all. The reason is because wishes always come true and we do not really know what is best for us. Life might have more interesting adventures in store for us than what we can imagine with our limited minds.

One more cup of tea and another biscuit on my little porch. The sun is shining on the tops of the trees and I see that Nandano's windows are already closed. He must be getting ready for White Robe, our evening meditation. Time also for me to rush! After a good scrub in the tiny shower, Amiten and I get ready and walk to the ashram. My hair will dry in the still warm air.

We lock the gate and walk towards the street behind the daughter of the chai shop owner. She balances a brass water-jug on her head, holding it with her right arm. Swinging her hips from side to side she carefully sets her golden sandals on the rough surface of the dirt path. She walks like a queen. Her yellow Punjabi outfit is decorated with red and gold embroidery around the hem of the long blouse and tight ankle cuffs. She carries water from a tap behind my neighbour's house to the cart across the busy street. I wonder who will be the lucky guy to marry her.

We say 'hello' to the Kashmiri sitting in front of his shop at the corner of North Main Road, like a guardian of our little neighbourhood, the Ragvilas Building Society. I feel safe at night when on my own because the shop stays open until late. He sells, as do all his compatriots along the street, painted papier mache boxes, bronze statuettes, lapis lazuli earrings, Shiva statuettes, Tibetan singing bowls and the like, displayed on cheap wooden racks covered with lengths of bright red satin. If you seat yourself on the carpets inside the shop he will show you his gems. From a tucked away wooden box he unpacks them from neatly folded papers.

On a cart near the chai shop, pakoras are frying in fuming oil. They are made from chick-pea flour and smell delicious. Many men gather around at this time for a quick snack before going home. On the other corner the fruit vendor calls his wares. It is mango season. Mango is not just a fruit, it is a passion. This fruit should be called passion fruit. There are many varieties, cheap ones and big ones for chutneys, but the Alfonsos are the best. Just a whiff of the aroma overwhelms my senses.

We walk over shady patterns cast by acacia trees, past the open-air toilet for the construction workers of the luxury villa up the road. We hold our noses and stop breathing. The cambered asphalt is about a foot higher than the dirt verges, eroded by pedestrians and monsoon rains. A worker from the sugar factory rides along on his squeaky bicycle with his wife balanced on the bar between his outstretched arms.

Across from the white-washed Parsee house, the coconut *wallah* calls out "Eight rupees only!" His shop consists of a board on four bicycle wheels; four pillars on the corners hold up another board forming a roof. Carved and painted strips decorate the *gadhi* and keep the coconuts from tumbling down. "For eating or drinking?" Flicking his middle finger against the shells and listening to the sound it makes, the seller chooses the nut corresponding to my order 'for drinking and eating'. I like the way the man swings his machete and cuts off one end. With the tip of the knife he gracefully cuts a hole into the exposed white flesh. In goes a coloured straw from a dusty plastic bag. "Seven rupees!" – because we are his daily customers.

A foot high stone bench around a tree serves as the customers' eating place. There is a bit of flesh in my coconut and I take it back to him. The *wallah* whacks the globe apart with his hooked knife – with sudden splashes of milk flying around – and cuts a bit off the nut's green shell to serve as a spoon. He hands me the two halves with the 'spoon' and back on the bench I scoop out, with glee, the gelatine-like, almost transparent flesh. We watch a couple of boys collect the empty shells in a big raffia bag. They haul it onto a bicycle and push it home to their village. Their mother will be happy to sun-dry the shells and burn them under the cooking stove.

On the bridge students sit on the stone wall trying to chat up female students on their way home. We can peep into the Osho Teerth Park through a gap in the fence netting covered with purple morning glory. Approaching the ashram, something changes in the air. We are no longer in India. We are walking into another space. Silence and aliveness flows from the campus. A buzzing tranquillity.

The guard inspects our passes. We split up and rush to our lockers. I change into a white robe, pick up white socks, a white shawl and my cushion. Each time I enter the ashram at this time I feel stunned: the queue waiting to get into the hall seems to disappear into the white marble path. It is as if the whiteness of robes and marble has merged everything and erased all boundaries. When it envelopes me it draws me into a space of lost non-existence. The trees sing their own evening song in green.

The queue is short. The gate passes are checked again, then through a metal detector and a sniff to check if I have washed my hair with scentless shampoo. Lifting the mosquito net I enter the vast hall. Amiten, in his usual spot, sits like a Buddha meditating with closed eyes. Although we met only a few weeks ago, and are already sharing my little flat, we have come to such an understanding that I do not feel that his presence next to me interferes with my meditation. This is the first time I sit next to my beloved in the Buddha Hall.

A girl gives last cleaning touches to the podium with her dusting cloth. In the light from the ceiling she can detect, leaning to one side, any specks of dust she has missed. With closed eyes I recognise the rumbling wheels of the cart with Osho's chair. Two fit men will carry it in, place it in the centre of the podium and take off the cover. When I open my eyes I am almost blinded by the glossy upholstery of Osho's chair, the same chair he sat in during discourse. Now an empty chair. Chandra, who a few years ago travelled with me for her first time to Pune, thought it was odd to bring an empty chair to the hall every night. I replied to her that even when Osho was sitting there in flesh and bone we had the impression that the chair was empty.

There is an expectancy in the air like before a theatre play and the stillness is deepened by the crows chasing each other between the branches with their 'crawck'. The sunset is turning a majestic purple. A very low note comes from the speakers. It slowly moves up to a higher note, goes down again, even lower, to find its way back to the root note. One sound which embraces a whole scale within itself! I look over to the musicians' podium and see my friend Kalyan playing his newly-discovered instrument: the *rudra veena*. Now the light-footed rhythm strings come in, just in between the heavy sounds. The tempo picks up. The raga now sounds as if it is played on a sitar. Osho would have loved to hear this – he had often enquired why none of us played this instrument.

The lights go off in the back and the main gate is closed. Nobody can enter or leave until the discourse is over. The first rhythmical pickings on a guitar make me sway from side to side while remaining seated in my spot. Then Narayani's resonant voice, like that of a black singer, starts the song and my swaying becomes wilder and wilder until – with a stop – we all shout with raised arms "Osho!" and remain still until the upbeat song picks up again, slowly moving into the next crescendo. After three 'Osho!'s, full of energy, we close our eyes. The arpeggios of the *tamboura* disappear in their own overtones, soothing like the sound of a waterfall. A crazy flute comes in, wiggling here and there. I can't really catch the line of the melody. It is like running after a rabbit. The *tablas* spur the tempo; the music gets faster and faster and more crazy than before – and suddenly stops. Silence for a few minutes. In the absence of the crazy notes I fall into myself, dropping into a restful place.

The flute starts again doing its performance: an acrobat under the circus tent. The *tablas* fly off, fingers flapping on the skin, grounded by the resounding and sliding bass of the *baya*. One more period of music and silence – and I am now waiting for the three drum beats which announce the end of the meditation. I don't want to be caught unawares, wandering in thoughts when they come. I remain attentive, listening to the silence in the hall. Three thousand people are gathered here in the same silence. The explosive drum beats are not just a signal. They hit deep in my belly and bring me back into myself. Was I somewhere else? Back to earth, we are ready to listen to Osho's words.

A screen unrolls by its own weight from the roof of the podium in front of Osho's chair. The title of the discourse is announced through the microphone. I wait anxiously to see Osho's face on the big video screen. I can see all his expressions and gestures clearly. Sinking into his voice I hope to come out the other end.

About an hour later, after a few jokes, he leads us into a meditation. He signals to Nivedano to beat the drum:

Nivedano...

Time for gibberish. We blabber along, talking to nobody in particular, gesticulating with hands and arms, in no particular language. Wild noises of insane people.

Nivedano...

His drum brings us back to silence.

Be silent, close your eyes, feel the body completely frozen.
Look inwards, as deep as possible, because the life source is not very far away. It is just in your empty heart. An absolutely concentrated look into your being, and you have encountered your Buddhahood. Your very life source is also the life source of the whole universe.
Deeper and deeper, so that you can gather the inner experience and bring it out into your daily life. Slowly, slowly your Buddha has to become your very expression, your very lifestyle.
Nivedano...

We lie back, almost onto each other's bodies.

Let go. Just be a watcher…

The mind is there, the body is there, but you are not the body and you are not the mind. You are just the watcher. The watcher is called the Buddha. Watching, witnessing, silently your heart becomes empty. And the empty heart is the Buddha.

Let it sink deep, in every fibre of your being.

This is the most precious moment – when you are just a witness and a tremendous silence surrounds you.

It is a great, blissful evening. Your recognition of your Buddha nature and your recognition that you are one with the whole…

There are not ten thousand Buddhas here but just one consciousness. Nivedano…

At his last drum beat we sit up.

Come back. But come back not the way you had gone in; come back more gracefully, more peacefully, more like a Buddha.

Sit down for a few moments to recollect the experience, to remember the space you have gone into, to remember the path that you have followed.

Whatever you have experienced in your witnessing is going to affect and change your twenty-four hours' life. Unless meditation becomes a revolution, a revolution of your whole character, it is not meditation.

Meditation liberates you from yourself and brings the new, original face which we have named the Buddha. Remember in your day-to-day work who you are. Let your inside affect your activities, your gestures, your language, your relations.

Okay, Maneesha?

Yes, Osho.

Can we celebrate the ten thousand Buddhas?

Yes!

Osho, *The Buddha: The Emptiness of the Heart*, Ch. 7

A quick progression of guitar chords introduces the song. A saxophone and a flute, playing the harmony, come in with the tune. The triangle drives the beat and we start clapping our hands. The *tablas*, the bass and the drums give the final boost. Osho rises from his chair and lifts his arms, conducting the tempo and our celebrating hearts with it. Then faster and faster until he stops with raised arms and remains immobile, no movement in his eyes. We all shout "Osho!" and remain still. Sometimes he looks into somebody's eyes. If it is Avirbhava we will know because she screams, out of fear or delight I do not know. Pretending to move on he might look back at her and we hear the scream again. Then more 'Osho!'s until he has greeted us all. Before disappearing into the small corridor between the marble backdrops, he turns around and greets us one more time. The last 'Osho!' shout, then gracefully he moves towards the glass door opened for him by two sannyasins. I hear the closing of the car doors and the start of the engine. The red back-lights disappear behind the trees. The video and the music fade until the screen goes blank.

In the darkness and silence I remain unmoving until I feel like standing up. Soon hunger calls. Many have gathered at the exits. I find my shoes, go to my locker and change, queue at the canteen and quickly find Amiten at our table. We meet some friends and have a chat; new friends and some old, known for years, like Vishnu, Satlok, and… I forget her name. No discussions, more of a sharing of what we feel and think, participating in each other's lives. A relaxing and alive family feeling. We carry our empty trays in single line through the umbrella-covered tables, drop them at the bussing station on our way out and walk to the main gate.

Tiny green fairy lights hang like necklaces on the trees around Buddha Hall and reflect their light onto the marble path, showing us the way, past the swan pond, to the bookshop. We check what is on display, maybe a new book. The publications department is still busy catching up with Osho's talks. A lot of books are being translated from Hindi, revealing new aspects of Osho's wisdom, and many previously published ones need to be reprinted. At present 650 books or more have been published, and many of them have been translated into the world's major languages: German, Italian, Dutch, Spanish, Portuguese, French, Russian, Japanese, Korean, Mandarin, etc. Each book has its own flavour, maybe from a question and answer series, or talks about Buddha, or Kabir, or Jesus – or maybe encouraging the intelligentsia to take care of our planet instead of letting the politicians go on with their dirty work.

In the next window we discover a new cassette tape. 'In Wonder' it is called. We have heard this song in Buddha Hall during White Robe. It is Miten singing with Neera, with Navyo on the keyboard. I love its jacket with Osho's black silhouette on a golden background. The song very much expresses my feeling when I saw Osho enter the hall, or even now when I see him in a video. I am still amazed that I have been so fortunate to have found my way to him or, I should rather say, that the ways of life have brought me to him.

Outside the gate we part from Satlok, my old friend from Zurich. He wants to have an early night. We get dragged by Vishnu to the bar. OK. We enter the compound on the other side of the street and walk past the queue for the Osho Café which reaches as far as the steps to the Post Office. We read on the menu: vegetable *tempura*, miso soup with tofu, *ohiruko*, an aduki bean dessert. No wonder there is such a queue!

The doors to Meera Barn are already shut. The play must have started. Jivan Mary from New Zealand has trained the actors. 'Antigone'. From the bar we hear the accented voices and the applause before the break. There is a play every few weeks. I haven't seen this one yet.

Vishnu and Amiten get beers, crisps and peanuts at the bar. I wait for them at a table under the light shining onto a colourful painting made by a child from the Ko Hsuan School who has attended Meera's kids' painting group. It is hanging on the outside wall of the Martial Arts Dojo. Yatro spots us and joins the table with a vanilla ice-cream floating in Baileys. We all look into her silver chalice and die of envy.

We are now all wearing our multi-coloured street clothes, no longer the unifying maroon robes we wear during the day.

Alcohol and smoking are permitted here at this time. It feels like anywhere else in the world at a bar. The checking with the eyes, who is here with whom, is she alone? Would he be available tonight? But there is a lot of genuine laughter interspersed with exclamations.

Recalling what duties are expected of us tomorrow and at what time we need to get up, we decide to leave.

Under the floodlights of the main gate we exchange last words of goodbye and goodnight.

I remember a scene which happened on this very spot, some fifteen years ago. I was sitting on the semicircular wall which was then part of our neighbour's gate, dangling my legs in mid-air – like angels do from their clouds – enjoying the coolness of the evening while watching who was coming in and out of the main gate. It was the same heavy wooden gate with the bulky brass knobs.

The *beedie* wall, as we called it, was a spot for a first date, or a potential date. And there we could smoke. The *beedie wallah*, the cigarette vendor, was just a few trees down the road. His goods were displayed in a wooden box and lit by a little wax lamp which we also used to light our *beedies*. As a special treat we would sometimes buy a foreign cigarette which he sold one at a time.

I heard Osho say that we girls could take the initiative and go up to men and ask them for dates, instead of us waiting for them to take the first step – very much contrary to what was appropriate in the outside world. We called 'the outside world' the world outside the ashram, the conventional world of set values, TV commercials and ways of behaviour which differed much from the rules and customs inside the ashram. There were times when relationships were 'in', then 'out' again – while Osho played his part, talking sometimes for and sometimes against them.

I would have loved to meet someone that night, so I was on the look-out. Maybe Santano would come by. I had met him here the night before. After swinging himself with elegance onto the wall he had asked me "So?" and was quite disappointed when, from this one word, I had guessed that he was Dutch. He must have tried, like many of us, to speak Queen's English which was in fashion then. Every morning we heard well-spoken Teertha read the *sutras* for Osho. (Now, after the sojourn in the States, we have given up all perfection in accents and relaxedly speak our sannyasin English. In fact Satyam, a teacher from England, is often asked what kind of accent she has, and she indeed speaks proper English!) Was I already getting attached to Santano? He must have felt it so he did not show up again.

On the one hand I wanted to be in a relationship and on the other hand I wanted to be free. I was afraid of relationships because they had often been painful. At one point I clearly saw the pattern: I would fall in love with men who wanted to be free and then suffer from not being wanted. On the other hand, as soon as someone was keen to start a relationship with me, I backed off, almost in disgust! Here Osho explains very beautifully what I was meant to understand then, but managed to many years later:

People become clingers, and the more you cling to the other, the more the other becomes afraid, the other wants to escape, because there is a tremendous need to be free. The desire for freedom is higher than any other desire, is deeper than any other desire. So one can even sacrifice love, but one cannot sacrifice freedom; it is not in the nature of things. Hence the real bliss can happen only in your aloneness.

Aloneness is an art, the whole art of meditation. To be utterly centred in one's own being without any hankering for the other; to be in such a deep rest with oneself that nothing else is needed, that is aloneness. It brings the eternal bliss.

If first you are rooted in your being and then you move into relationship it is a totally different phenomenon. Now you can share, you can love and you can enjoy this love too. Even though it is momentary, you can dance, you can sing, and when it is gone, it is gone – you don't look back. You are capable of creating another love, so there is no need to cling. You are thankful to the lover, you are thankful for the love that is no longer there because it has enriched you, it has given you some glimpses of life, it has made you more mature.

But it is possible only if you have a certain grounding in your being. If love is all you have, with no meditative grounding, then you will suffer, then each love affair will become a nightmare sooner or later. Learn the art of how to be alone, and blissfully alone – then everything is possible.

Osho, *A Must for Morning Contemplation*

The *beedie* wall was my favourite spot to go to after Music Group, mainly when I was not on the 'look-out'. I was happy, full of energy after the dance, light-headed, fresh and alive and often used to fall into a particular mood. Everything seemed normal – the dark trees along the road, the lights at the main gate – until someone approached me. Only then did I realise that I had fallen into a strange, but not unpleasant, space where I felt that everybody was very far away from me. It was difficult to talk and connect to people, as if the cords between me and people had been cut. But I enjoyed the parade of orange people streaming out of the main gate and tried to recognise each individual from the way they walked. Relaxing, as if sitting at an outdoor café in the Galleria del Corso and watching the elegant shoppers passing by…

When I had cooled off, I walked back through the gate, along the now silent concrete path between the boutique and Krishna House, around the translators' hut and past Lao Tzu gate. The 'to-ing and fro-ing' under the hot sun, with buckets, tools and boxes carried from one part of the ashram to the other, was a faraway memory. The ashram was sunk in a deep velvety darkness. This darkness had a feel to it. Do the words 'magic in the air' express this inexpressible feeling?

The crunching gravel path along Buddha Hall and beside Manu's exquisite bamboo hut took me to the bottom of the stairs of Jesus House. Every night I asked myself if I was really living here. Not that I felt excluded, unwanted or foreign to the place, just that I never took it for granted that I had the privilege to live in the ashram, just a few steps away from Osho.

The full moon's glow through the small square windows gave enough light to see the steps of the spiral staircase without the need to switch on the lights. I walked up to my room, carefully so as not to make any noise with my sandals. I gently opened one side of our double door with its heavy bolt and, still in the dark, brushed my teeth and climbed up the ladder to my bed in the loft. I had always been able to go to sleep immediately after going to bed, the moment my cheek touched the pillow I was gone – but since I had come to live in the ashram it took me at least an hour to fall asleep. It was as if there was a buzz or a hum in the deep silence, an adrenalin-boosting energy in the air. Sometimes I covered my face with the light blue towel Osho had given to me. This helped a bit.

Before going home, Amiten and I stop for a moment and admire Raghuvira's fountain – as we often do – watching the water and listening to the different pitches of the splashing sounds. The feature is part of the wall on the left of the main gate, clad in horizontally laid stone slabs which protrude, in different places, for an inch or so, creating small, individual waterfalls. I remember when Raghuvira was working on it, with his usual determination and totality, not letting himself be distracted by any comments of passers-by – in the same way he had worked on so many projects in the ashram. This was his last one before he became ill and died, and also the most beautiful. Thank you.

The rickshaw drivers, waiting in the queue, hassle us with their night prices – twice and three times the regular day fares – and it takes quite some time to make them understand that we want to *walk* home. Walking down this road is now much safer and more pleasant since the commune built the slab stone pavements and also much prettier since, at the same time, we added the foot-wide gardens between pavement and garden walls. Now even neighbours in the back roads have started to plant flowers on the green patches between the road and their garden walls, almost in competition with each other. The street vendors have gone now but will be back in the morning to clutter the fences and pavements again. The blind flute player is sitting in his usual spot. Every night, year in year out, he begs, "Poor blind man" and repeats the first four bars of one of our old songs which many have already forgotten or have never heard before.

Along the busy North Main Road we buy Vim, bleach and a new broom for Rita, our house cleaner, as she had ordered on her note. Then a few ginger biscuits at the German Bakery for tomorrow's tea. The Kashmiris await their customers with expectant eyes in front of their brightly-lit shops. Home is just around the corner. This is home for the next six months.

What a treat!

Samadhi

The morning is cool and I enjoy the freshness before the great heat of the day descends upon us. The road under my feet echoes to the sound of my rubber flip-flops slapping against my heels. I want to sit in the *samadhi* this morning. The meditation starts at 10am, but I want to be at the gate by 9:45 at the latest. The ticket vendor with his funnily braided red beard hands me the slip over his table which he always decorates with a tiny vase of flowers.

The queue at the gate to Lao Tzu House already reaches as far as the bookshop. Everybody has their maroon shawl and white socks in hand. The *samadhi* is cold, quite strongly air-conditioned. The way Osho liked it.

The marble path takes us along the house to the porch which is now enclosed and covers the white Rolls-Royce stretch limousine. This car conveyed Osho to the discourses in Oregon and here in Pune. Two rows of chairs set across from each other allow us to put on our socks with dignity. The few white marble steps flanked by a miniature garden of shade plants and semi-precious stones take us to the corridor/library. On one wall are the translations of Osho's books and, in the corridor, displayed under glass, are a multicoloured variety of non-fiction books. I heard from Rabiya, the librarian, that the books are not filed according to subjects as in any other library, but according to aesthetic criteria: the colour of the jacket, the height and thickness of the book. The books should create a harmonious wavy line on the shelves. This was, of course, Osho's idea.

On the left a glass door opens to the dentist's room with a modern reclining chair in the middle and the right wall covered with cabinets and work surfaces. The wall on my left is panelled from top to floor with mirrors. I can see myself walking past with my shawl in train. In the green marble floor there are inlaid black squares.

In the ante-chamber I pick up a small cushion. Large square grey cushions are already laid out in front of the *samadhi*. Two rows of seats with back support are lined up on the edges a few feet from the windows. I like to sit in the front row and find space there. Most people prefer to sit comfortably and are on the outer rings. I adjust the small cushion under my bum to reduce the weight on my crossed legs. The maroon shawl covers my whole body like a cape keeping my body warmth inside.

I turn my head to see who is playing today. It is my friends Joshua, on the sitar, and Ageha, on the *tamboura*. When everybody is seated, he will be playing, accompanied by the *tamboura*, for about fifteen minutes, then they wait in silence for the second quarter of an hour and then repeat the pattern, until one hour is over. As Osho explains, music, and especially Indian music, helps deepen our meditation.

With unfocused eyes I see in front of me a photograph of Osho looking softly at the gathering. The picture in a grey cloth frame hangs on a mirrored wall. I can see myself in it and the people sitting at my side. I can also see the crystal chandelier sparkling in all seven colours of the rainbow, like dewdrops on a sunny morning. The dark green plants outside in the garden contrast with the white marble of the waterfall and the black round pillars on the edges of the hall. The dimmers lower the light of the chandelier and the cone-shaped lamps on the bedside in front of me.

According to his wishes, Osho's ashes have been put under his bed in this room. A year before he left his body, Chuang Tzu Auditorium was transformed into a bedroom for Osho. He used it for a few days only (apparently because of the loud air-conditioning) and moved back to his old, much smaller room. In the East, the place where the ashes of a saint are kept is called a *samadhi*.

The air-conditioning and the waterfall are switched off now. Tibetan bells signal the beginning of the meditation, leaving the hall in deep silence. The atmosphere is so still I hardly dare uncross my legs. Even thoughts become conscious of the stillness. I can hear my heartbeat speeding up, ready for action, ready to run. But there is nowhere to run. I do not wish to go anywhere anyway. Falling into myself I get lost in the meanders of the vast space I find inside myself.

First the *tamboura's* three notes on four strings sound, resonating into each other's pitches, then comes Joshua's sitar, slow at first but then increasing in speed and rhythm. The music brings me into another space, more present, but it does not interfere with the meditative raptness I had before it started. There is a long period of silence again until suddenly three touches of the bells with their dissonant overtones bring me back into the room, in front of Osho's picture – he looks lovingly, vaguely, openly and intensely into my being. My body wants to bow down and I allow it to bend forward. I touch with my forehead the glossy white marble floor – but only after covering it first with my shawl. "Do not touch the marble, please," we are reminded at the beginning of our visit.

In the garden, after slipping into my sandals, I pretend to admire the swans in the pond while waiting to find the ground under my feet again. I feel the velvet thongs between my toes, the breeze through the leaves and through my hair; I listen to the twittering of the birds and the grinding of a power tool. The path will take me back to the gate, past 'English' Yoga Punya, who I see is guarding the entrance to the house today. She will understand that I will not feel like talking.

I remember that on this very path, then still covered with gravel instead of marble, every night there were about fifteen wooden benches put up in neat rows for us to wait on before going into darshan. And because of Osho's allergy to dust and scents, Radha had to sniff our hair at the gate. If the perfume was too strong from the shampoo we had used, we had to come back another day. The only way to get rid of the smell was to wash the hair out several times with lime juice. But if it was only a slight scent then it could be covered up with a scarf. Neerja, with her flair for fashion, was soon appointed as the 'scarf lady' and a pile of scarves was always at the ready at the gate. She did a wonderful job and always made us look reasonably handsome, adequate to be sitting in front of our master.

While waiting on the hard benches our excitement before darshan expressed itself in giggles and chatter, but we became silent when we joined the queue which wound itself onto the tiled path alongside the house. We slipped out of our sandals before entering Chuang Tzu Auditorium and again made a mental note of the spot where we had left them. Sometimes we were given a special place to sit but mostly we just sat behind the ones who had come in first. To wait for Osho was always special, a bit like the way we feel when we wait for a lover.

I remember a darshan – this was quite early on, when darshans were still held on the porch – where a girl who had just come back from Goa was in front of Osho. She had unwrapped from a red silk scarf a set of tarot cards she had painted herself. She showed her cards to Osho and asked him if she should go on using them. He suggested, if I remember well, that she paint more cards and that it was good for her to keep exploring the unconscious. In her deck there was even a white card with nothing painted on. Osho asked her to try them out and give a reading then and there. He called up a little boy and motioned him to sit at his feet, facing the girl. It was Somendra's son, maybe six or seven years old, with big, bright blue eyes. With her thin fingers she shuffled the cards the boy had chosen and laid them out in a cross. Turning them face up she started. "This is the issue." Then, "This is behind you" – it was the white card. Osho poked his toes into the boy's back and said, "Look who is behind you." The boy turned around and looked up at him and Osho responded with big eyes and a significant smile. I guess behind all of us Osho is nudging us with his toes, a pure emptiness in a neatly pressed white robe.

The next morning I was expected in the sewing room which was 'on the other side', that is, in Mariam Canteen. Deeksha had shifted her total energy into Vrindavan and had appointed 'Proper' Sagar to take care of the workers' canteen. He was a bailiff in Deeksha's feudal estate and had to account to her for the food stock and other expenses. The sewing department was in one of the rooms close to his kitchen, but we were independent from him. We enjoyed our freedom, working at some distance from Vrindavan, and therefore not under Deeksha's constant vigilant eye.

Our veranda was a girls' world. We enjoyed giggling, as girls do, although in Deeksha's world laughter was 'not on'. If she caught anyone laughing, they were scolded. According to her, our laughter was unconscious and about stupid things anyway. We should rather put our energy into the work at hand. I could see her point, but to have some respite from the regimented discipline was pure heaven!

My bosses were Kumud and Jivan Kavya. I was in total awe and admiration at their dexterity with fabric. They slung pieces of orange polyester over their shoulders and talked in jargon about pinches here and cut-outs there. They were the ones who sewed the robes for Deeksha.

I couldn't quite make friends with this slippery material. As a graphic designer I was used to working with paper; it was easy to cut and when cut it did not change its shape. But fabric stretched in all directions, which was good over breasts and other round parts, but was too unpredictable for me. My mother had learned to be a seamstress when young. Maybe she was talked into the job by relatives – but she was not naturally talented at it. This meant that she never managed to sew a dress without a lot of fuss and many mistakes. This convinced me from early on that sewing was beyond the capabilities of a common human being. Now here I was sitting at an electric sewing machine. I learned to sew straight lines but had an additional challenge of rolling the seam while the machine whizzed along, i.e. without any pre-stitching by hand. So I learned to make the blue food-covering cloths, the red aprons and do all the mending which was sent to us.

I am not sure for how many months I did this job, but at some point I became bored of sitting down. I wanted to move my body and thought that a cleaning job in Vrindavan would be just the thing. But to ask to become a cleaner would have been very odd; in Deeksha's kitchen one became a cleaner only as a 'punishment'. (She 'punished' us if we were caught manipulating, sleeping on the job, or if we did something wrong out of unawareness.) But it happened eventually in a roundabout way.

Long-term workers were receiving individual aprons and it was one of my jobs to embroider their names on the front pockets so that after washing, the owner could find his apron again. Sometimes I embroidered a little flower in front of a name or a leaf at the end, and with Prem's apron something really 'bad' happened. I added a golden Star of David next to his name. Far from being intended as a branding, it was a recognition for me. I was so fascinated by everything Jewish – their past, their rituals, the Chassids – and I never failed to be attracted by their physical appearance: the intense look, the dark beards, the pronounced nose. Osho had gathered around him many intelligent people and among them, of course, a lot of Jews. So there were a lot of them around to fascinate me! In the discourses he teased them, trying to break their conditioning and beliefs and – in doing so – went through their huge collection of jokes. I loved jokes and this one which I sent in for Osho, made me famous for the day ("Are you the Punya of the joke today?"):

Punya has sent me a joke. She says, "This is a real joke. I heard it on the main street of the ashram between the boutique and the bag check.

One sannyasin said to another sannyasin, "What I can't stand about this ashram is: wherever you look, there are queues."

The other said, "What? Jews?"

Osho, *Zen: Zest, Zip, Zap and Zing*, Ch. 10

The next day, of course, I was in Vrindavan, cleaning the floor. Deeksha had asked, "How would it be if you had made a cross next to a name of someone who comes from a Christian background?" Indeed, that would have been very, very strange. I was now at the very bottom of the proletariat. My range of action was the kitchen floor with its eight or ten kerosene stoves which were placed in the middle of the cooking area. Each of the stoves had its own aluminium tray to catch any kerosene splashes, spent matches and broken pins. It was a dangerous place. When water or oil got spilled I immediately sprinkled sawdust over it and swept it up. Mukul, my roommate, was one of the cooks. She reminded me of my little sister and I wanted to make sure she was safe and that she would never slip on the wet floor with one of those heavy pots in her hands. So I spent my days sweeping the grey-blue tiles, crouched on the floor with an Indian broom in my right hand and a dustpan in my left. I loved these soft brooms with their long silvery grass whips. They were so flexible and agile that with one flick I could catch a stray vegetable wedged between the stoves.

One day I felt like booking a darshan with Osho. I sneaked out of the kitchen and went to the front office. This time it was Garimo, Laxmi's secretary, who was giving out the appointments. In her calm but authoritative way she made it clear, that if Osho asked me if I had anything to say, I should absolutely say "no." I guessed that, because of the ever increasing number of visitors we, the workers, should keep more in the background and use up less of his time. When my name was called I sat in front of Osho and, of course, said "No" to his question. "Come closer." Without getting up I shuffled my bum two feet closer to him. "Fold your hands and lift your arms above your head. Close your eyes. Now, feel prayerful," were his words as I remember them.

Almost in panic I searched inside myself where the door to 'feel prayerful' was because I had never associated this word with any feeling inside me. The word 'prayer' was not even in our vocabulary as sannyasins. If he had asked me to feel angry or tearful I would have immediately found the right button. But prayerful? I suddenly saw the grey-blue floor of the kitchen and the whip of my broom. So I remained with that calm picture for a while. Before I knew it, I was called back by Osho with a, "Very good, Punya."

Living in the ashram, with all the relating and working together, it was difficult to hide our ugly sides. All the hurts and pains, stubbornness, anger and competition were always on the surface, so much so that in the end we felt this was all we were made of. In this darshan Osho gave me the gift of showing to me the forgotten beauty which was inside. (Even Mukta came to me afterwards and told me how beautiful I looked in front of Osho during this 'close-up darshan', something which was even conveyed in the photograph Krishna Bharti took from the back!)

Then Osho spoke to a new initiate:

Sannyas means putting your ego aside so you can understand. And sannyas is basically surrender to the whole.

The master is just an excuse. You surrender to the master because you are not capable of communicating directly with such a vast universe. You need some small window through which to look at the sky. The open sky is frightening, scary, but once you have looked through the window, the indication of the stars will take you into an eternal journey. The master is only a window, a window to God. That's why in the East we have worshipped the master as a God, for the simple reason that he opens a small door through which you can enter into the whole. You learn the art of surrendering in the company of the master, then finally you have to do it with the whole.

It is just like when you go to learn swimming: you first learn in the shallow water, very close to the bank. You cannot go into the deep water directly. But once you have learned swimming then you start adventuring towards the depths more and more. And then one day one knows how to swim; then it does not matter whether the water is one mile deep or five miles deep. It doesn't matter; it is the same for the swimmer, it makes no difference at all.

The master is just the bank, the shore where, without any fear, you can learn the basic art of surrender – and then the journey begins.

Osho, *At the Feet of the Master*

4

Hits

Vegetables 100mph

Returning from the *samadhi* with my folded shawl and white socks in hand I savour the last few minutes being close to Osho's house. The trees and bushes and the marble path had felt Osho drive past every night. Oh lucky ones! A blue five-pointed flower star falls in front of my feet. I pick it up, press the petals between a piece of paper and keep it in my wallet. Amiten will be happy to receive it, from Osho's garden...

Mukta, having a rest from her gardening work, greets me from the guards' hut with a smile; we feel like companions on a long journey and at the same time we discover each other's eyes fresh again, with a new understanding and love. Yoga Punya, in the meantime, is on the phone dealing with a visitor to the Meditation Academy, the offices of which are in this house.

Outside the gate a busy world flows over me. Maroon robes rush past; the blinding white marble path is as busy as a street in downtown Bombay – sorry, Mumbai. Such a contrast to the silent pond in the shade. The swan attracts my attention by flapping its wings. A mirror leans against a tree trunk on the little island. There the swan thinks he sees his mate whom he has lost. In the evening he even comes over to the bookshop where he mirrors his gentle movements in the glass panes.

Osho Times magazines are displayed for sale on a table set on the winding terraced marble landscaping. Further on, in the egg-shaped enclave, costumed and made-up actors are selling tickets for their evening show, like vendors in a market square. Better walk in a big circle around them else they will stop you and ask if you have bought a ticket. Unless you can say "Sorry, I have already seen the play," you have no chance!

The vegetable-cutting table is already buzzing with talk and wit like an early morning party. The talkative leader tries to attract the attention of passers-by and to motivate them to join the table. He already has half a dozen disciples chopping away on the carrots, whose funniest formations – gnarly specimens like double-rooted ones which look like crossed legs – are exhibited above the sign saying 'Daily Veggie Chopping Meditation Happening Here', with an arrow pointing to the table.

A few more yards to the left and quite a few years ago I see myself chopping these same woody carrots. But then there was no talking, mind you. Merely the pounding of the Solingen stainless steel knives on the imported plastic chopping boards. Standing upright in front of our blue square buckets we quartered tomatoes, parted cauliflowers in bite-size flowerets, chopped carrots Chinese style for the wok, cut more carrots in big chunks for the soup, halved and then quartered big potatoes. At the next heavy wooden table another crew, sitting down, worked its way through heaps of carrots, potatoes and *doodia* (an Indian vegetable resembling courgettes). Their Swiss peelers created, under their rapid movements, a metallic and high-pitched rhythm that sounded like a swarm of mosquitoes or a field full of crickets.

Some vegetable choppers had freshly arrived from California or from the Findhorn Community. They thought that to work meditatively meant to move slowly like in a Buddhist walk. No such thing in Deeksha's kitchen! The speed resembled that of a factory; the faster we worked with the sharp knives, the more we were on the edge, no time to talk or even think.

Sometimes mothers had come to the ashram with the intention of taking their offspring back home with them, but they eventually fell in love with Osho and joined the commune. They participated in the one job they had done proficiently their whole lives... but unfortunately here there was no such thing as 'I have always done it this way'. There were astonished faces and quite a few tears because it had to be done the way Deeksha had decided. Haridevi was there to make us follow the rules.

Haridevi was the vegetable boss and her cold blue eyes would not let us get away with anything. Just her name made us shiver. She had grown up in a German Protestant family and her father was a preacher. Although she was our age her body had the shape of that of an older woman: a pear-shaped bottom, grey skin and rings under her eyes. And her straight mousy blond hair... well, we did not consider her as a rival in our race for the good-looking guys. We could not relate to her much and she probably did not wish to relate to us either. If I could spend a whole day at the same table with her and survive, that was proof enough that I would be able to survive in hell as well!

The vegetables had become respectable beings under my hands, from the day Deeksha caught me and Vadan with the carrots dumped on the storeroom floor. "Look at these poor vegetables, they are more enlightened than you! And look at your stupid faces!" Later, these enlightened vegetables would gracefully follow me to the commune in America, where the ladies' fingers were replaced by courgettes, the dirty spinach by our home-grown kale, the small and sweet speckled bananas by perfectly rounded Chiquitas in their ripening boxes.

The cooks wanted the vegetables cut each piece the same size so that they would all be cooked through at the same time. This fuelled long discussions at the big chopping table: which was the correct size and who had been able to comply with the 'standards'. I kept myself awake in the monotonous hours finding the best ways to cut through the oblong potatoes, keeping in mind that all pieces should be of the same volume. Whenever I cut potatoes now I can see myself falling back into this mind puzzle.

Our rhythmical thumps on the plastic cutting boards resonated in the empty buckets underneath while above our heads we heard the mantra *'chapatti, chamaui'* – or at least that's what the words sounded like to me. It was Prasad's Centring group on Jesus House roof; like many Pune houses built in that period the roof was flat and covered with mosaics made of tiny white broken tile bits (very slippery when wet!). I was told the participants had to walk around and do complicated exercises while chanting these words. They could only do it right if they were present; just a thought and they would be out! Down below, if our thoughts came between us and the knives, it meant cut fingers!

Therapy groups, and even the meditations, were faraway things for us. There were two categories: workers and 'groupies'. As workers, our meditation was the work, Osho's discourse in the morning and darshan or Music Group at night. We ate in Mariam Canteen. The 'groupies' ate in Vrindavan Cafeteria. If we happened to eat in Vrindavan and at the same table with them we felt like outsiders. Their language was so different: they were going through a 'process'. Our talk was just plain gossip: who was with whom and what did so-and-so say.

Many therapy groups included verbal and physical expression (which might have been easier for Italians than for the Brits...). The idea was that through expression we would uncover – from underneath our put-on masks of 'good behaviour' – our more authentic self. This trend had also trickled down into the kitchen; for instance, the word 'nice' was considered the worst in our vocabulary. Deeksha often told someone to 'fuck off' and rarely dropped an appreciative word. Whatever she said was always a criticism or a button-pusher. And of course we copied her... Poor newcomers had a hard time. They were not welcomed with a smile, the way they would be in any other religious community; they immediately had to deal with our rough behaviour. If they remained, it was solely because they had fallen in love with Osho.

One day the Main Office gave Deeksha the use of a tiny room around the corner from the storeroom, facing Osho's garden. It was tiled in white and a high table was built to fit from wall to wall. So there I found myself on a high stool crouched over an enormous accounts ledger. I had drawn vertical lines for grains/milk/dairy/

pulses/vegetables to break down the expenses. I did not know why we should be interested in knowing how much we spent for each category, but I had seen lists like that when Mr. Bolli was doing my father's company's black accounts in our home in Milan.

Mr. Bolli worked for over a year at a big wooden desk in our entrance hall. He would come in the morning, eat lunch with us, and leave at night when my father came home. Then he returned to Switzerland and we lost a friend to tease. He was so Swiss! As he had done, I entered the bills from the markets (e.g. tea, flour and cutlery) on the left page and the amounts that Venu got from the cashiers on the right. Of course it was my professional ambition to make figures square, but Deeksha often came in and took some of the money. When she heard me protest she just said: "Make it work!" To materialise her dreams she needed cash: a tool shed upstairs for the handymen, fabric for their red dungaree shorts, a tofu and *tempeh* factory on Jesus House roof, and so on. So some of the money went to pay the bills, including the ones for the workers' kitchen; some went to Laxmi in the Main Office and some was kept for more interesting improvements.

Among the improvements were stainless steel cups, bowls and plates, which replaced the chipped earthenware. Anyone in India could lodge and eat for a whole day for the cost of one single stainless steel cup. The risk of having them stolen was therefore gigantic. As my mind had shown itself to be too inflexible to muddle Deeksha's accounts, I was sent with a "You are too Swiss!" out of the tiled cubbyhole to the newly-invented job of checking people's bags for cups and bowls at the exits of Vrindavan. There were two guards: one at the entrance, in case someone walked back without paying for food and drink (and maybe with a stainless steel cup in their bag…); the other was in the garden, at the exit of the eating area.

I remember sitting at the entrance on a high stool with my legs tucked under, waiting for the rush to come. Next to me was Aranyo in front of her hot urns with fresh *chai*. Both silent, just sitting, unmoving, aware of each other's presence: nowhere to go, nothing to say. All our dancing body energies were sitting still, dense, like lionesses waiting for their prey. Through this stored energy I saw the serving room shimmering in psychedelic colours. Aranyo might have had a similar experience, but we never talked about it.

The high stool in the garden was in the shade of a young tree. Whoever left the garden had to show me their bag – this was years before airport security checks became routine! Sometimes I could feel the contents from the outside; but when it was a swelling bag, I had to plunge my hand in and feel for a hard and round object. Everybody visiting Vrindavan became more aware of their bags. Many told me that they went through their bags more often and carried around only what they really needed, and even gave them a wash now and then. I somehow overcame my initial uneasiness and enjoyed having those little chats which would continue – like cartoon strips – the next time they came by. These bits of conversation turned this ungrateful job into a delight...

And this delight we learned from Osho's very being, seeing him at night. More and more people had gathered around Osho and the evening meetings had moved to Chuang Tzu Auditorium. Sometimes we had department darshans: we were invited to just sit there watching Osho talk to newcomers and give sannyas to new initiates.

The lights shone onto Osho and a group of people around him. On his left were Nirvano, his caretaker, and Laxmi, his secretary; on his right was Mukta, whose job was to call people by their names to come up and meet Osho. Next to her was Shiva, a ginger-head from Scotland who had become Laxmi's bodyguard after an unfortunate incident. The man who'd attacked Laxmi, first trying to strangle her and then biting her nose, was angry at her because she had not given him permission to see the master. Now Shiva was also present at all darshans. He helped those who came up to Osho to find the right spot to sit down. Next to him was Maneesha who took notes for the commentaries to Osho's words which were now recorded and transcribed daily. A darshan diary per month!

I enjoyed watching Osho when he talked to people. He behaved so differently from anyone I had ever seen and I can describe what I perceived only with these poor and inexact words. Whenever someone was sitting in front of him, it seemed to me that no one other than this person existed for him. Osho was totally there for that person. When the dialogue was over, Osho was ready with new eyes to welcome the next person, pouring the same clear attention into that being. The past conversation was gone and did not linger on in the air.

If someone had booked to be initiated, Osho asked him again if he wanted to become a sannyasin. He sometimes also asked those who had come with only a question. They often said "Yes!", to their own surprise.

For the sannyas initiation Nirvano would pass Osho a clipboard with a pen. He held the pen in a way we were not allowed at school: between forefinger and middle finger. With the same intensity with which I had seen him look into the eyes of those sitting in front of him, he slowly wrote the sannyas name. I knew he was drawing his signature when his hand was moving up and down and from side to side with that tiny scratchy noise of the pen. Leaving the clipboard on his lap, he returned the pen to Nirvano who handed him the mala. With both hands he slid it gently over the head while the initiate bowed forward. Then he held the locket of the mala in his left hand while with his right thumb he touched a point between the person's eyebrows, his fingers resting on top of the head. Master and disciple looked into each other's eyes.

Osho unclipped the paper and turned it around for the sannyasin to see. 'Rajneesh Foundation' and the address of the ashram in the header in blue print and the black and golden logo embossed on the top right. It was the symbol Osho had designed for his neo-sannyas movement: a point within a triangle, within a nonagon, within a circle. The sannyas name was in neat writing with no capitals (or sometimes all capitals), the Hindi spelling underneath. That day's date was written to confirm the event and Osho's always-changing, scrawling calligraphy signature was the seal.

I loved following the ritual which was the same for each one: "Your new name is Ma… Will it be easy to pronounce?" So caring. "It means…" and Osho revealed the significance of the name, its implications. He then talked to the new initiate and to us listening from farther rows. Asked about the meaning of the names, Osho said:

The names I give you are just like lovers' sweet nothings – don't make such a fuss about them. In fact, once I have given you the name, never come and ask me about its meaning again, because I forget it! It is in that moment that I create the meaning around it. How am I supposed to remember? I must have given thirty thousand names... or more!

A name is just a name! You are nameless. No name confines you, no name can confine you. It is just a label to be used – utilitarian – nothing spiritual in it. But because I pay so much attention to your name and I explain it to you, you get hooked by it.

That is just my way of showering my attention on you, nothing else; just my way of wooing my love to you, nothing else.

Osho, *The Diamond Sutra*, Ch. 10

Once an Indian man came up to take sannyas. He was crying, sobbing, his whole body shaking. I saw myself in his place. I remembered walking into Osho's room in Mumbai, sobbing, receiving the mala, sobbing, and then sitting in his living room/library, sobbing for the rest of the afternoon. After Osho had given the man his mala and new name – without commenting on it – Osho said to us what I remember as: "This comes from the heart." I was taken aback. I had felt very foolish about crying then and was touched by what Osho said. I judged myself as a heady person; but maybe my heart was not as closed as I had imagined. I remembered again the moment I was sitting in front of Osho receiving the mala, my eyes closed and crying. My body was sobbing but I was somewhere deep inside. Behind the sobbing and the embarrassment there was a calm and clear space. Later I learned that what is behind thoughts and emotions is called 'the witness'. Is there any other way to be in front of truth, in front of the master, if not in tears?

Outside the gate, friends waited for those who had just taken sannyas. "What is your new name?" They had to take a peek at the paper to find out. Flowers, hugs, tears. "Welcome to the club!"

To fall asleep with the feeling of darshan was exquisite. I would never take a shower; I wanted to take the sound of his voice, the evening lights, the magic moments with me into dreams and into deep sleep.

Next morning I could go to lecture again – I was on late shift. Osho was talking in Buddha Hall. Its temporary roof had meanwhile been taken down by the rental company which usually builds these structures for huge wedding ceremonies. It had been a rusty tin roof – though from underneath decoratively hidden by a white cloth – supported by wobbly-looking, gnarled wooden poles wrapped in strips of multicoloured fabric. Deeksha's handymen replaced the roof with white boards and glossy white four-by-four pillars. A new warm brown backdrop behind the podium gave the discourses a sunny feeling.

Osho was driven to discourse – from his porch to the back of the podium – by Laxmi in a grey Mercedes. There was controversy about whether it was proper for a spiritual man to be driven in such an expensive car. It is interesting that we always associate spirituality with poverty, as if a man living in a hut without bathroom or kitchen is more conscious than someone who actually lives in the 20th century. It is fine for a film star or anyone else living in Koregaon Park to drive a fancy car. Someone even had a yellow Maserati!

The approach of Osho's car was always announced by that crunching on the gravelled path. It was time to open our eyes and greet the master. One morning, however, it was Laxmi's little grey and black Ambassador approaching the hall. The Mercedes had broken down and Osho had insisted on giving the discourse. Of course, we all laughed – our great master in this utilitarian car, almost a Mickey Mouse car. So human – so beautiful.

I loved to see him walk into the hall, lifting his robe a little with one hand as he climbed the few steps to the podium, greeting us in *namaste* and sitting down in his chair, sometimes adjusting the distance of the microphone. There was a message in the grace of his movements, as important as in the melody and meaning of his words.

That morning I was not sitting in my favourite spot. I was on watch duty as an 'angel' near the entrance, my back leaning against a pillar. After Osho had been attacked by a man who had thrown a knife at him – my friends in the late shift, who had been at the discourse, told me how the knife clattered horribly to the ground between the rows of people – Shiva organised a group of guards and I was now one of them. The compulsory weekly karate classes were one of the reasons why I joined.

On that fateful morning, although the ashram office had been warned of the threat, Osho had come to the hall to give his morning discourse. Police in plainclothes were in the hall but they had not protected Osho. It seemed rather that they had come to protect the man with the knife, fearing he would be lynched by the sannyasins. We suspected he was from a right-wing Hindu group who was offended by what Osho had said about the then prime minister Morarji Desai (and his urine drinking). But Osho had many enemies as he was so outspoken about priests and politicians, and other 'idiots' – as he called them. I am not sure if the man even went to court; but I know he was not convicted of attempted murder.

The newly-formed corps of Lao Tzu house guards, now called samurais, sat in their wide maroon *hakama* trousers, facing the audience on both sides of the podium and watched each single movement in the hall. They trained in martial arts every day and were handsome and tall men. (To have a boyfriend who was a samurai was really 'in'.) Between them and us 'angels' there was a secret sign language to communicate from post to post. If someone had to leave because of coughing, an 'angel' escorted him out of the hall.

For many years I was frightened of Osho. Perhaps the fear was that I might be asked to do something I was not willing to do, but – as far as I remember – there never was such an incident. I might have been afraid of being exposed, in front of others and myself. I knew Osho could see through my soul. Attraction on one hand; fear on the other.

I saw Osho gliding up the steps – greeting us so gracefully – and the fear had suddenly gone. Seeing him from afar, he appeared even more delicate, and I heard myself say: 'My lovely teddy bear'. Present in discourse, listening to Osho with open eyes and alert to the outside world and looking simultaneously with relaxed vision at the crowd for the full 180 degrees was an exhilarating experience. On the one hand Osho's voice hypnotised me to my very depth; on the other hand, the guarding job kept me alert and in touch with the outside world.

In this space of attention I was suddenly hit by Osho's words which I remember as: "A master is not a teddy bear," pronouncing the word 'bear' like 'beer'. So, that was not the way to love the master either. And how could he hear my thoughts?

The master's work is really not of giving something to the disciple but of taking everything that the disciple has, leaving him utterly poor in spirit; and that is the journey and the arduousness of it. When a disciple comes to a master he comes hoping that he will get something; a real master is bound to frustrate it.

Only the pseudo-master gives you solace; the real master gives you fire. Only the pseudo-master pretends to give you something – knowledge, wisdom, enlightenment.

The real master knows that nothing can be given to you because in the first place all that you need is already there. It is hidden behind a great heap of rubbish; the rubbish has to be taken away. But you have cherished that rubbish very long, you have saved it like a treasure, so when it is being taken away it hurts, it leaves wounds. One wants to escape from a real master.

A thousand-and-one times one wants to escape from a real master. A thousand-and-one times one is frustrated with the real master, because basically he never fulfils your desires.

Osho, *God's Got a Thing About You*, Ch. 10

I am walking over London's Hampstead Heath to meet up with Amiten on the other side of the park. He comes off work at 4pm and I will walk back with him. High grass, sparrows, mature trees and bushes surround me and the whole city of London is at my feet. The Radio Tower and the many spikes of the churches try to hide behind the summer mist. The sun shines onto my face and a slight breeze from the south twists my hair and refreshes my brow. It still amazes me that not all towns are as flat as my hometown, Milan – that some can have empty spaces, high, bright blue skies between the boroughs.

We have now been living in London, between Islington and Camden Town, for a few months and it definitely seems that I will not go back to Mill Valley in sunny California, the place where I was living before meeting Amiten. We are renting a bedroom and a studio from a friend, Yashen and his partner, Farida. He looks so much like Amiten that everyone takes them for brothers; but if Amiten is the practical one then Yashen is the academic one. He is presently working as an accountant for a publisher, a sannyasin company here in London, whilst Amiten is an electrician on a conversion job of an old rectory.

My studio is full with newly-discovered papers and cards for the last photo album of a series I have created for a businesswoman in California. These albums are almost three-dimensional; using thick paper as a base I make a composition with the photos and small *objets trouvés*. I would then bind the pages into a book, with thin decorative papers between the pages. So for me to find a good source of paper is an unspeakable blessing. This is how I discovered 'Paperchase'.

I would never have believed it if someone had told me that there is a shop four stories high full of paper! Papers from all over the world: handmade paper from Indonesia and very fine (and expensive) decorative paper from Japan, as well as the full range of Fabrianos. I have also found blue metallic card which reflects very well not only the face of the onlooker but the favourite hobby of my client's husband: fishing. Amiten gets embarrassed when I look into skips to find interesting bits and pieces for my collages and even more when I tear off strips of posters even if – in the end – they look good in the album.

I had not cooked for a few years because in the commune we

had our lovely canteen with its delicious vegetarian food, but now in London I find delight in cooking again, so much so that I regularly cook dinner for all four of us in the house and try to recall our old recipes while walking on the Heath.

Hot Croissants for Afternoon Tea

Life must have been getting too easy for me, so Deeksha sent me to the bakery. I will be in charge of one of the shifts.

I had absolutely no idea of baking because my mother's gas-stove never worked well – either the back was too hot or the front did not warm up. I grew up without home-made cakes or gratins. It seemed I had to break through another preconceived idea which I carried from my childhood.

The bakery was about a fifteen-minute rickshaw drive from the ashram, behind the busy shopping street M.G. Road (M.G. stands for Mahatma Gandhi. He never acquired great popularity in this city – in fact he was murdered by a man from Pune, so his street had to make do with his initials only). We rented the premises from a local baker who used it during the night.

At 6am we cleaned his dough crusts from tables, walls and floors with scrapers, scrubbing brushes and buckets full of water. In the meantime Nigama built the fire in the oven balancing the logs on a long-handled wooden peel, the special bakers' shovel. Then we prepared the croissant dough with the butter, flour and water we had kept in the fridge overnight – in this way boosting the impact of hot and cold to puff up the pastry. The dough stretched over the surface of a whole table and required two people to fold it after the butter had been spread on. Someone cut the dough in even triangles. But at the rims, where the dough was thinner, we had to cut wider triangles to create a croissant of the same volume – again the mental exercise we were used to when chopping vegetables. We rolled them up, one under the palm of each hand, bending the tails with thumb and small finger. They looked like crabs! One of us scooped them up and placed them evenly onto an oiled tray. When the croissants had risen well, they went, sprayed with ice water and covered with a lid, into the hot oven. After some time the lids were taken off to brown their puffed-up tops.

The pressure from Vrindavan was heavy: 300 croissants had to be delivered before the end of Osho's discourse. Ideally, they had to be all the same size, have the same hazel-brown crust and be well cooked inside. When they were ready one of us took them to the ashram while the rest of the crew enjoyed the rejected, ill-shaped, but still delicious croissants with home-made jam. No wonder that under the comfortable red aprons our shapes were curving, loosening the androgynous shapes dictated by Vogue, into an easy feminine roundness. I am not only talking about myself: Mukul whom I remembered in Geneva as having a young boy's body was now turning into a woman.

Sometimes it was my turn for the morning run. When I arrived at the ashram with the croissants packed in metal boxes and loaded into a hired rickshaw, I asked the driver to stop the engine and, while Osho was giving his morning discourse in Buddha Hall, we pushed the rickshaw silently toward the kitchen. This moment was very precious to me. I could hear Osho's voice from the loudspeakers – a few sentences or a fragment of a joke – and feel the presence of his silent audience around him. The rest of the ashram was empty except for the Main Gate guard and us. I walked alongside the rickshaw, steadying my load from slipping off the seat. It would be a disaster if the boxes slid off and clattered on the floor; I could prevent that, but I couldn't do anything to prevent the fragrance of the croissants entering Buddha Hall!

After breakfast we prepared cakes for afternoon tea. Deadline: 2pm. We compensated for time pressure with ingenuity: we invented tools and set up work spaces with ergonomic considerations. Almost every day Nigama came up with a new invention or a new system. They always worked. I learned to set up my work straight in front of me, easy on my body, and avoid unnecessary movements and unnecessary thoughts. The movements became fast, without hesitation, and the attention was totally on the work. There was no time to dawdle, to think twice, or go through the argument you had with your boyfriend or girlfriend last night.

One of the deadly sins was to be 'spaced out'. We had learned under Deeksha's supervision to be where the work was. It was also not acceptable to be so lost in the work as to be unaware of our surroundings. Many a time we got busted in the kitchen if the lights were still on from the early morning or if she found a pot of yesterday's grated cheese under the table. "I didn't put it there," was no excuse. Our energy had to be with the work but the attention not so focused that the broader vision of things was lost.

The cakes… The physical was counterbalanced with the mental: vanilla sponge cake mixture three times the recipe. It took quite some concentration in the hustle and bustle not to make mistakes with multiplication and adding up of the numbers on the faces of the scale weights. I remember Satdeva had a total block about this. Many of his cakes turned out flat with a gooey look and a toffee flavour. If we liked his new invention, he unfortunately did not remember what exactly he had done wrong. To his disappointment he was never taken off the weighing job.

We baked white and brown bread for the whole commune and preparing the bread dough was my favourite job. I measured and sifted the flour onto the bread table and parted a well for water, oil and yeast. My attention was totally there: it would be a disaster if the walls collapsed and the water ran off the table. I enjoyed working the moisture in and kneading the dough with my strong arms; stretching the dough, folding it over and stretching it again.

The dough soon rose in the Indian heat under its white covering sheet. With the tips of our fingers we checked to see if it was ready to be rolled into loaves. Our fingers became very sensitive. We could decide if the dough was good just by touching it. We had discovered a new sense, a new dimension of delight: sensuousness. As painters would talk in colours we talked in touch. Nigama would confide in me, "That French girl last night was just like sweet dough, mmmmm…," expressing with his hands what he was saying.

When it was bread-rolling time the bakery turned into a noisy factory: everybody stopped their chores – cleaners included. Premananda had oiled the tins which were strapped together in fours and stacked in towers. Nigama was at the scales; the game was to cut the dough to the exact weight in one go. Everybody else stood ready at their corner of the floured table. A few stretches and a few folds, a roll into shape and the loaves were ready to be put in their cradle. When they had popped up their heads through the covering sheets it was time to put them into the oven.

The wood oven was about ten feet deep and had a small iron door which lifted up like a guillotine. The handle of the peel had to be ten feet long to reach the farthest corners. The oven master of the day – always aware of what was happening behind him, where cakes were decorated, cookies stacked and pastry dough mixed – stood ready at the oven gate. The bread tins had to be handled gently. If dropped onto the peel, the bread collapsed over the edges – a dreadful sight.

Even while busy with weighing out ingredients or scraping dirty trays we had an 'ear' for the oven. A timer would not have done the job as the heat of the fire varied too much from day to day. We had to sense the moment when the wet dough turned into bread, just at the right time, before it turned into coal. There was a telepathic connection between the bakers and their creations. The cakes called us when they were ready to be taken out. I do remember burnt bread though – and coming home late after spending hours scraping black bottoms off burnt loaves.

At the end of the shift we scrubbed hands and feet with brushes (Nigama found out that Vim was the best foot-cleaner on the market); in turns, we took a cold shower in the two shower rooms at the back of the bakery and slipped into clean robes, ready to show ourselves in the ashram again.

On our arrival, Deeksha, who never came to the bakery herself, could always tell how the day had gone just by looking at the cakes and breads. Their vibes would tell the story without me saying a word. I remember one evening when she asked me to have a cup of tea in her office (there was beer in the tea pot – just what I needed!). "Who do you have in your shift?" she wanted to know. Among the list I remember mentioning Ojas from Holland, a former minister, and Rupesh, a Mexican teenager, our conga player and a notorious rebel. He was loved by Osho and respected by Deeksha, who allowed him to get away with almost anything. Deeksha confessed that she had recently sent me quite a few people whom she could not deal with in the kitchen and – to make my life easier – considered sending me some 'good' workers the next day.

Deeksha was aware that, for some, the bakery was equal to Siberia and she used that as a threat. It was far away from the ashram and had very primitive facilities. If you were a cleaner, your place was in a tiny open courtyard bent over big plastic tubs full of scrapers, pots and bowls. Your clothes were wet below the stiff plastic apron and your arms and feet were immersed in water. In monsoon time you had to wear an anorak.

During celebration days departments like Translations and Publications sent their workers to help out in Chiyono, the cleaning department, or in Mariam and Vrindavan. Sometimes a dozen workers turned up with astonished faces at our bakery. Some helped with the packing of the biscuits and the cutting of the cakes; for others I had to find a job. Finally there was some manpower to clean the ceiling fans and the high windows that we never got around to doing. With buckets full of water and sponges in their hands, they balanced themselves on wooden stepladders while I watched that they didn't drip their dirty water onto the working tables. They must have asked themselves: "How could anyone work in such a place?"

The bakery was wild. Our long hair was kept tight on top of the head with rosewood hair-sticks or Chinese chopsticks, our bodies were simply covered with loose, full aprons. Sandals or shoes were too dangerous – with bare feet we could feel each oily patch or piece of dough. If the kitchen was hell, the bakery was freedom, almost too much freedom. Once I saw 'proper' girl Mukul, lying on the floor laughing, throwing her legs in the air and holding her belly with both arms. Rupesh stood over her, teasing her. Or Anupassana in a tantrum, shouting and screaming at the top of her voice, jumping up and down on both legs, red in the face. Everybody else went on with their work – "nothing special, so and so has had a freak-out." In these cases, as Deeksha had taught us, the message was: "Go and take a shower!" Water calmed and washed away the bad moods.

For many workers it was a beautiful playground to experiment with new recipes. We had total freedom in what we were going to offer on our menu. Each one of us contributed the breads and cakes we knew from childhood: Nigama brought bagels, sesame crackers and brownies from the States; Anasha, focacce and grissini from Italy; Ganga, apple strudel, and Veetmaya, Black Forest cakes and pretzels from Germany; Ageha, Danish pastries; Chanda, flutes from France; Anupassana, trifle tarts from New Zealand; Premananda, poppy seed cakes from his Polish grandmother... All these and the Engadin nut tart from my ski holidays in St. Moritz became part of our recipe book.

Working there I realised how different the learning process was with Osho compared to the world. In Switzerland a youngster was trained as a baker for four years. Here we became proficient in all jobs, even those of a pastry maker, in three months. But, unfortunately, we only had a few people who stayed that long. Others had to learn quickly under Nigama's supervision and soon were gone again to work elsewhere.

Anasha and Veetmaya were two of the steady workers. Both eventually became Osho's mediums in the energy darshans. Anasha was Kavya's sister who got to know about Osho through my little centre in Milan. Veetmaya was my best friend. If I was thirty-five she must have been twenty-five, but we used to walk around like teenagers: holding hands, going everywhere together, telling each other all our secrets as teenagers do. When the message came that Osho had asked for croissants to be baked for him, Veetmaya was the one to have the job. Osho ate them in the late afternoon and so they had to be prepared separately. We cleaned Veetmaya's table as much as it was possible for the old cracked wood to yield to our scouring brushes. She took a shower and changed into a fresh apron. A small hot fire was built in the oven especially for these three croissants. When they had cooled down, Veetmaya jumped into a rickshaw and took them to Lao Tzu gate.

Every two days I met with Renuka who was leading the other shift. I often went over to her room in Eckhart House. Together we estimated what we had to produce the following days. The amounts fluctuated with the new arrivals before the festivals and, interestingly, when Osho didn't speak because he had a cold – then more cakes and cookies had to be prepared.

We had three celebrations in a year: Osho's birthday, his Enlightenment Day and Guru Purnima, the traditional Indian festival at the first full moon in July, when the masters are celebrated. Thousands of Indian sannyasins who lived in the villages streamed into the ashram and remained in Pune for these few days. The kitchen cooked extra spicy dishes for them. Many western friends came to Pune for Osho's birthday, which falls on the 11th of December, and then stayed for a month or two. Or if our time in India had come to an end, we waited to leave until after a celebration. It was a way of going home: riding high on a big strong wave.

For one of these celebrations I remember that, after having cut and delivered all the cakes, I took a bath and put on, for the first time, the orange robe with yellow piping that Padma had designed and sewn for me. I squeezed my way through the queue waiting to get into Buddha Hall. It stretched all the way into Jesus House garden. Many had stood in line since morning to get a seat close to the master. If it was not possible to sit on his lap, or at his feet, then at least in the first rows...

My hair still wet from the shower, I looked for my cushion which I had left with the ushers. Just to be able to sit down and do nothing was a blessing. In front of me a few girls with lists in their hands were busy placing the lecture cushions of the regular front-seaters around the podium. I watched the moving forms under the golden light the way I used to watch the passers-by at the Biffi in the Galleria in Milan, sitting at a little marble table with a Martini Secco in hand.

I was relaxed until my mind came in with the boring and disturbing programme: "Why does so-and-so have a front seat? He does not live in Osho's house, nor is he a therapist or a co-coordinator of a department. Moreover, he just arrived a few months ago. Why don't I get recognition?" Always the nagging feeling that I was not getting enough and much less than others did. I forgot that many had queued for hours and saw me now sitting in front of them. I judged myself, saying that my energy was too gross and my mind too busy to ever get close to Osho. Or consoled myself that I would not be able to withstand the strong energy of the front rows. But when I closed my eyes everything was perfect: I was sitting in the right spot.

The musicians rolled their drums and we sang the songs we had learned in Music Group. Osho arrived in his white robe, greeting us with a big smile. He sat down in his chair and closed his eyes, his audience a choir. We sang one song after another. Soft songs like waves in the ocean, and fiery songs to melt our hair. I was aware of the still-starched crisp cotton of my new dress, of my friends sitting close by.

Sometimes Osho opened his eyes and I thought he might have looked straight at me. I did not know if I was sitting or flying. I was swaying my arms in the rhythm of the song, fluid like a flame in water, lost in the meanders of the flying melodies, almost fainting, but still aware of where I was, boundaries blurred. Osho, a brilliant sun shining onto me. Enveloped in a warm blanket of love, with the freedom to fly high into the sky. I could not remember ever experiencing so much bliss. Or could I?

Yes, the first time I had felt so much awe and wonder was, at age four, the moment grandmother had opened the door to the living room and the Christmas tree was standing there: the light and warmth from a hundred lit candles overwhelmed me while I was still standing in the other room. How could little Jesus have created it without my hearing the slightest sound? From my three-foot height I was gazing up, eyes open wide, jaw hanging, in wonder...

When for the first time something starts happening which is beyond words, life has happened to you, life has knocked at your door.

And when the ultimate knocks at your door, you are simply gone beyond words – you become dumb, you cannot say; not even a single word is formed inside. And whatsoever you say looks so pale, so dead, so meaningless, without any significance, that it seems that you are doing injustice to the experience that has happened to you.

Osho, *Tantra: The Supreme Understanding,* Ch. 1

I was aware that at the present moment all worries and fears had gone, that I was swimming in an ocean of bliss, and that my humanity down in the valleys of sorrow was also a reality. I felt the vast distance between possibility and actuality. I also knew that tomorrow anger would be back to torment me and my bakers again.

On the Very Edge

One day I decided to have myself sterilised. Now thirty-five years old and considered to be past the age for having babies, I was more interested in being a sannyasin than a housewife and mother. My appointment was scheduled for just a few days before the summer celebration. I then postponed it, imagining that Deeksha would not appreciate my absence from the bakery at such a busy time. I was wrong. For a reason I do not remember I was sacked just before the celebration with a: "All these two years you were a terrible boss." What a failure!

Then something went badly wrong. I was already recovering in our own medical centre along the river and having my first meal after the tubal ligation, when a terrible pain gripped my belly. I only remember being lifted into Veda's van and transported back to Doctor Saraswati's clinic where I spent, I later calculated, three days shouting "Please do something!" whenever I was conscious. Nurses in saris scolded me for waking up the other patients. And then something did finally happen. X-rays were taken and I remember seeing the many round lights of a convex lamp above an operating table, but not much more. Feeling pressure on my belly I wanted to tell the doctors that I was waking up, that more anaesthetic was needed, but could not speak. I tried to signal with my hand and all my body energy went into the left index finger, but could not move it. Shortly afterwards I heard someone say, "It is all over, Punya."

Deeksha and her secretaries, Anando and Venu, pushed my bed out of the operating theatre. From the number of people present I suspected it must have been a serious affair. I drifted off and when I came to again, I found myself in a hospital room. A laminated picture of Osho was hanging from the drip stand in mid-air in front of my face. I was hearing recorded music of Music Group, Anubhava singing, and the wooden box Osho had given to me, strapped in gauze, was dangling from the metal bed within arm's reach.

Digambara was in the room and he told me that he had been sent to clean my floor with soap and brush. He was a bit scared because I was breathing very fast. I did not remember him coming in.

Then I noticed the bed linen, which was certainly not the regular hospital linen, so suspected Deeksha's touch there. My head was on a huge feather pillow with a purple and blue flower print and my body was covered with a matching sheet and a soft white woollen shawl. I loved this shawl very much and caressed it to feel better. Our sannyasin doctor Amrit came for a visit and I complained bitterly about the pain. He told me to let the pain come and cover me like a dark blanket, welcoming it. It was difficult. The pain was so alarming. It came in strong waves. Deeksha also came for a visit and her instructions were clear: she wanted the room to be aired in the morning and the curtains opened as soon as the night had vanished. She wanted light in the room – but only later did I understand why.

Shahido, a strong and smiling nurse from Australia, was sent to take care of me. When I asked something she never replied until I realised that I was talking to her in Italian. It was difficult to form sentences in English. Soon I felt that there was another way of communicating, not through words but through the heart. I felt protected when she was there. Before she had come, the Indian cleaning ladies had been into my side table drawer and stolen the money for the medicines. They would even take a ring from a dying man, given the chance.

Twice a day a worker was sent from Vrindavan with a *tiffin* containing liquidised vegetables, papaya pulp and curd. I managed to eat only a few spoonfuls of each, with my heart racing at 120. Every afternoon a sannyasin physiotherapist slapped my back and the sides of my chest to avoid infections in the lungs. As my mind was too confused to read, I was happy to have visitors. Veetmaya came almost every day on her way home from the bakery. All visits felt like food for healing. They gave me encouragement and entertainment.

Doctor Saraswati dropped by on his way to Osho's discourse every morning. He sat at my bedside holding my hand for a long time. I felt a lot of energy from his hand streaming into mine and I became very silent and usually fell asleep. He had explained to me that an ulcer had opened after the sterilization and that this had created peritonitis. (I never knew I had an ulcer!) His son-in-law, who had fixed the mishap, checked on me regularly. I asked him in detail what he had found inside my body and what he had done there. He kept saying words I did not really understand: "If the patient wants to live he will recover quickly." I was blissfully unaware that I could have died. My focus was: 'I have to take care of myself and get better'. I even used to call the nurses to bring new drip bottles when they were getting low.

The seriousness of the illness became clear to me only a year later when I found some records which showed that my pulse, blood pressure and the circumference of my belly had been measured every hour. When asked, Doctor Amrito confirmed – with a "We were very worried about you" – that I had really been on the edge. Pradeepa, who was running the Vipassana groups in the ashram, visited me and – apparently on Osho's instructions – taught me the Vipassana meditation, to watch the breath coming in and going out. To her disappointment I had to tell her at her second visit that I hadn't done the meditation because it always made me fall asleep.

Soon my bowels started working again and it felt like giving birth to a child. I encouraged myself to go for little walks around the room, putting the scented flowers on the balcony at night and rearranging them in the morning. One day I felt a familiar feeling in my belly – it was anger – when the cleaning ladies had come to beg for money with their slimy smiles. I reckoned it was a sign that I was getting stronger. The printed sheets had gone and also the beloved woollen cloth. Many years later I discovered it was a shawl Osho had worn and then given to Deeksha as a present.

The vegetable soup came now in big chunks, my fingernails had started to grow again and the visits of my friends were less frequent. Veetmaya was sometimes the only visitor in a whole day. One evening she came with a radiant and astonished face: "I just saw Osho in the Mercedes right outside this hospital. It felt like

Christmas." We savoured the Christmas feeling together. Through her, Osho had visited me as well. The next day I heard he had gone to see his dying father in the hospital across the street.

In four weeks I had lost two stone. I exercised my weak muscles every day on an always longer excursion, up and down the stairs, and sometimes even ventured outside as far as the doctors' car park. A few times I visited Upassika upstairs; she had come down with the same condition. She was skin and bones, big eyes flickering in the candlelight. I soon noticed that it was not good for me to stay with her too long. Each time I left I felt drained and weaker. Her curtains were always closed and the room was always dark, day or night, except for the few candles. Was this the way to invite life back? Well, not for me. That's when I understood why Deeksha insisted that I drew the curtains and open the windows first thing in the morning – this might have been the best medicine for me! Seeing Upassika so skinny, for the first time in my life I appreciated the fact that I had been on the chubby side before the operation – at least now I still had some padding left round my sides. Although I was getting better by the day I was convinced that I would remain a cripple for the rest of my life and would never be able to run or dance again.

After a final operation to suture the incision for a second time I was brought back to the ashram, to my room. There was now a bed waiting for me. I would not have been able to get up from a mattress on the floor. My new bed had two big drawers on castors underneath where I could store my belongings and reach for them without getting up. But my plant had gone.

The fern had been standing on a low side table at the top end of my mattress. My head just below, I had loved to see the many light green curled-up shoots unroll in a spiral motion. The more I admired her the more she sprouted vigorously, seeming to outpace my compliments. It was her way of repaying my love. The more she propagated, the more my admiration grew, a circle of love. I had thought of her in hospital and wanted her to be brought there but I was too embarrassed to show my attachment to a plant. Mukul, on her one-time visit, had assured me that Sagara, our third roommate who was a gardener, had been watering it regularly. But finally Sagara had to plant the fern in the garden as it was overrun with aphids. The plant must have felt that I was ill.

I am so very grateful to the doctors and nurses and all the friends who had come to visit me at the hospital over that whole month. They contributed to my coming back from the edge of the abyss of no return. Thank you!

I would have expected to get a sitting-down job in one of the offices, but soon I was again in the kitchen playing with knives and aluminium serving trays. The doctors had recommended no weight lifting, no constipation, to watch my weight and to wear a belt around my belly, as a hernia had started forming. I felt so terribly unattractive, I thought I would never find a lover again. My hair had gone all scraggly as if it had undergone years of perms. To compensate, my eyes often rested on the strong wavy long hair of other girls. Deeksha made me show my still red scar to the guests in her office: "Punya, show your scar!" she commanded, and that took much of my shame away. There was really nothing to hide.

A few weeks after my return, on 8th September 1979, we heard that Osho's father had left his body. We had all loved seeing him walk through the ashram with his walking stick or sitting on his chair, watching the traffic of sannyasins streaming through the main gate, 'like a shop-keeper in front of his son's business', as we lovingly joked. We thought that one day Osho would look like him when he got old – but this was obviously never meant to happen.

In the evening, as usual, the musicians set up their instruments in Buddha Hall. We sat down in the centre of the hall and danced around the edges. Dadaji's body was brought in on a bamboo stretcher and laid on the podium. Osho knelt down, placed a garland of leaves on his father's chest and touched his head. Mataji, Osho's mother, was crying by his side, a desperate lament on top of our songs.

I felt as if I was stuck in a box, my energy still contained to heal myself. I could not reach outside my body to connect with the celebrating songs, Osho's presence, and the feeling of a woman losing her husband. I stood there like an outsider, watching things happen somewhere on a screen.

As my hernia was getting worse and the wound would not close, Deeksha decided to send me to the West to have it fixed. She gave me enough money to pay for the ticket and operation and my sister arranged for a surgeon friend to see me at her home. When I found myself again tied to tubes and drips I understood that more work than just fixing a hernia had been done. Apparently the surgeon had still found pus around my guts, and as he was at it, he cut out a cyst which was attached to my right ovary, the (healthy) appendix, and finally tied the tubes (the job which should have been done in the first place).

My father had invited me to come and stay with him in the mountains for my convalescence. In the mountains, while Father and his wife were skiing the slopes, I went for walks in the woods. The pines were heavy with snow and the paths crunched under my feet. Cool thin air filled my lungs. Magical, but I hated it all. I wanted to be with Osho.

The ashram was so important to me that in my imagination it was as big as the world, a whole galaxy. When I returned, after a three months' exile, the ashram appeared so small in its physical reality. Vedam carried my suitcase the few yards from the back gate to the house and up the stairs to my old room.

But it was a totally transformed room. As a surprise for my return, Deeksha had torn down the loft near the door and built a new one for Mukul in the far right-hand corner with comfortable stairs. Underneath was our tea area with a few cushions, space for our hanging clothes and Mukul's shelves. There was now even a little window, broken through the wall high up above the loft, for her to look into the garden. My bed with the drawers on castors was moved to the left, straight under the window and a second bed near the door with the same drawers was for our new roommate: South American Samiyo who was running the boutique. The beds had matching throws, the room had been freshly painted and looked so aesthetic that we always kept it immaculately tidy.

To go to bed and look at the stars, to fall asleep while feeling the cool breeze touch my face was a delight. It was like sleeping outdoors. We never closed the window, not even in winter. A philodendron, on its way into the skies, had wound itself around the middle post. We would not have been able to close the window anyway.

I often sat on my bed and admired the enormous bodhi tree in the estate across the street. Its fluttering leaves, disturbed by the wind, glimmered like thousands of mirrors reflecting the light of the sun, in always-changing patterns. Once there was a party on the lawn in our garden underneath. It was Maneesha's birthday. An elephant leaf was held over her head as an umbrella to protect her face from the sun. They were having tea and cakes. Musicians played the Happy Birthday song. I could watch the scene as from a balcony seat.

Back at work, while I was helping at the food counter, Deeksha noticed that something had changed. I could not work in harmony with the others. There was an edge somewhere. When I was in hospital in India I was blaming myself for falling ill because I had not been looking after my body well enough; after talking to the Italian surgeon I started blaming my doctors in India for causing the peritonitis. I was called to Laxmi's office. She told me that if I could not fit in with the others and would not stop the blaming I could have my donation back – which was an exception, she said – and was free to go. This woke me up.

I became a cashier and could finally go to discourse every day. The rule was to leave as soon as Osho had left the hall and run to our posts: a line of tables near the exit door into the garden. The four of us, sitting on hard stools, a small table and a little teak cash box in front of us, waited like sprinters to withstand the breakfast rush. Croissants and chai, slices of white and brown bread with peanut-butter and home-made jam passed under our eyes. Just seeing all this food, my hunger was stilled.

Unknowingly I had begun to add up in an intuitive way, much faster than using my brain. I had not been aware of it until a customer, with a German accent, said to me: "Zis must be wrong.

How kan you calculate so fast?" I was taken aback. I did not know how I had done it. We went through the numbers slowly and came to the same result.

So many meals passed under my eyes that I also started seeing the quality of the food without tasting it, as if I could see the aura of it. I knew it was good if it looked happy; that it was a warmed-up leftover if it was asking for consolation.

When the rush was over we helped the counter people dish out the soups and *dhal* into the stainless steel bowls. One or two cashiers remained at their posts. There was time to space out into the lime green of the mosaic walls or watch the newcomers choose their food. I enjoyed seeing their steps becoming bouncier from day to day, their eyes widening and shining with a sparkling glow, a happy smile just ready to pop out unawares. What a transformation after just a few days of Dynamic and meeting with Osho! Then finally they would appear in orange clothes, ready to become part of this mysterious journey.

More and more people were coming from the West to see Osho and to participate in the work, the therapy groups and meditations. We joked that sometime in the future Mukta would have to call up a whole row of people in the evening meetings to take sannyas. We didn't have to wait too long for this to happen – one evening five people were initiated at the same time. Osho spoke individually about the significance of their names, each one waiting for their turn, a few feet from him. At times he even gave the same middle name to the whole group, which confused our theories about middle names: apparently the 'yogas' were the heavy workers, the 'prems' the emotional ones, the 'anands' the head cases and the 'devas' the nut cases.

Darshans, the personal interviews with questions and answers, had been transformed into an energy phenomenon. Osho had often invited Krishna Radha to act as a medium when someone had come up with a question. She was asked to kneel behind the guest and hold his hands with arms raised while Osho was pointing his pencil torch on parts of the body or touching the third eye. The person would then shake, laugh, shout, cry or all at once and fall back into Radha's arms. Sometimes she even had a strong man behind her to prevent her from falling over as well.

The evening darshans had now developed into an even more dramatic event. Osho had chosen twelve mediums to participate every night and help with the energy play. The guests were called up, Osho motioned to them where they were to sit, sometimes facing each other or in a semi-circle, and the mediums placed themselves where Osho directed them, behind the guests or around them. They were sometimes holding the hands of the guests or of another medium.

I remember one of these 'energy darshans', as they were called. I was seated cross-legged facing another sannyasin and we held each other's hands. I closed my eyes and felt my head resting on soft, welcoming breasts. Osho switched off the lights. We were in the dark. The black velvety darkness fitted with the enveloping energy I was feeling from the medium behind me; we were in a female receptive mood. The flutes and drums went wild. The lights were switched on again, first like a stroboscope, as if to chase out the ghosts from our souls. Did Osho have a switch next to his seat? He might have enjoyed the trick.

Everything was in confusion, in a purposeful chaos. The mind was stunned. The only way to survive was to go into the soft space within, soft and welcoming as the breasts. Suddenly the lights came back, glaring in contrast. Osho touched my forehead with a finger. Male energy – assertive and intruding – a male mood, almost aggressive, penetrating my being, uncomfortable – waking me up from a comfortable slumber.

We could book an energy darshan every two months, and every couple of weeks we could sit in the audience. In the darkness we could sway and were invited to hum. It was a mind-blowing experience even from a distance.

If instead we were dancing in Buddha Hall, the music stopped and we sat down in the dark; if we were in our room we meditated until the lights came back. The whole ashram was involved in the darshans now. The lights in the whole campus were switched off. There was nothing else to do other than to meditate. It had become a sacred time.

To those who have really lived long with me, and have become intimate, to those with whom the barrier with language has disappeared, just a look into their eyes or just a touch of my hand, and there is communication – not only communication – but communion.

That's why just recently I have started a new way of communing with my sannyasins; just to touch them, just to let them feel my energy. The more you become intimate with me, the less and less will words be needed – because you will start hearing me and then there will be no need of words. I will continue to speak for the new people, I will continue to speak for those who will be coming – more and more will be coming, thousands are on the way – but those who have been here with me long enough or deep enough... depth can happen even in a single moment. It is not a question only of time, it is a question of intensity.

Sometimes it happens that when a person comes to me for the first time, with the first moment of contact he becomes intimate as if he has been with me for many lives. And not only do I feel that, he also immediately feels that he has come home, that this is the place he has been searching for his whole life or for many lives. Then communication immediately happens. Then there is no conflict. In fact, the moment that there is communion and there is no conflict, it is the moment of your real initiation.

Osho, *The Secret of Secrets*, Vol. 1, Ch. 12

Finding My Own Light

A year after my operation I came down with hepatitis. There had been a few cases in the commune in spite of our hygiene efforts in the kitchen. After nibbling a deep fried cheese cube for the famous palak paneer dish I felt so sick in my stomach I had to go and lie down. Soon high fever came over me, almost hallucinogenic. I threw my orange winter blanket over the window cross-beam. I was shivering and could not close the window because of the climber. Megha, our Dutch doctor, looking into my yellow eyes, said to me with sympathy: "You have hepatitis." I sternly looked back into his eyes and said: "No." I did not want to be sick again.

The very same day I was moved to the isolation ward. Only doctors and nurses were allowed in the room, no visitors. I was upset to hear that because, just a few days before, I had finally met a man I liked. He would certainly forget all about me, I thought.

The first ten days I spent deep-cleaning the ward and rearranging magazines and books, showing to myself and to the rest of the world that I was not sick – the doctor must have made a mistake – until I gave up my fight. Tired, I surrendered to the leisurely life my five roommates had been enjoying all along – lying on their beds reading spy stories and browsing through old magazines. I also became particularly interested in the adverts for food products and in the recipe sections with the glorious close-ups of succulent meat dishes. In our heads we had all become non-vegetarians, while our stomachs had a hard time absorbing just the blandest vegetable broth.

Yatri, who at night was visited by Ambu, his girlfriend – she was small enough to crawl through the window – was drawing a new comic strip collection about hepatitis. I remember in particular the cartoon where Osho, striding as a waiter past a hospital bed, with a wicked smile carried a roasted turkey on a tray high above his head, a napkin on his left arm instead of his customary towel. In another cartoon the skinny hepatitis sufferer was under the shower happily washing off his yellow colour which disappeared down the drain. This was everybody's longing: to get rid of our yellow skin and eat proper food again. Even just to be able to eat the boiled vegetables we were served would have been a treat!

When I felt my energy coming back, Tanmaya, my new friend from the bed next to mine, came for walks with me in the deserted streets around the Medical Centre. When we looked at each other it was like looking into a mirror. Some even took us for sisters: broad Russian faces, long brown hair, yellow skin and yellow eyes. She would sometimes come and sit on my bed, or I would sit on hers, and we discussed – and argued – about the interior decoration and landscaping of our hypothetical house in Tuscany. With the help of the glossy magazines we explained our visions in detail. Funnily enough, at the time of writing, she is working for *Architectural Digest* in Los Angeles.

Back in my room, inspired by Yatri's cartoons, I ventured to draw a collection of cartoons about my life with Deeksha. It was a thank you for what she had done for me all those years and a way for me to acknowledge what we had gone through together. Many times I had wanted to disentangle myself from her clutches. I didn't do it, scared to be thrown out of the ashram and feeling safer under her care. The dozen square cards were assembled in a cardboard box which I presented to her when I went back to work.

Walking still shakily to discourse one morning, I was stopped by Vidya. She used to sit at the entrance of Buddha Hall checking for any nuisance people. Nonchalantly she asked me, in her peculiar South African accent, to come by the main office sometime. I couldn't make out what kind of message it would be. It did not sound like a reprimand. So it took me a few days to show up at Laxmi's desk. She told me that the office had decided it would be best for me to go back to the West and recover my health. To my ears this sounded like a death sentence. I ran back to my room in shock and tears. My despair was so immense it seemed to fill the whole ashram, enveloping the trees and the sky between the trees. I did not want to go.

During the next few weeks I went back a few times to the office with the argument that it did not feel right for me to leave and that I would recover very well in India. Each time Laxmi was firm and her answer was a steady: "You have to go back to the West." This all while I was asking myself *why* I did not want to go, one question at a time. When the answer was a 'no' – a 'no' experienced in my whole body and not just in the mind – I would dig deeper and ask the next question.

Was it maybe because I did not want to part from my new friend? Asking myself this question it appeared that this was not the reason: I could let go of him. Was I afraid of being out in the world and facing it with my own strength? Trying to prop up my physical weakness with Parle Gluco biscuits, I travelled to Mumbai to apply for a visa to the States. I had never been there and thought it would be a great place to be. I was confident that soon I would be strong enough to make money, get better and come back.

In reality there wasn't even a penny in my pocket, not even to buy a one way ticket to anywhere in the world. It felt like baking a cake without ingredients. Then Gayatri from Geneva, on her winter holiday in Pune, entrusted me with a loan so that I could go. Now that money and survival were taken care of and there was no hindrance to following Laxmi's orders, I went to see Garimo to book my leaving darshan. She gave me an appointment for a few days later. When I walked down the marble steps of her office a loud "No" welled up in me. It reached the trees and the sky between the trees: "I do not want to go!" Not knowing what to do next about myself in this confused state I sat down on my bed and wrote a letter to Osho, explaining the suggestion of the office and – with a "No" covering half the page – conveyed my feelings about it all.

The next morning I was on late shift and could go to discourse. It was one of the question and answer discourses which were alternating between Osho's comments on the Isa Upanishads. I relaxed into the melody of his words, assimilating as much as I could what he had to say to my fellow travellers. He was not really answering the questions, rather he was bringing light to the issue from many angles so that the question eventually disappeared.

I woke up when I heard Osho say:

The third question:
"Osho, would you please say something about sincerity?"

This was my question! I had sent it in a few months ago and had totally forgotten about it, never expecting a reply anyway. I was used to receiving an answer to my questions, which I had either written to Osho or which were just brooding in my head, in a roundabout way, while he commented on a *sutra* or answered someone else's question. I did not know why I had asked this question in particular. Maybe I had heard Osho use the word 'sincerity' and had not been able to find the place where this word lived in me.

Yoga Punya, Man can live in two ways: either he can live according to the dictates of others – the puritans, the moralists – or he can live according to his own light. It is easy to follow others, it is convenient and comfortable, because when you follow others they feel very good and happy with you. [...]

My full name was like a call: he meant me. Looking up I could see him look straight into my eyes. He knew that I was this Yoga Punya and that I was sitting right there. His first sentence went straight to my heart. I knew perfectly what he was talking about. I had been trying my whole life to please others, to pass unnoticed, to be nice and kind in the hope of being loved and accepted.

Sincerity, Yoga Punya, means to live according to your own light. Hence the first requirement of being sincere is to be meditative. The first thing is not to be moral, is not to be good, is not to be virtuous: the most important thing is to be meditative – so that you can find a little light within yourself and then start living according to that light. And, as you live, it grows and it gives you a deep integrity. Because it comes from your innermost being there is no division.

I was sitting erect, my orange robe tucked under my legs, aware of the grey concrete where the square markings imitated a paved floor. His words ignited my life energy: I felt my body expand and fill with light and heat, my heart beating fast. Nobody around me noticed it. Nobody knew I was the addressee. Although Osho was talking to hundreds of people I felt it as an intimate communication between him and me. I trusted that he would not hurt me with his words. I could not relate to his words 'to be meditative' at all. For years I had just been working and had forgotten all about meditation.

When somebody says to you, 'Do it, it should be done', naturally it creates a division in you. You don't want to do it, you wanted to do something else, but somebody – the parents, the politicians, the priests, those who are in power – they want you to follow a certain route. You never wanted to follow it so you will follow it unwillingly. Your heart will not be in it, you will not be committed to it, you will not have any involvement with it. You will go through it like a slave. It is not your choice, it is not out of your freedom. [...]

I knew: 'I can stay now, I don't have to leave. I can stay, it is so fantastic, I can stay. This is my home. I don't have to go!'

Even to choose hell is beautiful, rather than to be forced to live in heaven. If you are forced to live in heaven it is hell, if you choose hell it is heaven – because it is your own choice. It brings your life to its highest peak.

Sincerity means not living a double life – and almost everybody is living a double life. He says one thing, he thinks something else. He never says that which he thinks, he says that which is convenient and comfortable, he says that which will be approved, accepted, he says that which is expected by others. Now what he says and what he thinks become two different worlds. He says one thing, he goes on doing something else, and then naturally he has to hide it. He cannot expose himself because then the contradiction will be found, then he will be in trouble. He talks about beautiful things and lives an ugly life.

This is what, up to now, humanity has done to itself. It has been a very nightmarish past.

The new man is an absolute necessity now because the old is utterly rotten. The old is continuously in conflict within himself, he is fighting with himself. Whatsoever he does he feels miserable. If he follows his own inner voice he feels he is going against the society, against the powerful people, against the establishment. And that establishment has created a conscience in you; that conscience is a very tricky procedure, a strategy. It is the policeman inside you, implanted by society, who goes on condemning you that: "This is wrong, this is not right. You should not do it, you should feel guilty for it – you are being immoral." [...]

I remembered that just a few years back, each time I had heard Osho bash the priests and politicians, my mind fought against him with an 'Oh no, you cannot say such a thing; then everybody would be free and could do what they wanted. It will be such a chaos'. I was astonished to see how deep these thoughts had been ingrained in me, how much I was conditioned, although, in my mind, I had long understood that we were manipulated by the rulers, church and state, and that we had lost freedom.

And everybody is guilty, and the priests want you to be guilty because the more guilty you are, the more you are in the hands of the priests. You have to go to them to get rid of your guilt. You have to go to the Ganges to take a bath, you have to go to Mecca, to Kaaba, so that you can get rid of your guilt. You have to go to the Catholic priest to confess so that you can get rid of the guilt. You have to do fasting and other penances and other kinds of austerities so that you can punish yourself. These are all punishments! But how can you be happy? How can you be cheerful and blissful? How can you rejoice in a life where you are constantly feeling guilty and punishing yourself, condemning yourself?

How many times I had heard him say these words. Abstract concepts. But now they touched my very bones. This time it was real life.

And if you choose not to follow your inner voice and follow the dictates of others – they call it morality, etiquette, civilisation, culture – then too that inner voice will start nagging you, it will continuously nag you. It will say, you are being untrue to your nature. And if you feel that you are being untrue to your nature then your morality cannot be a rejoicing; it will only be an empty gesture.

This is what has happened to man: man has become schizophrenic.

My effort here is to help you to become one. That's why I don't teach any morality, any character. All that I teach is meditation so that you can hear your inner voice more clearly and follow it, whatsoever the cost. Because when you follow your inner voice without feeling guilty, immense is going to be your reward, and looking backwards you will find that the cost was nothing. It looked very big in the beginning, but when you have arrived at the point where sincerity becomes natural, spontaneous, when there is no more any division, no more any split in you, then you will see a celebration is happening and the cost that you have paid is nothing compared to it.

You ask me, Yoga Punya: "Would you please say something about sincerity?"

Sincerity is the fragrance of meditation.

Osho: *I Am That*, Ch. 2 (later entitled *Living in Your Own Light)*

After the discourse I was flying high, feeling invigorated, strong in myself and was dead certain that I did not have to leave although, strangely enough, none of my friends had understood Osho's words my way. The next day I received the answer to my letter saying, if I remember well: 'No need to leave'. No thoughts of righteousness arose when I saw Vidya and Laxmi again. I felt grateful to them for putting me through this troublesome learning time.

I was used to things in the ashram happening in a flow: the right job would be vacant at the right time, the right person would come round the corner when we wanted to see them, a series of events like this. Some time later I heard Osho say that he knows what is happening in his ashram and it crossed my mind that maybe he had enacted the whole trick and asked Laxmi to tell me to leave. This way or that, it was the only way – this existential way – to understand what sincerity is.

From then on I became more attentive and questioned myself to see if I really felt like doing what I was doing or if I felt like being where I was. I often took the liberty of walking out of situations the moment I became aware that I did not enjoy being there. For many years I followed this rule. When my body felt like moving, I used that time for cleaning my flat; when the head was excited and wanted action, I could take care of the accounts and when meditation wanted to come, I sat down and closed my eyes. Later on I read in *Glimpses of a Golden Childhood* that for some time Osho did only what he felt like doing as a meditation and an experiment. And as total as he is, when he did not feel like walking any more he stopped then and there and sat down in the middle of the road.

Vimalkirti Departing

One afternoon rumour spread that Vimalkirti had collapsed during his morning karate class in Buddha Hall and had been taken to hospital. We knew him as a samurai, one of the guards in Lao Tzu House, and as the husband of Turiya – one of the leading therapists – and as the father of little Tanya. But for me he was my next door (or rather next window) neighbour, the trickster.

There was a funny ritual between Vimalkirti and us girls in our room. His head would suddenly appear in our open window, his long blond hair falling sideways from his shoulders while he craned his neck from his own window, and ask: "Do you have a spare *beedie*?" Startled by his sudden appearance, we would search in our bags to see if we had one of these little Indian cigarettes. He must have enjoyed startling us, because to smoke his *beedie* on the bench outside the ashram he would have had to walk past our door anyway.

After a few days we heard that he was not likely to come out of his coma and that Osho had gone to see him. Many of his closer friends went to the hospital to sit with him in silence.

For a few months now all workers were entitled to have one day off per week. Our bodies had become weak: it was easy to catch amoebas that then dwelled in our bellies eating away at the already poor nourishment of the vegetables grown in the depleted Indian soil. For years Deeksha had managed to make us work eight-hour shifts while the rest of the ashram worked six, and now the days off were a chance for her creativity to materialise further projects. My day off was on a Saturday. That Friday night she told me that the following day at 7am I was meant to meet Prakash at the main gate and go with him to Vimalkirti's hospital. It happened to be my 7th sannyas birthday and I could think of no better way to celebrate it than seeing Vimalkirti. I was glad to be able to repay, even just a little, what I had received from my friends when I had been sick.

Prakash climbed behind the steering wheel of his white shopping van and, sitting next to him, enjoying the ride, I wondered what our special mission was all about, as we were not carrying any food with us. Vimalkirti's hospital room was a free-standing bungalow separate from the main building. When I became accustomed to the darkness inside, I hesitated to believe what I saw: his beautiful blond hair had been shaved off, also his beard, where now stubble had grown back. Winding tubes were attached to his body, connecting to different machines, to glass bottles and plastic pockets. In a grey blue rhythm a machine pumped air into his lungs and with a sharp click reversed the valves and expelled his breath with a sibilant noise. I was astonished to see headphones over his ears. I guessed he was listening to an Osho discourse. Even if his mind were no longer functioning in such a way as to understand the words, he would have no doubt sensed the loving melody of our master's voice.

That morning in discourse, answering Garimo's question: "Is there anything you can say about what is happening to Vimalkirti?" Osho said:

Nothing is happening to Vimalkirti – exactly nothing, because nothing is nirvana. [...] 'Nothing' sounds like emptiness – it is not so. [...] Break the word 'nothing' in two, make it to 'no-thingness', and then suddenly its meaning changes, the gestalt changes. Nothing is the goal of sannyas. One has to come to a space where nothing is happening; all happening has disappeared. The doing is gone, the doer is gone, the desire is gone, the goal is gone. One simply is – not even a ripple in the lake of consciousness, no sound. [...]

I was so deeply touched when I heard his words a week later on the video:

Vimalkirti is blessed. He was one of those few chosen sannyasins who never wavered for a single moment, whose trust has been total the whole time he was here. He never asked a question, he never wrote a letter, he never brought any problem. His trust was such that he became, by and by, absolutely merged with me. He has one of the rarest hearts; that quality of the heart has disappeared from the world. He is really a prince, really royal, really aristocratic! Aristocracy has nothing to do with birth, it has something to do with the quality of the heart. [...]

We suddenly became aware that he was a prince. We might have known it in the back of our minds but had even forgotten that he was German. He was as much part of the commune as anyone else, with no special privileges.

The day he had the haemorrhage I was a little worried about him, hence I told my doctor sannyasins to help him remain in the body at least for seven days. He was doing so beautifully and so fine, and then just to end suddenly when the work was incomplete... He was just on the edge – a little push and he would become part of the beyond. [...]

Seeing us standing there helplessly and empty handed, Puja, the nurse, asked us to clean the room. We looked around and wondered where we should begin: it was definitely an Indian hospital. We opted to go for the floor. In the adjoining storage room we found heavy-duty scrubbing brushes, a can of Vim and a metal bucket for water. On my knees I attacked with determination the years of dirt in the cracks between the terracotta tiles. Looking up at the narrow bed with Vimalkirti's thin body I said in silent words: "You see, Kirti, I am just a kitchen worker. What else can I do for you than clean this floor?"

All of a sudden Puja shouted in distress: "The pressure is dropping, the pressure is dropping!" and waved us to immediately clear our gear and leave the room. We both sat on the bench outside, leaning against the wall of the main building. We had no idea what was happening: puzzling scraping metal noises came from the room, as if heavy furniture was being moved about. A gust of warm wind blew across our faces, swaying us from side to side. Its delicate whooshing sound erased all thoughts in my mind and the world bleached in front of my eyes like an over-exposed photograph.

Steadying ourselves again we held on tight to the rim of the concrete bench. We looked at each other, speechless, trying to find out what this was all about. Prakash's stare confirmed he was plunged in the same dizzy vacuum and revealed no further clue.

Amrito walked towards our bench with a folded piece of paper in his hand. His inexplicable smile did not help us in solving the mystery either. He asked if one of us wanted to deliver a note to Nirvano. I was unable to move and said I wanted to remain there. Puja called us back to help. While we walked down to Vimalkirti's room we saw a girl jump into a rickshaw and drive off to the ashram with the letter in her hand.

Many questions have come to me about what I think of living through artificial methods. Now, he is breathing artificially. He would have died the same day – he almost did die. Without these artificial methods he would have already been in another body, he would have entered another womb. But then I will not be available here by the time he comes. Who knows whether he would be able to find a master or not? – and a crazy master like me! And once somebody has been so deeply connected with me, no other master will do. They will look so flat, so dull, so dead!

Hence I wanted him to hang around a little more. Last night he managed: he crossed the boundary from doing to non-doing. That 'something' that was still in him dropped. Now he is ready, now we can say goodbye to him, now we can celebrate, now we can give him a send-off. Give him an ecstatic bon voyage! *Let him go with your dance, with your song!*

When I went to see him, this is what transpired between me and him. I waited by his side with closed eyes – he was immensely happy. [...] So last night when I told him, 'Vimalkirti, now you can go into the beyond with all my blessings', he almost shouted in joy, 'Farrr out!' I told him, 'Not that long!' And I told him a story...

The crow came up to the frog and said, 'There is going to be a big party in heaven!'

The frog opened his big mouth and said, 'Farrr out!'

The crow went on, 'There will be great food and drinks!'

And the frog replied, 'Farrr out!'

'And there will be beautiful women, and the Rolling Stones will be playing!'

The frog opened his mouth even wider and cried, 'Farrr out!'

Then the crow added, 'But anyone who has a big mouth won't be allowed in!'

The frog pursed his lips tightly together and mumbled, 'Poor alligator! He will be disappointed!' [...]

This accident is an accident for the people who are on the outside, but for Vimalkirti himself it has proven a blessing in disguise. You cannot get identified with such a body: the kidneys not functioning, the breathing not functioning, the heart not functioning, the brain totally damaged. How can you get identified with such a body? Impossible. Just a little alertness and you will become separate – and that much alertness he had, that much he had grown. So he immediately became aware that 'I am not the body, I am not the mind, I am not the heart either.' And when you pass beyond these three, the fourth, **turiya,** *is attained, and that is your real nature. Once it is attained it is never lost. [...]*

There was silence in Vimalkirti's room. The breathing machine had been stopped. The struggle to keep life going was over. His body, now wrapped in a red cloth, had come to rest. A few people had arrived from the ashram and had brought a bamboo stretcher. They asked me to help lift his body onto it from the bed. The body was light and I could feel its warmth through the soft velvet cloth. His chest, I saw, was no longer breathing. Anando spread drops of Osho's camphor lotion around Vimalkirti's body. It was the beautiful scent Osho used in earlier years. Coming close to him in the darshans we could smell it. Once I got a whiff of it on the beach in Goa, with no one around.

Vimalkirti's body was carried away. Prakash and I were left behind to help clean up the room. The nurse told us what to pack and what remained with the hospital. I was happy to have something practical to do. We loaded the van with boxes of gauzes and pieces of equipment. At our medical centre we dropped everything off as quickly as we could and rushed to the burning ghats.

These are the 'three L's' of my 'philousia': life, love, laughter. Life is only a seed, love is a flower, laughter is fragrance. Just to be born is not enough, one has to learn the art of living; that is the A of meditation. Then one has to learn the art of loving; that is the B of meditation. And then one has to learn the art of laughing; that is the C of meditation. And meditation has only three letters: A, B, C.

So today you will have to give a beautiful send-off to Vimalkirti. Give it with great laughter. Of course, I know you will miss him – even I will miss him. He has become such a part of the commune, so deeply involved with everybody. I will miss him more than you because he was the guard in front of my door, and it was always a joy to come out of the room and see Vimalkirti standing there, always smiling. Now it will not be possible again. But he will be around here in your smiles, in your laughter. He will be here in the flowers, in the sun, in the wind, in the rain, because nothing is ever lost – nobody really dies, one becomes part of eternity.

So even though you will feel tears, let those tears be tears of joy – joy for what he has attained. Don't think of yourself, that you will be missing him, think of him, that he is fulfilled. And this is how you will learn, because sooner or later many more sannyasins will be going on the journey to the farther shore and you will have to learn to give them beautiful send-offs. Sooner or later I will have to go, and this is how you will also learn to give me a send-off with laughter, dance and song.

My whole approach is of celebration. Religion to me is nothing but the whole spectrum of celebration, the whole rainbow, all the colours of celebration. Make it a great opportunity for yourself, because in celebrating his departure many of you can reach to greater heights, to new dimensions of being; it will be possible. These are the moments which should not be missed; these are the moments which should be used to their fullest capacity.

Osho, *Zen: Zest Zip Zap and Zing*, Ch. 15

At the burning ghats I found a space on top of the wall at the end of the slope. From there I had a clear view onto the wide river, the lit funeral pyre and the hundreds of sannyasins, in their fiery colours, who had gathered around it. Anubhava's song *Step into the holy fire, step into the holy flame*, took on a tangible reality for all of us, *Oh, hallelujah, Oh, hallelujah.* Singing my heart out I addressed Vimalkirti's beautiful memory. My torso swayed from side to side, covering my face with my heavy dark hair. At times lost in the feeling of love and bliss, at times aware of the astonishment and wonder in my mind, I felt the cells of my body vibrating finely, giving me the sensation of growing in size. Was Vimalkirti leaving his life energy behind for all of us to savour? Like a balloon I was carried in swirls and lifted off into space, as if he had wanted to take me with him wherever he was flying off to.

The feeling of expansion followed me for the next few days. I tried to hide it: maybe others would also see the light I felt burning inside me. Deeksha's sharp eyes immediately detected it and I got a special job. Now aware of my artistic talent, she asked me to lay out the inscription for Vimalkirti's *samadhi*. There was going to be a marble grave for his ashes in Lao Tzu garden. With quick pencil strokes and with the help of a wooden ruler the words given to me on a little piece of paper found their place, size 1:1, on a big sheet of architects' paper. I was amazed to see that the line under 'Swami Anand Vimalkirti' should read – in brackets – 'Prince Welf of Hanover, Germany'. Later I heard that he was a cousin to the Prince of Wales and that Osho had invited the Prince of Wales to come and visit the ashram. I think Vimalkirti met him in Mumbai. The ashram was probably too hot a spot for a future king.

There was not much creativity involved in the drawing as Deeksha already had her own idea how the inscription should be: the same as on Dadaji's *samadhi*. Not until I was half way through the job did I become aware that I was involved in an ugly competition between Deeksha and Samudaya, the ashram calligrapher. He was a stern man who was working for the publications department. I later heard that he had survived Auschwitz. His layout was presented in beautifully rounded, old-fashioned letters, drawn to perfection in black ink. But still ours was chosen, to Deeksha's delight and triumph. It made sense just because it was easier and more practical for the Indian stone carver.

My next special job was to dispose of a heap of aluminium pots which had been collected outside Deeksha's office. Instead of taking the job fully into my hands – finding out by myself who would buy them from us – I asked her: "But where...?" and that was the end of my 'special job'. I was put back into the ranks of all other kitchen workers. I so much wanted to have a demanding job, but somehow always managed to mess it up. On the one hand I was safe hiding in my little black hole but on the other hand regretted not having taken the challenge.

Looking out of my office window I see the evening sun giving shape to the forest and gorse patches and the crags of 'our' hill. This is the way the people in the village call the Staerough. It is not much of a hill as far as height is concerned but it certainly has personality. Amiten points out to me when the greys of the crags change depending on the slant of sunlight or the depth of cloud and when the mists rise from the Scots pine forest in the morning.

We moved to Yetholm in the Scottish Borders after Amiten looked greyer and greyer in the face when a diesel excavator started digging into the foundations of the rectory he was working on. It was his choice to come to this nook of the world and I certainly love it. After long walks in the Pennine Hills it always amazes me that we do not have to return to the city, that we live right here amongst the hills.

From my window I also see a corner of our front garden. Amiten has planted a snake bark acer and a cherry tree and he is very proud of them. I have been religiously watching Gardeners World on prime time TV (Fridays at 7.30pm) to learn as much as I can about plants. I was not aware that there were perennials, annuals and even bi-annuals; that some plants love to live in full sun, others in partial shade, some like it dry and some others love to have their roots in a boggy patch. And then the rhododendrons, they love acid soil... what a stressful situation!

Despite all these difficulties and minor fights between us to determine the best place to plant a new acquisition, the garden looks stunning – so much so that it has inspired many neighbours to take up their hoes again. I have tried to integrate into village life as much as possible but in Scotland an 'incomer' remains an 'incomer' for the rest of his/her life. But then, we are not really living an ordinary life either: we are teaching Reiki and Osho's meditations in the middle of the village.

When I first saw the cottage I was aware that it was much too big for the two of us. We have a guest room which also acts as a session room (perfect as it has a pink carpet) and a second front room where we do the meditations. It also has a few guest bathrooms (the previous owner was an American). But the cottage had a nice feel and it could become a meditation centre. Looking into the sky, I said to an imaginary Osho: "If you want this house, you make it happen." This allowed me to remain unconcerned about the outcome of the bid. The seller eventually withdrew the cottage from the market but put it out again after a few months...

Today I spent the whole day deep-cleaning rooms, bathrooms, stairs, kitchen and passageway, even the steps in the back garden which for some strange reason always have to be spotless. I am excited about the Reiki weekend which starts tomorrow. I know only one of the guests – Pat, my journalist friend, who has been correcting my English for my Reiki brochure – but all the others will be new to me. They have spotted my course maybe at a holistic fair, from an ad or from my brochure of which I always have plenty with me to place in all those restaurants, shops and venues which have a notice board or a brochure rack.

The printer has finished rattling next to me. The last sheet of the manual can now be compiled with the other pages and with the laminated cover. The manuals look nice and neat. I love to give out material which is aesthetically pleasing – I think this is the Osho way – and I go a long way to create the best I can. The manual will give the participants the feeling that they can hold something in their hands while the Reiki energy is working on them in its mysterious and inexplicable ways.

In the meantime the details of the Staerough Hill have vanished into a two-dimensional dark blue shape outlined by a lighter shaded sky. On its summit the arrival of the full moon is announced by brightly lit clouds – until it peeks through and shows its white face.

5

In the Desert

The New Commune

There were rumours that Laxmi had left the ashram in search of land in the north. Osho had been talking a lot about how he wanted "the new commune" to be. We started imagining a new commune so big that we needed buses to go to work and, of course, had a good laugh at such a picture because we were so used to our small cramped ashram.

Then, suddenly, I heard that the publications and translations department had been moved to Saswad.

The previous year, on Osho's Birthday, many of my friends had joined the caravan of buses heading for Saswad to inaugurate a new commune – I had still felt too weak to venture off on a hot and dusty ride. On their sides the buses wore white cloth banners saying: 'Rajneeshdham – Neo-Sannyas International'. The logo, bearing a drawing of Osho in the middle, said at the bottom 'This Is That' and what I think was the Hindi original on top. People told me of an abandoned fort in the hills and a few acres of dusty land. The whole project fell into oblivion, at least in my mind. I was unaware that a group of Indian sannyasins – headed by an old disciple of Osho, Swami Yoga Chinmaya – was now living there.

"Osho, you can send me to the West, but please not to Saswad!" I was myself astonished when I heard this sentence formulate itself in my brain. I couldn't really say why I was terrified that I would also be moved there as I had not heard any horrible stories about it. Although I kept my fears a secret, Deeksha's antennae caught them and with an alluring, "You don't really have a proper job here, why don't you run the kitchen in Saswad?" she organised my move into the hills. As I resisted so strongly she let me come back to sleep in my old room in the ashram for the first few nights, and sent one of her aides, Venu, to help me get acquainted with the place.

In Prakash's van we headed towards the outskirts of the city and then finally we were in the countryside. I hadn't left the ashram since I had gone to Mumbai the previous year in an attempt to get an American visa when I had been asked to leave. Unlike the times I spent in the West when I was always happy to travel from one corner of the world to the other, here, at the feet of the master, any enthusiasm for travel had disappeared. I heard that Teertha hadn't left the ashram for over a year. He had not even been to M.G. Road to do some shopping or dine at the Chinese Restaurant or at Latif's, nor even at the close-by Blue Diamond hotel. So much was happening around the master, so many journeys, that the idea of actually physically travelling did not interest us at all.

Behind us the handles of the aluminium kettles with the rice, *dhal* and vegetables for the Saswad people were rattling in synchronicity with the potholes in the road. We heard the drinking water splash against the walls of the stainless steel drums. The jeep passed fields of sugar cane, their silvery brushes waving in the wind behind a small farmhouse. A poor place, but with a dignity: front porch neatly swept, not a piece of garbage in sight – so unlike the ugly and dirty misery people have to endure in the towns. One of the brown 'table' hills, the ones we could see on the horizon from the ashram roofs on a clear day, was now in front of our noses and the road started to become steep and winding.

After a quarter of an hour of gear-changing on the switchback road, Prakash said, "Here you are." In front of me stood an imposing dark grey stone wall. The round logo I had seen on the buses the previous year was blown up to a diameter of ten feet and hung like a medal in the middle of the wall. A flag was up on a mast. So this was it. In first gear, we drove up the ramp on the right which led to the gate in the middle of the north wall. Above the gate was a balcony with small ornate round arches supported by round columns. Maybe in the past this was the guards' lookout. It was the only decorative and mogul feature of this huge, square flat mass of stone.

In Deeksha's dining-room in the ashram, I had heard rumours that the Saswad project was not going to last for too long – maybe a few months at the most. No wonder that, when stepping into the castle and looking up at the pointed arch of the entrance gate, I said to myself: "This is so absurd, it must be the right thing," and it felt like taking sannyas again – so absurd and so right.

The stairs which led into the courtyard and those winding along the central tower all the way up to the second level were carefully laid out in black stone. The strangely slanted steps were about six inches high and three feet deep. It took someone's explanation for us to understand that they were built for horses – for us humans their step and rhythm were quite awkward. Across from the tower, half a dozen tiny doors opened into the courtyard on the left. They had just been whitewashed and 'Indian ladies', hired from close-by farmsteads, were spreading cow dung on the floors. Soon this would dry, with no trace of smell, and keep out all the bugs.

We carried the food kettles up to the tower. On the side of the steps, Venu had already set up an improvised food line with paper plates and plastic cups. Through an archway, which gave our position a pleasant breeze, I saw Indian Mukta, one of the persons in charge of the castle project (the other was the more delicate Homa), encouraging her crew with shouts and commands. In heavy heat and choking dust, lines of translators and editors, with rusty *ghamelas* on their heads, scrambled back and forth over the rubbly ground of the flat roof. On the edge they ruthlessly dumped gravel and rock over the top of the wall – a fifty-foot drop. (I don't remember that we ever used that cleared ground for anything later on…)

A stone bridge connected the second level of the tower to the rooms on the second floor along the east wall. A long wooden balcony connected the stairs to the living quarters on the left and, on the right, to what was going to be the kitchen and the dining-room. Deeksha's handymen were busy laying down flagstones, whitewashing the walls and connecting the new water tank on the roof with pipes to one corner of the kitchen. Soon four kerosene burners were blasting at 2,000 decibels for most of the hours of the day; our drinking water had to be boiled for a full 10 minutes. It was then cooled down in spouted stainless steel drums in a draughty spot with wet towels wrapped around them. Luckily we had Bhaven who was strong enough to carry the urns to the most strategic positions for the castle dwellers to drink the vital liquid. Colourful plastic cups were stacked next to them.

It was time to be inventive and creative – as quickly as possible. An Australian architect built wings from wooden planks which – attached to the outside of the castle – channelled fresh air through the slit windows into the kitchen, to the delight of our Korean cook. He had stoically deep-fried wok-loads of paneer squares at 50° C without a blink. Asutosh and Robin (a bird's name for a middle-aged English scientist?) proudly showed me the lengths of a black rubber hose they had laid out on the roof in the sun. We would have hot water in our new showers that very night!

Thrilled by the responsibility and freedom of action given, I often found myself in the middle of the night designing trolleys and gadgets to make kitchen life easier. Some of these I only saw materialised a few years later in our next commune, our ranch in Oregon. Some dormant intelligence was triggered in me. I suggested to Vishvasa how to build our kitchen sink unit: on legs with welded square pipes, because I saw him desperately looking for a sound piece in the wall to hang the sink. He looked up in astonishment, "That's a great idea. It would never have crossed my mind."

Body energy seemed unending, too. Not yet having got an organised routine, I often had to run down to the gate to catch the next shuttle to Pune, handing the driver a new order for Deeksha: a bag of carrots, a drum of ghee, another wok or the definitive measurements of our dining tables – and then carrying up the goods of the previous order: sacks of white rice, drums of cooking oil, salt and spices. Why on earth had we decided to build a kitchen on the second floor?

Finally the long serving table, which would separate the serving area from the kitchen proper, arrived, as well as the tables for the dining room with the little stools. The dining room was bright and happy and reminded me of one of those fashionable small Italian restaurants with a rustic look. (We would only have needed to add red and white chequered table cloths and a few bottles of wine.) We also used the dining room to prepare the vegetables when nobody was eating. Being at the south end of the wall it had windows on three sides. After a month, the carpenters built a new flight of stairs from the dining room straight down into the courtyard. This kept the flow of the diners in one direction: up the stone staircase, through the kitchen past the serving line, dining room and out via the new wooden staircase.

My bed and my few belongings, stowed away in the drawers on castors, was eventually shipped to the castle and placed in the last empty space of the 'girls' room'. It was the square room at the left end of the east wall. From the rings in the walls and the narrow slit windows into the valley, a visiting male had concluded that it must have been the cannon room.

At night I hooked up my mosquito net to feel some kind of privacy. I enjoyed falling asleep with the little noises in the room. It felt like being part of an extended family or a tribe in harmony.

On my right was Big Prem's bed. She had left Pune for Saswad a few weeks before, leaving behind her boyfriend Rakesh. Every morning she received the tape of the darshan of the previous night with the first shuttle. Seated cross-legged at a low table between our two beds, headphones clamped over her head, she typed it off at supersonic speed. She told me that many of the typewriters had broken down as they were not fast enough to catch up with her fingers. I would have enjoyed listening to Osho's words, but that was not allowed…

The flawless manuscript plus copy went to Maneesha, the editor of the darshan diaries, who slept and worked in and on the bed right next to Prem, across from the narrow split window with the view onto the plains. Maneesha, as well as Savita, who had a room just along the balcony, had been living in Osho's house for many years and had been mediums for the energy darshans. That these hitherto unbreakable arrangements were now disrupted was disconcerting for quite a few people, not just for them.

Pankaja, the English novelist who had been my next-door neighbour in Jesus House, had her bed in the corner diagonally across from the door. And next to her was Hari Chetna, Chaitanya Hari's former girlfriend and – as I heard later – a former actress who had worked under the name of Mascha Rabben in some of the Fassbinder movies. She had arranged a colourful corner with saris and shawls around her mattress on the floor.

Amito's mattress was hidden by the clothes hanging on a pole over the staircase leading to the room downstairs (we used it just once for a prank to frighten Nirved in the middle of the night). Amito was actually a man but fitted well with the female energy of our room. He had come to Saswad to be in charge of the soap department.

Sometimes he played the guitar at night. It was like a lullaby, mingled with Hari Chetna's giggles and Big Prem's whispers. A candle was lit to read her lover's letter for a second time. The cool moonshine cut through the open door. I fell asleep blissfully as part of a family; joined to everybody else – as children like to fall asleep, surrounded by loving people, reassuring voices – not disconnected, alone in a room. For many years to come I missed this secure, womb-like feeling when going to sleep.

One early morning I woke up at the sound of my bed cover flapping like a flag. So much draft through the windows! I saw the first sun rays shine onto the yellow barren hills: "Yes, I am still in the desert!" and with a feeling of 'home' went back to sleep for a little while longer.

On another morning we girls had all decided to stay in bed and pretend to be sick. The doctors from the Health Centre of the Commune in Pune were sent up in weekly rotations, while we had a permanent nurse. This week it was Amrit's turn and we all loved him. He was slight and sort of knotty-looking with a wispy light brown beard and an acne-scarred face. Sex appeal has not much to do with looks apparently. When he discovered the prank he playfully hopped into everyone's bed to the uproarious laughter of everybody in the room. All the girls became well pretty soon.

Every doctor came to me with their idea about how the meals should be planned: one emphasised that the high protein meal should be served at lunch rather than at dinner; the other that cabbage and other bloating ingredients should also never be served at night. My aesthetic eye also wanted the colours of the different dishes to complement each other, which meant no white rice with cauliflower in a white sauce or carrot salad with spaghetti in a tomato sauce.

In April and May, during the months before the monsoon, the produce offered in the markets was limited to cabbage, potatoes, tough yellow carrots, red beets, pale cucumbers and more cabbage. It was a miracle we managed to prepare colourful and doctor-correct meals each time. From the commune we received tofu from the tofu factory on top of Jesus House as well as some greens from our hydro-culture project at No. 74 Koregaon Park.

Many workers from the ashram, on their days off, came to give a hand with the building of the castle project. (Deeksha told me later that when asked what they liked best there, they often replied: "The food.") As soon as the busloads had arrived, I checked the numbers with the gate guard to adjust quantities for lunch. As there were no nearby restaurants – there was not even a village – it was our job to prepare enough food and hot drinks for everybody. A few nights before, it had happened that Indira arrived late for dinner. She had done some overtime work and there was no food left for her. She broke into tears like a child and could not be consoled for hours. Her worst fear was to be left without food – and every kitchen worker's worst fear was to run out of food.

After what was, for me, three weeks in the hills, the day came when we could see Osho again. We all showered, washed our hair and put on our best clean robes. Just walking down the ramp to meet the buses on the flat ground in front of the fort we gathered dust on our sandals and feet. The thin padding under the brown vinyl seats hardly weakened the sudden bumps of the mountain road. In the bends – real hairpin bends like in the Swiss Alps – we were thrown sideways against the hard green panels and the windows or against the neighbour on the adjoining seat.

"Sorry, Pushpa!" I said, bumping my shoulder into her strong upper arms. She smiled back, tiny wrinkles in the corner of her eyes above her sunburned cheeks. Her hair had gone all frizzy in the dry winds of the hills. A few days before, she had stopped me in the courtyard and showed me how she had decorated her living space in one of the rooms on the first level. There we stood, a Dutch translator and a kitchen boss from Italy. We felt deeply connected, beyond job or nation. What was happening to us was greater than our minds could ever have imagined. Her smile acknowledged that she could see that whatever was happening to her was happening to me as well. The high energy created in the castle by the intense physical work was bubbling in our veins. In this abundance of life energy, not only did all competitiveness and petty judgements disappear, but hearts could no longer stay closed.

We felt as one, as a tribe again where the feeling of being a separate individual had not yet been learned. I also felt a 'yes' from Satyananda who, in the seat in front of me, was listening to Nirvano's interpretation of the in-depth meaning of the Saswad experiment. (Before he met Osho, Nirvano was a professor of German and English and his outlook on things was always rational...) Satyananda had come to Pune a few years before as a journalist for the German magazine *Stern*. Being a sincere man, he tried out the meditations before writing his story and soon fell in love with Osho. Knowing that he could never sell a positive article, even less so to the snotty *Stern*, he had the courage to give up his prestigious life as an international star reporter, become a disciple and move to India to permanently live in the ashram.

We heard that he was keeping a diary of his life in Saswad (I wish I had his notes now!) and that a book about his first years with Osho was going to be published. His *Ganz entspannt im Hier und Jetzt* became a best-seller and all of the German speaking sannyasins gulped it down as soon as it came out. A passage where he describes Deeksha walking through the ashram stunned me the most. I never thought that words could be so accurate and give a complete picture of a person in just two sentences. With his permission I have translated them here, hoping to do justice to his art:

Deeksha is a well-rounded Italian beauty with long black hair and an energetic chin. She pushes the low centre of gravity in her large short body along the paths of the ashram with vigorous steps and powerful rowing strokes generated by swinging her arms out sideways.
> Jörg Andrees Elten, *Ganz entspannt im Hier und Jetzt*

After a long stretch in the plains the rattling bus finally halted at the ashram gate. Like a loud bunch of tribal people we jumped off and collected our bags for the overnight stay, leaving in our wake a cloud of dust. The workers in the boutique stopped with their needles in hand to watch the scene. They all looked so pale, skinny, clean, a bit distant, a bit aloof. What had happened to us? We had become pagans, peasants, with sunburned rough hands, clear eyes, laughter in our bellies and warm, simple hearts. We felt a bit out of place, though, like a peasant from Oberägeri might have felt on the Bahnhofstrasse in Zurich on a Sunday afternoon.

I was astonished when I was directed to a front seat in the darshan that night, an honour only 'certain' people had, such as therapists, the people living in Osho's house, or special guests. Of course, I was now the 'person-in-charge' of the Saswad kitchen. My mind explained it away: I was sitting there because I needed extra energy for the project in Saswad, and not because of anything to do with me personally. But I was lucky to get this unexpected treat. Next to me was Indira who was taking care of the cleaning department and further along were Indian Mukta and Homa. While waiting for everybody at the back to be seated and for Osho to come and sit in our midst, Greek Mukta leaned over and asked, "Do you have electricity?" "Oh yes, we even have running water, and warm water at night!"

Osho walked in, greeting the people sitting silently with their hands folded and their eyes gazing at him. We had seen him walk in so many times – I have described it a few times already – but each time it felt like a miraculous event. We must have all looked silly, with faces like that of cats being tickled under the chin.

Sitting so close to him I felt his energy very tangibly and I was not quite sure if I wanted to be exposed to it too often. The sensation on the skin was that of a fine rain and inside I felt a soft calmness with an edge of excitement. The evening had brought fresh gusts of wind into the assembly and goosebumps had appeared on my arms. They were quite in contrast to the warm, enveloping feeling.

When the last group of new disciples had gone back to their seats, the mediums prepared themselves to be called up. The atmosphere became electric with expectation. Osho silently motioned a medium to each side of himself. Kneeling with their backs to the wall they had in front of them four or five girls, one of which was me, who were seated in a semicircle around Osho. I happened to sit in front of Nirada, Anasha's small sister, and my head was resting on her warm chest. I was happy it was her. Brushing my bangs out of my face she showed that she was also pleased to have me there. This made the already intimate feeling of the darshan even more cosy. In front of me, my hands were resting on Astha's shoulders. Under my fingers I could feel her long, neatly-combed blonde hair. I thought she must be special because she cleaned Osho's room.

The lights went out and the music increased its frenzy. Something was meant to happen to me, but nothing did. I felt very clear in my mind. There was the cold marble floor under my bum, Nirada's warmth behind me and Astha's swaying shoulders under my hands. Although it was dark and my eyes were closed, I seemed to see the hall in front of me, the swaying and humming participants of the darshan, the dark marble pillars at the edge of the hall and the trees beyond in the garden. I was aware of, and almost saw, what was happening beyond the hall: all lights in the ashram had been switched off. Even the dancing had stopped in Buddha Hall during our daily 'blackout'.

My mind still clear and alert, undisturbed by the crescendo of

Chaitanya's squeaking recorder and Rupesh's wild bongos, I was aware of Osho sitting just a few feet away from me. The lights were switched on again and in their warmth shining on my face I felt my head being held still – I guessed it was by Haridas – and then Osho's cool fingers on my third eye making my perceptions even more clear-cut.

While the darkness had reminded me of a velvety, cosy, womb-like softness, the energy on my forehead almost felt like an intrusion, a very male affirmation like a lightning bolt. An uncomfortable wake-up call.

Supporting me under my right arm, Haridas escorted me to my seat, while Shiva and a few other strong men were carrying, literally carrying, the girls on their arms to lay them down on the edges of the hall. 'I am so hard and stuck that I don't feel anything, no bliss attacks like everybody else,' I judged myself. Osho *namasted* the assembly and disappeared into his house. We silently gathered ourselves, left the hall, slipped into the sandals left on the side of the path and made our way out of Lao Tzu gate.

I looked down at my feet to see for sure if they were touching the ground. It felt like I was wearing those plateau shoes my mother had worn after the war, which are in fashion again right now. But these were soles made from air. 'So maybe something did happen to me.' When a friend saw me and asked, "Did you just have energy darshan?" I sensed that whatever had happened was visible even from the outside. Light-footed and full of energy I ran back to the room where I was going to stay that night.

In the following weeks, buses from Saswad were also arranged for the morning discourses. But after a short time they were stopped. There was a chickenpox epidemic in town and Osho's doctors had decided that it was too risky for him to leave his room, so discourses were cancelled. Maybe this time also Nirvano, his caretaker, locked him in as she apparently had done before when he had had a cold.

This interim period gave Deeksha the opportunity to re-make the podium. As Osho's back had been troubling him more and more, he found it difficult to climb the few steps leading up to his chair. All handymen available were gathered to build a ramp for Osho's car to park on a raised level behind the podium and – while they were at it – they broke down the old podium and replaced it with a larger and higher one.

In the heat of April the message came to the hills that from now on Osho would remain in silence and would no longer give discourses. He would instead sit with us every morning in a silent heart-to-heart communion. Every change is always accompanied with the disappointment of losing the familiar and the excitement of the unknown. I pondered the implications: 'I might be missing the harmonious melody of his words, the expressions on his face when he tells an anecdote, the piercing eyes, the expressive gestures of his hands, the smiles which make his cheeks go round.'

On the other hand, I felt very grateful to see that he trusted us, that he felt we were ready to listen to his silence. I had always been touched by the story of Buddha who one morning comes to discourse with a lotus flower in his hand. He looks at the lotus flower and does not start speaking. The disciples become restless except for Mahakashyapa who is sitting silently at a distance under a tree, smiling. Buddha gives him the lotus flower and says to the audience: "What I could say in words I have said to you. What I have said in silence I am giving to Mahakashyapa." So maybe we were now all ready to receive the lotus flower.

This silent gathering was called satsang and started with an invocation first used in Buddha's commune:

Buddham Sharanam Gachchhami
(I go to the feet of the Awakened One)
Sangham Sharanam Gachchhami
(I go to the feet of the commune of the Awakened One)
Dhammam Sharanam Gachchhami
(I go to the feet of the truth of the Awakened One)

It was intoned by Taru. On the repeats we bowed down towards Osho's podium. This was followed by a passage of music – which changed every day and which was maybe improvised that very morning. This helped deepen the silence of the silent phase. Amrito's deep voice and soft-spoken manner gave a very new dimension to the passage read from one of Osho's books or from Khalil Gibran's *The Prophet*. Then there was another period of silence, intensified by the squawks of the crows.

We had our eyes closed but sometimes I looked up to see if Osho was really there, in the distance, in his chair. The veneered sliding doors acted as a warm backdrop to his white figure. They were flanked by beautifully curved walls sheathed in white marble. Asheesh, an Italian engineer who had become a carpenter and later also a knitter, had added handle bars on the arm rests of Osho's chair so that he could get up more easily at the end of the meditation. It was a clear sign that his back was not in good shape and confirmed the rumours that back doctors from abroad had been visiting.

Six thousand people humming under one roof, in the presence of an enlightened master, felt at times like eternity and other times a short but intense few minutes. The *satsang* ended, as a mirror reflection, with another reading passage, silence again and the 'gach-chhamis'.

It felt a bit as if Osho had moved some distance from me. But it was now up to me to make the effort to come closer to him. I had to find him by becoming as silent as he was and merging with this silence.

The participants of the meditation weekend are enjoying the Scottish summer sun on the lawn of our garden. They have taken their salad plates and kombucha drinks with them. One of our neighbours, a professional gardener, commented earlier that it is a meadow rather than a lawn. But the flowers and grasses are too pretty to be cut and our guests do not seem to mind. Chandra, an elderly sannyasin, has come from Edinburgh, together with Rona and Satyam. Chakori, in her faithful red Lada, has driven all the way from the Isle of Mull.

I take refuge at my desk in the office where I can see them

through the small window, sunbathing, chatting and being silent. Chandra has just returned from India and told us that, earlier, during the Nadabrahma Meditation she had felt as if she were in Buddha Hall in Pune and was astonished to see that she was in Scotland when she opened her eyes.

Soon it is time for everyone to gather in the meditation room again. My grandfather's colourful carpet covers the whole floor and makes it a happy place. The beams which Amiten has painted in a light wood colour give the sensation that the ceiling is not as low as it really is. Just recently we have exchanged the portrait of Osho on the main wall for a photo of Osho's empty chair on the podium and today we hear that in the Commune in Pune they have eliminated most of Osho's pictures, a change which has apparently created a worldwide stir. Somehow, even living in far-off Scotland, we are connected with what is happening there.

Breaking Down

For quite some time Sheela had been a secretary to Laxmi, Osho's secretary, together with Vidya and Garimo. I could often see her in Deeksha's private dining-room behind the kitchen where special food was served. Walking by, I had heard a lot of laughter and a lot of what sounded like gossip. Laxmi was away from the ashram and the Saswad project was under Sheela's management.

One evening she came up to the castle for a meeting in the courtyard – we had brought our lecture cushions to sit on. She announced that more people were going to move up to the castle and that for them more accommodation was going to be built. We were encouraged to work for longer hours and beer was served free that night.

There had already been beer on sale at the little kiosk in the courtyard. This had astonished me because an ashram in India is traditionally alcohol-free. The kiosk was a cute little room with a bright strip light, run by Yuthika. She was a bright Australian girl who was so tall she barely fitted when she needed to stand up. There were Cadbury's chocolates on sale, blue aerogrammes and pens, Vicco toothpaste, our own homemade scentless shampoos and soaps, hair sticks and whatever other items were in demand in that remote place. It was a lovely place to have a chat. While she remained seated in her chair behind the counter, I could tell her, from under the door frame, what I had experienced during the day and hear what she had done.

It soon became routine that the days did not end with dinner, but with some working 'party'. When the soap department had more orders from the ashram than they were able to cope with, we had a 'soap-wrapping party' at night. We sat at long narrow tables and wrapped different kinds of soap bars in different decorative papers. With all corners neatly folded the wrapping was held together with a sticker and a label. It was a mindless job, so we could chat with the children (yes, we had now a few children in our hilltop community) and with the weavers who had just moved up with their bulky looms (how could anyone be interested in *weaving*, I asked myself?) and sip homemade ginger beer. A Swiss-German soap-maker had found a better use for some big plastic containers. The fresh 'chincher' (ginger) beer, as he advertised his product, had matured in the dungeons under the soap department. It was delicious and refreshing. We drank alcohol only at night, after work or at these parties.

When the day was really over, I could go for a *beedie* outside the castle. A few days earlier I had been given a cigarette lighter (it was a classy, silver, piezo-electric Colibri), a present from Osho. I do not remember now who brought it over from Pune, but it was a great surprise, in particular because I would never have expected that Osho would have okeyed my smoking habit with this gift. But now was the opportunity to use it!

The gate was a relaxing place for smokers and non-smokers of all nationalities. I remember an incident when discussing the events of the day with American Ashoka. First we spoke in Italian, then adjusted our conversation for a Frenchman by speaking in French, then in German and English for others who later sat down next to us. A girl who had been sitting behind us for some time made us aware of our language shifts which had happened spontaneously and without our awareness. (At that time I had not known that Ashoka also spoke Swedish: "I grew up there." He was one of those proverbial wandering Jews.)

The open sheds opposite our bench had recently been turned into cow sheds. The cows had arrived one day to the delight and enthusiasm of many castle dwellers. I could not care less, maybe because I was busy with the dinner, and it did not really matter to us kitchen people where the milk was coming from – the main concern was not to burn it. But for many it was an adventure and they booked themselves in for the milking as early as 5am. Dwabha, an actress from Hollywood, was the most enthusiastic of them all. Now the shuffling of the hooves of the cows became the background to our evening conversations.

Late one morning I was called down to the gate where a jeep was waiting for me. We drove up a dusty path towards a not-so-distant farmhouse. I had not been aware that along with the castle we were also renting some fields and a few cottages. There was not much of the 'fields' to be seen at that time of year. The sun scorched the rubble and one would think the rocks would split in half under the heat. I was glad I was driven and did not have to walk under the sun. The reason for our excursion was for me to meet Chaitanya Hari.

Chaitanya Hari was already an acclaimed composer under his legal name Georg Deuter. He was probably the first New Age composer ever. Under Osho's supervision he had composed the tracks for our meditations: Dynamic and Kundalini (two versions), then Gouri-shankar, Nataraj (two versions) and Nadabrahma. More recently he had become one of the 'court' musicians playing at night for the energy darshans. I was used to all sorts of surprises, like seeing Maneesha with us in Saswad; for years she had been present at all the darshans as a scribe and commentator. And now Chaitanya Hari was here as well.

He stood there like a wounded giant. His long blond hair had fallen over his high forehead and I followed his lost eyes. They wandered between the still-unwrapped instruments and electronic equipment, to the small empty space on the dirt floor and the mattress in the opposite corner. Dust flew in through the open door and I tried to picture in my mind how he could ever do any recording in this tiny and dusty space. It seemed his stooped posture was not because of the low roof, but rather an expression of: "What have they done to me?"

I was brought there to make arrangements for his food: he needed kerosene for the green stove which was there already, then tea, milk and sugar. Maybe we also discussed whether he wanted to have vegetables delivered or eat his main meals at the castle. I have no idea what became of him after that because I did not see him again – he must have left shortly after that, or maybe even the same day.

Living at the castle was not a delight for all. Some had to leave behind their boyfriends or girlfriends. They could only write to each other or see each other for a short while when we went to Pune to sit with Osho. No special arrangements were made for people who were in a relationship. If someone's department moved to Saswad, tough! The boyfriend who happened to be a therapist had to stay in Pune.

Relationships were not respected much, mainly by Deeksha. She often made a couple work together side by side or interrupted their private life with no remorse. But her own was untouchable: she loved and cared for her 'amore' in a typical Italian mama way. Krishna Bharti was the 'court' photographer and had the chance to be in darshan every night to take the photographs of the newly-initiated. He also photographed the energy darshans when the lights came back on. The photographs, taken in black and white, were developed and enlarged in the darkroom where he was to be found during the day. The photographs could be ordered the day after the darshan from contact sheets.

I remember vividly that Deeksha had a special robe made for him with an insert of foam in the back. Unlike for the lectures, cushions were not allowed at the darshans – to avoid dust. The only exception was for Teertha who had a medical condition, maybe piles? But Krishna Bharti had an 'unofficial' padding under his bum which he must have welcomed in the winter months.

For many years I had the feeling that being in a relationship was a way of avoiding: avoiding being alone, avoiding meditation and work, avoiding a one hundred percent commitment to the commune. I felt that being in a relationship was like saying "Yes, but…" Certainly this idea helped me to stay at it, to stay with Osho, to give priority to meditation and leave all relationships, which might have taken me in another direction, aside. For others it must have been a totally different story but that's how it was for me.

On one of my last 'shopping' visits to Vrindavan kitchen I was climbing the wooden fly-over stairs to our roof space when I came to the height of Deeksha's room that was right above the kitchen and connected to the stairs. I saw her figure through the sliding glass doors and stopped. She had spotted me as well and looked back. She was surrounded by gaping suitcases on the floor, ready to be filled;

clothes were in disarray on the bed and over the bamboo armchairs. I had heard rumours that she was getting ready to leave for New Jersey in the USA with a group of handymen and other 'chosen' people to prepare a place for Osho to stay. So, this must be it. She was standing in the middle of the clutter with – what synchronicity! – the comic booklet in her hand – the one I had created for her as a thank you for the care she had taken while I was sick. She was maybe deciding between throwing it out or taking it with her. At that moment I could see in the eyes of this very determined lady, this 'dragon master', the soul of a little girl anxious to know how her future would unfold.

She called me in and asked me to show my scar to Sheela who was sitting on the corner of her bed. I was still embarrassed about my red scar which travelled from my belly button with a curve all the way into the pubic hair but Sheela, of course, was not particularly interested in my very shy display. There were no goodbyes or hugs. The next day a big black truck left from the ashram for Mumbai. I did not know then that this was the last time I would see Deeksha.

Although she had suggested that I have my hernia repaired in Switzerland by a specialist, I decided that now was the time and I arranged to have it done in Pune. I was tired of wearing my orthopaedic belt in this heat. The Saswad kitchen was functioning well by itself and it was no problem for me to leave the job. Afterthoughts only came when I walked into the operating theatre. With the narrow operating table covered in brown leather, worn at the edges, it would have been the perfect set-up for a retro movie. Leila, a doctor from Geneva, had asked me if she could assist during the operation. Seeing her standing there with a big smile gave me the courage to go for this next adventure despite my fears.

The human mind has difficulty in recalling traumas and pains and forgets them very quickly. But, after the operation, the forgotten pain was back again in all its might. Leila was talking about 'many adhesions', which at that time did not mean much to me. A good friend came all the way to this distant hospital, at least three quarters of an hour by rickshaw, to visit me with a bunch of scented flowers.

They looked like a wedding bouquet. There was not much talk; there was not much to say.

Despite the physical impairment I was happy to spend some days in civilised Pune, meeting friends at the restaurant at No. 70 (one of the properties we had rented), visiting friends and staying out at night without returning to the ward until late. I enjoyed my stray-dog life until the office found me and arranged for my return to Saswad.

The mala shop had been moved to the fort and a big shed was built outside the castle along the front wall, below the emblem with Osho's picture, to accommodate the lathes and a few working benches. My next assignment was the 'mala shop' which, being a sitting-down job, would suit my physical condition. The procedure for making a mala took me a whole ten minutes to explain to a friend after I had learned how to do it. Despite the acute humour of Shanti, our Austrian boss, for the very first time in my life I experienced what boredom meant. I could not feel any interest in cutting Osho's black and white pictures in circles, nor sanding the edges of the Plexiglas pieces. The best part was maybe the cutting of the beads out of rosewood sticks on the lathe. It made a lot of noise and it was dusty. I had never felt bored while baking the same croissants every morning or cleaning the same stoves after each meal. Maybe wood was really not my element.

One day the dreaded but expected news arrived that Osho had left the ashram and flown to New York. Although we had seen Deeksha leave with her crew to prepare Osho's residence in New Jersey, we still hoped it would be just one of those ideas. It is amazing how the human mind hangs on to its wishes and does not want to see reality as it is. All the signs were there, black and white, as if in print. That night in the girls' room we got drunk, which I felt (afterwards) was not an elegant way of sending off our beloved master.

My idea of the future was that Osho would return to India after his back was in better condition and join us in the new commune, the property for which Laxmi was searching in the north of India. After a few days Sheela came to the castle for a meeting. By now the population in Saswad was such a crowd that it filled the courtyard to its edges. She announced that all new structures were going to come down and that some departments would be moved in stages back to Pune. Although I had known from the very start that Saswad was just an experiment, I still could not believe that what we had built with so much effort and money was now meant to come down after only a few months. Swiss conditioning says that you build a house not just for the next fifteen years but for a few centuries. We Swiss believe in the perpetual!

We heard rumours – this word was now in the vocabulary of everyone, even of those who were just starting to learn English – that the neighbouring villagers had become hostile towards us. The wood from the north wing, which had been taken down, had been piled in front of the castle ready for the scrap people to pick up. One night this heap of recycled wood was set on fire, apparently by some neighbours. My wound was hurting too much for me to scramble down and join the others around the bonfire. I could see it well from the slit window of our bedroom, though. Later we heard there had also been fires in some of the warehouses in Pune where we had stored Osho's books.

We were put on high alert, watching all suspicious movements outside the gates with particular attention. Strangely enough we still had Dutch Taru (as opposed to Indian Taru) as a guard. She was a spirited, tall lady with a condition in her legs. She would have had big problems trying to run after some hooligans, but maybe her height and the fierce expression she could put on her eagle-nosed face would have managed to scare them away. Late one night I visited her at the gate and although we were chatting about bosses and boys and all the new events, we remained on the alert in case neighbours came to disturb the peace. Suddenly and simultaneously we turned our heads and stared into the empty courtyard. But there was nothing to see. We would have expected to sense the 'enemy' on the outside of the castle rather than on the inside. We both looked at each other: "What is that?" Taru remained at the gate on duty and I got up and walked towards 'it' in the darkness. The presence I felt was much bigger than what I would have expected from a human intruder. It filled the whole courtyard and I could sense it surrounding me when I walked up the stairs to find someone 'responsible' to whom I could report the incident. Everybody was asleep or in an embrace with their lovers. I turned around and went back to Taru to discuss this quite astonishing event. We came to the conclusion that it must have been a ghost from the dungeons. In comparison with my later encounters with ghosts this one did not have that hair-raising 'yukkiness'.

Shortly after this event I recall being woken up one morning by the sun filtering through the trees. When I opened my eyes I noticed that above me there was only sky, below me a hard mattress, my clothes folded neatly next to me on a white mosaic floor. I recognised this kind of tiling we had on roofs in the ashram. They always intrigued me, in particular the edges which were rounded off at the parapets, most probably, I deduced, so that the monsoon rains would run off instead of seeping into the outside walls. But this was not one of our houses. It was probably No. 8, a grandiose but old Maharaja mansion I heard the ashram had rented to accommodate some of the workers. I do not remember anything of how and when I left my 'desert paradise'. Either it was so un-traumatic, or so traumatic, that I did not retain any of my usually faithful photo slides. But I knew that our five-month experiment in Saswad was over.

After getting dressed I looked around and saw there was no trace of my belongings. So No. 8 was not going to be my final destination. That same day, after checking with the main office, I found the rest of my things in one of the rooms behind the *godown*, the warehouse where we stored Osho's books (we literally had to take a dozen steps down, reason why I always thought it was called like this because it was half-underground...). My new place was a single room. A room all to myself? It used to belong to Prashantam, a Portuguese football player who was now a body-worker and a passionate lover of all things Japanese. He had even learned to play the *shakuhachi*. I used to hear its long notes in the night from the rooftops. No wonder this tiny room was decorated, floor and walls, with bamboo mats. With their black piping they imitated the Japanese *tatamis* perfectly. This was Prashantam's Zen way of emptiness: a clothes-hook hidden by a bamboo mat, a shelf and an Osho picture. The rolled-up futon in the corner was going to be my bed.

I was plunged into someone else's dream. A stark room to be filled only by the emptiness of my soul. The dampness of the undergrowth and the rustling of chickens in the neighbour's garden came in through the netting of the large window, and the nights seemed very lonely. I was pleased to see the familiar face of our washerman, the *dobhi*, who brought me my clean but still damp robes. "Too much rain today." I was wondering if he knew how good-looking he was? After a week he had to find me in yet another room. Prashantam's place, along with all the temporary buildings behind the *godown*, was going to be demolished.

My next room was in Jesus House, exactly below the room I had lived in for three years. It had belonged to Helen, a wealthy lady from the States. She had made a home for herself with proper furniture: table, chairs and a sideboard, all beautifully crafted in rosewood. I had not seen a furnished room in Western style for such a long time. It looked very bourgeois to me, and odd. I was again plunged into someone else's dream. My partner in this movie was Vimal, an actor from England, who had travelled all over India with our theatre group playing Shakespeare's *A Midsummer Night's Dream*. When I arrived he was reading a book under his bedside lamp stretched out on his bed. Not much was said but I felt welcomed.

To complete the absurdity of the situation there were wooden *nunchakus* on the side board, just inside the door. *Nunchakus* are a very simple weapon from Japan: two eight-inch sticks held together by a couple of chain links, one for each hand – very effective, as I would find out! They were lying there as if someone had just been practising with them and walked out for a moment. They grabbed my attention immediately and, although I had never seen *nunchakus* from close up before, they felt like old companions in my hands. Each time I entered the room I could not resist giving them a swing, from armpit to armpit first, then over the opposite shoulder, grabbed under the armpit by the other hand, watching carefully not to hit knuckles, elbows and skull. Later on, Vasant, one of the Lao Tzu samurais, showed me a few more tricks. They were the perfect antidote for the crazy job I had in the kitchen – they kept me sane and centred. I had to be present, without thoughts, if I did not want to be hit around my ears.

Yes, again the kitchen and this time it was Mariam Canteen, the workers' kitchen. For years it had been under the supervision of 'Proper' Sagar – until he left. He was called 'Proper' (there was also an 'American' Sagar) as he was so very proper and British. Osho was amused when he found out that this tall, straight, blond gentleman was actually German by birth. Now Mariam Canteen was run by Durga. Durga is another name for Kali, a fierce Hindu goddess, so you can imagine what we had to deal with. She was strict, exacting and looked fierce like a Kali.

The main office was juggling numbers between who was leaving for the West and when, who needed to be moved to a new location, how many portions we still needed to cook, and how many were needed to prepare that amount of food. Many sannyasins from other departments were appointed to work in the canteen; they were graphic designers, translators or accountants and had not undergone Deeksha's rigorous and disciplined training.

When I called back the workers from their break in order to finish off the clean-up at night, I was amazed that they would just laugh at me and keep on smoking. They were not at all impressed by the fact that I was their shift leader. In the kitchen we had not known any rebels (except for Rupesh) and I was not used to dealing with them. It was sad that I was the one who had to take the blame from Durga for their disappearance and finally had to clean up the kitchen all on my own.

On the other hand, Durga pointed out to me that I was too bossy and made people work too hard. I tended to overestimate their strength and have ideas of 'perfectly clean' even during monsoon time. Although my body had gone through quite a few hits in recent years I used it like a bulldozer and nothing could stop me. And I certainly thought that everybody else could do as much as I could. But it is unfortunate that, because of this, many would remember me as a tough cookie for a few years to come.

The people in the main office, who had worked out the strategic plans for the closure of the ashram, had suggested that I leave on the 5th of August, so with the help of a friend in Holland I booked my ticket for that date. That was the end of my stay in Pune where I was meant to stay 'forever'. Maybe I was suppressing my feelings because I do not remember what was in my heart. However, what occurred the day before my departure might give me a clue: I took a rickshaw to M.G. Road to buy a few presents for the folks back home. A lilac jacket with a red satin lining on a stall in the street grabbed my attention. I bought it although lilac was, at the time, not included in our colour scheme. Neither did I think about the practicality of it: it was filled with lumpy cotton wool and the outer cotton layer would certainly not be waterproof or washable.

But there was this thought: 'Osho, if you can leave me behind then I can also buy this dumb lilac jacket!'

Through the small cottage window I am looking at the shiny silvery crags of the Staerough in the midday sun and into our front garden with its begonias still in bloom. I have already said goodbye to each plant individually, as well as to the ones in the back garden. Amiten's contribution there is a water feature running in a steep slope towards the house which, after many months of disruption, has just recently come to completion. It was inaugurated with a party to which we invited the retired ladies of the neighbourhood and a few friends. I thought that a cup of tea and a few biscuits would have been suitable, but, at the suggestion of one of the ladies, a bottle of Amaretto had to be bought for the occasion. So, in a way we have said good-bye to our neighbours already.

Amiten has now gone for a walk to 'the top' to say goodbye to the hills. Crossing the river Bowmont he would have passed the scented cypresses and cooing doves that live in them, then the black church faced in whinstone and then maybe he would have looked into Christine's window to see if she was in. She is our best friend here. I admire her for her courage to go for what she wants (i.e. practise Shiatsu) with a young child in tow.

'The top' was, for us, the place where the road behind Kirk Yetholm, the start of the Pennine Way, to the east of Staerough Hill, reached a summit before it plunged again into the valley where to the right it ended at two farms. At that spot the bare hills with their smooth rounded tops would suddenly come into view. We always felt overwhelmed by a wall of silence coming from the hills, so tangible that it held us back from walking any further but also allured us to step into it and disappear forever.

We have often stood there together, speechless, in wonder. We know that for miles and miles there is nothing except hills and hills and hills. No town, no village, no people, except for a few hill walkers. The Pennine Way (260 miles long) which is best walked from south to north (in order not to have the sun in the eyes) ends in Kirk Yetholm.

Up there I once met a walker who said to me, very softly and slowly: "Hello, you are the first person I have met in one week." I felt honoured to be this first person: he appeared to me like someone just coming out of a Zazen retreat. No wonder – these hills emanate such a silence.

I am packing books, notes, files into cardboard boxes which we have received from the movers who will pick them up tomorrow. My unused painting paper has already gone to an artist friend, the frames for papermaking to my teacher of the art, but the files in the metal cabinet will need to be sorted at our destination in Edinburgh. Because of its size one book sticks out of the box: *Mojud – The Man with the Inexplicable Life*.

Osho has commented on this Sufi tale and Vibhavan has published this beautifully illustrated book of the discourse. Interestingly, I had received the book free of charge from a book stall in the ashram during a celebration because the pictures were missing, and was later given a set of the coloured illustrations from a surplus of the Italian edition. It was easy to paste the pictures into the right spots. If you have to read a book it will come to you even from different directions…

I find solace (and confirmation that it is OK to make irrational decisions) in the story of Mojud now that my life is again taking a turn into the unknown. The decision to move to Edinburgh came suddenly, the flat which awaits us there appeared unexpectedly and the sales contract for the cottage will be signed shortly. And all this happened in less than three weeks.

Here is the story: Mojud is an Inspector of Weights and Measures. One day he meets Khidr, his inner guide, who asks him to take off his clothes and throw himself into the river. Being a swimmer he does not drown and is pulled out of the waters by a fisherman. He lives with the fisherman and helps him with fishing. After a few months he again hears that he needs to move on.

On the highway he meets a farmer and lives with him for a few years. Again he is guided to leave, this time for Musil, where he becomes a successful fur merchant. Then Khidr asks him to give him all his savings which he wanted to use to buy a house. In Samarkand he works for a grocer and heals the sick in his spare time. Clerics and philosophers who visit Mojud ask under whom he has studied and all he can say is: "I jumped into a river…"

I am ready to leave this beautiful cottage in the Scottish Borders where my family thought I would live until I die, a place I thought I might live in for another 'forever'.

Watching the Clouds

Sitting in my window seat heading for Zurich, my mind went back to what I had left behind. All temporary structures in the ashram had been taken down, like the boutique on the left of the main gate. I had loved the airy wooden structures of that two-storey building: the shop on the ground floor with the sewing room on top. It had been my roommate Samiyo's domain. The carpenters' shed was gone as well as the monstrous two-storey bamboo hut of the translators and the press office. It was most peculiar to see our beloved Buddha Hall without a roof: a grey expanse of concrete surrounded by shrubs and gardens. The newly-built podium was also broken down and many of us kept a piece of the white marble – a tangible piece of Osho to take home. We were clearing the ashram the way one would clean up after a big party: washing the glasses and throwing away the rubbish. The ashram was going to be an Osho Meditation Centre after we had left.

So here I was enjoying my plane ride, ready for a new adventure. Seeing the clouds float by over the Indian Ocean I remembered a meditation Osho had given to me many years before. At a darshan I had told him that there were many feelings and thoughts which were bothering me and that I did not know what do to about them. He suggested, if I remember well, that I look at my thoughts and feelings as if they were clouds and that they would disappear just by looking at them. I could also experiment in a plane – looking down at real clouds I could find out if physical clouds also disappeared. I do not remember if the clouds actually disappeared but this exercise certainly brought my mind to a calm and relaxed state.

Looking back at the time spent in the ashram – a bit over three and a half years – I could see with new eyes the many incidents in the kitchen, like, for example, when Anu, who was in charge of one shift, would ask her subordinates to 'drop their ego'. This sentence – stolen from Osho's discourses – appeared in situations where someone did not want to execute her orders: "Drop your ego!" We had to learn to let go of our ideas about how things had to be and had to be done. They had to be the way Anu wanted them to be, which in the end was how Deeksha wanted them to be.

Sometimes I have to put you in a certain work where you have to drop your ego and you think it is a kind of punishment. It is not a kind of punishment; it is a challenge, it is a situation where you will have to drop the ego sooner or later because it will be creating misery again and again for you. It will make you clearly aware that your ego is causing your misery.

Just the other day, Anshumali wrote saying, "Beloved master, working in Vrindavan under Deeksha seems to be a punishment." It is not, Anshumali. It is a reward, not a punishment! It is a punishment if you want to cling to your ego; if you let the ego fall, it is a reward. And then you will be able to see the beauty of the work, and you will be able to see the beauty of Deeksha too. She is a beautiful Italian mama! She loves her workers, she loves her people; she is utterly devoted. Of course, she loves so much that she shouts also, she screams also. Her love is such that she trusts that you will understand her screaming too. But she is a good device; she has been of immense help to many people.

There are one hundred therapy groups here, but Deeksha's is the best! Although it is not known as a therapy group – it is a secret therapy group.

If you drop your wilfulness, your ego, then hatred also drops because hatred is nothing but the shadow of your ego. If there is no ego there is no hatred; if there is ego, there is always hatred following it. Whosoever comes in the way... and everybody will come in the way because egos cannot adjust to each other. Egos are always in conflict, egos are always quarrelling; they are quarrelsome, hence the hatred.

Drop the ego and see the beauty of egolessness. Then there is no hatred, no anger. You become so silent, your energy becomes so calm and quiet, that suddenly you start seeing the world in a different light, in a different perspective. Then this ordinary world is no longer ordinary – it becomes sacred.

Osho, *The Dhammapada: The Way of the Buddha,* Vol. 11, Ch. 5

Deeksha's sense of cleanliness, perhaps due to her long stay in Switzerland or to her sun sign, Virgo, brought the Indian kitchens to a comparatively high hygienic standard. The unspoken motto was 'cleanliness is next to godliness'. We were often cleaning surfaces and walls which were clean already. There was not much professional satisfaction in it, but it certainly helped the 'drop your ego' factor.

There was also the deep-cleaning. This meant moving tables and chairs to clean the walls behind them, the beams, the ceiling fans, anything whether reachable or unreachable. The corners were even scrubbed with a used toothbrush.

I vividly remember Swiss Astha crouched on the cold floor in our health centre scraping the yellow dirt along the corners of the marble floor. The pieces done looked fantastic and made a big difference. She is the one who used to cut our hair in the health centre's garden with the customer sitting on a wooden chair under a tree, its lovely branches like a fan protecting us from the sun. I always felt this was a much more luxurious way to have my hair cut than in the top notch place in Zurich where she works now.

Not only did Deeksha's sense of cleanliness and aesthetics influence the ashram – from Chiyono, the cleaning department, to the construction of the boutique or Osho's podium, to the quality of the fabric from which Laxmi's clothes were made – she also believed in luxury. The workers often received robes for the darshans made from raw silk and her private room featured beautifully handmade pieces of furniture. We had oregano imported from Italy in the kitchen storeroom. We had our own French cheese maker and a tofu and tempeh factory. There seemed to be no limits.

But there was a downside. It all started when Deeksha turned her boyfriend, Krishna Bharti, from a hippie into a well-groomed man. Her aesthetic influence then extended to all kitchen workers. There was no reason to look sloppy and dirty because one worked in the kitchen. When Bhakti, another hippie, would not be persuaded to throw away her ragged and faded pink cotton robe, it was literally torn off her body. She screamed and sobbed: "No, no, it is my favourite dress." Instead she received a beautifully tailored robe in expensive polyester (lasts forever, dries quickly and needs minimum ironing). Maybe as a sign of rebellion she keeps the ends of her long blonde hair jagged to this very day.

'Zenning out' (a practice which 20 years later is accepted world-wide and is mistakenly called 'Feng Shui-ing') was also executed in our rooms: old clothes were thrown away or given to the painters, clothes which did not fit went into a recycling bin (that word did not exist at that time either) and the books went to the guards' library. The *raison d'être* of each item was questioned to its root: was it really necessary or was it just occupying space? And space was certainly not greatly available in the ashram. No wonder that I religiously held on to the few items I loved: Osho's box, the little wooden Buddha statue which loved to sit on top of it, Osho's picture in its decorated bronze frame and maybe a plant. As so little privacy was left, there was an unwritten law that you would never sit on a bed which was not that of the friend you were visiting.

Working in the kitchen I had also learnt to be more focused on the present. It happened quite often that we were suddenly called in the middle of a job, e.g. while decorating a cake, and asked to go chop carrots, only to discover that there was no delay whatsoever in the vegetable preparation and that there was no apparent need for us to be there. Maybe it was just a way for us to learn *not* to say: "Let me finish the cake!" It taught us not to be too much involved with the outcome of a job and helped our minds to gain a certain flexibility in making a sudden shift from one rhythm to another.

Many workers in the kitchen were Italians because they were friends of others working there already or because Deeksha grabbed them the moment they entered the ashram gate – as it happened to me. (Although I am of Swiss descent, at that time I regarded myself as Italian.) From being an Italian to being a good cook there is not much of a jump and as most of them only spoke Italian, they were useless in other departments anyway. They could not become great group leaders, PR people, administrators and secretaries without speaking English properly.

Osho spoke a lot about us Italians, more than about Jews and

Polacks put together. After discourse, Nando often confided to me: "Today he told three of my jokes." He used to send in all the jokes he remembered from his childhood. And Pierino was our hero.

Pierino comes home from school and asks his father, "Papa, what does 'simultaneously' mean?"

"It means at the same time," replies the father. But Pierino still does not understand, so the father explains it.

"Well," he says, "if you were born from a relationship between your mother and another man, not me, what would I be?"

"A cuckold!" replies the little boy.

"Right!" says the father. "And simultaneously you would be a son of a bitch!"

Osho, *Come, Come, Yet Again Come*, Ch. 13

Four men are in a bar talking about their professions.

The first, a German, says, "I'm a coke-sacker at the coal yard. I fill sacks with coke."

The second, a Frenchman, says, "I'm a sock-tucker at the clothing warehouse. I tuck socks into packages."

The third, a Dutch man, says, "I'm a cork-soaker at the barrel factory. I soak the corks so they'll make a good fit."

The fourth, an Italian, says, "I'm the real thing."

Without the Italians the world would not be the same; they are the most earthly people. And I love the earthly people; they are the most rooted in the earth. They are not abstract people, like Indians; they are not metaphysicians. That is their beauty.

And my work here is to create a synthesis of the sky people and the earth people. I would like my sannyasins to be as earthly as the Italians and as unearthly as the Indians, because unless your roots go deep in the earth your branches cannot reach to the stars. The deeper the roots go into the earth, the higher is the reach of your branches. Then you can whisper with the stars. Up to now there has been a split. The earthly people have been condemned by the religious people as materialists and the materialists have condemned the spiritualists as hocus-pocus. Both are true in a way, but both are half. And a half-truth is far more dangerous than a lie because it looks like a truth.

The whole truth is that a real, authentic man, the whole man, will contain contradictions. He will be vast enough to contain contradictions. He will be a man and a woman together. He will be earthly and unearthly together. He will be materialist and spiritualist together, with no conflict. Unless this synthesis happens the world is going to remain schizophrenic.

My sannyasins are not to be unearthly, they are not only to be earthly either; they have to be both. I am giving them the hardest task ever: they have to be materialists and spiritualists, spiritualists and materialists. They have to drop the whole division of this world and that, of this shore and that, of this and that. They have to make a bridge between the two. And once that bridge is made, man will be whole for the first time. And a whole man is holy. Neither the spiritualist is holy nor is the worldly man holy because both are not yet whole. They are unholy because they are half, and any person who is half is bound to suffer. He cannot rejoice, he cannot celebrate, he cannot know what a blessing life is.

You have to know that even dust is divine, that your body is a temple. You have to become Zorba the Buddha!

Osho, *Tao: The Golden Gate*, Vol. 1, Ch. 4

Maria has six sons, all dark-haired. The seventh, however, is born redheaded.

Giovanni is furious.

"I know you have betrayed me!" he shouts in anger. "Confess that this is not my son!"

"I swear, Giovanni, he is your son. I swear it – I swear it!"

But Giovanni, in a blind rage, shoots her. Before dying, the woman asks him to come close and whispers, "I have to confess something to you, Giovanni. He is your son – it's the others that are not yours!"

Osho, *Tao: The Golden Gate*, Vol. 1, Ch. 4

Mrs. Carbotti went to the doctor complaining of fatigue. After the examination, the doctor decided she needed a rest.

"Can you stop having relations with your husband for about three weeks?" he asked. "Sure," she replied, "I got two boyfriends who can take care of me for that long!"

That's why I like the Italians – they are so human, so truly human!
Osho, *Come, Come, Yet Again Come*, Ch. 15

One thing is certain: without the Italians the world would have never been so beautiful, would have never been so interesting. Italians have contributed much. Another thing is absolutely certain: without the Italians there would have been no commune here – impossible. I am dispensable, but Deeksha is not! Even if I am not here you can sit in silence, but without Deeksha how long can you sit in silence?
Osho, *Tao: The Golden Gate*, Vol. 1, Ch. 4

But in the end we had to understand that:

At least here, drop your German-ness; that is your disease. And it is not only about you. The Indians have to drop their Indian-ness; that is their disease. And the Italians have to drop their Italian-ness; that is their disease.

Nations are just man-made boundaries; races are stupid discriminations; religions are man-manufactured. And they are all dividing man against man.

Sannyas is an effort to bring a new world into existence, where nobody is a German and nobody is an Indian and nobody is a Japanese; where nobody thinks that he is superior, where nobody thinks that women are inferior and slaves, where equality and equal opportunity to grow is simply accepted as natural.
Osho, *Sat Chit Anand*, Ch. 26

The jumbo jet approaching the Zurich Kloten runway brought me back from my memories. Morning mists were rising from the surrounding fields and buildings slowly defined themselves. A welcome thump and here we are back in civilisation. A civilisation of neat blue-grey, wall-to-wall carpets, ten foot high aluminium light cases with panoramic views of Swiss mountain resorts, of odourless toilets with flushes that work, water taps with combined cold and hot water, blowers to dry the hands. While appreciating the aesthetics, workings and cleanliness of the airport, my eyes were caught by a pair of waving arms. I was not expecting anyone to come and meet me at the airport: I thought nobody knew I was arriving.

Shanti Lisa had heard from Sidhai that I was on this plane. He had been washing *thalis* and cups at Mariam Canteen and left Pune the day before me. He happened to remember my flight number and so I was now invited for breakfast at Osho's commune in Zurich. How could I resist the prospect of fresh *Weggli* and crispy croissants with Swiss butter and home-made jam? Shanti Lisa drove past the arts and crafts school where I had studied and stopped the car just a block away. The commune was in a newly-renovated tenement house over-looking the Limmatplatz. Just coming from India I found it very luxurious and I was particularly struck by the tan wall-to-wall carpets and the colourfully tiled bathrooms.

At the breakfast table I met the centre leaders, Chandrika and Premyogi. They remembered me from the one time I went to visit the Meditation Centre in Fribourg. It was a short trip from Geneva where I lived then. The centre was run by Parigyan, Premyogi's brother. Parigyan was studying Maths and Premyogi Geology and they were dating two sisters, Chandrika and Majida, who were also there. All four were of stunning beauty, in particular the youngest, Majida.

Over an aromatic cup of coffee I was asked if I wanted to participate in the Zurich commune. It appeared that the commune wanted to expand and was looking for new members. My plans were to go back to Italy and work there, but I promised to consider the offer and make up my mind after visiting my parents.

It turned out that my mother had other things to do the coming weekend and could see me only after a fortnight. This felt odd, as I thought she might be happy to see me after four years. (We had always been on good terms and I never felt her as my mother with a big M, rather as an older sister.) Or was it maybe her way of punishing me for staying away all these years? I never asked. In our family we never asked straight questions about things like these; indeed, now that I think about it, there were many unspoken feelings, resentments, hidden thoughts. On the other hand, to my even greater astonishment, my father, who was on holiday in St. Moritz, invited me to come and see him the very same day. "At what time does the train arrive?" he asked immediately.

When we were clearing the breakfast table, the local newspaper *Tages-Anzeiger* called. They wanted to write a story about the closing down of the ashram. Chandrika thought I would be the best person to give the interview as I had just come back from there. It was arranged for the next morning in the Meditation Centre, and my father was quite upset to hear that I would delay my arrival for a day.

The article eventually appeared as a full page story with a photograph of myself with my long no-style hair parted in the middle. It had already been our experience that, however positively we talked about our times with Osho and however carefully we used our words, the journalists managed to make a bad story out of anything.

During the interview Chandrika had to help me with my Swiss German which I had not spoken for years. I did meet some Swiss in Pune, but I was so self-conscious about being Swiss that, if there was no other way to avoid talking to them in this rather guttural dialect, I used to step aside and make sure nobody heard us. In fact, as I already mentioned, if Deeksha wanted to insult me all she had to say was: "You are so Swiss!" To be Swiss, to me, meant to be stubborn, self-righteous, stern, inflexible, and a perfectionist, all qualities I could very well identify with. To be Swiss also meant to be law-abiding and to check that others also were, to be organised (better than anyone else) and to work hard as a duty and a suffering. I preferred to be identified as an Italian. This was synonymous with fun, long nights out with friends, eating good food – no wonder Osho suspects that the brains of Italians are made from spaghetti! It also meant spending the money we had (instead of saving it like the Swiss) and also spending the money we didn't yet have.

Italian was the language I spoke with my sisters and Swiss German was the language I spoke with my parents. It was like living in two worlds.

Father surprised me by taking me, his wife and Lucia, my seven-year old stepsister, to a posh dinner at the Muottas Muragl Restaurant on top of a mountain ridge. We had a table with a view – and what a view! Three small lakes in a row like beads on a string reflected the turquoise and golden evening sky between the black silhouettes of the square-topped La Margna and, across the valley, the imposing Piz Julier. If I had to describe paradise this would certainly be it.

To my father's delight – who reckoned that the oddest thing in my life as a sannyasin was the fact that I had become a vegetarian – I ordered an entrée of Parma ham and salami, and trout as the main course. My body must have craved protein as it digested everything with ease. A special night service of the funicular took us down into the valley to our car.

The next day we met some of my father's business friends at the same station and I was introduced as the daughter who had just come back from India. We started off, heading towards Piz Languard. All were quite impressed by my fitness, as I made an easy ascent at the beginning of the queue, talking and laughing with the kids. Nobody knew that I had run up and down the flight of stairs at Mariam canteen for months. As I was such an outsider and rarely fitted in with the values of the family, I was always on the lookout to gather a few positive points for myself, but this one came as a surprise.

Even though seven years had already passed since I had first met Osho, my family still hoped I would give up my 'life in orange' and come back to a 'normal life'. Maybe now that the ashram in Pune had closed, there might be a chance? They could not see that this was the very best choice I had made in my life. It almost seemed as if my father thought Osho was his personal rival, as if by loving Osho I could not love him as well. Also I could not understand how they could love me and at the same time reject what was most important in my life. The fact that, despite everything else, I was physically fit impressed everybody though…

The next day brought us into the Rosegg Valley, which was an easy walk and a rest after yesterday's climb. The slowly ascending path was soft, covered in rust-coloured pine needles. The awe-inspiring sight of a full range of snow-covered peaks with their imposing glaciers plunging into the valley was always in front of us, the midsummer sun high in the sky, tanning our cheeks. I shunned the small talk about things which happened to so-and-so two years ago with the excuse that the rumble of the river was too loud. The milky glacier water was gushing furiously from rock to rock close to the path for most of the time. There were too many things to be savoured in silence: a variety of mosses at the bottom of the trees, tiny alpine flowers wiggling their heads in the drafts. Tits flew boldly around my head, begging for food.

At the end of the two-hour walk an incredible reward awaited us: a garden tea room, with a table under a canopy, covered with raspberry tarts, bilberry cheesecakes, strawberries with ice-cream, apple pies, fruit salad, meringues with cream. The owner, and probably the baker, stood proudly behind the table in her white lacy apron and served the international clientele.

Just before I had left for the mountains Premyogi had received a telephone call. He had been asked to organise a celebration day in Zurich for all Swiss sannyasins. A few ladies were going to come for some announcements and he was to prepare the entertainment for that day. On my way back to Zurich, sitting in the narrow-gauge train that meandered down the valleys, my eyes wandered between the sunlit scenery and the notes on my pad. I had started to write a cabaret. It was about our situation: Sheela persuading Osho to go to New Jersey and us waiting to know what to do next. The sketches came very easily, although I had never done work of this kind before. It was similar to sketching comic strips, yet quite another realm. I was amazed to see how the script flowed effortlessly onto the paper.

Almost the whole commune, of which I had now become a part, was involved in the rehearsals of my cabaret piece and this was the best way for me to get to know each one of them. I also persuaded Abhilash, who was living by himself and working as a waiter in town, to join the commune because we needed him as an actor. Another new commune member, Virena, got involved in a few scenes. I taught him all that I had learnt in my mime school years. He was an excellent student and we did good work together.

Other groups were rehearsing at the same time in other rooms: the men joined the yodelling club and the girls revelled in Ursula's modern dance performance. Pastel tulle was stitched into flower petal dresses and suspenders with edelweiss embroidery were bought by a mathematics professor who helped the commune in her spare time.

When the day of the dress rehearsal finally came I was amazed at the authority of my instructions to the lighting engineers, as if I had done this job before. Then the ladies arrived. They turned out to be Garimo, Sushila and Turiya. They were angry that we had planned so many shows and had left almost no time for their own events. I guess there must have been some communication problem during the telephone call. I did not mind if we had to scrap the cabaret from the programme. In my eyes it had been a beautiful way for the commune to come together creatively. I had learnt that results did not count, but Dipo, our accountant, blamed me that he had sacrificed his after-work time 'for nothing'.

Heart Dance with Turiya was planned for the afternoon. She was one of the most prominent therapists, still is, and was Vimalkirti's wife. We sang in circles with eyes closed and arms over each other's shoulders. She kept insisting over the microphone to 'open our hearts'. We always think that our hearts are open because we fall in and out of love, so all this talk did not make sense. But, unexpectedly, I felt a sudden click in my heart and it opened like a rose flower. It was a lovely feeling. I opened my eyes and met hers looking straight at me. Could she observe what was happening to me from the outside?

Between the performances on stage the announcement was made that we had bought a ranch in Oregon (on the northwest coast of the

USA, we were told) and that the new commune was going to be built there. Slides were shown of the Muddy Ranch: rolling hills and valleys without a sign of vegetation. Pratibha, who had come all the way from Ticino, was disappointed and commented: "There are such beautiful places in America, like California..." I had no preference. Wherever my master was going to be that was OK for me; moreover, I had a particular soft spot for barren lands.

Sushila, a voluminous woman with a myriad of wild grey curls, sat in real American fashion on one of the tables and was soon surrounded by an audience sitting on the parquet floor. I had met her for the first time in Geneva while visiting Deeksha, back in 1974. We went to meet her at the airport while she was changing planes (Chinese Alok was also on that flight) – as I remember Deeksha had something for her to take to Osho. In perfect lotus position on the table she was talking about the need to find donations to sponsor the project. If money was lying in the banks why not invest it in this experiment?

Garimo, tall and contained, had been Laxmi's right-hand woman for many years. I enjoyed observing her face soften while giving initiation into sannyas in one corner of the hall while we danced barefoot on the shiny parquet floor. Many had applied for initiation by mail and she had brought the certificates with the new names. But one name was missing, the one for François. This handsome professional from Geneva was inconsolable: he was sobbing like a child and none of the women who gently patted him on the back were able to stop his tears.

The next day the ladies moved into the upper floor of the commune in the Limmatstrasse and we cramped together – dormitory style – into the first floor flat. Each one of them had a room: bedroom, sitting room and office all in one. Sabha and Shanti were appointed to be the ushers for the guests who were coming for their appointments. Tea, coffee and biscuits were served.

In the commune I was trained to follow someone's orders immediately and with no questioning. If scrambled eggs still soft inside were preferred, I would go back to the kitchen and make them again the way they had to be. If the ladies needed wastepaper-baskets I could run and find pot covers which would do the job. This way of working was alien to my new friends in the commune and we probably thought that both ways – the laid-back and the servile one – were quite odd.

The atmosphere in the upper floor was thick for the next few days and the ladies would tease each other about whose room was thicker than their own. The interviews were about money – donating or investing money to build the Ranch, as the new commune was called. Although money was available in abundance in Switzerland at that time, it was also kept safely and securely hidden away. It needed great speaking skills and charm to loosen up the bonds between owner and owned.

Nishkam, the commune dentist, was certainly charmed – you could see it. He was allowed to sit on Sushila's bed from morning till evening while she was discussing money matters with the other visitors. After a few days I saw his glowing face and I knew that his decision to sell the villa in Ibiza was insignificant compared to what was happening inside him now. In exchange he was offered a place on the Ranch as soon as accommodation was available there. Similarly, Leeladhar, a successful plastic surgeon, was delighted to be caught. This tall handsome man, who had turned up in dungarees, was also invited to work at the Ranch where he could prepare himself for the US medical exams.

Before they left, the ladies organised a breakfast with croissants and sherry – yes, you are reading correctly. Why alcohol was introduced at that time of day is still a big question mark. We were asked to follow the new trend which was to integrate into society: to find a job instead of being on the dole, to have good haircuts, throw away all hippie clothes and to say no to all drugs. They pointed out that the meditation centre at the Seefeldstrasse was way too small and that we should look for a new place.

In fact the meditation centre was in a converted cellar with small windows high up near the ceiling, with the entrance at the back of the building accessed by long and steep stairs. Although it was newly-carpeted it gave the impression of a hide-out. They also asked us to find different ways to make money for the Ranch project.

The very next day Chandrika and Premyogi announced, to my great astonishment, that they were leaving for a holiday abroad. The events of the past weeks had given so much juice to the centre that in my eyes it was a shame not to take advantage of it. One day I woke up with the brilliant idea of inviting Chaitanya Hari to give a concert in Zurich. This would be a great start to the money-making project, I thought. It was easy to find his phone number in Germany, but unfortunately he was busy with concerts for the rest of the year, except for a date at very short notice – in three week's time. This meant that we had to take a decision on the spot...

Now I was in a dilemma: either forget all about it or say yes without the centre leaders' consent. Dipo encouraged me to go on with the project and so I studied the availability of halls, the rents and how much we should charge for the tickets. I also placed advertisements in the newspapers and had A3 posters designed and printed. Considering that Zurich was still a city unknown to me and that I had never organised a concert before, it was certainly a risky thing to do.

When Chandrika and Premyogi returned from their holiday, nicely tanned and relaxed, the project was in its last stages. It must not have been nice for them to come back and find things happening without their consent. They reckoned that more advertising was necessary, so two of our guys were sent to the Bahnhofstrasse as sandwich men and Premyogi organised an interview with Mr. Schawinsky, owner of the popular, but pirate station, Radio 24. The studio was at the Limmatstrasse just a block down from where we lived and Chaitanya Hari talked to him about his own music which was also played between parts of the interview.

Eventually the whole commune was involved with the concert – to Dipo's great disapproval. Ticket checkers, ushers, wardrobe ladies. Sidhai and his crew set up tables in the foyer for the display of Osho's books and Chaitanya's tapes. Chandrika wanted me to take care of the musicians, their food, drink and physical well-being, and during the concert my place was in the wings. I watched Harida's fingers drumming on the *tablas* and Renu stroking the *swarmandal*. Chaitanya was busy hammering on the *santoor*.

I stood there, just a few feet away behind the curtains, checking on the level of water in their glasses, when suddenly I felt tiny ripples rising from my legs up into my face. It felt delicious and disconcerting as I had not expected anything of the sort to happen right there. When I shared my experience with Chaitanya during the break, he muttered: "Did you think this was just music?"

The next morning I was called in to see the centre leaders. Dipo and Ursula were also there. The concert had been a financial flop, I was told. We had just managed to cover the expenses with the sale of the tickets. I was also blamed for gambling with the centre's money. Only later on I got to know from Sidhai that after the concert we had sold as many Osho books as we normally would in twelve months – but that probably did not count. They unanimously decided that from now on I was going to be a cleaner.

From the way the vacuum cleaner was yanked around the corners, it was obvious to anyone that I had taken it as a punishment. It was my opinion that I could have contributed to the centre in a more creative way but this was how it was going to be. When Yoga Priya came to Zurich on her massage tour I confided my disappointment to her. It was not easy to hear what she had to say: "If you, as an old disciple, cannot show that cleaning can be done with humility who else should be able to do that?" Well, my ego was hurt and I could not do any cleaning with humility.

At this point in my story I stopped work on my book for over a year, postponing it with one excuse or another. I did not want to expose myself as having such a horrible and pushy character and also I still had thoughts like "They have been so horrible to me."

By coincidence I found these words by M. Scott Peck who comments on this dilemma: *"A significant portion of our lot of existential pain throughout life is the anguish of continually and accurately discerning what we are responsible for and what we are not responsible for."* In retrospect, I can see that my having been kept in check at that time has spared me from burning my fingers in any future power position.

Soon I became creative in my cleaning and enjoyed making surprises for my commune mates when they came back from work: I neatly tidied their small living spaces, which sometimes were merely 20cm around their mattress. But Chandrika made me aware that I always needed to draw people's attention to what I had done. I was unable to just do things for the sake of doing them – silently in a corner. I was a performer. I needed other people's attention and approval. To make life even more uncomfortable I kept comparing myself with her, seeing myself as a bulldozer while she appeared more attractive with her loving and gentle character, allowing people to have a good ("*lässig*") time.

One might ask why I did not leave the commune if I was not happy. I somehow knew that this was the right place for me even if my ego had a hard time with it. There were also all these lovely new friends: Svarna and Maja with whom I was living in one room, later joined by a German lad, Martanda. From central Switzerland came Svaraj, whose inability to cope with city life became clear to me only when I saw him run down a steep ravine. He had legs like those of a mountain goat. And there was my friend, Tanmaya, with whom I had designed fictitious villas while recovering from hepatitis. She had paid me a visit on her stopover and, waking up the next morning, said to me, "I am going to ask if I can stay," and so forgot all about going home to Los Angeles.

Other friends also, coming back from the ashram, stopped and remained at the centre: Shantidharma and our graphic designer, Shivananda, both tall skinny guys. Kalyan Mitto, a clerk who had lived in the top floor flat, also decided to integrate his flat with the commune, which meant that he lost his private bedroom and private bathroom but gained an involvement which had attracted so many like myself.

Leopold Place, London Road, Edinburgh is our new address.
We are expecting the group of meditators which has formed

through our Reiki workshops to turn up for our housewarming party and we hope they will all find it. The large living room with its conspicuous fireplace and high ceiling (so different from the cottage in Yetholm) can comfortably accommodate our colourful carpet. Amiten is adjusting the lights in the glass cabinet between the two bay windows and rearranges the crystals on the glass shelves. The pillows along the walls are ready for those who want to sit, but I suspect that everyone will cram into the kitchen and then spill out, standing, into the long corridor which the landlord has painted in a vivid purple colour.

I give a good sweep down the stairs which lead from London Road to our basement flat and the flagstones of the tiny courtyard. I have planted a few colourful annuals in wooden tubs to make it look inviting. Just above, beyond the buses and the traffic, is Carlton Hill, my new friend. To keep fit I have been climbing it every morning, from the top admiring Edinburgh Castle and Princes Street on one side and on the other side, the always changing colour of the water of the Forth of Firth with its little island I call 'Alcatraz' because of its shape. Back below I am met by the low-hanging fronds of the mature chestnut trees lining London Road. City life after all is not that bad.

Purnam and Deva Dhyan have arrived a day earlier as they have come all the way from Germany. They help me prepare the drinks, the plastic cups and paper plates for the finger food we have bought. Our friends will be here in half an hour. Probably Mairi and Jamie will come, Audrey who often brings a new friend along, Laura and Nicky, Shirley, for sure. Maybe others whom we have not yet met. Then we will hear the clattering of Paul's bicycle being dragged down the steps. I once admired his regular attendance at the meditations twice a week and he said: "It's downhill, and the bicycle just takes me."

The Big Muddy

Before leaving Switzerland, I visited Grandfather. I always made a point of visiting my family before travelling to see Osho, as I never knew when I would be back. It could take years for me to see them again, and – who knows – at their age they could decide to leave this world any moment, or I could die from illness or in an accident abroad.

Grandfather lived about an hour's train ride from Zurich and his house was a stone's throw away from the small railway station of Rupperswil. I used to take an intercity train to Aarau and then switch to a local train which travelled back on the same track. This was faster than taking a local train from Zurich. While on the intercity I could always catch a glimpse of Grandfather's house: its red roof, its white front looking from a distance like a friendly face, and the little garden, just perceptible behind the pear trees.

On the local train out of Aarau I got a glimpse of the school where I had spent four years ploughing through Greek and Latin declensions, feeling a foreigner with my Italian accent and my many mistakes in the German essays. The campus looked very much the same as it had twenty years before. I wondered if the students still walked in circles on the dusty gravelled forecourt during their breaks.

The Rupperswil train station had been totally automated and no station master was living upstairs anymore. My childhood friend's family, who used to live there, must have moved on. Trains now looked more like trams, with a driver and a ticket collector who now blew the whistle, and there were machines on the platforms for the tickets. No more kiosk for sweets and magazines.

Grandmother had died while I was in Pune. Nobody had informed me and I was shocked to hear the news from my mother when I came back. "I did not want to upset you. You could not have done anything from there, anyway."

Was it really consideration or had they plainly forgotten me? Had I become such an outsider in the family?

I felt apprehensive about approaching the house without grandmother being there.

Grandfather's old pale blue Opel stood in the drive, as usual. I showed myself in and found him finishing his lunch in the kitchen. He lived on canned vegetables and sausages. The house had turned into a bachelor's place, untidy and uninviting. If I were a filmmaker I would choose the kind of lighting used for scenes in submarines or spaceships to describe the desolate atmosphere. The house had lost its spark. The colours and scents my grandmother had brought into it were gone.

I remember in particular the tarts she made when she expected me to come on my days off from grammar school. She baked them especially for me: savoury onion, cheese and spinach tarts; then the sweet ones: apple, apricot, plum or pear. There weren't enough windowsills to cool them on. Whatever I had not managed to eat during the afternoon I could take with me for the next day's snack during breaks.

The garden around the house was her domain. Still now when I read names of flowers I hear them with her intonation: forsythias, fuchsias, begonias, petunias, African marigolds (the smellies, as she called them), geraniums, gladioli, and sweet peas climbing up the fence. Starting our garden in Yetholm I often wished I had asked her a few questions about gardening, but can you expect a teenager to be interested in gardening? My only contribution was the weekly grass-cutting with the manual push-me-pull-me. It made a dreadful squeaky noise but who cared – as long as it was not a Sunday (no such noises are allowed in Switzerland on a holy day!).

Grandfather ushered me into the living room. It had always been cramped in there. The extendable table with six chairs was squeezed between a grey patterned sofa and a heavily decorated sideboard. One had to walk sideways to reach the cane chair with its reading light, near the window across from the pedal-driven sewing machine. Near the door was the equally dark and decorated desk where paperwork was kept. Among books and papers was his black typewriter. It was an antique piece, maybe one of my uncle's finds from a dumping ground. It had white keys with shiny metal rims. If you did not hit them well in the middle, your fingers plunged into an array of metal-work and got stuck there. Quite a painful experience.

Grandfather had typed a folder full of poems for grandmother. Rhyme and rhythm according to Schiller and Goethe, some in dialect and some in High German. He had used words found in romantic poems and reshuffled them in trite but sometimes creative combinations. The poems were addressed to a young woman, as if he had just met her. While reading them to me, tears flowed from his eyes and his drooping lower eyelids reddened even more. But I remained unaffected by his emotional outburst as I had seen him treat Grandmother with disrespect and scorn so many times.

She had been a simple country woman, short and plump – looking very much like Nikita Khrushchev's wife. As a student I had also pitied her for her lack of education, as teenagers do. She could hardly write in High German much less speak it. But, on the other hand, she knew many beautiful words to describe the wind and the weather in our very simple, down-to-earth dialect.

Grandmother had always accepted me the way I was and had no particular idea of how I should be otherwise. She had taken care of me when I was four, when my mother had her hands full with my two smaller sisters. While I was a student in Aarau she did my washing, ironing and mending as a matter of course. In a few words: it was a grandmother's love. She had bestowed the same selfless care and attention on Grandfather despite his misanthropic behaviour. Unfortunately a few years before her death she had a stroke. As a result her mind went out of sync, she spoke strangely and treated him as a stranger: "There is a man who lives in the house as well." Was this maybe her revenge?

Although Grandfather was now pushing ninety, his doctor signed his driver's permit every year. He knew well that he was not going to drive further than to his little holiday home – where we were heading now – or the pub where he used to meet his friends for the daily Jass, the Swiss national card game. At 20mph my fingers were clutched into the seat out of fear. We drove to the cabin on a new route the forestry department had put in which allowed him to drive all the way up to it. He confided to me that he was glad about this change. "I would hate it if people saw me on my wobbly legs." So much pride, I thought. And we knew that the moment he lost the driver's licence he would start dying.

There had been quite a few changes since I last saw the place. The raspberry and blackberry bushes were gone. No more collecting berries with the aluminium milk kettle through the prickly branches. No more fresh berries with cream, home-made jams and jellies. Also grandmother's strawberry patch, producing those huge red fruits giving off such a delightful aroma already from a distance; Grandfather's asparagus experiment and uncle's snail farm behind the shed were gone. I remember grandmother bent over the potato and onion beds, groaning about her back pain. She used to sun-dry the onions and then sell them to the butcher for his sausages. The apple, cherry and quince trees had grown so large that no badminton game could end the evenings anymore. Potatoes, French beans, onions, parsley, chives, Swiss chard and rhubarb, once safely protected by a fence against the deer, had made space for a large patch of grass. "There is nobody around to pick them and to eat them," he moaned. Still I regretted all the changes.

As travellers moving from place to place, and as meditators constantly changing moods and thoughts, we pretend that whatever we have left behind should remain unchanged in time and we regard any change as an offence to our sense of security. As if the past has to remain frozen in time to give us the roots to fly off again.

Also the log cabin had changed. The inside walls had been torn down to make space for one well-proportioned, tongue-in-groove finished room. It was inconceivable that in this small space, which was at that former time divided into a living/eating room, a bedroom, kitchen and utility room, my mother and my two sisters and I had spent all our summer holidays. It was 'goodbye town' and 'plunge into water and grass' for a whole three months.

We sisters used to spend the day in the public swimming pool at the bottom of the hill and, when the children's time was up at 5pm – signalled by a dreadful honk – we returned to the cabin after a strenuous climb. Grandfather and uncle joined us, bringing with them the catch of the day from their fishing trip. The fish were cleaned and eviscerated at the drinking water fountain in the woods. Glittering fish scales stuck in grandfather's hair and the stink was quite disgusting. Some of the fish were fried for dinner and some went to the communal freezer in the village the very same night.

The cool and dark woods welcomed us, so much in contrast to the sun and heat we had felt on our skin the whole day. We walked the narrow deer trails, in wonder at the thought that, unseen at dawn, real deer walked on this very path, brushing against these very beech branches.

We knew almost each single tree, but certainly we knew all the spots where mushrooms could be found in September. With the help of a multi-coloured pocket book, I knew all the mushrooms by their names and had learnt to distinguish the good ones from the bad ones. Grandmother was very good at making delicious sauces to accompany noodles or rice. "Well, this has saved us again from spending money on meat," she used to say.

When once asked in a visualisation session to imagine my most favourite place, I saw the meadow next to the cabin. In those years (before weed-killers were used on such a large scale) we could still see a variety of multi-coloured flowers, many different kinds of grasses, a multitude of insects and grasshoppers, white and yellow butterflies – and grass up to our knees. There was a view onto the plain where the Rupperswil church tower and the castle of Lenzburg were the most distinguished features. Distant hills turned blue and the peace was deepened by the cries of huge crows with their black shiny feathers.

At night, tucked into our bunk beds, we could hear the approaching buzzing sound of the odd mosquito, the owl calling in the echoing wood, drops falling onto the leaves, or mother turning the pages of her magazines out on the veranda. She loved to sit there by herself, peacefully smoking her cigarettes, protected by a roof come rain or hail. She particularly enjoyed watching the thunderstorms – a free sound-and-light show. This was a delight for her but a threat for Donnar, our retarded pedigree dachshund, who would hide under the bench shivering and whining with fear.

Grandfather brought me back to reality, showing me the wooden birds' hut on the maple tree, confirming that this year again the same couple of thrushes had come back to rear their offspring. Could he recognise them from the pattern of dots on their feathers? In contrast to how much he disliked human beings – he had quarrelled with all his relatives – he loved birds and animals dearly. Probably I was also included in this special selection of beings.

During one of those long stretches of time when I had stayed with my grandparents, most likely the time when my second sister Kätti was born, barely a year after Annamaria, my grandparents wanted me to see the fox they had spotted in the woods. They put out a few fish just below the cabin as bait and the three of us waited patiently and quietly in the dark at the window. In the twilight I could eventually see the vixen approach cautiously. And as a great surprise she was followed by her three cubs, who also walked away with a fish between their teeth. What wonderful bushy tails they had!

Never during those visits was I asked about my life. Not about India where I had spent so many years, or the States where I was going next. Traditionally, in Switzerland, at least for Grandfather's generation, the youngsters had no say. But I was still a bit disappointed that he was so self-centred and was not interested in knowing what I did and how I was.

On the train back to Zurich I went through in my head what I had to do at work the next day. Dipo had found the perfect premises for a meditation centre – but it could be financed only if some of us went to work 'outside'. Two top floors of an office building in the shopping centre in Örlikon, one of the main suburbs of Zurich, were going to be converted into a meditation hall, coffee-shop, bookshop, offices, plus canteen. I did not mind leaving my cleaning job in the commune and found work in an advertising agency. My ego felt restored when

I realised that my salary was double what others brought home from their jobs as waitresses or nurses.

Mr. Abächerli was a decent boss despite his habit of smoking Havana cigars. Being a Freemason, he must have felt some affinity with me as I was openly wearing red clothes and the mala necklace. I felt respected by him (and not by one of the graphic designers who kept waffling on about 'sects' and the 'sex guru'). The outward signs of belonging to a group had created a certain discipline in me. So although working under intense pressure I managed to keep my composure and never lose my temper. It was like being an ambassador for this red wave of sannyasins. I had my own office and enjoyed researching for industrial magazines and items we needed to publicise a chemical industry or a political party.

I had my final hernia operation as my invitation to work on the Ranch clearly stated this was a prerequisite for going there. By chance I had discovered that Leeladhar had graduated with a dissertation about the very operation I needed and he introduced me to his professor. He was working at a hospital in Männedorf where I spent ten days of agony, lying flat with a heavy wheat berry bag on my belly. But now I was ready to leave the nest and go to the Ranch.

In New York, on my one-day stopover, I felt very much at home. New York reminded me of my hometown Milan. It was pure bliss to look up at the skyscrapers with my head tilted backwards. The approach to Portland, Oregon, was highlighted by a close view of Mount Hood from the plane. It swerved around the cone-shaped mountain and we had the impression we could touch the snowy slopes by stretching out our hands.

I was to be picked up at the Greyhound Bus Station in Madras, Oregon (not to be confused with Madras in India, as Chennai was called then). To my surprise the driver was Shanti Sagar whom I knew well from Vrindavan kitchen. He was standing next to a blue diesel van and was already surrounded by a group of newcomers dropped off by another bus. Amongst them I spotted Digambara from Milan, an old friend whom I had first met just before his graduation from Bocconi University. We had been travelling companions before, from Pune to Milan, where he was so kind as to help me with my suitcases after one of my operations.

From the back seat I bombarded Sagar with countless questions about the Ranch and could not wait to get there as fast as possible. My old roommate, Veda, had written a few letters to me in which he told me about his isolated job harvesting wheat on a remote hill and stressed that being on the Ranch did not mean being with Osho a lot. He could see Osho only once a day when he drove past for his car ride and I should not pity myself for not being there yet. But I knew that I was going to feel very different just being near Osho.

We had been driving for an hour on a flat barren plateau when Sagar suddenly stopped the van. The plain was eroded into wrinkled crevices and valleys which looked deeper with the black shadows of the setting sun. With a grand gesture Sagar announced: "Whatever you can see from here belongs to our Ranch." A multitude of rolling hills were turning blue in the distance. "All this?" we asked incredulously.

A narrow dirt road plunged steeply into the valley in front of us. When it levelled out, Sagar swerved to the right and drove up to a set of trailers hidden behind trees. With his accommodation list in hand he unloaded my suitcase and that of Digambara and showed us our spaces: two futons covered with colourful duvets in a room finished in dark fake wood. After a hot shower, we prepared ourselves a cup of coffee in the breakfast kitchen and, sitting on the porch, finished the remains of our travel snacks. Tired and excited we looked into the cool darkness. There was an unfamiliar scent in the air. They later told me it was sagebrush.

Purnam has come to Edinburgh not just for the housewarming party but also for an initiation meditation we are going to do together. Amiten is not keen on doing it but, to be nice to me, has agreed to participate. I take a shower very much like before going to a darshan and the same feeling of excitement wells up. Osho is present right here in our beautiful front room in Edinburgh. Tears are rolling down my cheeks as they used to do for many years, each time I saw Osho walk into the auditorium – and there is the same sense of embarrassment.

It happens many times: every day I watch many people who yet have a living heart in them start feeling awe, but they start repressing it. It feels as if it is a kind of weakness and you are not to show it. If they want to cry, they stop their tears. They have come with many questions to ask and suddenly those questions are not there – because in an awe-filled mood, questioning stops. They forget their questions. And they are very worried about where their questions have gone, and they start searching hectically inside to find something to cling to so that awe does not become too overpowering. Sometimes they ask foolish questions, just to ask, so that nobody becomes aware that they have lost their grounding, that they have fallen into something deep that they have not been strong enough to resist.

Osho, *The Beloved*, Vol. 1, Ch. 2

After the meditation Purnam, with pendulum in hand, tells Amiten that he has a calling: to paint individual meditation pictures. Purnam is astonished at his own revelation and looks sheepishly in my direction to check the expression on my face. I know well that Amiten has a good eye. When we first met in Pune, and I was painting for the photo album, he could always detect the best of the day. He also impressed my calligraphy master, Qui Zheng Ping, when, in an exhibition, he walked straight to one particular scroll. I also thought that it was the best calligraphy, as did someone else because it was already decorated with a red dot.

To test if the dowsing is accurate, Purnam suggests that Amiten prepare a painting right then and there for Sheila. She came to our housewarming party yesterday and Amiten had seen her briefly but does not know her at all. Sheila is being chosen as the guinea pig because Purnam is going to meet her tomorrow for a session and we will be able to see if she can relate to the painting or not. I drag out my painting gear, the watercolour paper and even my very precious and beloved Chinese calligraphy brushes. The painting is quickly made under our eyes. We silently watch light blue watery patches being adorned by unwavering rapid red strokes. The atmosphere is calm and warm and none of us moves. We enjoy the creation unfolding before our eyes until it is completed.

When we show the painting to Sheila the next day, Deva Dhyan mentions that it looks like water and fire flames dancing together. At that, tears suddenly come to Sheila's eyes and she says: "Many years ago a shaman gave me a name which means 'fire within water.'"

I guess Amiten and Purnam passed the test!

6

Celebration

Finishing off

A yellow school bus was going to pick us up in the morning, we were told. We waited on the steps of the porch with a steaming hot cup of tea. The sun was just peeping over the hill and shining straight into our eyes. Invisible moisture and specks of dust became visible against the dark hill in front of us. Digambara pointed out to me that the same trees next to our trailer were also scattered on the hills around, and we came to the conclusion that these must be the junipers we had heard of. The scent reminded us of the cypresses we knew from the cemeteries in Italy. The air was fresh and I felt frisky and excited about what was going to happen next. I was glad that I could share my first impressions and little apprehensions with this old travelling companion. It was all the more lovely because we could speak Italian to each other. To me he was like a little brother taking care of his big sister.

At breakfast in Magdalena we met old friends we had last seen in Pune.

"So finally you have arrived!"

"Wow, you look so healthy!"

"It was about time you came!"

"Wow, you look so healthy, I hardly recognised you."

The healthy Western food and the outdoor work had changed everybody for the better. We were offered a lift on the back of a pickup truck, a kind of vehicle I had never seen before. Holding desperately to the rim of the side panels we enjoyed the breeze despite the bumps in the road.

In the work department we were greeted by Vidya who told me I should help the Twinkies. These were the tour guides, our Ranch hostesses, named after a popular sweet sugary cupcake called Hostess Twinkie, because – it was said – a sweet smile was permanently glued to their faces. I would have preferred to have a job outside in the fields and not again in an office, but I was intrigued that Vidya chose this job for me, a job which – unknown to her – I had done for many years in the past. It was actually the very first paid job I ever had. (When Veena, while editing this book, came across this passage, she apologised and had to admit that on that day, after spotting my name on the new arrivals list she dashed to Vidya's office to ask them to assign me to the Twinkies. She knew of my office and language skills from the time she came to visit me in Geneva and thought I could be of help to them, as well as being a very good tour guide. So this explains, in the end, the mystery of this job assignment.)

The Twinkies had their office 'downtown' in an air-conditioned trailer between the main house and the barn. Isabel, Veena, Sunshine, Rosalie and Sarita (a selection of beautiful girls, all as beautiful as their names) welcomed me with a cup of tea – they had a small corner with an electric kettle, drinking water and a few settees where visitors could wait for the tour to start.

Soon I was invited to participate in one of their tours and wrote down the information (in order of appearance) that I would need to memorise, underscoring the new words for my new American-English vocabulary. I would start with:

-    Ranch size: 126 square miles, 64,229 acres (of which 15,000 acres was rented from the Bureau of Land Management)
-    20 miles from closest town = Antelope (population: 39 in 1980 census)
-    Bought in July 1981 for 6 million dollars
-    City incorporated 18th May 1982

From the Ranch's past I would mention that it was locally called 'The Big Muddy' or 'Muddy Ranch' (now called Rajneeshpuram i.e. 'Essence of Rajneesh') and that John Wayne had starred in the movie

Big Muddy which was filmed here (which, as I check today on Google, was not absolutely correct; there was no movie of that name although he starred in several movies filmed on this ranch).

I had already noticed a spot where I could stop and talk about the environmental issues we had on the Ranch. It was on a bend of the main creek where flash floods had created a twelve-foot vertical drop, taking with them a wooden fence which was now hanging in mid-air. Every now and then I saw a new lump of earth lying at the bottom of the creek. The sight was so deplorable – each time I passed by I felt so sorry for the land – that I thought that the environmental message would have the best impact if I mentioned it here. I would then talk about the 50 years of overgrazing, particularly by sheep which uproot the whole plant.

I could also tell the story of a visitor to the Ranch, an American Indian chief, who could still remember knee-high sweet grass growing here. Once the roots had gone the topsoil was washed off forever. For forty years the Ranch had changed hands for tax write-offs. Nobody had lived and farmed here for a long time – but it was our intention to restore the land. 'To live in harmony with nature' was a great slogan and fashionable at the time.

Along the county road, the visitors would have already seen the airstrip which was 4,500 feet long. I would now drive them through the 'downtown' area with the original farmhouses. One of them was our first cafeteria with a seating area under the trees. Sarita remembered how, during the first winter, the ice which had formed on top of the tables caused the warm plates to 'skate' across the top and slide off the edge. The old water tower, its white paint flaking off, was standing on a small hill like a landmark. Just below it were the old sheep sheds which we used to store machinery and the like. Opposite the road the visitors could see the original barn which had been beautifully restored (Anu, the one who was in favour of 'dropping the ego', was the controller of our security radio system – which would not be disclosed to the visitors although the huge antenna on the barn roof would have certainly given it away). We now lived in 44 prefabricated trailers, some of which the visitors saw during the tour. They were in brown and grey-green earthy shades which blended in well with the landscape (another details we would mention on the tours).

My list continued with:

- Zarathustra Valley with Patanjali Lake and distant wheat fields
- the nursery and the geodesic dome greenhouse (named Yari)
- the new greenhouse 2.2 acres (88,000 square foot), not yet in use

At the bottom of Magdalena Cafeteria we would come to a halt to show the impressive kitchen building and, on the other side of the valley, the trailers high up on the hills. We would tell the visitors the story about when the still unassembled trailers had arrived and the contractors, too scared to drive up, let our dare-devil boys do the rest of the job. The long houses looked grand up there. What a view, and what a climb to get home!

Further entries in my notebook read:

- Atisha chicken farm (we eat unfertilised eggs only), geese and emus from Australia to keep coyotes at bay
- Vineyard project with drip irrigation
- Rabiya dairy farm with 52 Holsteins – there is a huge Swiss cow bell hanging outside (a Swiss man is in charge)
- Surdas vegetable farm near the John Day River (now renamed 'Radha River')
- Mention the waste water lagoon project which recycles treated sewage water for farm irrigation via long pipes

We gave tours to the guests who visited the Ranch from as far away as Alabama – and their accent was the most difficult for me to understand! On the other hand, I was always asked what accent *I* had. Maybe they thought I was from some remote US state.

I tried my best to blend in with the surroundings (as I had always done – in Switzerland hiding the fact that my home was Italy and in Italy hiding my Swiss origins) and had started to adopt the American way of pronouncing words, with all the open vowels and the hot potato rolling of the R's.

I was amazed to see how tour parties travelled for hours on end to get here (similar distances would have crossed Switzerland from one side to the other and back!) but then this was America, and America was big. They had maybe read something about us in the papers and wanted to see things for themselves. Most visitors were attracted by the pioneer spirit, the results of which they could admire on the tour. (Nobody had yet mentioned 'meditation' in any of their questions.)

I learned how to start and drive our blue automatic diesel van and was allowed to use our tiny school bus to drive myself home to the distant trailers of Desiderata. I practised double-declutching (this was the official excuse) while exploring the bee hives on the single track beyond Surdas. There was freedom, exploration, pioneering, enthusiasm and excitement in the air. This was the Wild West dream come true.

Lawyers putting up fences in remote valleys and getting sun-burned faces and scratched arms from the wood-chipping machines; businessmen, sitting high on yellow excavators, preparing the ground for culverts to go in; musicians on Mac trucks, dentists on dozers and clerks on graders which caused all the dust on our papers – were the unlikely workers. And girls on backhoes, forklifts and front-end loaders were very much appreciated by the mechanics as they were gentler on the levers and switches and caused fewer breakdown problems.

We had already started preparing for the arrival of our summer guests and occasionally I was asked to help the tent crew. (We were given a break sometimes – to enjoy a change, some fresh air and some muscle flexing.) It was run by an exuberant Italian, Francesco. Under his commands we heaved, in synchronicity, the wooden platforms onto the four levelled posts which were already wedged into the ground. Soon neatly aligned wooden squares were shining in the sun on all the flat areas of the valleys. A tent would be set up on each platform, leaving a ledge around it where you could take off your boots. It would have been absurd to place the tents directly on the ground as they might have slid away in the mud. With the first rain drops, the limy, reddish-brown earth turned into slimy mud which stuck in inch-high wedges onto the soles of our boots. This was the reason why the Ranch was called 'The Big Muddy' and why all this earth moving was going on: we needed proper roads.

The Twinkies were also given some security jobs. On an extra evening shift Rosalie and I staffed the Mirdad guard hut not far from our trailer. We were equipped with a radio, clipboard, a handheld torch, which I learned is called 'flashlight' here, and a lot of gossip. One evening a truck came to a halt under a cloud of dust in front of us. The driver swept his brow and looked at us in distress, "I have a delivery of a few hundred mattresses in my truck. They must have given me the wrong address. There is nothing here." Little did he know that in the next few weeks we would be putting up thousands of tents for our guests who would join the upcoming Celebration. He thought someone had played a practical joke on him.

One day after work we Twinkies packed ourselves into one of our blue passenger vans and drove out to Patanjali Lake which was in the south part of the Ranch, maybe half an hour's drive. It was a small reservoir which we had inherited. As it was so far from any public road we could bathe in the nude. It was a delight to feel the cool water around the body after the hot summer's day. I remember Isabel mentioning that she did not like to have sun marks on her body from a bikini. I wonder if she had also bathed in the nude in Tahiti where she had lived before. She often mentioned the islands with nostalgia as if she had left her paradise.

The First Annual World Celebration was from 3rd to 7th July, 1982. The wording felt like an exaggeration when I first saw the bookmarks which we had started to give out to the visitors and journalists, but – to my surprise – over 5,000 people came from all over the world. Each day Osho came to meet us in the big greenhouse for morning satsang. The fertile soil was now covered with a huge stretch of uneven linoleum and a wooden podium was installed. Upbeat songs at the beginning and end of each gathering replaced the instrumental pieces we were used to. They were more fitting to the new locale. In fact we were encouraged to openly express joy and ecstasy (there was even a terrible song with 'ecstasy' in its lyrics) and to smile into the cameras, as if we had to prove something to somebody. It took me a few days to be able to sit still in meditation without effort after the hustle and bustle of the preparation work. Osho's drive-bys at two o'clock reached kilometrical proportions. It was a long walk to get to the end of the line of people if you didn't want to be hidden three-deep behind the front row. The highlight of the Festival was on Master's Day when thousands of rose petals were released from our little Piper plane onto Osho's car (which now was a Rolls-Royce) and onto those standing in line.

When the Festival visitors left, I was relieved. I was not so happy that these visitors had come in the first place, as if their presence could have taken something away from me. Of course, this was not a feeling I would share with anyone. In my eyes, it was not acceptable to think like that, but the feeling was there nonetheless. I used to watch how Sheela welcomed the Festival guests with a beautiful smile, meeting with them on the lawn in front of her house. This was the way to behave, I told myself. I slowly came to realise that all this had something to do with the time my sisters were born. Not only had I lost my four-year status of being an only child, but I was sent for months at a time to stay with Grandmother, because my mother could not cope with two babies plus me (the help of a nanny was then beyond our financial means). Grandmother was living in Switzerland, a day's journey away, international phone calls were too expensive to waste on evening pep talks with parents, so to be suddenly cut off from the family must have been quite a drastic event for such a small girl. Until I understood this aversion to 'newcomers' – in this case the Festival participants – I had always considered these stays abroad only in a positive way: a good preparation for becoming more independent, happy to travel on my own and, ultimately, going on the journey with Osho. (As with many things, there is always a positive and a negative side.)

After the Festival was over, the tents were cleaned and folded and sent to storage, the platforms collected from the fields, and rumour had it that they were going to be used to build cabins. Whose crazy idea was that? The colourful rented tents which had been used in different areas as serving stations for Magdalena Cafeteria were rolled up and returned.

The Festival had run smoothly and everybody had enjoyed sitting with their master again. The school buses had coped with the many runs from the tents to the greenhouse/meditation hall, the food was rated delicious, the shower trailers had worked to perfection, and the shit-truck had coped with all the portable toilet units – no reason not to have a Second World Celebration next year!

While everyone went back to their professions or to their jobs at the 500 meditation centres which had sprouted up all over the world, I went back to sorting the many press clippings about the 'red-clad followers' according to country, title of newspaper and date, the way Jayamala, our Twinkie receptionist, had shown me. The other Twinkies were mesmerized to see that with one 'swoosh' I could retrieve, as if by magic, any given article from one of many steel cabinets. I am still wondering what was so special about that. "It is just a matter of filing them in the proper place," I kept telling them…

I settled nicely into all that was new around me. I loved the fresh, unpolluted air in the valleys and the scent of sagebrush and juniper. The evening skies were spectacular: a deep orange red sky behind the black outline of a square-topped mountain, a view such as in a Western movie. It was a joy to work, participating in this common project and to be close to Osho. The daily drive-by gave us a break from what we were doing and was really the reason why we were here in the first place. Osho was now wearing a knitted hat and white gloves for driving and, as always, I felt that his gestures, together with the choice of the materials and colours of his robes, were an expression of his grace.

Digambara and I were soon confronted with the stark reality that we had to leave this paradise sooner or later as our visas were running out. If only we were Americans! Needless to say, we cried our eyes out the evening the work department told us the date of our departure. It felt like a death sentence. As a consolation and a treat, instead of flying straight back to Europe, we decided to stop in San Francisco, Boulder and New York to visit some sannyasin friends.

Mr. Abächerli was delighted to have me back in his agency, as my substitute had just resigned (good timing), and I served as his assistant for many more advertising campaigns. The commune in Zurich had successfully developed the centre in Örlikon into a thriving meditation and therapy centre, offering well-attended week-end courses and various sessions during the week. Switzerland was full of cash to spend on antiques, holidays in the Alps and now on self-discovery groups. The reception and bookshop were tended by old friend Radhika, and the airy and welcoming coffee shop by an exuberant Italian beauty, Barkha.

Bland and boring New Age music played in the background all over the centre – there was no escape from it!

The floor below the huge meditation room teemed with busy offices. Ursula planned the groups and scheduled the workers' shifts on big maps on the walls. Shivananda created the centre's leaflets as well as graphic layouts for new clients. The centre had also taken on board Nirvikar's business which had been distributing Osho's books in Switzerland for the last few years, while incorporating the previous owner as its team leader. The innumerable cases of books which lined the walls and cluttered the floors of the distribution centre were testimony to a thriving business.

After my day at work in the city I joined the centre workers for supper and, while waiting for the 'dinner is ready' signal, plunged into the busy, golden whirlwind of the commune. 'Loud as a Jewish school' would have been the expression any Swiss would have used to describe the chaos and noise. Very much in contrast with the almost Prussian education we had had in Switzerland, this commune was on the unruly and wild side. It would have taken a lot of courage to take any one of us to a posh restaurant. "Can't take you any-where!" I loved to see that, given the chance, the Swiss could also behave like Italians – and to see all this freedom of expression.

I would like to mention at this point that the main centre in Italy, Miasto, in Tuscany, went completely the opposite way and was famous for its regimented and Spartan ways.

The canteen offered delicious vegetarian meals which I enjoyed in the company of my Italian friends who had recently joined the commune along with many others from European countries and the States. At their table, my Italian gestures came back from nowhere, to the great bewilderment of my Swiss friends who had only heard and seen me talk in Swiss German. They felt they were now looking at a completely different person.

Fritz and others were away, working on a construction assignment near Sargans. Also Tanmaya, my American friend, and Shakur, Dipo's boyfriend, were missing; they were running a vegetarian 'nouvelle cuisine' restaurant in town. It was called 'Zorba the Buddha', the name Osho had suggested our restaurants should be called.

During my visit to the Ranch, the commune had left the flats at the Limmatstrasse and had moved to a newly-built complex on the edge of town, a place called Höngg (a name which no foreigner could pronounce even after long practice). It had an inner courtyard, a passage with an arch and it felt very much like the fort in Saswad. It was a new development with some of the buildings still damp with fresh concrete and wrapped in rustling plastic sheets.

I heard that eventually there would be shops and cafés across from us and that the terminal of the bus would be moved to just below the complex, but for now we were still living in a muddy building site far from everything. It had the advantage, though, that we also had freedom of expression and movement at home. We almost had our very own village.

One of the flats was converted into a nursery for the small kids and a place for the bigger kids where they could do their homework after school. Another flat was the 'common flat' which included a kitchen for the cleaners and a tea room/common room for anyone wanting to socialize at night or to find a comic book they'd still not read. Asterix and Lucky Luke were our heroes. Tushir, a teacher, who had just joined the commune and was in charge of the Sunday flea market stand, was appalled by the level of our reading material. In the hope of changing our habits he set up a library of 'proper reading material', as he called it, in one of the wood partitions we had in the cellars but, to be honest, it did not attract much attention.

To accommodate some newcomers who wished to participate in the commune spirit while not giving up their jobs, the commune had reserved a few flats for 'hotel guests'. Those who were working for the commune had food, accommodation and pocket money, but the hotel guests paid for their room, their dinner and the evening meditations at the centre. As with all the other rooms, the hotel rooms were also shared by two or three people and had mattresses on the damp concrete floors. The scheme suited me well and this is where I met Passiko, a girl with whom I was later going to share a flat and innumerable trekking days in the mountains.

Coping with the Media Coverage

I had suspected that the work on the Ranch would have continued at the same supersonic speed I had witnessed during my first visit; nevertheless, on my return, my jaw dropped – and remained dropped – throughout the whole tour that the Twinkies gave me to update my notes.

The previous evening, driving down into the Ranch from Madras, I had already seen the new earthen dam and lake. Imagine going to visit your family and after nine months of absence you discover a huge lake at their doorstep. The road which had taken me to the Desiderata trailers the year before was now below the water level and the county road had to be rebuilt higher up alongside the waterline. In the middle of the lake floated a two storey wooden construction with diving boards and a shop (for ice-cream, I hoped) which suggested that this place was going to be fun as soon as the weather warmed up. As it was along the county road I was told we would need to wear swim suits. Nude bathing was restricted to Patanjali Lake. (I slowly came to realise that Americans were totally different from what I had thought they would be. In my eyes, being the New World, they should have been more liberal than we were in historic and traditional Europe. I thought accepting nude bathing would be a matter of course.)

The reason for building the dam was, in the first place, to collect water. The lake was in fact a reservoir. The main concern of our neighbours was that our presence would lower the water table, which would affect their farming, and the lake was one of the means to avoid that.

Another water-saving measure had been introduced from the very beginning: all showers had a button on the head to stop the flow while soaping or shampooing. We also learnt to turn off the tap while brushing our teeth (which is now being advertised 20 years later by the UK government on TV: 36 litres of water saved). We also did not flush the toilets each time, except in particular instances; but this was not something we would reveal to our visitors.

The dam and lake had been opened with a ceremony, which I had missed, and marble plaques in honour of two great mystics and masters of the 20th century (of which our visitors had never heard) had been placed at the edge of the water:

- Krishnamurti Lake
- Gurdjieff Dam

Further information about the 45-acre lake which I had to memorise was that it had filled up in less than 6 weeks (which overcame everyone's concerns about low rainfall, even ours), its capacity was 330,000,000 gallons (for those who needed numbers; for me it was just enormous) and the height of the dam was 80 feet. Soon I had to become acquainted not only with gallons and feet, but also with inches and Fahrenheit degrees. Later, working in construction, I realised that this way of measuring the world was much closer to the human body. An inch which in Italian translates into 'un pollice', actually meaning 'a thumb', is a measurement which, to my feeling, has more to do with real life than one centimetre.

Later I got to know '2x4 eight-footers', a description of a piece of wood difficult to translate into metres and centimetres. The drawback was that calculations in multiples of twelve were beyond my mathematical training.

The tour notes also listed details about our restoration programme and erosion control:

- 1 million willow trees planted along the creeks
- 200 silt dams (check dams) built

I knew that this was the result of Raghuvira's crew working in distant valleys. I had admired in photographs the clean and aesthetic design of the dams and was intrigued by the fact that they built them so beautifully knowing well that nobody, except themselves, would ever see them.

Then there were all the new buildings in the industrial area (11,000 sq. ft.):

- RBG, which stands for Rajneesh Buddhafield Garage

- Rahul petrol pump
- Gorakh recycling centre (paper, cardboard, cans, glass, compost) in a remote valley
- the welding shop (3,500 sq. ft.)
- Saraha, the carpenters' workshop

On the right we could already see the 23,000 square foot foundations of RIMU, Rajneesh International Meditation University. This building did not really make sense to me as everybody I knew was a worker; but the plan was that soon we would have visitors to attend courses in meditation.

We also had a new garage for heavy-duty machinery. Interestingly, its name was Mahavira, a very gentle saint from the Jain tradition, so gentle that he used to sleep only on one side, concerned he would kill any ants if he rolled over. Also the fire department, with the one huge red fire truck, had the name of a 'cool' mystic, of Buddha himself: it was called Siddhartha.

While I was in Switzerland, there had been disputes about the validity of the incorporation of our city. We were suddenly living in an illegal city. (I had heard of illegal drugs and illegal gun trafficking, but had never heard of an illegal city.) In one of the press clippings, which I later filed, Bob Stacey, an attorney for the watchdog group, 1000 Friends of Oregon, said: "Rajneeshpuram does not exist." How surreal can you get?

Apparently Wasco County was worried that it had to come up with millions of taxpayers' hard-earned dollars for sewage, water, electricity and roads for a city consisting of thousands of residents of a religious 'sect' which was not even Christian and was headed by a foreigner. All we had actually done was to ask for help to upgrade the county road which runs through the property. We financed everything else ourselves.

The incredible success of our commune had triggered a lot of jealousy in our neighbours. (I heard they were even jealous of our lake.) They started to campaign against us and it looked as if they could not live in peace until they had destroyed our creation.

As we had lost our city status, I was no longer allowed to mention the sewage lagoon which was now illegal. With the incorporation, our 2.2 acre 'greenhouse' had become a 'meeting hall', our Rajneesh Mandir. What would it be now that the city was dis-incorporated? While I was away, the construction team had enclosed it with solid walls and glass at each end to give shelter for the winter celebrations.

I was happy to see that cows and chickens were thriving although I was not particularly interested in the farming side of the commune. On the other hand, I was delighted to see that wild birds had finally begun visiting the Ranch – some staying on – although my enthusiasm was soon dampened as these red-winged blackbirds were already considered pests: they had gathered in big numbers and were behaving in a rowdy manner, very much like starlings do back home. I had to mention the 700 laying hens (Osho had suggested we eat eggs as they contain a protein important for our brains – "no vegetarian has ever won the Nobel prize," I remember him saying) and the new methane digester which produced fertiliser and gas from the cows' manure.

We never drove down to the Surdas vegetable gardens with the visitors, because there was a danger of getting stuck on the steep road and because the tour would have lasted too long. However, we always mentioned the nurseries, greenhouses and the salad washing unit, as these were part of our pioneering image and our desire to become self-sufficient. I was lucky to see the Surdas gardens now on my introductory tour. It was a totally different world down there because it was green: rows and rows of greenery the details of which my horticulturally ignorant mind could not identify. At the edge of our fields I could see the white-water river which was the border to the east of our property and more fertile fields beyond, dwarfed below an imposing mountain. I recognised some of my friends under their straw hats which confirmed that this green world also belonged to my world. We were far from being self-sufficient, as the number of inhabitants kept increasing at a rate with which the vegetable gardens never managed to keep up, but we were always pleased to see on our dinner plates what Surdas had sent up to Magdalena Cafeteria: it was fresh, organic and, above all, home-grown.

The Twinkies' office was now fifty yards down the road from its previous spot which had become the main road over Kabir creek. (The advantage of a trailer is that it can be moved!) It was now located close to the new ponds. I had seen them being dug out the previous year and had discussed the daily progress with the drivers of the heavy equipment. While I was in Switzerland my longing for the Ranch became a heartache whenever I passed by a building site and heard the high-pitched beeps of the heavy machinery. Now the excavators had gone and had left behind two beautiful ponds teeming with wildlife.

Instead of hitchhiking to Magdalena Cafeteria on the back of a pickup truck (which was now forbidden) we patiently waited, and even queued, at the bus stops for one of the new yellow school buses. (These were decommissioned, but new-to-us, school buses which had been purchased to run a set of routes around the Ranch.) It was clear that as the number of citizens had grown, some new rules had to be introduced to avoid accidents and to maintain order.

From the turnaround of the buses at the bottom of the hill to Magdalena Cafeteria there was a fairly steep walk which always helped to work up an appetite. The mudroom had been designed specifically for our personal needs: the passage in the middle was for those with muddy boots on; the steps on both sides of the channel were seats to take the boots off, and high up on both sides were the shelves for the boots. That's where the 'socks only' area started. If I remember well, there was heating under the floor of the cafeteria; at least I never felt uncomfortable walking around in my socks.

The choice of food could either be different every day or always the same, it was up to you. There were the regular staple foods like brown rice, tofu, salad and sprouts (for the health freaks) and the changing menu of main dishes cooked according to recipes from all over the world. Here I was introduced to Mexican enchiladas and Japanese tofu pockets. And new for us Europeans were also – at breakfast – multivitamins, peanut butter, sunny-side up (or over easy) eggs on toast; and at lunch yeast powder and Bacobits (ham flavoured vegetarian 'bacon' bits) to sprinkle over the salad. With dinner came draft beer served in big colourful plastic mugs. We could go back to the food lines and serve ourselves with as much as we wanted, but for the beer there were tokens and everybody got only one of them. Beer was not one of my favourite drinks and often my token ended up in the hands of a begging construction worker. Unfortunately, the girl serving the beer had a good memory for faces and often spotted the unlucky scammer.

Magdalena was not only a canteen but, in the evenings, also a common room, a place to meet new friends, catch up with old friends and share what had happened during the day. But this evening this was not for me! Tired from all the excitement of my first day back on the Ranch, it was time to walk down the hill and catch my bus home.

Home this time was Walt Whitman, a valley across from the airport which descended at a right angle towards the county road and which divided halfway up, where the bus turned. The tent platforms of the first summer celebration had indeed been transformed into houses: they had become the roofs. The cabins were called A-frames as the roofs touched the floor on both sides. One wall had the window and the other the door. The A-frame was mounted on a platform on stilts which was accessed by a few steps. The little landing in front of the door allowed us to take off our muddy boots or to smoke the occasional cigarette. Each A-frame housed two people. As in a tent, it was comfortable to stand up only in the middle. There were a hard, but healthy futon under each sloping wall, some hanging space and a few shelves, enough to be comfortable. My roommate was working as a guard. I do not remember her name but remember that she had been a nun before taking sannyas – the vibe of the nunnery was still around her and filled the whole cabin. It would have been totally inappropriate if I had brought a man home even just for a night!

Showers, toilets, and laundry were in the trailers down at the bus turnaround. Our A-frame was called E11, and all my clothes and linen had to be marked with this number using a special pen. "Tomorrow the clean laundry will be on your bed," my new roommate explained. The cabins were cleaned during the day, apparently by elves... A belated thank you to all the lovely, invisible cleaners. From their side, they might have known me only by my sexy under-wear or by the size of my bra; they had never seen my face either.

Coming home that first night, I looked up at the unpolluted sky and tested myself to see if I could find the constellations among the millions of stars which looked down at me. I had never seen so many stars in a sky (later a visitor exclaimed in wonder: "Wow, so many stars in America!" Everything is large and in big numbers in America, why not also the stars?). It was much easier to find the constellations back home when, as a 10-year-old, I had studied the night sky with the help of the little Hallwag booklet and a torch to see the images and had learned and memorized the exotic, Arabic names of the stars. Apart from the Polar Star which I loved for its usefulness – I always liked to know where North was – Sirius and Betelgeuse were my favourites. There were no constellations in the Northern hemisphere which I did not know as a child. But now here in America things were so grand I could not distinguish anything in all this abundance.

Amiten is sitting next to me on the marble bench across from the bookshop in the ashram (which is now officially called Osho Meditation Resort) and admires the new window display I had set up earlier. The previous day I had noticed a beautiful, chunky piece of bamboo lying near the Lao Tzu guard hut and asked Mukta if I could have it. I hauled it over to the bookshop, washed it and placed it on the tip of a carved marble block. It immediately balanced, without any adjustment! Underneath the bamboo I stacked a few books from a Zen series, with their elegantly designed covers; a tableau lit from the top by halogen lights and from the bottom by the reflection of the newly-polished marble ledge.

We both agree that it is a window display worthy of any shop on Fifth Avenue, and he pats me on my back because I had managed to create it at zero cost. But the housekeeping department will have to come up with a lot of money for the many repairs which need to be done to upgrade the shop, fit for the only author on display: Osho.

How did I come to work in the bookshop? Initially my intention was to finish writing this book while in Pune but plans changed, as they often do around Osho. It was probably my mistake to book a Tarot reading with Gandha. During the session she notices that there is too much emphasis on 'finishing' rather than 'writing' the book and tells me that it is OK to have unfinished matters. I remember a quote from Osho where he says something like "death comes like a semi-colon, never as a full stop." This sounds so very uncomfortable to me.

Maybe my concern about unfinished things originates from the time when, giving in to my creativity, my wardrobe was always bulging with half-done knitting and sewing projects – which my poor mother ended up finishing for me. It can be that her grumbling voice still roams inside my head. But thanks to her I have now disciplined myself and do not start on projects I know I cannot finish within a reasonable stretch of time.

It happens that Gandha is also in charge of the work department (all work is voluntary). Maybe her reading is a bit biased as she asks me to come by her office the following morning and tells me that she has a nice project in mind for me. From her office window we look at the bookshop and agree that it needs some attention. In her view I am the right person for that. Both in Yetholm and in Edinburgh I was passionate about our tiny bookshop: a few shelves with books, tapes by Osho and the CDs for the meditations – and now my kingdom is going to be a full-sized bookshop!

I spend many nights after the White Robe Meditation cleaning, scrubbing, dusting, re-arranging and re-organizing books and tapes. With fingers white from acetone to remove the stains of the ubiquitous scotch tape, I eventually drop into bed just before midnight. I am glad to see that the lethargy which had befallen me after menopause has lifted and that I am again strong in my arms and full of vigour in body and mind.

I tell Amiten I have discovered that the bookshop comes with a window display studio, now abandoned and in a desolate state. I can clean it of the glitter which has infested nooks and crannies; and now that the suitcase which we had sent by cargo from Edinburgh, full of papers, acrylics, inks and even a spray compressor, has arrived, he could paint there for my bookshop. I will ask Harito in the book production department to give me the mock-up covers of the new books and Amiten could then make me a backdrop which would suit the colours of the newly-published volumes.

With this resolution in mind we get up from the cold marble bench, massage our bums, and – arm in arm despite the slight stickiness in the air – walk back to our room. On the way, in the Multiversity Plaza, we check which new advertising boards Chetna has put out today. Lacking any other visual input from shops or TV it has become a pastime of ours to visit the display as the pictures often relate humorously to the title of the courses.

Along the path in the dark I become aware that this place has the same feel as it did twenty-five years ago, when Osho was still in his body and living in Lao Tzu House next door: a cool darkness with a velvety softness to it. Again I do not take it for granted and am aware of the great privilege it is to be living here: we have been granted temporary accommodation in the Tilopa pyramid (the one with the Zen bridge in the courtyard).

In the morning I was greeted by a faint mist and a brisk coolness, scented with juniper and sage. The junipers were considered a weed on our Ranch as they had very deep roots and therefore took nutrients away from everything else growing nearby. But they were great survivors. The two junipers next to our A-frame emerged from anonymity and became 'my' junipers. I could imagine them in winter, covered in snow – they would look like Christmas trees. It was not just my impression but also that of others, that even the junipers looked greener than when we first came. Maybe they had tuned in to the celebration and the nature restoration programme.

We had started to ship in and plant trees along all creeks and in two other designated areas. One would be below Magdalena Cafeteria and the other would be a fruit orchard behind Sheela's headquarters in Jesus Grove. I met the girl who watered the new trees daily, or twice daily, with her yellow, rusty water truck. She was very passionate about her mission and, while holding on to the hose with her sunburned hands, explained to me the procedure with pride. She filled the hollow around the trunk with water, allowed it to be absorbed and then filled it again – three times in total.

The Second Annual World Celebration was now being prepared. As more than double the number of guests were expected to come (at least 15,000), the tent city spread deeper into the valleys. Wherever there was a spot of fairly even ground, we could already see platforms set up for tents. In the Zarathustra field a stretch of concrete was laid down. This was going to be the Festival kitchen, roofed and partially enclosed. The Twinkies were informed that five-gallon stainless steel pots and thirty-inch woks were going to be stirred on fifty gas stoves by the 'professional cooks' – one of them I later spotted was a famous Indian movie actor – and by countless Festival volunteers. What a crazy idea! The seating for the guests was going to be long wooden tables with benches and as fridges we would have free-standing refrigerated trailers. Later on, when I visited the kitchen with a journalist, I had to admit that it was a very good set-up indeed and, to my astonishment, I saw in front of me the exact same pot trolleys I had designed when I was in charge of the kitchen in Saswad, as if they had materialised out of the drawings I had made there.

Devateerth Mall was the other project which would certainly astonish the visitors to the Festival. It was also, in my view, a way to show our gratitude to all those who had given many a substantial contribution to the commune. It was a wooden two-storey building totalling 30,000 square feet. The panels and roof beams had been prefabricated in the carpentry shop and were being set in place by cranes. It happened so fast that if you had not been downtown for a few days you got a shock on your next visit. Prefabrication was the only way for us to build houses: we only had a few skilled carpenters but a lot of very willing, but unskilled hands. This was also something I would mention on my tours.

The top floor was to be dedicated to departments like Publications (Osho's books and our weekly newspaper *The Rajneesh Times)*, and our lawyers. The ground floor was going to house a pizzeria, a gourmet restaurant, an ice-cream parlour, a pancake house, a beauty parlour, a jewellery workshop with its sales shop in front, a travel agent and a bank. On arrival the Festival visitors could leave their money with the bank and in return receive an electronic cash card with which they could do their shopping and eating out. "We do not want to use dirty money," I heard Sarita say the day before, during her tour. This was a very modern arrangement as everywhere else in the world we still paid with cash; plastic money had not been invented yet.

We had a red and white plastic card which I did not use too often as my bank account was practically empty. This was the fate of most participants in the commune project. Either they had donated their money and their cars to the commune or they had spent their savings on their airline ticket.

But nobody missed out on anything vital, because lodging, food, bus fares and working clothes were all given to us. So, in a way, the mall was a tribute to the Festival visitors who could afford to shop at the jeweller's and dine at the fancy restaurants.

Near the second crossing over Kabir creek, the concrete crew had started laying foundations for a bookshop dedicated to the exclusive sale of Osho's books, and a boutique for the sale of clothes in the shades of the sunrise: from salmon pink to maroon. Between the two shops there was a passage to the new Zarathustra Cafeteria. The post office remained in the refurbished old shack. Its symbol was a heart with two wings. Mail was delivered directly to the departments, but I visited Pragito, our friendly postmaster, for the occasional letter I wrote. I am still the proud owner of an envelope with the postal frank saying: Rajneeshpuram, OR 97741.

It was the year that the Ranch was infested with flies. Undeterred as we always were in adversities, we faced this problem head on: everybody was equipped with fly swatters and attacked the pests in this way. We followed the method Red China had used when it encountered the same problem. I eventually became very proficient in killing flies without squashing them and without leaving a mark on the wall. Caught on the swatter, the dead flies were dumped with an elegant move into the waste-paper basket I held in the other hand. To kill two at a time with the same technique was my secret challenge. The flies didn't dare to return a second year.

Then suddenly the Festival had begun and the first visitors flocked in from other US states and from abroad. Registration tents were put up at the bottom of the dam, which the gardeners had decorated with the new symbol of the sannyas movement by planting flowers of different colours. The symbol was two birds, a white and a red one flying together. I always imagined that Osho was the white bird and I was the red bird, high up in the sky, flying together next to each other.

The line of the drive-by was getting longer and longer, and, on peak days, it was 4-deep. We now had our own police force, which we called Peace Force – several of whom had graduated from the Oregon Police Academy – and their first job was to accompany Osho's car either on foot or in the Bronco behind. I knew the driver of the Bronco, Arpitam – we had worked in the old M.G. Road bakery together – and sometimes our eyes met. At that moment I always heard my name being called out, loud and clear. When I first wrote this down one of my editors doubted this would be the case; it would have been too much of a distraction from his security duties, she thought. So when I recently met Arpitam I asked him if I was imagining. I was not. He remembered that as part of his security job he would scan the crowd and spot his friends (those people who would most likely intervene in case someone would get too close to Osho's car) and in doing this said their names in his mind. This procedure certainly worked because I heard the call, "Punya!" I immediately felt energised, more alert; a welcome wake-up call. (And just the other day I discovered in a book by Osho, *The Secret of Secrets,* that Lord Shiva had spoken on meditating on one's name and this reminded me of this incident.)

Sometimes standing in the perfect spot, you were right where Osho would stop the car, roll down his window and hand out a present. One day our hired Peace Officer, Harry, received a Magnum of champagne which he accepted gracefully and with a big grin. (According to Osho we should say "Harry, Dick and Tom" and not the other way round – Harry should definitely be in the first place!) An older disciple – it was our postmaster – was presented with a pair of pink slippers with bunny ears. His face expressed something between awe, embarrassment and delight. One day the lucky ones were the toddlers who had gathered with their parents under the trees in front of Naropa, the old farmhouse. There were so many of them that Osho had to get out of his car to give them their presents. Another day it was the older children's luck to receive gifts and the grown-ups' delight to watch Osho carefully wind up the toys and set them in motion before handing them out.

During one drive-by I was lucky to be standing next to Maitreya, one of Osho's oldest disciples who had previously been a politician. He had just arrived from India, with a fractured leg, and was leaning heavily on a Zimmer frame – a walker, as they would say in the States. Osho stopped his car when he spotted him and Maitreya explained what had happened to his leg – at least this is what I thought they were talking about by following their gestures. They spoke to each other with reverence and kindness but in a very casual way, the way I have always seen Osho speak with his Indian disciples.

We had also started to place roses on the bonnet of the car while Osho drove by. It soon created a big pile of vegetation which hindered him from seeing where he was driving. Every day he chose to stop close to our Twinkie, Sunshine, who then scooped up the bounty with a blissful smile. Sunshine was 'family' and so I felt the blessings pouring over me as well.

The slow drive for these few miles in the desert heat brought even so well engineered a car as a Rolls-Royce to boiling point and at different stages a new car had to be brought from the garage. This technical hiccup, a nightmare for security, was a delight for the rest of us: Osho had to get out of the car and walk to the new, cold car. Such an occasion was also a lucky moment for one press photographer whom I was accompanying. He got a full-size picture of Osho instead of a furtive shot through the car window with all its reflections. It was a lucky moment for me as well, as Osho looked straight into my eyes with a beautiful grin. I bowed my head, but was not able to greet him – as I wanted to – with hands folded in *namaste* because with my left I was holding onto the belt of the photographer and with my right I was carrying his 400mm lens which he wasn't using at that moment. This intrusive holding-on technique was introduced by us Twinkies to ensure that the photographers did not crowd Osho too closely – which they liked to do! But for many of them it was OK to be held as if on a leash because they could concentrate on the eyepiece and not worry about their distance from the subject. One of our photographers must have been there on that occasion as well, because later I was able to buy a postcard of this scene. Osho was wearing a white robe with golden embroidery down the sleeves. With such a close encounter one's memory is engraved with minute details, even those of the decoration on the robe.

Another day, a photographer assigned to me wanted to climb up to Socrates building, despite my reservations. He looked around like a sniper for a suitable window and finally set up his look-out post on the outside stairs. He was grumpy, nervous, and deeply stressed out. What a contrast to the celebrating crowd! He was there to do a job, a good job, and maybe his career depended on this very photograph, as he mumbled something like "I need a breakthrough."

We sat on the steps and waited in silence for Osho's car. It finally appeared from behind the bend and the photographer got ready. We saw the car approach, and then, beyond all hopes and expectations, the car stopped and Osho got out. Bingo! He got the shot! Osho, dressed in a black robe with long white stripes, was standing next to the Rolls and greeted the crowd with both arms raised. Behind him were a few hundred yards of the winding line-up of the 'red-clad followers,' as the caption later read. The photographer could barely believe his luck – a flicker of light did show in his eyes momentarily – but his mood hardly changed. The following week I filed hundreds of clippings from all over the States with this very photograph. One of the main press agencies had chosen it as *the* photograph of our celebrations. A breakthrough indeed!

For the satsangs that year Osho wore flowing robes in soft colours – beige, light blue, light green – colours which blended in with his long grey beard. One day my mind got caught up in thoughts about the allocation of my reserved seat. It was in the fourth row, which was quite a good spot considering that there must have been at least thirty rows to the very back. But Nada, a friend of mine, was in front of me in the third row. Not only did she have a better place, but she was sitting on her heels hiding Osho from my sight and while singing and moving, her hair slapped in my face. I could have easily told her to tie her hair back and sit on her buttocks, but I was frozen with guilt about my petty jealousy.

"I should be more grateful for what I have and not always wish for more," the monologue went on in my head. "I should accept things as they are." To be accepting, invisible and accommodating was my Swiss conditioning which was fighting with a part in me which likes to be seen and acknowledged. Inevitably the meditation, the humming and Osho's words read by Amrito went over my head due to this internal fight. I was aware that I was missing the satsang and this provided even more fuel for the turmoil. (In the meantime I have learnt to reveal my inner self, as you can see. Is there anything more exposing than writing about this 'pettiness'?)

The next morning, for satsang, I had a photographer in tow. He chose to sit at the back next to the exit, because he wanted to quickly dash out of the hall at the end of the meditation and catch Osho when he walked to the car. From forty yards away, Osho was just a blur with my short-sighted eyes, but his presence was so tangible and real it was as if his body had expanded to the edges of the hall and I was sitting inside him. It required my greatest effort not to close my eyes and space out. I was 'on duty' and had to remain aware and alert, with eyes open like a guard. And the more aware I became, the more his presence overwhelmed me. What an eye-opener! The row numbers really do not matter much, do they?

On Master's Day the celebration started at lunchtime on the main street along the mall. There were jugglers, clowns, tightrope walkers, hot air balloons – to the delight of the visitors and workers alike. The distorted music from the speakers reminded me of a country fair. 'Welcome Home' said the banners and the words in the song. Rajneeshpuram was meant to be the home for all the sannyasins in the whole world.

Before the Festival I moved to the Alan Watts area of A-frames which was in a valley parallel to Walt Whitman. The architects, in their creativity, had come up with a further sophistication of the A-frame model: four A-frames, on a single deck, were held together by a shower-kitchen unit. (Another new word for my Twinkie vocabulary: quadruplexes.) These now had luxuries like running hot and cold water, as well as air conditioning and heating. Unlike any commercial developer, the Chuang Tzu building crew had not shunned the extra work and trouble to place them in the most beautiful locations with the most stunning views down into the valley, onto the Mandir meditation hall and into the distant hills. In case we did not get enough exercise during the day, living up there certainly kept us fit.

Isabel introduced me to Lani who had just arrived and was going to move into the same A-frame as me. Out of hearing, Isabel asked me to show her the way to the Mandir for the evening celebration. As she felt like 'family' immediately, it felt awkward to have to explain to her the words of the *gachchhamis* and the routine of the celebration. After a shower and in our best clothes, we descended into the valley and crossed the creek over the footbridge. I loved this bridge. It was built with rough juniper trunks. Did it gently sway? But certainly it sounded great under our footsteps. The paths leading to it and then winding up to the Mandir were covered in wood chips, kept in check by rough beams on both sides of the path. This material was soft under our feet and, most important of all, had the scent of juniper bark! (If it had rained we would also have reached the Mandir without muddy shoes.)

We left our trainers on the racks in one of the shoe tents, memorized their location and descended barefoot towards the Mandir on the tan carpets which stretched from shoe racks to hall. To avoid the disgraceful habit of running through the hall to get a seat up front, we held each other's hands in a long chain and walked into the hall in a more civilised manner.

Guru Purnima has for millennia been the day Indian disciples pay their respects to the master and traditionally it is celebrated on the first full moon night in July. The full moon had fallen the previous year – for the First Annual World Celebration of 1982 – on the 6th of July, and this date was kept for all celebrations to come, regardless whether the moon was full or not. Why this was so, I have no idea. At the time I thought that maybe this date was important to Osho. At any rate, when asked about why, the spiel was: 'It is now an international Festival.' That was the cliché answer we Twinkies were meant to give.

This year's celebration offered us a particular treat: before sitting down in his seat, Osho called up Gayan and asked her to dance on the podium. Despite her formal training as a dancer, her movements were very natural and fluid. There was never a hint of a performance. Her dance was rather like the innocent flutter of a leaf in the wind or that of a butterfly searching for a flower. Osho danced through her for us and with us, while we sang the songs and swayed our arms in the air. For the silent part she sat down on the podium at some distance from him. Such a graceful sight: male and female at rest. But I was meant to have my eyes closed and be meditating!

Again I had the sensation that I was totally alone and that I was sitting all by myself in the big hall with no one else around. I was shocked when I opened my eyes again. Such a mass of red, so many thousands of people around me. I remembered Lani. She was still sitting close to me and was getting ready for the final *gachchhamis*. Taru's velvety voice led the mantra – one could not imagine the *gachchhamis* without her.

Osho got up, greeted everyone and walked from the podium to his car while we sang to our hearts' content. Many got up and moved to the edges of the hall to get a closer glimpse of Osho's smile while he drove around the Mandir (anticlockwise as in Pune – in case this should have an esoteric meaning).

To avoid an over-flooding of the canteen, the kitchen moms had invented the famous 'celebration box'. Beautifully arranged white cardboard boxes, containing a savoury snack, cake, fruit and a drink had been previously stacked on tables at one end of the hall.

In the style of a *'déjeuner sur l'herbe'*, small groups scattered around the huge hall, sitting gracefully on the linoleum floor, hardly talking, just enjoying the food and each other's company. It was a more festive atmosphere than at a Queen's Christmas banquet, although we were eating cold food and sitting on the floor.

The next day I escorted the photograper of the *Stern* team to Krishnamurti Lake. My job was to make sure that his lens was not pointing onto a subject which could be misused. An innocent hug between friends would certainly receive a caption mentioning the 'sex guru' and we wanted to avoid that. But it escaped my attention that a girl was wearing her mala around her waist; while swimming it was probably safer there than around her neck. Such an innocent thing, but the published photograph which spread over two pages showed her sun-tanned belly button, Osho's face in the mala and a sexy, wet, red bikini bottom.

We introduced a few Festival visitors from Germany to the *Stern* journalist. She became very enthusiastic about Chaitanya Hari, applauded our ways of living and – I think – would have loved to stay with us forever. When she finally had to depart, she lost her keys and we had to organise a carpenter, in the middle of the night, to force the door of her room to retrieve her luggage. Despite her obvious Freudian slip, the negative article which was eventually published turned out to be worthy of the aggressive and cynical journalism of *Stern*, and the choice of the photographs and the text of the captions belied her positive feelings. The last paragraph, where she quotes a passage from a discourse by Osho, was the only thing that seemed true to her real feelings. Maybe as an apology, she wrote me a card from New York to thank me for taking her around. I felt betrayed and certainly did not reply. *Stern* would not have accepted a positive article about us, but – in my view – she could have been true to herself and given up her job. But then, not everybody is as courageous as Satyananda had been.

Then came the filing of all the articles about the Festival. We had to get bigger premises for the new filing cabinets and we moved to the airport building. Our crew was enriched by a new member: Ma Margaret. She also happened to be Swiss and had grown up abroad, in England in her case, and, having married an Italian, had spent many years in Italy. All three languages were on hand for us to use, but, for some unknown reason, we had the unwritten rule that English was the language for professional matters, Italian for our private conversation and Swiss German was an infinite source for 'funny expressions' which lightened up our tedious job. We sat at two grey desks next to each other like two archivists in the Vatican library.

The local newspapers wrote so many articles about us that soon we had to have a separate drawer for each: *The Bulletin* from Bend, The Corvallis *Gazette Times*, *The Register-Guard* from Eugene, *Hood River News*, *Herald and News* from Klamath Falls, *Madras Pioneer*, *The Oregonian* (Portland), *Willamette Week*, *The Dalles Chronicle*, and last but not least the *Statesman Journal* from Oregon's capital, Salem.

The national newspapers had their own place. They included the *New York Times*, *Washington Post* and the *San Francisco Chronicle*. We were lucky to have a positive two-page article from the latter. This clipping was laminated and often photocopied. It was the best part of our press kit.

Soon Margaret's desk was adorned by an enormous Rolodex file with a dark grey metal cover. Her new job was to read through the articles (she was in fact a writer – how jealous I was about that!) and mark the cards with the relevant topic including date and name of the newspaper. This cross reference would enable our lawyers to quickly identify the articles they needed for their research. We started to file the articles with a photocopy attached behind each clipping, so that the lawyers could take the copy with them right then and there. We had often seen them walk out with the original without the slightest sense of wrongdoing.

Past my eyes came many names. Among them was the oft-recurring name of David Frohnmayer, Attorney General of Oregon, who, according to what I had heard Sarita and Sunshine discuss, had boosted his political power with his campaign against us. His platform was the issue of separation of Church and State. Then there was the name of Rick Cantrell, the Mormon Wasco County judge who had accepted the incorporation of our city and who subsequently lost his job and moved abroad. We understood that the Mormons could move their people about like missionaries, but in this case the timing was obvious.

Then there were the dreaded 1000 Friends of Oregon. I felt them menacing like daemons who wanted to destroy my home. The aim of this land-use watchdog group was to ensure that Oregon remained lush, green and beautiful (but our poor Ranch was none of the above). Their attorney, Bob Stacey, said: "We are against urbanization and development in this case because their plans are inconsistent with existing state law... Sure they have done a good job, especially at identifying adequate water sources, but their use is still inappropriate." I just wondered what they feared we would do in these forlorn desert valleys and why they invested so much time and energy in having our city dis-incorporated.

Many of the articles spoke of the 'red-clad followers of The Bhagwan who had taken over the city of Antelope' (where Bhagwan was often spelled with the H in the wrong place). Taken over a whole city? But then few if any of the newspaper readers had ever been to Antelope and no article had ever mentioned that 'the city' of Antelope was practically a ghost town.

I am now looking at an aerial photo of Antelope in one of our publications: I see four roads, each about 100 yards long. Between them are three rows of properties. There are no more than fifteen houses, if I also take into account the fact that some might be hidden by the trees. At any rate, the population numbered just 40 – mostly retired folks – before we came, and many properties had been standing empty and up for sale for many years. When we first arrived we were interested in having a base in Antelope for the handling of book distribution, a business which would not have been permitted on a farm. Now that the legality of Rajneeshpuram as a city was disputed, there was more reason to take root there.

The 'Antelope Store and Café' soon became the vegetarian 'Zorba the Buddha', a stopover for visitors to and from the Ranch (the avocado pita bread was memorable) and the population increased to 95 (inevitably sannyasins outnumbering the original inhabitants). In autumn of 1982 the new Antelope elected our Karuna Kress as mayor. It was funny to see some of my friends playing politics, but Karuna looked very good in the position of a matronly mayor. (The change of name from 'Antelope' to 'City of Rajneesh' was decreed much later, in autumn 1984.)

I had a friend who lived in Antelope but worked at the Ranch. He had to take the early morning shuttle which took him to work on the 20-mile-long route including the 7-mile-steep descent on the narrow, unpaved county road. In the evening the same bumpy ride awaited him again. The waitress at 'Zorba the Buddha', on the other hand, lived on the Ranch and so also got a taste of both worlds. But for most of us Antelope was a place far away, somewhere in the outside world, not worth a visit or even a mention. In a way we did take over Antelope, even introducing recycling – to the horror of the old residents. No wonder I often found in my clippings defamatory articles signed by the former mayor of Antelope, Margaret Hill, who was trying to fight her way back into office.

I usually tend to deal with adversities by moving out of the way or giving in, but here the sannyasins were defending themselves tooth and claw against the cult-hysteria which was encouraged by the fundamentalist Christian, Ronald Reagan government. Sannyasins were standing their ground and fighting for their rights.

This country had cherished constitutional guarantees – the rights of religious liberty and freedom of religious expression – which were being flagrantly violated left and right. This was a good lesson for me, but I can also understand that the poor old people in Antelope experienced quite a disruption in their lives. Because I was more of a submissive person, I admired the courage of the leaders of the commune in fighting for our legal rights, but I thought that there could have been a more diplomatic way to do things.

Other names our Margaret had highlighted in the clippings were those of the Jefferson County District Attorney, Michael Sullivan; a group called the Concerned Citizens; and a high-level government figure called Edwin Meese, who was counsellor to Ronald Reagan and later became the Attorney General of the United States. The pathetic Eckart Floether, an ex-sannyasin who had found solace in a Christian sect where he 'saw the light', became famous with his 'insider's account' in which he accused Osho of mental instability. His book was used by many as confirmation that there was something wrong with us.

Aware that it is much easier to write a controversial book (hate is a very energetic and active drive) and much easier to find a publisher even if it should lack any literary grace, I had the desperate conviction that it was absolutely necessary for the story to be written from the other side as well. But I never thought that I would be one of the people doing the writing.

The most frequently highlighted name was that of a redneck housewife called Donna Quick-Smith, the ex-wife of Antelope resident and unsuccessful mayoral candidate, Don Smith, who accused us publicly of selling pornographic material. What a mind she must have had to come up with such an idea!

Another housewife (I always imagined them with big pink curlers) was Joanne Bois from Albany. She spent her life organizing rallies against us, collecting signatures at fairs and parties (once she came up with half of the 62,000 she needed for getting a measure on the election ballot) and calling us an alien cult, a New Age movement (what an insult!) and naming Osho the 'antichrist'. She even suspected that we worked with the CIA and that Osho might be a Jew.

To confirm the saying that pictures speak louder than words, I was most affected by a bumper sticker which often appeared in the headings of the articles. It said, 'Better Dead than Red'. This might not have been such a big deal but on the right side there was a drawing of Osho's face with beard and hat over which was superimposed a shooting gallery target. The first insight into the psychology of the ranchers, who were the ones distributing the sticker, came to me while driving to the Ranch for the first time. On their fences along the road they had displayed several coyote hides, legs stretched in all four directions, as if this ugly sight would deter other coyotes from entering their farms. But it said much about the rednecks and their rough manners. This bumper sticker had the same insensitivity – and was difficult to stomach.

I knew well that I was on the Ranch out of love for Osho and that I came to visit the place to be close to him, but this constant negative input made me wonder if maybe somewhere the media were right. I do not understand this psychological twist, but maybe it is a survival mechanism, similar to the way an abused child blames herself for her parents' bad behaviour. I was in such turmoil that I decided to write to Osho. The answer just said: "Love your work." I wondered how such a simple device as loving one's work could stop this negativity from affecting me, but it must have done its job, as, with no effort on my side, I came back to my true self the very same day.

Most of my friends were doing things like driving food trucks or sorting bolts in the plumbing shop and were blissfully unaware of the content of the articles piling up on my desk. They had no idea of what was going on in the media and would not have been particularly interested in knowing it either. We had *The Rajneesh Times* as a source of information, but this was more of a party publication with our view of things. We had no television and just a few of us had a subscription to *Time* or *Newsweek* magazines. Everybody was happily working along in our much more interesting world of spiritual pioneers.

The filing of the articles was interrupted around 2:30 by the visitors' tour, which was a welcome change. Although I'm not a very articulate person (apparently due to having Saturn in Gemini which stunts speech and song), jobs very often came my way where I had to talk, a lot. (Later I would be a radio dispatcher, a psychic reader and a call centre agent under a headset.) Maybe the esoteric people call this: 'the lessons of this lifetime'.

The afternoon tour coincided with Osho's return from his drive out to nearby Madras. We were asked not to line up for his return (I never understood if it was for his privacy or because it interrupted our work), but it was OK to greet him when we accidentally crossed his path or were working close by. Some of the roads were blocked until he had passed and this was the occasion to stop our blue diesel passenger van, form a line by the road and wait for him. I always left it to the visitors to decide if they wanted to see him or drive on, but they always opted for what most women openly expressed as "we might as well see the man himself." Osho usually slowed down and *namasted* the visitors with the same smile with which he greeted us. Very often there was silence for a while in the group and nobody knew why.

During the Festival I had given my most memorable tour of the Ranch. A yellow school bus full of Festival visitors from Italy had driven up to our meeting point and on the tour everybody was so enthusiastic about all the changes which had taken place since their last visit, that I often had to silence them in order to give – over the PA – the details of the new construction in front of us. I could leave out the entire political rap which was of no interest to anybody and injected the talk with lots of humorous bits which made the bus almost jump off the road. With them I was flying like a kite. Only later I realised that it had been so easy because I was speaking in my mother tongue, so close to my mind, so close to my heart.

But with our daily visitors it was a different affair and more of a challenge. They had heard about us in the press and wanted to see for themselves what this place was all about. I appreciated that they had made the effort to drive to do that instead of just believing the press. Inevitably, their questions were provocative, but soon enough I learned how to use the energy behind their questions, turn it around and find an answer without becoming defensive – a skill which became useful in all my future 'talking' jobs. Most of the time the visitors left with a hearty handshake and a "Keep up the good work!"

A frequent question was why we were working without pay for this man and for so many hours. I could always see a glint in the women's eyes when I explained that it was easy to work all these hours as I was taken care of in other ways: my laundry would be ready on my bed when I came home, the trailer was cleaned while I was away, breakfast, lunch and dinner were served in the canteen. Most probably these women worked more than 12 hours in their house and garden and had no money they could call their own. I could devote many hours to my job and still have the time to chat and meet friends after work. All my needs were covered, including medical expenses, and I felt there was nothing more I could ask for.

The more courageous mentioned the eternal 'free sex' issue. I had heard Isabel answer a journalist with: "Well, we do not charge anything, if that's what you mean," and I sometimes used the same pun. Nobody would have believed, if I told them, that because of the exhausting physical work, mainly in the following year during the intense construction spree, it often happened that lovers fell asleep before any action had taken place. We had a joke where an Englishman goes to the pharmacist and asks for seven condoms, for Monday, Tuesday... Then an Italian asks for eight condoms for Monday, Tuesday... and twice for Sunday, and then a Ranch resident asks for twelve condoms for January, February...

Other visitors asked if another Jonestown could happen here. To my unknowing stare, my American colleagues informed me about this well-publicised tragedy: the preacher Jim Jones, founder of a Christian church called the Peoples Temple, had created an agricultural project in Jonestown, Guyana. When rumours had leaked that followers were prevented from leaving and that the place was run like a concentration camp, Leo Ryan, a Congressman, visited Jonestown for a personal inspection. On his departure, a few of the Temple members had joined him and they were shot by the Temple's security guards. Following this, Jim Jones asked the whole community to commit group suicide – almost 1,000 people died. This was still alive in people's minds as it had happened only five years earlier, in 1978, but I could not understand why we should be associated with this tragedy just because we were also a religious agricultural project. Osho's vision was so life-affirmative that a mass suicide was out of question. (There were similar tragedies which followed and are mentioned in the same breath as Jonestown: the raid on the Branch Davidians at Waco in 1993, and the mass suicide of the Order of the Solar Temple in Switzerland in 1994.) Inevitably also the journalists drew parallels between the mass suicide in Jonestown and our commune and Isabel then organised an interview with Leo Ryan's daughter, who had been a sannyasin for many years and who spent a lot of time on the Ranch, so that she could show with her own presence that this was something totally different.

The media had also mentioned that the commune 'takes the kids away from their parents'. This was a delicate issue and was easily misunderstood. I avoided showing the kids' quarters on the tour to avoid the question but sometimes it came up. We also never showed the location of Osho's residence, but that was for security reasons (as if the CIA did not have detailed aerial photos of our place...). In comparison to the population of the commune, which in that year would have reached about 1,000, the kids were a minute percentage. In the very first year, when the infrastructure had not reached a civilised standard, no parents with children were invited to come to the Ranch. Later children were living in a conglomeration of trailers with a playground in the sun, with teachers, helpers and the nightly watch, which consisted of parents staying overnight on a weekly rotation. They ate with us in Magdalena Cafeteria and had the privilege of a special kids menu, skipping all boring adult food. They got pasta with tomato sauce, French fries, bean burgers, vegetarian sausages and a delicate hint of some seasonal vegetables. This was all lovingly prepared and served by a New Zealand actress and theatre director, Jivan Mary. My stern Swiss German food education condemned and envied them. (These two always go together.) Not fair! Many parents then spent the time after their meal together with their kids and went to Osho's drive-by together. In my eyes, this loose but still close connection with the parents allowed the kids to grow up without being limited by the preconceived ideas of their parents; they had the possibility of adopting a variety of 'uncles' and 'aunts' to widen their view of how people can be. On the way to Magdalena Cafeteria I often met one of the kids and we used to have grown-up conversations in the back of the bus. We told each other what we had done during the day and what was ahead of us. It was an enriching communication for us both. Often during drive-by I used to chat with Meera, a teenager, and we became close friends. Only months later, when I saw her chatting with another friend of mine, did I become aware of how much they looked alike and discovered that they were mother and daughter. Always seeing them separately, I was not aware of their kinship. This had allowed me to know Meera independently from her mother and appreciate her personality on her own, without reference to her mother, without the limitations of 'being the daughter of so-and-so'.

Osho had never encouraged us to have children and these were the children who were born before the parents had met Osho. (I understand that this suggestion was not only for the sake of the parents, for whom it would have been more difficult to combine the duties of rearing a child with the discipline of meditation, but also for the sake of the children. All children like to be number one in their parents' eyes. Being second to Osho and to a parent's spiritual path is not easy.)

When we later 'took over' the dilapidated school in Antelope, the teachers – with the help of the pupils – turned it into an awe-inspiring, aesthetic, intelligent and free institution, worthy of the new name: Rajneesh School. Coloured sofas filled the rooms instead of hard wooden benches. Not fair! Not fair!

While Margaret and I busied ourselves with the Press Office 'household', i.e. filing the new clippings and preparing the press kits, Isabel, Veena, Sunshine and Sarita spoke to the journalists and the VIPs. I remember hearing the name of Ted Shay, Ph.D., a professor of Political Science at Willamette University who came to study the commune. He was accompanied by his wife, Cari Shay, Ph.D., also a professor of Political Science, but at Western Oregon University, who later became Ma Amrit Roshani and a beloved friend of mine.

Other names I heard mentioned in our office were Kirk Braun (*Rajneeshpuram: The Unwelcome Society*), Dell Murphy (*The Rajneesh Story: The Bhagwan's Garden*) and James S. Gordon. They all published well-informed books and the latter's *The Golden Guru* became a point of criticism against him when he was chairman of a Complementary Medicine group under Clinton. I vividly remember the German philosopher, Rudolf Bahro, who stayed with us for a few weeks. I was introduced to him because I spoke German and was delighted to meet an intelligent, unprejudiced man. Although a philosopher, he looked more like an artist or a poet, more a person functioning from the heart than from the head, as his profession would suggest.

The girls also arranged interviews, and paved the way for Ronald O. Clarke of the Department of Religious Studies, Oregon State University, to work on a Summer Research Project (sponsored by the Oregon Committee for the Humanities) which had as its intent an objective analysis of Osho's teachings and their social and ethical implications. If I remember well, the study took a whole year to complete and the results showed that the IQs of our people by far exceeded that of the average Oregonian. Mr. Clarke must have belonged to our more intelligent category: on the back of an Osho discourse book we printed his words as an endorsement:

"Rajneesh is a man of gifted intellect and extraordinary erudition. His published discourses are a source of much wisdom, insight and poetic beauty. And I regard his teaching to be a significant contribution to humanity's enduring quest for spiritual understanding, growth and fulfilment."

Another study group was led by Lewis F. Carter. Apparently the group encountered problems in evaluating the results as each interviewer had his or her own perspective derived from individual religious upbringing, nationality and gender. Moreover, the interviewees, although all wearing shades of red, gave such diverse answers to the routine questions that they were too difficult to assess. Then, from the University of Oregon came Norm Sundberg, Dick

Littman and Carl Larkin, psychologists, and Mimi Goldman, a socio-logist, all of whom later wrote several articles about Ranch residents.

These were the few stars in our sky: intelligent people who were willing to see – even though it was through their own coloured spectacles – and to investigate with an open mind what was happening on the Ranch. But still there was a big difference: we were living the experiment; they were just observing it, like scientists trying to study wildlife from afar.

At the back of the Osho Meditation Resort, behind Mirdad and the Pyramids, lies Osho Teerth Park. It used to be a barren stretch of land belonging to the city of Pune, with a putridly polluted brook, called a 'nalla', running through the middle. It was, in fact, a garbage dump and much neglected. Osho wanted to create a garden and we got permission to plant trees and bushes in exchange for opening the park to the public during specified hours. The park was completed around the time Osho left his body. Sannyasins holding a commune pass can go there at any time and enjoy the opportunity of being able to meditate in nature without being disturbed.

To keep fit and healthy I have started to walk in the park every morning. In India, people always talk about 'going for a morning walk' which sounds strange to us, but it is indeed the best time to be out here. The heat of the day has not yet touched the stones and the cool morning mists are still in the air. The white sky behind the dark fronds of the trees announces that the sun is not far from hitting us again.

Right inside the gate stands a frangipani tree, still small but full of flowers. The scent is overwhelming. The flowers fall onto the ground still fresh and intact. I pick one up and admire its slightly twisted petals, their sheer whiteness, and the delicate yellow centre, and bring it up to my nose. In this position I walk down the gravelled path towards the river which, after it has spread out into a pond, leaps over rocks and passes below the curved wooden bridge I stand on.

The garden is full of small paths which end in hidden corners with benches from where, as if from a window, we can admire stunning views. I come to a bamboo forest and admire the green lines down the chunky yellow stems; just past it a black statue of a female Buddha greets me with its silence. Every morning I discover new things even if my route does not change much. Today it is a tree. Its roots seem to start a few feet up from the ground then, as if afraid of leaving the tree, form a connection between the tree and the ground like a curtain. I had never imagined that trees could be so creative and come up with such forms. I think it is called an Arjun tree. In the same patch are gathered some extraordinary palm trees with huge bulging stems. I wonder where our gardeners, Nivedano, Rashid and Neehar, had found these beautiful specimens.

Along the winding path, I am accompanied by a stretch of Bird of Paradise flowers in bloom. A businessman on his morning walk is looking at the sky and a lady in a sari but with white sneakers strides with energetic steps towards me. She swings her arms high with stiff elbows like soldiers do. It could be that her doctor told her she needed to lose weight and has advised her to walk this way. Back up on the other side of the Nalla, returning to the southern gate, the path leads me alongside spectacular palm trees: four traveller's palms. The leaves remind me of those of banana trees. They are neatly packed in two opposing rows and open like a fan. I have to stop and have a good look at them, and admire the whiteness and geometry of the interwoven stems. So many miracles!

Back in the Resort I turn towards Jesus House. Amiten and I have recently moved and are now living in a room on top of the roof. It is airy with a lot of light but, unfortunately, it is next to a very loud water pump which keeps us awake at night. (Can't win, can you?) The stairs are the same circular stairs with the same round wooden banister which I had climbed twenty years ago. I am astonished to see how my body's memory has stored the information so clearly, and for so many years, so that I can walk up the stairs with closed eyes. But it has the downside that, on my way out, I often turn right at the bottom of the stairs and find myself at a sealed-off wall.

Padma's Buddha, painted on the wall, greets me on the second floor and I climb higher to the exit onto the terrace. On the left is our door. Down eight steps is our room, and up four steps again is our bathroom. Like an archaeologist, I once thoroughly inspected the outside wall from the terrace to see if there were any signs which would reveal if the room had been added at a later stage or if such an in-between level room was planned from the very start – but I didn't find any clues. The room had been there in the old days but was something of a forbidden zone as far as I remember. Shashi, who works in the kitchen, and always kindly informs me when there is a treat like carrot *halva* or mango chutney (which I am not meant to miss), confirms that it was indeed out of bounds as it was used to store the master tapes of the discourses and that her husband, Arun, one of Osho's brothers, who has now also died, duplicated them in this room.

Up until now the Twinkies sent out press releases and invitations to journalists only once a year, just before the Summer Festival. But suddenly we busied ourselves, in the middle of the year, with dispatching two photographs (one of Osho and one of a line-up of some of the 65 Rolls-Royces we owned at the time) and a short caption to press agencies and to all local and some national papers.

Within a few days both my and Margaret's desks were snowed under with heaps of bulky envelopes containing hundreds of press clippings each – sent to us by the clipping service we had hired. They were from all over the States, not just from our local papers. The other Twinkies stared in disbelief, elegantly covering their wide open mouths with both their hands.

The clippings all showed a 6x4 black and white photograph of the Rolls-Royces, neatly parked in parallel at an angle on the road leading to Osho's house. In the background were the garages to house the cars and in the front, the creek flowing under the culvert.

In one corner, mostly boxed into an oval, was the bearded face of the 'owner' of the fleet. The title and the three-line caption mentioned: number of cars, Rolls-Royce, Silver Spur, Osho's name, Rajneeshpuram, OR, and certainly the 'red-clad followers'.

We had never expected that the photo of the cars would attract so much attention. With my experience of working in the media department of a major advertising agency like the one in Geneva I could easily calculate that an advertising budget covering the whole of the United States would have been much more expensive than the cost of the cars. And considering that an advertisement on meditation would not have attracted any attention whatsoever in a country where money and riches are number one on the priority list, an absurd and extravagant display of so many cars, all of the same make, all being used by one person only, did the job of putting the Ranch and Oregon on the map. Osho was now a household name in the US. And maybe, I thought, if the right person saw Osho's portrait, they could be attracted to come and join the caravanserai.

The usual procedure of pasting the articles onto individual sheets, marked with title and date of publication, was quickly abandoned. We decided to file them according to States and created special folders called: Rolls – Ohio, etc. The number of clippings could then be measured by the bulking of the individual folders. In this way I learnt the names of all the states of America.

The acquisition and display of the Rolls-Royces did not go down well with our neighbours and also found a lot of criticism among sannyasins, even those who had been with Osho for many years. Gaveshana, for instance, never came to the Ranch for the festivals because of the cars. Osho's (apparently) absurd ideas had always found a soft spot in my heart. I trusted that behind the absurdities he might have a reason, and if there was no reason, motivation or scheme, they were all the more welcome.

Unfortunately, in the West as well as in the East, spirituality has always been associated with poverty. The picture of a saint living in riches was suspicious from the very start, as if living in hunger and discomfort helped meditation. I knew from my own experience that while fasting I started dreaming about food. It even happened that towards the end of a week of fasting I found myself, a vegetarian for years, staring at a poster showing a raw steak in the butcher's window. I also remember my hippy and penniless friends in Goa who spoke about nothing else than food every minute of the day. I came to the conclusion that it is not possible to meditate or to empty our rich minds and to enjoy life if we have to worry about our basic needs.

Already in Pune journalists had called Osho not only the 'sex guru' but also the 'guru of the rich'. I remember his answer when someone had asked: "Are you not the rich man's guru?"

I am, because only a rich man can come to me. But when I say 'a rich man' I mean one who is very poor inside. When I say 'a rich man' I mean one who is rich in intelligence; I mean one who has got everything that the world can give to him, and has found that it is futile.

Yes, only a rich person can become religious. I am not saying that a poor person cannot become religious, but it is very rare, exceptional. A poor person goes on hoping. A poor person has not known what riches are. He is not yet frustrated with it. How can he go beyond riches if he is not frustrated with them? A poor man also sometimes comes to me, but then he comes for something which I cannot supply. He asks for success. His son is not getting employed; he asks, "Bless him, Osho." His wife is ill, or he is losing money in his business. These are symptoms of a poor man, one who is asking about things of this world. When a rich person comes to me, he has money, he has employment, he has a house, he has health – he has everything that one can have. And suddenly he has come to a realisation that nothing is fulfilling. Then the search for God starts.

Yes, sometimes a poor man can also be religious, but for that, very great intelligence is needed. A rich man, if he is not religious, is stupid. A poor man, if he is religious, is tremendously intelligent. If a poor man is not religious, he has to be forgiven. If a rich man is not religious, his sin is unpardonable.

I am a rich man's guru. Absolutely it is so.

Osho, *The Discipline of Transcendence*, Vol. 3, Ch. 10

The commune on the Ranch was already showing signs of luxury. We had a beautiful mall with elegant restaurants and shops; we had just celebrated the arrival of two Convair CV240s which we all welcomed on the air strip like new babies. The era of holes in our socks was definitely over. But there was talk of even more comfortable houses for us, beautiful clothes, individual cars, the prospect of which made my brain go blank in mid-air. Christianity with its poverty mentality, with its story of the camel and the eye of the needle, was still well ingrained in me. Why should I not deserve the very best? With such a mental attitude how could I aim for enlightenment, which I hear is the ultimate luxury? I am sure that had Rajneeshpuram been a poor, hand-to-mouth, hippy commune there would not have been so much political controversy and hostility from our neighbours.

Not long after the Rolls-Royce press release there was a second one which generated a response of the same magnitude. A meeting was announced one day and everybody was bussed to the Mandir. Osho informed us, through his secretary, that the time of sexual carelessness, now prevalent in this modern age, had ended, because the lives of two thirds of the world's population was threatened by AIDS, a newly-discovered viral disease which had no cure.

Osho offered the following solutions so that we could take responsibility and care for our health:

If you are ready and can drop sex altogether through understanding and without repression, this is the safest protection from the disease.

Or remain with the same partner; merge into the same partner, move more and more into intimacy and less into sexual activity.

Even if you are with one partner, or if you have several partners and choose to have sex, at least make use of the scientific knowledge available: use condoms during the sex act and latex or rubber gloves during foreplay. Oral and anal sex should be completely avoided, since there is no way to protect ourselves from exposure to AIDS.

The final thing is to thoroughly wash yourself after any sexual exposure.

(from a leaflet given out to all Festival participants)

The press release was picked up enthusiastically by the same number of newspapers and, this time, we had to get an altogether new filing cabinet to accommodate the equally bulging folders, now called: AIDS – Ohio, etc. Unfortunately, the world media's enthusiasm did not reflect Osho's concern, but rather ridiculed the prediction. They were happy to have another go at Osho.

In our trailers and houses, in the cabinets beneath the wash basins, next to tampons and spare toilet paper we now had condoms and the latex gloves, which came in two sizes. The women learned how to slip on the condoms as they would, in the end, be the ones who would insist on their use. Even today, AIDS awareness in Third World countries is in the hands of the women, as they are proving to be more responsible and health conscious than men. The introduction of condoms also brought an end to the propagation of other less deadly, but still uncomfortable, venereal diseases, along with the resulting embarrassing tracing procedure which would reveal the names of who else your lover had also entertained. This procedure aimed to limit the number of people catching and passing on the complaint.

The press release, dated March 1984, was strongly ridiculed, although it must have left a mark on the international collective unconscious. Three or four years later these exact same preventative measures were proposed to the public in posters and advertisements all around the world – without, of course, mentioning Osho's initial contribution.

The previous winter, while I was in Switzerland, a booklet called *Rajneeshism: An Introduction to Bhagwan Shree Rajneesh and His Religion* was published by some people (on Sheela's instructions) in Rajneeshpuram. When I saw it later I could not believe my eyes. First of all the word 'Rajneeshism' in the title: I knew how Osho loathed anything with an -ism at the end. The text, which described the celebrations and their dates, with dogmatic values and ideas as if we were a church, reminded me of the Catholic catechism booklet I had to learn by heart when I was a child. The churchy feel was perfectly reflected also in the outer appearance. I remember it as being an unaesthetic little paperback booklet of about 50 pages. There were two editions; one had a red-and-white cover, the other maroon. The text was printed on glossy paper in a calligraphy font. The only way to stomach such a thing was the thought that this publication could have helped Osho receive the status of a 'spiritual leader' which he deserved and which would have given him permanent residency in the States.

In fact, that winter, Osho appeared in Portland for an interview with the INS, the immigration service, with the request that he be granted residence status as a religious teacher (the application was 8,000 pages long and included 3,000 letters of support). And, sannyasins had participated in peaceful demonstrations and presented petitions to US consulates and embassies in all major cities in Germany, UK, Italy, Spain, Holland, Switzerland, Sweden, USA, India, Japan and Australia.

On a clear but cold winter's day I had also marched with my commune friends, carrying posters and heart-shaped balloons, through the streets of Zurich where we caught the attention of journalists and midday shoppers on the Bahnhofstrasse. We ended the procession at the Lindenplatz, nicely warmed up by the steep ascent on the cobble-stoned path, and gathered under the age-old lime trees. We stood there in silence for a while, without making a sound despite the gravel underneath our soles, before we let go of the balloons. They carried the words 'I love Bhagwan' like a flock of pink birds across the Limmat River, over the squat towers of the University and the Polytechnic, slowly gathering height and spreading out over the city. Even my very pragmatic Taurus mind came up with the words: "It's like giving a blessing to the city." It must have been in other people's minds as well as there was total silence until the balloons had disappeared behind the dark woods of the Zürichberg.

Fifteen months after the INS interview Osho was apparently given permission to stay, an occasion we celebrated in the Mandir with chocolate cake and champagne. (I read this from the caption of a photograph I have recently found but I don't remember much of the event.) I say 'apparently' as I had started to mistrust many announcements made by Sheela and feared this celebration was more wishful thinking than a reflection of true facts. I knew that the trouble was not over. Similarly, I only have a vague memory that we eventually destroyed the Rajneeshism booklets in a public book-burning ceremony together with Sheela's 'pope' outfit, a satiny red robe which she had worn for her public appearances.

My friend Nirvano commented on these events during one of his Festival visits with words like: "Historically seen, you see, this is very important. Our master is a real genius! He creates a religion while he is still alive, without waiting for us to do so after he has passed away. And then he destroys it again. In his own lifetime! Even if we were foolish enough to create a religion out of his words we could not do so as he has created and destroyed it already. The possibility is gone."

Or is it that Osho had not even seen the booklet and Sheela's robe? I do not know.

In Pune, on the terrace outside our room we have a few old wicker chairs. They have lost all paint and lustre but are comfortable enough to relax in after work. I bring out a pillow and sink into it. Above me are the fronds of a poinciana. I always wonder at the contrast between its dense canopy of tiny confetti-sized leaves (which drop in their millions in winter), its height and girth (it shades our terrace which is two storeys up) and its big, orange star-like flowers. Some flowers have fallen and I arrange them in a pattern on the old coffee-table in front of me. In the distance I hear the music of the Kundalini Meditation which I have missed because of a latecomer in the shop, but this view also counts as meditation: high above in the sky the kites are coming together to bathe in the last rays of the sun and take advantage of the last upwind of the day. They circle higher and higher in the company of each other, yet each one enjoying its flight alone. I wish to believe that they fly up there out of sheer pleasure and delight. In this they are so like sannyasins.

7

Worship

Temples and Gachchhamis

How I came to get my next job I don't remember: carwash girl at the
gas station. In those days we were no longer working in a 'department' but in a 'temple' – to keep up with the 'religious' twang! So my
'temple' was named after Buddha's son, Rahul. This was the gas
station where we filled all the vehicles with gas (without paying, of
course). I was equipped with a straw hat, Wellington boots and a
high pressure water gun to wash off mud. There was a lot of splashing on legs and arms, but the hot desert sun soon dried it all off. I
enjoyed sculpting the dried mud off the wheel arches of the pickup
trucks with this magical tool and transforming neglected brown
trucks into sparkling, colourful vehicles. What a wonderful job I had!
But I was naive not to hide my smile – that of a cat who had got the
cream – when a few 'moms' walked past! A few hours later I was
called into the office and was told that from tomorrow on I was going
to be 'Gemini'. This was code-name of the operator at the radio base
of our taxi service.

The taxi fleet consisted of the pickup trucks in which the first
Ranch residents travelled from their homes to join the commune.
They had now become assets of the commune. Some were bulky,
with a row of lights even above the windshield; others were smaller
with only three-litre engines. Quite often top and bottom had different colours. The only thing they had in common was that they all had
a number, marked in bold black transfers, on the side of the bonnet.

Bhagawati, who was leaving the post in order to help out the
Twinkies at Mirdad Welcome Centre, showed me the key hooks, each

marked with a number. If a key wasn't there, I would see that the driver had not yet come back to base and I was to wait for their return. "Most drivers have their preferred car but this should not be a standard rule," she said. In the various columns of the logbook I had to write the date and time, name of requester, starting point, destination and then the number of the car to which I had assigned the job. There was also space for annotations like 'long-haul' and 'number of passengers'.

In order to understand the conversation across the static of the radio, we had adopted an already existing code language where, for example, 10-4 meant OK. People requesting a taxi called me with "Gemini come in," a sentence I had to intercept among all the other radio conversations that were being held between crew leaders scattered all over the Ranch.

In my eyes, the boys carrying a motorola were the 'cool' guys (although the expression 'cool' was not widely in use back then) – until I tried to have a more personal conversation with one of them outside the garage. His radio overpowered our words and his attention was constantly distracted by incoming calls. Many of my friends' names still end in my head with '...come in', like 'Sumir come in' and 'Premgit come in', because so many times I'd heard their names in this phrase.

It did not take me long to realise that there were not enough taxis for the many requests which came in to 'Gemini', e.g. a repaired saw from the tool shop had to go to the 'top of the Ranch' which was almost halfway to Antelope; a compressor from Mahakashyapa to Zarathustra, a food order delivery from Magdalena dock to the 'tea mama' downtown, the whole pipe crew with their gear to be transported to the next project's location... Only rarely did I hear the taxi drivers call me back. I had a picture in my mind where the different taxis were heading and where they might be and managed to add a few extra pick-ups on the fly. It was like playing chess and I was delighted when I could cross a few extra runs from the list in this way. Quite often people had to wait a couple of hours but this could not be avoided. Most of the time I took their complaints personally, as if I were responsible for their irritation. This exhausted me, adding emotional stress to the job.

'Gemini' was a lone figure: sitting on a high bar stool, facing a wall, log book on a narrow ledge, swamped by the grey noise of a radio mounted above her on the wall. There were no friends to chat with or look into the eyes of. The drivers appeared only briefly in the morning to get their keys and in the evening when, wordlessly, they threw them back onto my ledge. I was under the impression that nobody in this world would have wanted to swap their job with mine but, on the other hand, I was sure that the person before me had coped much much better. At night, I walked out of there like a tired warrior, but still felt a hero, because I could say to myself: "I made it again!"

Then Durga (the 'Kali' I already knew from Mariam Canteen) was appointed to be the 'mom' of the garage. I was used to making decisions by myself for the smooth running of the taxi service, mainly because decisions had to be made instantly. Now things became more complicated: Durga wanted to have her say, even in small matters, but on the other hand she dismissed me each time I wanted to ask her something. She called it 'pestering'. It was a real *koan* to work this way, one of those no-win situations Zen masters used to set up for their disciples.

I was torn between my customers to whom I wanted to offer an efficient service and the prospect of waiting for the appropriate time to ask my questions. I must have expressed my frustration quite loudly because one day I was called into the office by top 'mom', Su, to discuss the matter. Not much of a discussion; it was rather an inquisition. The office was stuffy and, to my surprise, crowded with another five or six moms from other temples, as well as Durga herself, all looking at me. I had taken a seat near the door and saw everybody just as dark silhouettes against the bright light streaming in from the window: an invisible court of judges. What I said in my defence I do not remember, but the fear I felt is hard to forget. I would not have been sent to the gallows, but I could have been asked to leave the Ranch which, for me, would have been the same as death, if not worse. The verdict of the session was that I was to attend Dynamic for a week. Meditation as a punishment!

One day, at tea time, I was drawn, as if by invisible threads, to go for coffee at the Multiversity. This was just across the street but not within my 'territory'. Next to the coffee shop there was a small boutique which had a display cabinet full of crystals as these items were now coming into fashion. I instinctively pointed to one of the crystals and asked, "How much?" It was a useless question as I had no money in my account but the shopkeeper, a lady from Chile and an old acquaintance of mine, simply offered to pay for it from her own card. The crystal, which was later analysed and reported to be a very special specimen (it has marks from Atlantis, can you imagine?) became my mascot next to my radio.

Once again I am sitting with Amiten on the marble bench across from the bookshop in the Pune commune. With a paper napkin we wipe dry the marble which is damp from the drops that have found their way through the cracks of the corrugated roof. People seeing me here at night might think I cannot have enough of the shop but, for once, I am not concerned about what they think of me. I am getting used to being exposed. Is there another working place in the Resort more exposed than the bookshop, in the main street, with windows on three sides? I now understand why my predecessors tried to hide behind heavily-draped window decorations. But there is nowhere to duck behind: the shop mirrors the people working there just as the cakes used to mirror the awareness, or lack of it, in our old M.G. Road bakery. The bookshop is my baby and I love it. It is my place, my offering to Osho, the gift of my energy to him. This sounds very altruistic, but this offering makes me feel just great.

In the decoration studio we found a 4x4-foot board advertising the millennium celebration of the previous year, and under Amiten's brushes it turned into a moon reflecting its white light in the sea. It fits perfectly with Shunyo's blue and silver cover design for the new edition of *The Osho Upanishad*, a collection of discourses given in 1986 in Mumbai, and the best place for it is the corner window facing the main gate. A pile of books, some lying flat, some standing up, complete the composition. It is Harito's idea to let the shoppers serve themselves directly from the window display instead of searching for the books on the shelves. The big white moon on the painting invites people from as far as the main gate as it shines under the halogen spotlights from underneath the darkness of the *mandaps*, the temporary monsoon roofs we set up during rainy season.

We suddenly understand why so many sannyasins have turned up today. We realise it is full moon – although it is hidden behind heavy clouds – and not just any full moon but the traditional Guru Purnima, the master's full moon. The visitors come to pay tribute to their master from faraway villages – but this year they do not find the traditional marigold garlands on the main gate.

The four festivals which had been the highlights of so many years in my life as a sannyasin are no longer celebrated. The motto is: 'Every day is a celebration'. At a recent department meeting we were told that we need to accept these changes. Due to the reduction of work opportunities in the West and the higher exchange rates of the Indian rupee, travellers can no longer come and stay for months and years at a time as they used to. They now come and stay for a few weeks at most and it would be quite a coincidence if this week fell exactly on one of our celebrations. This all made sense to me as I knew this from talking to many visitors while serving them in the shop. Nevertheless, I am pleased that, by coincidence, we are inviting people to the Resort on an un-celebrated Guru Purnima day with a painting of a full moon!

During the meeting I was also amazed to hear that – according to the people at the welcome centre – nobody is in search of a master. This had been the main driving force which had brought my generation to travel all the way to India.

The Resort wants to emphasise Osho's message and his

meditations rather than Osho as a master: *We* have to make the effort and do the meditations – no guru, alive or dead, can do this for us. The Resort wants to be a modern and attractive place where meditation, relaxation and play are offered to the young, intelligent traveller and it certainly does not want to become a place for pilgrimage and worship of a deceased Indian guru.

Today I found this excerpt:

This always happens: when I say something, I create two groups of people around me. One group will be exoteric. They will organize, they will do many things concerned with society, with the world that is without; they will help preserve whatsoever I am saying.

The other group will be more concerned with the inner world. Sooner or later the two groups are bound to come in conflict with one another because their emphasis is different.

The inner group, the esoteric mind, is concerned with something quite different from the exoteric group. And, ultimately, the outer group will win, because they can work as a group. The esoteric ones cannot work as a group; they go on working as individuals. When one individual is lost, something is lost forever.

This happens with every teacher. Ultimately the outer group becomes more and more influential; it becomes an establishment. The first thing an establishment has to do is to kill its own esoteric part, because the esoteric group is always a disturbance. Because of 'heresy', Christianity has been destroying all that is esoteric.

And now the pope is at the opposite extreme to Jesus: this is the ultimate schism between the exoteric and the esoteric. The pope is more like the priests who crucified Jesus than like Jesus himself. If Jesus comes again, he will be crucified in Rome this time — by the Vatican.
The Vatican is the exoteric, organizational part, the establishment.

These are intrinsic problems — they happen, and you cannot do anything about it.

Osho, *The Great Challenge*, Ch. 9

I am glad that the outward-oriented people have been taking

care of this place in such a beautiful way but, of course, the change in the presentation of Osho's work has not gone down well with many Indian sannyasins with longstanding key positions in the commune. Many have left, not without voicing their protest internationally. Many western sannyasins, on the other hand, escaped to Goa where they 'grumble' about Pune.

But for us there are more tangible things that we grumble about, still sitting here on the cold marble bench: e.g. the Cappuccino bar is now a smoking zone after White Robe Meditation. Amiten hates smoke. We used to spend our evenings there chatting with friends, but this is no longer possible. Quite strange because there is already talk in some countries that they want to ban smoking in public places. I grumble about the loud music in the bar which is not only disturbing our sleep in the room on the roof but also the meditations in Buddha Hall. I will have to give up running Gourishankar Meditation on Thursdays because I am tired of having to walk out of the hall and ask the barman each time to turn down the thumping house music during the silent stage. (As I mentioned before, Buddha Hall is actually just a big tent with mosquito netting around it.) When I complained about the problem in the main office the comment was: "Do not make a difference in value between meditation and enjoyment at the bar, between the Buddha and the Zorba." 'There are so many places in the world where music and booze are offered, but not so many with meditation,' I thought to myself and walked out.

Here I go off on a tangent about being considered an 'old' person here. This comes as a surprise as, while living in the West and mingling with mostly young people, I never felt that I was from a different generation. All my young Reiki students have accepted me as their equal. Here in the Resort I was told that those who used to sit in the front rows have had to stop sitting there, except for Greek Mukta who still sits on her spot, so as not to give the impression of a grey-haired establishment! I still love to sit in front as the atmosphere is much calmer and people do not tend to lie down and snore during the video discourse, but then my hair is not that grey yet...

My grumbling goes on about my job: to run the bookshop turns out to be much more difficult than I had thought it would be. It is not so much the problem of not getting audio and video tapes ready on time before people leave, and their bad sound and picture quality, but rather the problems with the staff. They have never read a book by Osho and, if I am lucky, have just tried Dynamic once. Our working methods and attitude are miles apart. I like to constantly keep the place nice and tidy, aesthetic, and filled with books; they like to sit at the cashier's desk and wait for the customers to come to them.

To encourage people to participate in the Resort as workers, a residential programme was devised a year ago. It was first started during the quieter monsoon time and then extended to the whole year. Some of the group rooms are set up as dormitories with partitions and some of the old session rooms are allocated to the programme. It is open to the 'oldies' like us, but also to those turning up at the gates and enrolling on the spur of the moment. Some of these newcomers are my colleagues now.

Just today I was left alone in the shop for the whole day while one of the people working with me suddenly decided to change her job. (I assumed that she had wanted to escape my perfectionism – but she confided in me later that she just didn't want to be exposed to the public for the whole day seven days a week.) And the other, a young man who has just broken up with his wife, called me from his home saying that he wants to take his life (he came back after a few days as if nothing had happened, in case you are wondering).

At this point Amiten reminds me of the good times I also had in the shop: the charm and playfulness of my first helper – she was from Mexico; then the charm of Naman, a young man from Germany who helped me choose Osho's photographs (both attracted lots of male and female customers to the shop!); the silent presence of our 'old man', a retired businessman who took care of the audio and video orders with such grace; the wisdom of Amit, Osho's youngest brother, always ready to help out on Sundays and during the Indian holidays.

Although I feel very attached to the shop I start thinking about it in the past tense. Is my time in the bookshop over?

It is difficult for me to recall events of my life in a sequence, like a flow in time. Rather I see them as a slide show – not necessarily in the right sequence – with the brightest pictures at the front and some more blurred ones, with less distinct colours, floating around them.

The slides from the Ranch time are grouped in 'places of worship' and in one of them I see myself as a taxi driver (…but cannot remember who my 'Gemini' was). As the pickups were not assigned to any particular driver, every morning the surprise was to see which car one would get. But one car became faithful to me, 'Onethreeone,' an old battered red and white truck which was certainly a 'she' and not only because in English vehicles are referred to as female. She became so much part of me that I knew her dimensions as if they were my own body, managing to back up into narrow spaces leaving merely fractions of inches on both sides of the tailgate.

Then follows a slide of myself in a shiny brand-new pickup truck. We had bought a fleet of trucks, all of the same dark brown colour. They had been driven in from Ohio where some of my friends had gone to collect them. The old colourful pickups were still around, but they had been given to crews so that they could move their gear from place to place without waiting around. It made me happy whenever I saw them and each time I heard their 'name', or rather number, in my head.

With my shiny new taxi I see myself stuck in the mud in front of the soon-to-be hotel. It had been raining and the slimy mud around the construction site was knee-deep. The shell of the building was almost complete, but there was a lot of work still to be done inside. We wanted to complete the building as soon as possible and everybody who still had a sound back was recruited to Chuang Tzu, the construction temple. We were expecting to receive the final 'halt' to construction from the government at any moment. This would make all construction after that date illegal. In the interim we built as many projects as we could – and as fast as we could. We did not expect the houses to be actually bulldozed down once they were built but, in hindsight, this could very well have been possible.

Stuck in the car, I had a moment to take in the scene in front of me. I could see the dark brown wooden panels of the outside walls and the mud of a different shade of brown. The whole picture was dotted with red specks. These were the sannyasins working on and around the building. Each square inch of my vision was filled with at least five red dots, like those pictures in children's books where gnomes are all over the place. Someone was climbing up a ladder to the second floor with a toolbox, someone else was squeezing past that ladder with a big piece of sheetrock and someone on the same landing was fixing, on his knees, the floorboards with a nail gun. If you repeat this scene fifteen times and include the roof where a whole crew was fixing the final insulation, you will get the image I was seeing!

Not only was my truck stuck in the mud, but I had to give the electric saw I had in the back to Swami Chinmaya. How was I to find him? Was he maybe one of the carpenters I could see through one of the windows, the ones putting up the wall beams? Whom to ask? Who was in charge of this whole place? I felt helpless and desperate and close to tears.

How this situation got resolved, if I eventually found the recipient or took the saw back to 'Gemini' or who pulled me out of the mud I do not remember. But I remember another time when I got stuck with my same taxi. It was in deep snow, high up in a remote location of the Alan Watts A-frames. To the rescue came Arvind, our driving instructor who, at the test, made us drive in reverse through a maze of stacked tyres and who taught us to never leave the car doors ajar. He was an imposing personality, still a samurai in his gait, and I felt terribly embarrassed to have to be rescued by him. Luckily my tears had dried up by the time he had arrived.

Once a month there was a night shift. 'Gemini' closed down

before dinner but some of the regular errands could be done at night following a detailed schedule. With the job came the keys to several vans and trucks for the various tasks. One of the brand-new passenger vans for the Ranch tours was the ideal vehicle for picking up visitors from Reception to take them to their individual celebration tents. I vividly remember the arrival of lovely Nishi, teacher Tushir's girlfriend, who had arrived on her own from Switzerland. The moment she slipped on the slope from the road to the field I remembered that I should have held her by the arm. She had such a natural way of behaving that I had forgotten she was blind. She must have recognised me from my voice.

Experience told me not to use the fancy van on my next assignment which was to pick up guards from the 'top of the Ranch' at the end of their late shift: they would trash it out with wrappers, crisps and muddy boots. The old blue van used by the Twinkies, which had done its time by then, was good enough for this wild and loud bunch. They only quietened down when Arjuna, a great baritone trained in opera singing, told the story of the ghost. One night this ghost was apparently standing at the roadside, on the county road down which we were driving. He even showed us the exact spot where he had seen it. "It had empty white eyes."

Then, switching to a pickup truck, I collected the plastic bins full of used tablecloths from the back of Nagarjuna restaurant at the Mall and, saying goodnight to one of the waitresses who was closing up, drove the washing to one of the laundry trailers and placed the bins on the deck ready to be washed first thing in the morning. Except for the guards, to whom I brought very welcome late-night snacks in central and more remote posts, there was nobody around. The disco had closed at midnight, the last bus had done its final round – I was the only one roaming about.

On the back porch of the restaurant I had caught myself re-arranging the bins so that they were ready for the morning shift, as if I were going to be part of that shift. I actually did not even know anyone working at the restaurant – I was there just to take the full bins to the laundry. In the night the Ranch did not feel divided into different temples and I felt part of the Ranch as a whole. It was all my home, my ground; it was all under my care.

There were the dark moonless nights which had their own appeal and the mystical full moon nights with glittering ponds and black hills. The coolness of the air mixing with the warmth from the soil. Headlights on the dusty roads. Silence when I stopped the truck. I was alone, at home, with Osho close by.

Driving at night brought me the pleasure of meeting an owl who flew along the road for a long distance in front of my headlights. And my first sight of a raccoon. Of course, at the time I did not know it was a raccoon. I had not even heard the word before, nor seen a picture of the creature. From behind, it looked like a big cat with a very heavy gait (but we had no pets on the Ranch so where would a cat come from?) and when it turned round I saw the masked face. At dinner before my shift the next day I asked Rashid, an ornithologist and gardener, about it. He knew everything about birds so he might also know about unknown furry friends and so I described my encounter. "This was a raccoon! How fantastic, we have a raccoon on the Ranch, they have come now!" he exclaimed enthusiastically. Later, in a school book, I saw a (daylight) picture of a raccoon which confirmed my sighting.

When the hills thought that it had been dark for long enough they brightened up under the first rays of the sun slanting into the valleys at slight angles. The schedule got busier again, jumping from pickup truck to fancy passenger van and from fancy van to battered van, as if jumping from one horse to another. The many sets of keys made my trouser pockets bulge. People arrived from afar and needed accommodation, a new shift of guards was brought to the 'top of the Ranch'. My twelve-hour shift was over. Breakfast – then home to bed.

The pictures of the living spaces are on different slide shows, vivid pictures, but difficult to combine with the worship pictures. Where was I working when I was living on Nirvana Road? I remember walking to the trailer from downtown in the middle of the night as there was no bus service on that road. Nirvana Road had been specially built for Osho to drive from his house straight onto the county road without passing through the centre of town and we generally avoided driving on that road. He always used it on his return from the drive, but on his way out preferred to take the downtown road so that he could greet us along the way.

I shared the room with Aruna, an Indian sannyasin, who had just taken a course at the Multiversity. A set of tarot cards had just been published illustrating the many parables Osho used to tell us in his discourses. Aruna enjoyed giving me readings on the floor between our two mattresses, practising what she had learnt. One day she also told me that a tree along Nirvana Road was talking to people... I thought she was now completely over the top with her esoteric experiments.

On my way home next day I was indeed called back by a voice or pulled by little invisible fingers as if tugging at my T-shirt. I looked back and saw the trees lining the pond – the dam made by the beavers – but nobody else. The leaves of one of the willow trees danced in the sunrays in a particularly lively manner. Suddenly it felt like I was being embraced by grandmother: a soft and warm feeling. I thought that maybe Osho liked that tree in particular and looked at it when he drove by, but these were just rationalisations. Nevertheless, every day on my walk home I stopped at the tree and bathed in the lovely feeling. I started to call that energy 'the squaw's grandmother' because it would have been too much to think that it was my own grandmother wanting to say hello.

Then finally I was also called up to join Chuang Tzu temple. For me, it was the foundation crew. Saguna I knew from old Pune and so had a point of reference in him. We were going to prepare the holes for the stilts of the townhouses. This new project was a set of two-storied houses on the bank of the creek near Osho's house and another set in the little valley to the left. When I first heard that we were going to build houses so close to his residence I was touched that Osho wanted to have us so close to him.

The holes had been dug out by a machine with a huge screw similar to a giant's bottle opener. They now needed to be emptied of grit so that the concrete would touch hard soil. The holes were six feet deep and barely over two feet wide – I would not fit into one of them with my increased circumference at the time of this writing! With old Nescafé tins, we scraped the bottom and collected the loose soil; then standing up, heaved the full tin to someone above who then dumped the earth for us. Some holes were so deep that it took two people to lift the person out of them. This showed how much trust we had in each other. Before we went for a tea break, or for lunch, someone always made a round to make sure nobody was left behind down a hole. While sipping tea and eating an apple we discovered that everybody in our crew was thrilled by working so deep in the earth and that nobody was frightened by the tight space. We then realised that all members of the crew had either their sun-sign or ascendant in Scorpio or had Pluto in a dominant position. Esotericism was catching up.

The daily *gachchhamis* before and after work had been introduced after a general meeting held in the Mandir. We already knew the melody and the words from the celebrations. The salutation was to be directed towards Osho, which meant that we had to work out the direction of Osho's house, a bit like knowing where Mecca is. 'Oh, well, why not,' I thought – until I could not live without doing them. The kitchen workers and the mechanics did their *gachchhamis* on the clean linoleum floors in their temples, the pipe crew in the fields wherever they happened to be and the vegetable-pickers outside, still in the dark, on the loading bay.

With the foundation crew we reached corners of the valleys where we had never been before, but where houses were now going to be built. I remember one evening when we knelt down for the *gachchhamis* with a wonderful view of the main valley below. We were tired, exhausted, but felt as high as kites. Before the *gachchhamis* I was appointed to say the few usual reminders, but that evening there was only a 'Thank you!' which came out and I knew that it reflected the feeling of everyone in the team.

After a few weeks we came back to the same holes but this time as the concrete crew. In the meantime each hole was provided with four rebars neatly tied together on the top. I was aware, as anyone else was, that if I fell into one of these holes I wouldn't just fall into a hole but would find myself speared like a sausage. Another danger we became aware of, and not only through the admonition of our crew leader, was that the chute of the concrete truck, if unattended, moved sideways and could hit our heads and knock us over. In this dangerous situation we bonded very tightly as our lives depended on the awareness and care of our companions, a bit like, I imagine, being in a platoon during combat.

If we noticed that our attention was drifting or someone had their thoughts wandering, we came together in a circle, closed our eyes and started humming. This brought us back to the present and to our holes. Our crew leader was Samiyo, a journalist from Canada, then we had Gandharva, a dentist from Italy, Hari Chetana, the actress from Germany with whom I had shared the girls' room in Saswad, and Navanita, a happy girl from New Zealand whom I knew from the disco dance floor. Nowhere else in the world would these people have come together like this nor would they ever have dreamt about having anything to do with concrete. Not even the dentist! Hari Chetana, who remained fashion conscious in all situations, introduced the feminine look on the site: the girls always wore pretty pink scarves around their necks in interesting contrast with the heavy boots caked with concrete.

Even the truck driver, Deepesh, a soft-spoken lad from Germany, was dressed up in nice t-shirts. His concrete truck could be seen from a distance with its rotating red and white drum. We often had to adjust our lunch and tea breaks to his arrival, and sometimes even missed out on the drive-bys. At lunch we had to ask other crews to keep some sandwiches aside for us. (Since we started with the building crunch, the lunches were no longer in Magdalena Cafeteria but sandwiches, drinks and fruit were brought onto the sites to save time in unnecessary travel.)

Deepesh constantly tried to perfect his driving, day after day, and managed to reverse into the building site and avoid the holes by a few inches only. Usually Samiyo was the one giving him directions using the side mirrors. Thumb to the right or thumb to the left – and a grisly swipe with all fingers across the neck was the signal for him to stop.

Gandharva was on the rake, pulling the concrete from the chute or stopping the flow when the hole was full. I was on the 'vibrator', an eight-foot mechanical snake with a motor at the top. Its job was to bring the air bubbles to the surface and so compact the concrete. I had to slowly lift it while the concrete was poured in and make sure to switch it off just in time when it reached the top, unless I wanted to spray everyone with fresh concrete. After a short time we all perfected the job to an art, with perfect 'fillings' and without a spill. We often looked back onto the site and with a smile of accomplishment for a job well done, said to each other: "Not a spill in sight."

The next job for the foundation crew was to build the moulds for the pillars which were going to go on top of the plugs we had already filled with concrete. The moulds were made from four wooden planks so this was my opportunity to learn how to use hammer and nails. Not only had the nails to go in straight, which was an accomplishment in itself, but – the further challenge – in as few hits as possible, and without smashing one's fingers, of course.

We filled the moulds with concrete as we had filled the holes in the ground and when the pillars had set, we took the moulds off using the claw side of the hammer to remove the nails. This made an eerie sound reminiscent of a horror movie music track. After a good clean, the planks were reused for the pillars of the next set of houses.

We were fortunate that it was dry season. We preferred to work in dust rather than in mud – at least that was my choice – but with the dryness came a tremendous heat, as if the sun wanted to bake the life out of rocks and humans. As a personal present from Osho we had received straw hats with the invitation to wear them at all times. To drink four pints of water a day was also suggested by the medical staff.

Once the steel I-bars were lifted onto the foundation pillars (a back-breaking job done by another crew), a wooden beam had to be fixed to the steel as a connection to the floors to come. This was the job of Azad, a short, rugged and brooding man with a red complexion. Apparently he needed an assistant and that was going to be me. My job was to place the beams on top of the I-bars ahead of him so that he could just walk along the beams and shoot in the nails. We had our own truck which pulled our yellow compressor. The most precious asset was the high-powered Hilty nail gun which he stored in its immaculate bright red metal box. Needless to say, I was quite impressed by the power of this deadly weapon which could pierce a steel I-bar, and I knew not to distract him during his work. This made me feel quite lonely as he would not talk during our tea breaks either and I started missing my old companions. One day I quenched my thirst with a few cups of orange juice which had been brought to the site for refreshment. From a deep-frozen state they had melted and must have turned bad during the few hours under the blaring sun – and I suppose I was not aware enough to notice that the drinks were off.

Soon my guts responded in a violent fashion and I was taken to the medical ward by my new team leader, Bharti, who had been called to the site by radio. More people must have drunk from the same orange juice batch, I thought, because the head nurse, Puja, was called in to see me. Instead of having my stomach pumped out, I was shown in to the lady gynaecologist. I knew very well the location of my female organs and my guts and how they felt when ill, but Puja insisted that my pain was to be attributed to some monthly occurrence. This felt very odd. I was taken to the ward and given a few tablets but the pain did not ease off. During the night the spasms occurred every ten minutes – which I scientifically followed on my watch. Despite the moans and screams which I did not manage to suppress, nobody was woken up. Everybody was too sound asleep to hear anything – all recuperating from months of heavy physical work.

I was, however, better the next morning and Bharti picked me up and introduced me to the firewall crew. He explained the purpose of the job: "If more than two houses are built in a row (of so-and-so-many cubic feet), then we need to build a double wall between the second and third house to prevent fire from spreading. That's why these walls are called firewalls." He was the architect of the pre-fabricated townhouses and was responsible for the planning of these details. I heard him say many times in his melodious South African lilt: "I am so happy to be up and about, away from my drawing table, seeing if the things I had thought out really work in practice." Not only was his knowledge an asset to our crew, but so also were his physical attributes. He was slim, long-limbed and over six feet tall and, best of all, he was ambidextrous: he could whack in a nail to the right, or to the left, at heights nobody else could reach. This often spared us from building an extra platform.

The wobbly scaffolding with the worn, narrow, only foot-wide beam did not inspire much confidence in me. I was happy to cut the sheetrock on the ground with my sturdy grey Stanley knife (without ripping the protective paper) and pass the sheets up to those working on the platform or – on a new firewall – fix the first sheets on the ground floor with broad-capped nails. An extra hit made them disappear into the sheet.

Deepesh, whose concrete truck was garaged now that the foundations had been laid for all the townhouses, was also part of the firewall crew. I am not sure how he managed to persuade me to venture up onto the platform one day. Afraid of losing my balance, I was holding on to the blindingly white wall and looked down, past my brown boots, to the ground which seemed miles away. The platform was shaking with the movements not only of my tentative steps but also of the tread of Deepesh and of Niravo at the other end. Whatever his words were, they were of understanding and love, giving me absolute confidence that I could do it. I started to smile; I was so tremendously happy and proud of myself that I had gone up there at least this one time and I knew that, even after I had left, there would be no stupid boyish talk and laughter behind my back. This is real love. I am in tears while writing this. Only in a commune like ours could this have happened.

Soon the half-dozen firewalls had been built and we moved on to a new part of the construction process. In hindsight I am amazed at how well the whole project was coordinated: there had never been a day when we had to wait around before a job could be started – everything flowed smoothly from one job to another. Our next assignment was to paint and apply, on the outside walls, the bonding strips around the windows that would keep the rain from seeping in and nail on eight-inch fascia below the roofs. It was clear to everybody that I was going to do all the windows of the ground floors first and that the boys were going to do the fascia, but once the windows of the ground floors were done I could not escape having to climb ladders.

Once I had learnt to use the nail gun, the caulking gun (which was kept at the correct temperature in a 'warm box' between uses) and was comfortable in leaning over on both sides of the ladder, it was easy to extend the ladder a little bit further to reach the second floor. But when I had to move to another window, I took the time to climb down the ladder and reposition it under the next window. The boys, on the other hand, just 'walked' their ladder over rough ground, holding onto the roof with their hands while their nail guns dangled from the ladder.

When two more girls, and a new extension ladder, joined the crew, we organised ourselves in such a way that one person painted the lattices on the ground, a second person passed the lattices to the person on top who nailed them to the windows; and the last person did the caulking. It does not add up mathematically to make three, but it worked in practice. It felt like a dance. (One of the girls was from Brazil!)

One day our crew received a tool cart similar to a cart you would find in a farmers' market, with four wheels and a wide serving/storage area. This one had in the middle, between the two uprights which held up the canvas roof, a set of drawers for small hand tools and nails – and it could be locked up at night (crews would steal tools from each other…). I was meant to be the 'tool mama' and take care of it. Bharti thought this would be just the right thing for me, something on the ground.

It is true, I always liked to arrange, sort and store things in jars like an apothecary, but this time I was reluctant to accept the new assignment as by now I preferred the work high up on the ladders! I remember Bharti standing next to me disappointed to see my disappointed expression on my face.

Thanks to working in Chuang Tzu I had not only lost my fear of ladders but also of mud. It had rained heavily and the ground around the houses had turned into deep, slimy, slippery muck. We were all given yellow outfits with a pointy hood. I was safe from the rain, but the mud from the boots stuck on the rungs of the ladders and then the ladder caked my hands and my outfit with mud from top to toe. It was such a desperate situation for a city girl like me that there was no choice but to accept it as part of life and relax. And so I was healed of another aversion.

Our insulating touches to the windows were the last jobs on the outside of the townhouses, apart from the roofing. It was time to dedicate ourselves to the inside as well, so our crew moved on to building the bathrooms. This was welcome to all as it was getting colder and some shelter, even without heating, was a good thing to have. As usual I suffered from cold feet and complained very bitterly until Bharti, out of desperation, bought me a pair of blue insulated boots. One day it snowed – to the delight of Niravo, our middle-aged Aussie, who had never seen snow except in pictures. He did not work for the whole day as he made snowballs, hiding inside unfinished houses and targeting whoever came down our road. It was again the Wild West in Oregon. But soon rumour spread that it was dangerous down our way and Niravo's source of targets dried up.

It took some coordination to manoeuvre the eight-foot beams into the tight spaces which would be the bathrooms, but it eventually became second nature – like using chopsticks for noodles. One day it dawned on me that I must have developed 'tennis elbow' because each hammer hit was excruciatingly painful. I kept it a secret as I did not want to move on to another job; I would have missed my crew too much. But as things happen around Osho, the next morning Indian Mukta came to see Bharti and me and told us that there was a job they would like me to do: to be a hostess on the buses to Portland. Bharti was happy for me and suggested I should accept (also because of my cold feet…). Mukta instructed me to go, then and there, to the uniform temple and get my new outfit (it would be the mauve trousers and a light pink blouse which the guards and the Twinkies were now wearing). I should then be at RBG garage in the morning at 8am. I had not left the Ranch for a while and the idea of getting out of the confined bathrooms into more open spaces became suddenly very alluring.

The journey to Portland, after the steep ascent from the bottom of our valleys, was indeed through very open spaces. Everything seemed big – the vast flat desert with the few ghost towns and then the impressive Cascade Mountains. Even the mountains seemed to be bigger in America than anywhere else.

As so many times in the past, as a tour guide with Danzas in Lugano or Autostradale in Milan, here I was again sitting in the front of a coach with a friendly driver on my left, a rumbling engine below and a microphone in my hand. This time I also had to serve refreshments on the hoof. Not yet knowing where the road would straighten up, I stumbled over the passengers while serving them their neatly boxed snacks. Some were acquaintances from Switzerland returning home with tears in their eyes and some were workers back on duty at Hotel Rajneesh in Portland.

Our only stop on our almost 4-hour drive was on the Columbia River, a river as wide as a lake, severed at intervals by hydroelectric dams. There was a rest area with toilets and space for parking the coach, and there were seagulls to feed. The seagulls were huge compared to those I knew from Lake Geneva, but, unlike those, they were not able to catch pieces of bread in midair! Our air-conditioned coach was good-looking, standing there waiting for her passengers, clad in grey aluminium like the Greyhound buses, but with a big red 'Rajneesh Buddhafield Transport' on its side. The damp coolness made everyone come back to the coach without having to be called.

We dropped everyone at Hotel Rajneesh, helping with their luggage, and then parked the coach in a side street. The rest of the day was all mine. I finally had the opportunity to spend my very last savings on a pair of proper boots: Canadian Sorel boots! Many on the

Ranch wore them and I had envied these people for their warm feet. Now I was also going to be one of those lucky ones.

I was also pleased with the look of them and back at the hotel I walked up and down the room, admiring them in the long mirror on the wall. I particularly liked the white fur collar peeking out over the top. In the shop I had been shown how to pull out the insoles to air them and how to waterproof the leather part which was not sealed in rubber. I placed them next to my mattress on the soft carpeted floor so that I could see them first thing when I woke up, as I used to do as a child with all my Christmas presents.

The next morning new arrivals had already boarded the bus with anticipation in their eyes. These were people who had meditated in one of the many meditation centres we had around the world and were going to attend courses at the Multiversity; or the fortunate ones who had been invited to come and participate in the project as workers. Sometimes these were friends from the old ashram in India.

There were many I had to promise to sit next to once we were on our way, as they wanted to be filled in with details of all the changes on the Ranch. We also had on board the band that played in our Club in Portland during the week. They were now going back for a break on the Ranch. Satyarthi drummed fervently on a pad strapped onto his left knee in time to music he heard over his headphones. Milarepa and the rest of the musicians caught up with some much-needed sleep.

So now on the return journey we admired Mount St. Helens towering over the Columbia River – I was impressed to hear it was a volcano as it stood so serene and grand under its layers of snow – and stopped at Multnomah Falls. The story goes that an Indian maiden had jumped from the rocks, sacrificing herself to relieve her people of a deadly disease and, as a sign that the sacrifice was accepted, the Great Spirit had created the waterfall. It is said that sometimes the maiden comes back and is seen among the trees. From under the fine drizzling of moisture in the air the Falls is so awesome that it's easy to imagine seeing her standing there.

Up along the Deschutes River we reached the dried-out high

plateau en route to Madras, Redmond and Bend. But we turned left at a bent and battered sign saying 'Antelope' (it appears people in the West use road signs for their shooting practice). Travelling through abandoned towns and more barren land we finally reached the town we had 'taken over', where we made a quick stop at our Zorba the Buddha Café. As we climbed up the hills again I looked back at Antelope and was reminded of how small and insignificant a place it was compared to the big hoo-ha the newspapers made out of it. And the long and bumpy journey from Antelope to Rajneeshpuram reminded me of how far we were from anywhere. We were really living in the sticks!

The newcomers descended at Mirdad – the new pyramid-shaped Welcome Centre which had sprung up next to the Multiversity – into the care of Sarita and Rosalie, whilst the musicians hopped on a bus for an early dinner at Magdalena. I helped the driver wash and clean the coach, ready for the next morning's trip. A good dance at the disco was the best way to end the day.

With my face still hot from dancing I walked home along Nirvana Road. It was pitch black but I knew the road by heart. I was in high spirits, delighted to be walking in the dark, feeling the freshness of the air, the expansion of the valley and the blackness of the sky above. A darkness which for the first time in my life was also safe: we had no rapists, burglars or other characters a woman would have been scared of; no repressed sex and no perverted sex either. Whoever lived on the Ranch was also my friend and wanted no harm done. I knew I could walk in total darkness and be safe – as long as I didn't fall into a pond. For someone who grew up in Italy in the middle of the 20th century this was just incredible!

From far away I saw a light in my trailer: Aruna was still awake. Again sitting in front of a spread of cards and consulting the instruction booklet, she told me about the card she was studying. It was called 'Work/Worship' and depicted a tent with two men asleep and a camel walking off into the desert. The reading says: *'Don't shirk your responsibility! Be intensely alive in the work you do and go on doing whatever is humanly possible, yet at the same time create no tension, remain unfrustrated, trust and allow your doing to become prayer, without attachment to the outcome.'* The parable the card referred to comes from the Sufi world where the master says: 'Trust in Allah, but tether your camel first – because Allah has no other hands than yours.'

It felt awkward in the beginning when we stopped 'going to work' but rather 'went to worship' and one was no longer working in a department but in a 'temple'. Because Rajneeshism had been introduced for political (immigration) reasons, the concepts of worship and temple probably came from the same idea. But calling work 'worship' made us aware that this was no ordinary work but something more, something one was doing for oneself, where the gain was in the present and not at the end of the month in the form of a pay cheque. At times we forgot the meaning of the word and just called work 'worship' automatically as nowadays we use 'awesome' instead of the more plain 'beautiful', without remembering that 'awesome' means 'awe-inspiring'.

8

Play

On Four Wheels Again

Finally the townhouses were ready – we could move in. My home was going to be in one of the first houses in the little valley on the left of the gate to Osho's residence, outside the fence around it. In a room at the back, on the first floor. My new roommate, (another) Indira, had moved in a few days before and had just come back from her guard duty when I arrived. In my picture slide show I always see her in the uniform of mauve blouse and purplish culottes (both in easy-care half-polyester fabric, disgusting to many!) or, sitting up in bed reading a book under the light cone of her side lamp, with her reading-glasses halfway down her nose. She had prematurely greying short hair and deep blue eyes.

I always thought of her as being much wiser than I was in many matters; for instance, she had a deep knowledge of how to look after plants and she gave me lots of good advice. But – and this was strange – the plants on my side were thriving more than those on her side which were even closer to the light.

I was always happy to hop onto the buses to Portland, but one morning I felt reluctant to button up my pink shirt. I was aware of each little white button and of my fingers not wanting to perform this seemingly automatic task. The night before I had sat on my bed with a friend and confided to him my overwhelming feeling of not wanting to travel the next day. Every half hour I felt like calling Durga, my boss, and asking her to find another guide, but resisted doing so as I was neither sick nor had a valid excuse not to go. In the end it was too late to call. To make me feel better and in the hope of finding an answer to my unease, we shuffled my tarot cards and drew out one card: the Knight of Cups. Both ignorant in reading cards, we jointly agreed that 'giving support to the other' was an adequate meaning and that the 'other' would be Punito, tomorrow's driver.

Punito was a heavyset, strong woman who instilled confidence in all passengers thanks to her stalwart looks. After eating our boxed snacks and enjoying the refreshing stop at Columbia River we safely arrived at Hotel Rajneesh in Portland. We gave a good cleaning to the bus in the garage and returned to the Hotel where, according to new instructions, we had to help with the setting up of the rooms. In the laundry I was shown how to fold the corners of the stretch fitted sheets, but the meticulous way in which it was shown to me made me cringe – sometimes we just hate to be shown how to do things, don't we?

At breakfast I met Punito, who was sourly staring at her coffee. She had been feeling sick during the night and was not interested in any food. She would still feel fine to drive us back, she said. The stop at the waterfall was my favourite part of the journey. I loved to stand below the soft, long watery hairs of the princess plunging into the depths, dispersing moisture to the greenery around and into our hair. Punito had thrown up again while we were at the Falls, I could see that from the colour of her face.

The visitors from abroad were thrilled to see Shaniko, a ghost town, on the high plateau. The wooden beams had turned silver from wind and rain. The roofless houses looked like rotten molars. If it wasn't for the sound of the bus engine, we would have certainly heard the rattling of a half-closed door or the clanking of a shutter in the wind. Here we always slowed down, not only for everybody to admire this unusual place but also to turn onto the road towards Antelope.

This is where Punito said under her breath: "My brakes." This was for me alone and I understood that something was not quite right with the bus. I kept entertaining the passengers with facts and figures I had learned as a Twinkie and with anecdotes I had collected during the time I had lived on the Ranch. As most visitors had taken a year or more to save up money to visit and were now a stone's throw from their destination, the excitement became stronger the closer we came to our mecca.

As the bus was taking its first plunge into the valley I saw Punito stand up, still at the wheel, but pressing the gear stick with all her might to keep the bus in second gear. I understood that the brakes must have totally failed and that she was using the gears to keep the speed down. The moment she could no longer keep the second gear from slipping into neutral, I assumed, she would drive into the hillside and come to a halt. This would probably turn the bus over on its side and cause broken bones, maybe even a broken skull. A sudden calm overcame me at this dreadful picture. I sat silently, but on alert, just behind the driver, ready to turn around towards the passengers and shout with authority "heads down" just before the impact would occur. The tarot card: 'give support to Punito' came back to mind – it finally made sense – and I started projecting all my life energy into her as she stood in front of me pushing the gear stick with all her might.

From time to time I looked back and felt reassured when I saw that the passengers were enjoying the hilly scenery flying by their windows. I thought we had it all under control, until Nivedano, sitting next to me, understood the situation and started freaking out. He was jumping up and down, out of his wits with panic, but eventually I managed to calm him down. I did not want the panic to spread to the rest of the bus.

Each bend, each further downward slope, was an opportunity for the crash. But the crash never came. We stopped on the flat in front of Mirdad Welcome Centre as if nothing had happened, and the un-wary passengers disembarked and unloaded their luggage as after any other trip. One of the regulars asked what Nivedano's shouting was all about and I told her that the brakes had failed. All she replied was: "Well, I thought she was driving a bit fast down that narrow road."

The next day I bumped into Punito at Magdalena Cafeteria. Only the moment we saw each other we remembered, wide-eyed, the adventurous journey of the day before. Probably once you live something with totality there is no need to remember it at all. She had heard from the mechanics that the brakes had been tampered with and it was suspected that it was done during the night when the bus was parked in the garage. From that day on we changed our schedule: we drove out early in the morning and came back the same evening – no overnight stay.

I am sitting at a window looking out into the gardens of the Resort in Pune, imbibing the various greens of the leaves dotted by patches of light that manage to get through the canopy. The dots sway gently with the wind in the mature trees above. There is nothing for me to do other than wait. At this time most people are either in a group room, at work in one of the air-conditioned offices or meditating in the Hall. Through its mosquito net we can distinctly hear the music for Nadabrahma Meditation. Across from me sits Samadhana, also looking out of the window in a relaxed, meditative mood. We had a chat earlier and are now enjoying the space of being by ourselves even if we are sitting in the same room. This would be unimaginable anywhere else where small talk always has to fill the unease of silence. But silence is so beautiful and the presence of the other does not interfere if he/she also enjoys it.

We are the watchdogs of this little building containing the passports and travel documents of the many visitors. It is built with thick concrete walls, triple locks which can only be opened by the keys that are kept overnight under someone's bed. We always have to be two together, which means that we have to arrive exactly on time and go on tea breaks together. Samadhana has been a delight to be with. She is a Swiss girl with a strong face and eyes, strong curly, ginger hair and a big smile. To speak the Swiss dialect, which is one of my two mother tongues, after so long is a joy. It took only a few days to shed its rustiness and I am now fully enjoying the broad vowels and guttural sounds.

She had shown me how to prepare the document pockets for new arrivals: how to stick the little photographs onto the card, how to fill in the details (on card and in log book) and where to have the visitors sign. The visitors would then fill the plastic pockets with their documents, in individual paper envelopes, each one signed and closed with sticky tape. It all felt so familiar and logical and I wondered how on earth I knew already what she was going to tell me. Then I remembered that I had actually invented the procedure almost fifteen years ago, when we first opened the facility next to the stationery shop. Either my procedure was so comfortable and foolproof that it had survived all these years or nobody had bothered to invent a better system.

I came to Kuber, the name of our safety deposit office, after I had lost my job in the bookshop. Maybe the head accountant was not so happy with my spending so much money for the many renovations, maybe I was not the right person for the job, but a concrete reason for why I had lost the job was not given and I did not expect an explanation either. It was painful because I was informed of the move while I was giving a Reiki training – and this during a lunch-break. It felt as if I had been smacked in the face. On the other hand, if I had had the chance to sit down with my department leader, I would probably have opted for a change anyway.

My next job was going to be cleaning in Lao Tzu, the house where Osho used to live. I had a morning of detailed training (which bucket and which cloth was to be used for which surface) by a Japanese girl, but after lunch I was literally dragged to Kuber as they urgently needed a replacement. The idea of being enclosed in such a confined space made my whole body lean back and dig its heels into the ground as kids do when they do not want to move on.

I have now surrendered to sitting in here, dealing with the customers during their breaks and using my language skills with newcomers whose English is not up to scratch. Giving the plastic envelopes and having the IN and OUT files signed each time the transaction is completed... a little chat and laughter will not distract much from such a simple procedure.

My first three weeks as a bus driver (on one of the yellow school buses and not on a silver coach) were spent driving up and down from the Mall to Magdalena Cafeteria and back until our dispatcher, Narendra, realised that he had forgotten to change my weekly schedule. He apologized profusely for his mistake but I explained to him that to drive the same small route for weeks on end had not been a problem at all. I had seen the mornings grow brighter after each round until I finally saw the first rays of sun shine into the valley, the hills turning from black to grey and then to brown. It was a spectacle in itself. Brown hills, a brown dusty road – but still it was paradise if one could see the magic and if one wanted to be there. I think that paradise is where one wants to be, whatever it looks like. With sunshine came warmth and the flow of people getting on and off the bus – from their homes to Magdalena for breakfast and from Magdalena to their temples.

The training to become a bus driver was given to me by my favourite hairdresser, a gay lad from Australia with beautiful long curly hair. His instructions were as simple and competent as his cuts and his soft manner made me forget all my fear when I was asked to reverse with the help of side mirrors alone. As I had learnt to drive on a Fiat 500 the necessary double-declutching was no problem, but the leeway of the pedals and the strength needed to change gears – designed for a heavy man – were a bit of a challenge at the start. But soon my invisible body became as big as the bus and I managed to judge well how much space I needed on the bends and how close I could drive to the passengers waiting in line.

When 'Proper' Sagar became totally involved with crystals, I inherited his automatic bus No. 235 and tried to keep up his standard of cleanliness. There was a special place where we could wash the buses, a flat area with a water pipe beneath a big juniper tree, but it was so remote that hardly anyone ever used it. But that was the spot where you could find me during my breaks. I loved to move my body after the many hours of sitting in the driver's seat. It was a joy to splash with water under the relentless desert sun, in total aloneness away from everybody and everything. It was voluntary work as nobody ever checked on the cleanliness of the buses – but I preferred washing the bus to spending my break sitting in my room reading a book.

After rinsing down the bus inside and out and polishing what seemed like 100 windows I was ready for a rest. I had learnt to take a fifteen-minute nap in the grass before my dinner at Hassid Cafeteria in order to be fresh to start the second part of my shift.

Although I enjoyed a steady routine I also enjoyed being the 'jolly bus', i.e. being on call for special trips. This service was totally in the hands of the dispatcher, Narendra, who was on the motorola, receiving requests from all over the Ranch. His place of work was the central bus stop downtown and he was easily spotted in the crowd because of his orange Tibetan hat. Narendra timed the buses with a whistle and entertained bus drivers and passengers alike with his antics. He had apparently been an actor in Hollywood and fitted well into our multi-national mix of characters. If one evening there was an event at the Multiversity it was up to the 'jolly bus' to take everybody home. If it was quiet he let me go and have a five-minute dance at the disco nearby. He knew how much I loved dancing and how restless I could become sitting in the bus for too long.

After a few months as a bus driver I knew where everybody lived and who was dating whom. With working days of twelve hours or more, the passengers used to fall asleep as soon as they dropped onto their seats. It was therefore up to me to deliver them to the right place, to their own home or that of their girlfriend. At the correct stop for each passenger I used to shout out their names (if I knew them) or that of the locations. What a service!

In my slide show collection of that period, there is a very unusual picture. There had been a general meeting in the Mandir and Sheela had made the announcement, if I remember correctly, that "If we do not change and become more loving, Osho will leave his body on 6th July." At the news, my blood was bubbling but there was no fear, no worry, no panic. After the meeting, while waiting for my bus to fill up with passengers, I saw the hills vibrating in a wild dance all around. There was joy and excitement, maybe even laughter in that dance. What happened the next day was not my imagination, I am sure: when I drove past the heavy machinery garage I saw Ralph smile at me, for no reason at all. I had known him as a grumpy face – so much so that I was scared to even talk to him. I guess he must have been looking at a much friendlier face as well.

Rajneesh Buddhafield Transport, the bus department or, rather, the bus 'temple', now had an enlightened man in charge, Haridas. In Pune he had been the electrician in Osho's house and I had always seen him in the darshans, sometimes as a guard. Here he was my boss. Osho had recently published a list of twenty-one names of people who were enlightened and he was one of them.

I knew all those who were on the list. One of them was Maneesha who had edited all the darshan diaries and who had been with us in the Saswad fort. Each one of those on the list reacted in a different way. One of them, apparently, started giving satsangs and talking to people on a tent platform behind her house. Swami Maitreya, the man who had arrived at the Ranch with a broken leg, showed off on the Mall how he could enjoy smoking a cigarette in an 'enlightened' way. When he had received the news that he was declared enlightened, I was told that he said: "Osho is a rascal." And when I asked Haridas about his enlightenment he just gave a shy smile.

In the months to come further lists were made public, with avatars, bodhisattvas, mahasattvas and people in other stages of enlightenment. Everybody who was somebody had a title but, of course, my name never appeared. Maybe I was forgotten, maybe I did not deserve it or maybe I did not need it. From the thousands of us only about a hundred were 'on a list', so the same thoughts might have gone through other people's minds as well. Even people like Teertha, one of the first therapists and meditation leaders, was not on any list. This game created a great stir, some of it lived out in secrecy as in my case, some of it more publicly.

Shakers, Drums and Claves

During one of my bus-washing sprees I found a real treasure! I could hardly believe it when I saw a dollar bill wash out from the back of the bus. On close inspection it was a *five*-dollar bill! Instead of spending it immediately on ice-cream and pizza, as I would normally have done, I went to the bank and put it into my empty bank account, for the future.

The Third Annual World Celebration in which we expected over 20,000 people to participate was so well organised that we even had loudspeakers on each lamppost broadcasting celebration songs during the line-up for Osho's drive-by. It felt very phony and it was no wonder that my Swiss friend, Krishna, and some other daring musicians turned up the next day with flute and guitar and played a Sicilian song. One would have expected some repercussion from the peace keepers or guards but, lo and behold, Osho stopped the car and gestured to keep playing and did not move from the spot for an eternity.

If this was the way to get attention then I was going to try my best as well! I immediately went to the garage and, exploiting my Italian connections, convinced one of the mechanics to help me turn an empty spray can into a colourful shaker. As there were no music shops around for miles, one had to be resourceful even if it meant stealing some tiny screws and washers to fill the instrument. During the next day's line-up I asked Maniko, who had brought along her guitar, to show me how to hold and play the shaker. I was now playing music for my master, even if it was 'only' with a shaker. Rattly and noisy things must have been my kind of instruments because I vividly remember the fascination that I had as a teenager, for some blue *maracas* played in the dance club during my beach holidays in Sestri Levante.

It did not take long for the Purchasing Temple to have instruments shipped in and one day I saw a pair of *claves* for sale in the boutique. They were exactly five dollars and I had exactly that amount of money in the bank! Five dollars for two six-inch-long pieces of turned wood seems a lot, but the wood had to be either rosewood or ebony to create that clean sound when the *claves* were hit against each other. I joined a drummer, Sudhiro, a djiembe player who looked like a Native American and dressed like one, and played with him every day at the intersection across from the Mall – until I was 'discovered' by Nivedano.

When Osho drove off towards Patanjali Lake, on the road we had built for him in order to avoid the harassment (and the speeding tickets) he received on the road to Madras, he had left behind him a joyfully dancing crowd, slowly dispersing back to work, or maybe to the ice-cream parlour at the Mall. Nivedano approached me. "You have good rhythm," he said, and repeated it a few times. Then asked me to come and play with his gang, and explained to me where I should turn up the following day: just outside the gates of Osho's residence. Rumour was that he had been a drummer with not only Santana, Weather Report and Pink Floyd but also with Miles Davis and John McLaughlin – and to be invited to play with him was certainly an honour. But I just stood there and followed him with my eyes while he walked off hand in hand with his girlfriend, Gayan. All good news needs some time to sink in, doesn't it?

At the entrance to Lao Tzu, opposite the pond where I had seen my first and only raccoon, Taru was intoning an Indian chant. Her energy and enthusiasm were as big as her body. When someone (probably a woman) asked why there were eleven men and only ten women on the enlightened list, Osho replied: "Taru counts for two." Not far from her was Nivedano. He walked up to me and hung a snare drum over my shoulders and gave me two sticks. It felt awkward as my left hand was totally out of sync with my right and my brain could not keep up with the complicated riff I was meant to follow. Milarepa, a handsome Mac truck driver and singer of songs, was next to me. He did not have a much easier time either, judging from the expression on his face.

The instruments were stored in a small shed behind Mataji's

house close by. One day Nivedano produced a gourd the size of a big head with bead netting around it. He handed it over to me with a glint in his eyes and I was thus relieved of the drum. I soon figured out different ways of shaking and rotating the gourd to create certain sound effects and came to know that they call it *'shekere'*. Nivedano must have been satisfied with my playing as, together with Rupesh, a Mexican drummer, we left Taru's group to form a separate trio farther down the road. It was definitely a strange trio: an Italian/Swiss shapely secretary; a young, wild, short-limbed and balding Mexican; and a dark-skinned, lean Brazilian with a nose like an Arab.

Everyone wanted to be next to the musicians to see Osho as long as possible and there was always a great shuffling, so much so that in the end there was no space to move the arms and do the playing. Rupesh came up with a trick whereby we warmed up in one place and, just before the car came around the bend, we ran up the road and placed ourselves comfortably at the very end of the queue.

Our line-up was always the same: first there was me with the *shekere*, then Rupesh with the *doumbek*, a small drum made of clay, and lastly Nivedano with the *surdo*, the big, deep Brazilian drum. Osho always stopped in front of Rupesh and, waving his arms for us to play faster and faster, looked deeply into his eyes. Rupesh was asked to keep his eyes open, but always ended up closing them tightly. A glance from the master might have been welcome but a one-minute stare is a frightening affair!

With lovers I had experienced beautiful moments and while dancing I had felt exhilarated and weightless, but what was happening during the drive-by could not be compared to any experiences of the past. It was as if high-current electricity streamed from Osho via Rupesh into me, dissolving everything into a white-out. After Osho had driven on I had to wait for a few minutes on the side of the road until I could see the world around me in its proper colour scale again.

Arpita has invited me to play for a meditation after dinner in Buddha Hall. Not much time for dinner, actually, as we have to rush to be on time for the sound check. We will all be sitting on the floor, Indian style. For this I have a special black velvet cloth where I can spread my percussion gadgets out on the floor. My microphone is set up on a miniature stand and I test one instrument at a time to assess the best distance to avoid too many adjustments for Deekshant, our mixer. A small dim light over our heads tells us where things are and above the podium the lights are also dim. We can just make out the silhouettes of those coming into the hall: some still wear their maroon robes but others have changed into their street clothes. I love to wear my maroon robe during a meditation.

Instructions are given over the PA system – tonight it is the Mahamudra Meditation taken from *The Book of Secrets* – and the music starts. I listen carefully to what the solo instruments have to offer tonight. Then Arpita's harp – it is actually a *swarmandal* which she places flat on the ground – invites one of my little noises to come forward: a string of dried pod seeds rattle against each other, something shamans might use. I close my eyes and, as if in a trance, I let my hands grab whatever instrument they want and add a little spice here and some more there. It feels as if the musicians are just one entity, with no separation between them, all creating this one invisible happening lost in the air. We know we have helped people to go deep into meditation when they linger and remain lying on the floor for some time after the music stops. "Thank you, Osho, for letting me play," I whisper while bowing down towards the podium in gratitude.

We suddenly had a new kind of guest on the Ranch: the homeless people. A few of us had gone out into the cities of America to round up street people and bring them to the Ranch. They came in on school buses and coaches and were accommodated in the Walt Whitman A-frames and in the Zarathustra trailers which were empty at the time. Although we were informed in a general meeting that this exercise was a way 'to share our wealth' I wasn't fooled. This was only a means of gaining more voting power in the next local election. Somehow there was a jarring note in what was said; I had started to learn to sense what was behind the words instead of blindly believing in them.

Many of the homeless friends were black, which was a nice addition to the only three black residents we had, a conga player and two cooks. The new guests always sat at the back of my bus even if it was half empty. I did not understand that they were merely following an old habit. For so many years that was their place, I was told. When they found the courage to sit in the first row they told me how they had had their first warm shower in years and quite enjoyed it, despite initial reluctance. They felt respected and were happy to have a good place to stay. But now there were cigarette butts all over the ground and violent behaviour began in the houses. I was wondering how they would ever fit in with us, as they had no interest in meditation and no connection to Osho.

In the name of security we had introduced a badge system. Residents of the Ranch wore a golden (brass) bead on their mala; those from the meditation centres wore a silver bead – many of them worked on the Ranch in an exchange programme; paying guests wore a blue plastic armband and the participants of the 'Share-a-home' programme now had a pink one. Blue and pink armbands had no access to the townhouses where the residents were living. And as a bus driver I had to check that no one breached this rule.

I got to know our new guests a bit better when I changed jobs and was put in charge of vegetable cutting in Hassid Cafeteria. Many of the men in my team were veterans from the Vietnam War, with bone-fractures which had mended badly and with very fragile psyches. They needed sitting-down jobs and we could provide that. The team soon excelled in all the chopping chores. Tables, floors and hands all turned red when we skinned and cut the beets and everybody was crying their eyes out after two bags of onions.

We became so proficient that in the end we even chopped the vegetables for the big Magdalena Cafeteria. The vegetable area felt like a kindergarten/therapy/playground. We always had great fun and I loved each one of the men.

Nivedano appeared one day in the pot-washing area. Rumour was he was there for punishment. He must have opened his loud mouth, I thought. He soon created a good working team with a big black man – a great dancer despite his girth – washing five-gallon steel pots in the tiny dark pot-washing room. What made him more angry than washing pots was to know that for this year's celebration 'they' had replaced the professional musicians and singers with people who were 'in', regardless of their musical talent.

Another small elderly black man from New York, who was also working on a shift in Hassid Cafeteria, often talked to me about his daughter and one day showed me her photograph. I must have reminded him of her, I thought. He took sannyas and was so delighted to have by chance received the same name as mine. For my birthday he proudly signed his new name on a photograph of Osho, a present I still cherish. When I was eventually moved to Magdalena Cafeteria, some of the men protested, but it was healthy that the bond was cut and I was again free.

It is only now, while sorting notes and comparing dates, that I become aware that Osho started to speak publicly again, interrupting a silence of over three years, the same month the homeless people were brought in. At the time I did not make the connection between these two events. While Osho was in silence I felt that my connection with him was non-verbal and that the most important thing for me was to be with his people and to be in the same place as he was. Now that he was talking again I sensed that we needed a wake-up call.

The first words of his first discourse were:

It is a little difficult for me to speak again. It has been difficult always, because I have been trying to speak the unspeakable. Now it is even more so.

After one thousand, three hundred and fifteen days of silence, it feels as if I am coming to you from a totally different world. In fact it is so.

The world of words, language, concepts, and the world of silence are so diametrically opposite to each other, they don't meet anywhere. They can't meet by their very nature.

Silence means a state of wordlessness; and to speak now, it is as if to learn language again from ABC. But this is not a new experience for me; it has happened before too.

For thirty years I have been speaking continually. It was such a tension because my whole being was pulled towards silence, and I was pulling myself towards words, language, concepts, philosophies. There was no other way to convey, and I had a tremendously important message to convey. There was no way to shirk the responsibility.

Osho, *From Unconsciousness to Consciousness*, Ch. 1

In his house he spoke at meetings which had the subtitle: 'To the chosen few who are going to be the messengers for the world at large'. It was an expression which sometimes made me feel excluded and other times included, depending on my own degree of self-esteem. The people invited were those of his household and some workers on rotation and, most importantly, the cameraman. The discourses were recorded on video and shown the next night in the Mandir meditation hall. I would have expected our working hours to be cut in order for us to fully enjoy the discourses now that the construction crunch was over. But the videos were shown after dinner; I think it was around 9 or even later, which meant that we were already tired from the day's work. To stay awake, I remember us girls taking our knitting with us; but mostly everybody fell asleep after the first half hour, stretched out on the linoleum floor. And the hall was too well-heated, which had its own soporific effect on everybody present. Maybe Sheela did not really want us to hear what Osho had to say? On the other hand, to go home and skip the discourse altogether was a total no-no.

Once, bent over a salad bowl, I was approached by Nirmala, an old playmate from the Vrindavan kitchen who had worked herself up the rungs of power on the Ranch. She brought me the good news that that very night I was invited to go to the live discourse. There was just enough time to go home, take a shower and change my clothes. So excited was I that there is no trace in my memory of the path from the guard hut to the room where the discourse was held. For more than three years I had not heard Osho speak! I was asked to sit behind Nirupa, one of the cleaners in the house, who was already sitting cross-legged just a few feet from the chair where Osho was going to sit.

Seeing Osho again, up so close, was like seeing an old friend, an intimate acquaintance, who had changed a lot after a long absence, maybe after a long illness. His voice was so weak that, despite the short distance, I could hear him only through the small speakers on both sides of his chair. I was so worried about his lack of strength that I could not pay attention to what he was saying. I could just take in the walls and floors lined with wooden squares; the tan chair and his tan robe; Mukta sitting as usual on his right side; and the heavy clanking sound of the video cassette when it was removed for a new one. I was aware that I was not able to relax and listen to the words and I knew that he could sense this as well. Maybe this was the reason why always the same people were invited to the discourse, the 'chosen few'.

At this time of writing it happens to be the year we are celebrating the 60th anniversary of the end of WWII. I have seen some interesting film footage and can draw parallels between the Ranch and the totalitarian states in Europe. What impresses me the most is an interview with a German octogenarian who said: "We were so certain that we were the best." On the Ranch there was a similar feeling: we could see with our own eyes the tremendous feats we had accomplished, not only the beautiful townhouses we had built for ourselves, but also the hotel with over sixty rooms for our visiting guests – all in such a short time. From abroad, we heard of the success of our meditation centres with their discos and restaurants – mainly in Germany – where they had gained wide acclaim amongst the general public. Some of the war footage shows mass demonstrations of female gymnasts and meetings of the Nazi party; Hitler driving through the crowds; the euphoria and the tremendous energy created in the square by the flames on high columns; the symmetry of architecture and the imposing theatrical structures. I have known the same feeling those crowds must have experienced.

How similar and still how very different!

But Osho's discourses were refreshingly down-to-earth. They were all answers to our questions. He emphasized the importance of accepting our humanity and not striving to become superhuman. We even wrote a celebration song starting with his own words: "Just an ordinary man." He was so special to me that it was difficult to accept that he was just an 'ordinary man', but I got the point and, through that, felt him much closer to me again.

Priests and politicians were again on the receiving end of his verbal daggers, but this time I saw them not in Delhi or Rome, but right here among us, me included. I heard him talk about respecting the other and respecting nature, as if for the first time, and I took it to heart and decided to give more respect to the sannyasins around me. His hilarious recollection of his rebellious childhood and his student years was a wake-up call for me not to follow the crowd.

In the discourses he started to say that God does not exist. I felt a great relief and thought: 'He is finally saying what he always wanted to say.' I had always heard this basic message between the lines, but many sannyasins did not like to hear it so loud and clear. It caused a big stir, mainly among sannyasins living outside the commune.

One night, climbing up the hill behind Magdalena Cafeteria to visit my disabled friend, Bodhi, I overheard someone showing Osho's house to a meditation guest. Not to reveal its location for security reasons was so instilled in me that my knowledge of the whereabouts of Osho's house had almost been washed out of my brain. At that moment I understood what brainwashing meant and I was shocked to see that this had happened to me.

The discourses held in Osho's house were not only shown in the Mandir the next night but were sent out to the centres, where the sannyasins watched the videos also at the end of their twelve-hour shifts. But one day there was no discourse. Despite my usual *naïveté*, I immediately thought: 'Osho probably said something which Sheela would not like us to hear.' Interestingly, this was the first thought of my close friends too, although the official story was that the video 'got lost'. Sheela even called a general meeting and we were informed that it was absolutely *not* true that during the discourse Osho had given her a hit, as some people had insinuated, but that the video had truly disappeared. Amiten tells me that his friend, Zeno, who was the video operator that night, was sent to work at RBG garage the next day, and when we were all tested for HIV she was moved to Desiderata and kept in isolation (although, as it later turned out, she tested negative).

Desiderata, the few trailers at the far end of Krishnamurti Lake, where I had stayed the very first time I had visited the Ranch, became the home for those who had tested positive. Osho had expressed his ideas on how to keep this disease in check and one of them was to separate those infected from the main population. (The same had been done with TB at the beginning of the century, and Cuba adopted segregation for AIDS patients later on – with very good results.) It was imperative in Osho's vision that those who tested positive were respected and had the best possible food, entertainment and treatment.

I knew that Lazarus was in Desiderata and wondered how he was doing. He had been our nurse when I was kept in observation in the Zarathustra ward during the 'conjunctivitis epidemic'. As nobody felt sick really or felt any discomfort, I had a ball with my old roommates from Saswad: Pankaja and Maneesha. Lazarus, with his friendly southern slang, entertained us and helped us in our mischievous endeavours. Despite the fact that I had followed the doctors' instructions to keep the epidemic at bay, i.e. to climb onto the buses without touching the bars, and sitting down without touching the top of the seats in front, I had apparently caught conjunctivitis, although my eyes looked and felt OK. It struck me that while I was being checked at the ward, Laila, our Swiss doctor, used the same swab for both my eyes and when I drew her attention to this, she just shrugged her shoulders and looked away.

I remember Lazarus's death and cremation as a very beautiful, though sad event. I had never been to the cremation ground before. It was up a side valley on the left before reaching Krishnamurti Lake, and I was told that it had previously been a sacred site for the Wasco and the Walla Walla Indians. In deepening twilight we walked up the dirt road until we reached a flat space where the crematorium was. The tall copper chimney, reaching to the stars with its irregular spikes, was lit from all sides and cast a warm glow onto the slopes of the hill. What a beautiful structure it was! The roof at the base was held up by eight metal beams which then curved to a slender long chinmney, like a long-necked upside-down funnel. Many sannyasins had already arrived and positioned themselves on the hill-slope to get a better view. The musicians where up there as well, keeping our singing in rhythm. Garimo said a few commemorative words. I remained close to the crematorium and could see, through the glass panels, the blue gas flames under the flower-bedecked body. I could see the people on the other side of it seated in chairs and looking at the flames, their faces aglow. The subtle smell of burning flesh was faintly apparent. "Goodbye, Lazarus." I was sad to lose a friend but was happy that we could give him a regal send-off, truly worthy of this gentle and loving person. I would have liked to dance around the crematorium, as dancing helped me cope with sorrow and joy and I wished that when my turn came, friends would joyfully dance around my fire.

On the way back hundreds of candles lined the roads all the way down to the main valley where the buses were waiting. It was so overwhelming a night that to walk home in the dark was for many the right thing to do. While I walked, I felt on my bare arms the coolness of the night and at the same time the heat of the day still stored in the sunburnt rocks.

Soon winter came upon us with a lot of snow and a whole month of temperatures below freezing. The snow was so cold and dry that it was impossible to make snowballs, they just disintegrated. During drive-by we jumped up and down to stay warm in our lined dungarees and eiderdown jackets. The buses were full beyond legal limits as it was a sin to leave passengers stranded in the cold. With axles screeching the buses snailed along, following the tracks in the snow.

Added to this coldness was another chilling factor (or is this memory from the also-harsh winter of the following year?). Rumour had it that the US National Guard was stationed beyond the north boundary of the Ranch, on the ready. When we heard this we suspected it was one of Sheela's bogey stories to keep us in check, but many years later I found out it was indeed the truth.

Sheela had asked us in another general meeting to refrain from negativity and requested us to report people whom we heard speaking negatively at work or in the houses. The living room in our house was rarely used, everybody just went straight to their rooms, so the issue did not really touch me. In Magdalena everybody was so busy with their physical activities that I never overheard anyone talking 'negatively'. I understood what Sheela meant only when I went to help out picking vegetables at the farm and overheard some 'clever guys', as I called them, ranting about one thing or another. I understood how that energy did not help the work which needed to be done and – in good faith – thought she had a point. But I would certainly not report them!

Then I heard that some people were removed from their jobs and replaced the moment they had raised a few questions. Our fears were not only about being sent to wash pots, but about being sent off the Ranch, never to return. This would have been the worst possible scenario. To live away from Osho was not an option for me!

When the spring sun managed to warm up the roofs again, my place of worship was the Magdalena dock. I was happy to move my body: unloading trucks and delivering the vegetables to the choppers felt like a dance.

My great passion was the hydraulic pallet mover, and I tested myself to see if I could place a pallet full of tofu into the walk-in fridge in one go. I spent a lot of time in there, marking and dating the leftovers on the shelves. It was cold and dark and I had to work fast. The walk-in freezer, on the other hand, was reserved for those wearing winter dungarees, caps and gloves. I remember that once a pallet full of tofu landed in the freezer by mistake. The cooks tried the defrosted tofu and liked the chewy, meat-like texture and after that requested that for their Tofu Stroganoff the tofu had to be frozen first.

Dry goods were driven in from the warehouses at the 'top of the Ranch' and vegetables came from Surdas truck farm. The salads and sprouts had already been washed there. From Rabiya and Atisha came our eggs and milk, but butter and the dreadful cheddar cheese had to be brought in from outside. Ditto for the boxed bread, which for us foreigners tasted more like cotton than bread. The bakery only had the capacity to produce the croissants, rolls, chocolate chip cookies and fancy tarts for the restaurants and the travel boxes.

I enjoyed flattening the empty cardboard boxes and stacking them up ready to be collected by the recycling crew. I learned to check on the stock of bananas and, when needed, strip the plastic sheeting from the boxes to release the gas which had prevented them from ripening.

Whatever my job, the highlight of the day was playing music for Osho during drive-by. This was the focus of my life. Dreadful events like those of the bombing of our Hotel in Portland, and the subsequent apprehension of the person who had planted it, were somewhere far off in the background. We eventually acquired a helicopter for Osho's security and the sound of the approaching chopper had become a welcome noise, as welcome as the sound of car wheels on the gravel around Buddha Hall had been.

During the Summer Festival the main kitchen moved again to Zarathustra. I was going to take care of the plastics. Great! My love for containers of any sort was such that I had even thought of studying packaging design. Here I had ceiling-high stacks of white buckets for dry goods, grey trays for silverware, blue drums for clean vegetables and red vegetable buckets ready to be returned to Surdas farm. I was my own boss, working on my own and was happy to be in my own space. Then I was 'sent' – this is the term we used – to the bakery.

Up until now all changes had come at the right time and in harmony with my energy. No matter if I was happy with the change or not, it always felt right; but this time there was an odd-smelling, uncomfortable, jarring ring to it. I could feel in bone and marrow that it was not following the Tao and was not in harmony with the commune spirit. I felt no attraction for the little white breads my hands perfectly remembered how to roll, nor the mixing of the dough which was now done in stainless steel mixers with blades weighing as much as a ton.

The cake bakers' corner was a much more interesting place. I relished the female chatter between Aseema, a dark-haired South American girl and an incredible dancer, and Kavisho, a blonde French beauty, and admired their skilful decorations on the cakes. They welcomed me as part of the team and let me have a go at the mixing of the strawberry mousse, even if it was a tricky affair. But soon I was called back by Big Prem, my old neighbour in the Saswad girls' room, who was now the 'mom' of the bakery and therefore my boss: "I want you to help Arpana with the bread."

Arpana was a stocky American construction worker who had a passion for baking bagels, croissants and bread-rolls although, according to rumours, he had been sent to the bakery as a punishment. His enthusiasm did not infect me. I became more and more frustrated mainly because Big Prem kept asking, each time I walked past her with a bowl in my hand, where I was going and why I was going there. It became such a strain that my body reacted by swelling up my ever-so-present varicose veins, provoking so much pain that I could not stand on my legs. I remember sitting on the floor, leaning against the wall and cooling off my calves against the red linoleum floor. Swami Hassid brought me cookies and tea with comforting words.

The highlights of the week-long Summer Festival were the discourses in the morning and the evening celebration on Master's Day. The first morning Osho came for a silent *satsang* but, as the audience had been too restless and noisy with coughing, he decided to speak for the rest of the Festival. For dinner on Master's Day we had prepared celebration boxes with many goodies like spring rolls and brownies, as had been done for all previous years, but something peculiar happened that night. When I walked into the Mandir, I was called aside and together with other kitchen workers had to empty the fruit salads into a compost bin. They said the salad had gone off.

It felt odd, not only because the salad smelled all right to my trained kitchen nose, but because I had seen the fruit salad being prepared under disposable plastic gloves that very morning and had noticed the stacks of containers safely stored in the walk-in fridge. I could not imagine how the salad could have gone off.

After the celebration the morning discourses continued and Osho decided to hold interviews with the press in the evenings. These were held in a specially-built large room adjoining Jesus Grove where Sheela lived. It was spacious enough to accommodate the press people, the cameramen and a few dozen invited sannyasins. We had reporters from 'Good Morning America', *Der Spiegel*, '60 Minutes Australia', *Seattle Post Intelligencer*, *The Guardian*, and many others. There was an opportunity to be invited, either for the line-up at the entrance or, best of all, to the interview itself. For that occasion we had to dig deep into our winter clothes to find polo necks and long johns as Osho liked *very* cold air conditioning.

We lined up on the rose-petal-strewn path from car to house, and greeted Osho on the way in and out. Two Russian musicians, a fiddler and a guitarist, walked behind him and we all danced to the wild gypsy airs. Sometimes Osho stopped in front of one of us in the line-up and danced with that person. I would have loved him to stop for me, but it never seemed to happen.

One evening I was standing under the awning when Osho descended from his car. I had a strange vision: instead of Osho, I saw a Hassidic master dancing in a wood-panelled inn surrounded by his pupils. At this sight my body bent over double in reverence, something which had never happened before. I had the impression we were celebrating the departure of this master who was going to leave us for some time to visit another town. During the press interview, which some of us followed on loudspeakers from the entrance to the house, I remembered the vision and tried to overcome my sadness by holding onto a friend, but the feeling became deeper despite my reasoning that Osho was here with us and there was nothing to worry about.

Another evening I was asked to hold the door for Osho inside the house. I was so exhilarated and danced so wildly that I was afraid I would forget to hold the door for him. I saw Osho approach in his long light-coloured robe with the musicians following him and could hardly feel my feet touching the ground between the jumps. Holding the door I closed my eyes and when I opened them again Osho had stopped on the landing and, with a broad smile, looked straight at me. He waved his arms vigorously in an upward motion which accelerated my jumping and dancing. My eyes closed by themselves and a pink lightning-bolt passed through my body, swirling out at the top of my head. Or was that me flying out of myself? This was a joyous experience which happened all because I had forgotten about my year-long wish for Osho to dance with me and look into my eyes. Good things happen when we least expect them!

When the Festival came to a close and Magdalena was again our main cafeteria, I was put in charge of a cleaning shift. Working with me was Ambu from Chile who, like me, heartily disliked being told what to do. But she had a knack for handling one of our new crew members, Tarun. He was deaf, mute and severely autistic; nevertheless he was a good worker and always managed to entertain our crew. Messages for him, such as at what time the shift started the next day, had to be given in writing as none of us knew sign language. (The only sign I remember he taught us meant 'crocodile'.) He astonished us with his coordination at the end of the dishwashing machine, where he had to stack the clean trays on the correct pile: cups with cups and plates with plates. When it got too fast for him and his shouts became louder it was easy just to stop the machine. We gently pushed him to his limits as we had learnt to do with ourselves. His mother, Roshani, was incredibly pleased with his improvement since he had been with us. He had a great sense of humour. I remember he once walked off and started sweeping the tables with a large floor broom. He turned his wide shoulders and discreetly looked back to check if I had noticed, and he enjoyed the antics I had to play out to scold him for his bad behaviour. When Tarun turned 21 we celebrated his birthday with a huge chocolate cake at the end of the shift. He was now of age and was allowed his beer. He gulped down that of others as well and that night he had to be carried into the taxi.

This was the first and last time he touched beer!

The news that Sheela had left the Ranch with some of her closest friends reached me when I had just become a cook. I shared many tasks with Shakti, an Indian lady so tiny that I could pick her up and pretend to throw her into our huge garbage bin. I used to shout to the other cooks: "Open the lid, open the lid!" On the other hand she had such a charisma that not even our hugely strong black male cook dared dispute her orders. That morning we noticed an unusual quietness and came to the conclusion that we were the only cooks who had shown up. Not even the kitchen-mom, Karuna, made an appearance that day. Without stress, but at full speed, the two of us boiled pasta, fried up some leftovers and wokked the sunflower sprouts we had found in the fridge. The hungry came with their plates in hand directly into the kitchen where we served them straight from the woks. We had a good laugh and felt like two lonely warriors holding down the fort.

When Osho heard about a similar incident where cooks, waiters and bus drivers went to a celebration without having their jobs covered, he commented that without Sheela's regime we were not able to take responsibility for ourselves and that without her we would never have been able to build a city like we did.

Osho asked the FBI to come to the Ranch and make the necessary enquiries about the wrongdoings of 'Sheela's gang'. The evening talks to the press were moved to the Mandir meditation hall where everybody could follow the interviews. This meant that we heard Osho speaking morning and night – and he brought many things to light. For instance we learned that the fruit salad for the celebration had been poisoned, which was why it had been disposed of before it was served in the hall. Proof was that some guards in faraway posts who had received the boxes earlier got sick that night. We also heard of the poisoning by needle of Osho's personal physician, Amrito, while he was sitting in discourse (he luckily survived, after being rushed to hospital); of the discovery of a secret escape tunnel in Jesus Grove; of bugged hotel rooms. Even the poisoning of a salad bar in a neighbouring town came to light, and that the conjunctivitis scare was a set-up job arranged so that Osho's caretakers would be moved to the medical ward long enough to bug Osho's room. Other people like me were probably also confined there so as not to create suspicion.

Osho spoke about Sheela and her gang morning and evening, about the same events again and again, *ad nauseam*. Although I had detected some jarring notes here and there, it was difficult to believe that so many evil deeds could have been dreamt up and executed under my very nose. To see Julian drive around in his elegant brown pickup truck with the twelve-foot-long antennae did not create too much suspicion: it was all for security. Never would I have suspected that via these antennae he could tap into the bugs laid under Sheela's front room carpets (for so-called confidential meetings), in the hotel rooms and even in Osho's own bedroom.

On the other hand, most of us had something to hide, like an expiring visa, some food containers sitting on the ground which would have failed the hygiene inspection, a not-so-kosher electrical installation or the sewage pipes which were not meant to remain in the ground from one celebration to the other. Almost everybody was living with little secrets which we could not share with anyone. It was like breathing polluted air.

It was painful to hear about Sheela's wrongdoings again and again but it had the therapeutic effect of washing our laundry in public. Keeping secrets creates guilt, paranoia and self-pity. I was so bored with hearing everything described all over again that in the end I did not feel any grudge against Sheela and her aides. Of course I was pleased to hear when she was eventually tracked down in Germany, extradited, sentenced and sent to jail with two other women, but I was free from anger towards her. I remember that as long as I blamed the gynaecologist who had punctured my guts during tubal ligation and almost sent me to the creator, I could not be at peace with myself and be part of the ashram. It was good to know where we stood and that the sannyasin superman or superwoman had been a great delusion. We were no better than anyone else out in the world.

When I was conversing with one of the buyers about the number of celebration boxes to order for Osho's birthday, we heard over the motorolas that Osho had just flown out of the Ranch on a Learjet. This was about a month after Sheela had left. "Well, in this case, I will not need the celebration boxes," was all I managed to say, looking down at the sample in my hand. We had hardly managed to recover from the shock of Osho's departure when more worrying news came that same night. The two Learjets, when they had landed in North Carolina, had been surrounded and everyone in the planes was arrested at gunpoint. We later heard that there was not even a warrant for that almost military action.

A TV was installed in Magdalena for all of us to watch the news. My soul shrank when I saw the footage of Osho without the customary cap and robe but wearing a green prison uniform – jacket and trousers – which looked like it was made of very scratchy cotton. I had not seen his bald head for a long time and he looked delicate and vulnerable to me. But his expression had not changed. With fire in his eyes but still exuding his usual calm he gave interviews to the press. The many flowers outside his prison hospital ward showed worldwide interest and concern. Knowing him, he might have even enjoyed being a prisoner!

What could I do? I wanted to fly to Charlottesville and protest, but our new secretary, Hasya, who had called us together in the Mandir that night, spoke as if everything was going to be settled through the lawyers. It was difficult to judge what action would have been better. I did not want to jeopardise Osho's safety with a mass demonstration – that was for sure.

After a few days Osho was moved to another prison in another state and we followed his whereabouts on the news with anguish, until one day the track was lost. Even the media had lost sight of him and could not report a specific location. The deep abyss of the unknown started gnawing at our souls – everybody looked miserable, too miserable even to cry. Walking up to Magdalena for breakfast I looked into the sun; there was a beautiful rainbow-coloured ice circle around it. What could I do for Osho? He used to say that when we leave him he can be with us, so I thought maybe I could be with him when he was gone. So, with closed eyes I let the sunrays shine on my face and took a deep breath of fresh air, for him. I sent him health and joy in jail where he could not feel the beauty of nature.

A few days later we heard Osho was coming back to the Ranch. It was already dark when we lined up on the roads to welcome him. With my best friend, Tanmaya, I waited near the hotel, where from time to time I could have a seat in the lobby as I was plagued by horrible cramps in my belly. They were indeed in synchronicity with what I was going to see in the car. It was Osho, yes, but he looked so different. He was sitting in the back, looking straight ahead of him, not at all interested in seeing us. As if he just wanted to get home quickly. We knew little about what he had gone through until the next time he spoke to us.

In my mind's eye I see a slide of another drive-by, maybe a few days later and during the day, not on his usual route to Patanjali Lake but to the airport. The line was so thick that I was frustrated to have all these tall heads in front of me. I ran toward the runway, where a quick glimpse of Osho climbing onto the jet, waving to us from the top of the steps with a victory salute and seating himself in the dark, was the last I saw of him. The plane made a big extra loop around our heads and someone next to me said: "He is not coming back." "What? He is just going to Portland for the trial," I said. But he was right. As suggested by his lawyers, Osho had signed an Alford plea and left the country for India that evening.

It became clear to us pretty soon that the Ranch without Osho's presence was not viable because it would not attract the visitors it had in the past. We were dependent on them as we had no industry, no mines… nothing which could support our living there. In the evenings we sat together on the porch, discussing where we intended to go next or whether we had already made arrangements for our tickets. Some had bought school buses to turn into caravans for touring the States. A friend booked a flight ticket for me – for the 5th of December – as I planned to spend Christmas with the family in Lugano. Father would love to have all five daughters reunited for once.

I was not sad to leave and knew that others felt the same. We had lived our lives on the Ranch to our fullest and there was no remorse, no sadness for leaving it all behind. But when someone mentioned the *samadhi*, our beautiful crematorium, everybody burst into tears. We cried not only because we were not able to take that beautiful building with us, but because we had thought that our old bodies would eventually be burnt there. There was no chance of that now!

While packing my few red clothes which were good enough to wear at my father's place I saw the *shekere* in the corner of my cupboard. I looked at it in gratefulness but left it standing there. I thought that I would never have the joy of playing music for Osho ever again.

Here in Pune, during the first weekend of the month, we have three intensive meditation days. We still call them 'camps' as we did in the very distant past when Osho used to travel from Mumbai to locations in the countryside where the participants would find shelter overnight in tents, as already mentioned. Later the camps became more sophisticated and we all slept in hotels and guest houses, as I did at Mt. Abu. In Pune, before we moved to the Ranch in Oregon, the camps were also at the beginning of the month and lasted ten days, but later they were reduced to three days (I don't know the reason for this though). There were five to six meditations a day, finishing with White Robe Meditation and a video discourse.

For this occasion we would be playing live for Nataraj Meditation at 11am. Nataraj is the name of the Hindu god Shiva depicted as the cosmic dancer, and the meditation consists of dancing, on our own, possibly with eyes closed, letting ourselves go in the dance, drowning in the dance. It is the only active meditation for which we play music live – for all others it is preferred to use the recorded music as most probably it helps body and psyche fall into that meditation quicker. We are gathered on the musicians' stage which is on the right of the podium. Mikes checked, instruments tuned, my new *shekere* tight in my hand, we are ready to roll. For some strange reason people are facing us musicians instead of the podium as one tends to do for all other meditations. I am not afraid of being noticed up here. Everybody can see me in full daylight, particularly now that I have stopped hiding behind my percussion stand. I feel this is the perfect and only place to be! But it is a meditation and not a concert!

The musicians use as a base the melody and sequence of scales from the original music on the CD. But our forty minutes are filled with new variations created on the spot by the solo instruments – electric guitar, flute and keyboard – each one telling their story in turns as if in vivid conversation. The rhythm section just needs to have the stamina for that length of time. When I tire I look at the dancers. This gives me the energy to keep going and, in turn, my rattles make the dancers go wilder. This circle of energy is renewed many times. After forty minutes both musicians and dancers are happy to hear the gong for the silent phase. We all lie down, the dancers on the cool marble floor, the musicians on the sweat-drenched carpet over cables and leads. Before closing my eyes I see a crow, or rather, its shadow, fly over the Hall. It expands and slides down the other side of the plastic tent roof. The sound of the birds and of people passing by in conversation float into our interior space without causing much disturbance; they are close and far away at the same time. I lose track of the time and am not sure whether I am asleep or awake. Sometimes I feel turmoil – colours and sounds in some inner space – until that busy layer has been crossed.

Our drummer Purana makes a gesture in my direction that it is now time to play the Tibetan bells. Three even strokes, with even intervals in between. Such a sweet silvery sound to bring us slowly back to our physical entity. The guitars come in with their arpeggios and the keyboard fades in with a chord of strings. The dancers stand up slowly and sway to the gentle music, the drummer just slightly accents the beat on his hi-hat. The day, the present, is coming back to us with a sense of joy and celebration. Osho's greatest contribution to humankind is to combine meditation with celebration, to bring the two together.

The flight I had booked for my return to Europe was a cheap one, with an airline which sold sandwiches instead of serving meals during flights, a novelty at the time. Unfortunately it went bankrupt the following year. I had a long wait in the Brussels railway station standing sleepily and miserably in the cold wind, waiting for my train to Zurich. I was wearing my new outfit: corduroy trousers and a thick woollen pullover with a polo neck peeping out the top – all in a beautiful, vibrant turquoise green. Osho had revoked the obligation to wear red clothes in a discourse before he left and I had taken the opportunity of my stop-over in Portland to buy the outfit. It would also be easier to go through customs in disguise, I thought. Others had bought multicoloured clothes the very next day after that discourse and I remember hearing that Osho was sad when he got wind of it, particularly because these were people living in his own household. He might have felt that it was a sign that they had reluctantly worn red all these years.

But when Osho suggested we return our malas he happened to look at me and must have seen my stunned expression, so that he added: "unless you wish otherwise." (Probably I was not the only one he saw with that expression on their face.) Here is that part of the discourse:

And today I would like to declare something immensely important, because I feel perhaps this helped Sheela and her people to exploit you. I don't know whether tomorrow I will be here or not, so it is better to do it while I am here and make you free from any other possibility of such a fascist regime.

That is, from today, you are free to use any colour of clothes. If you feel like using red clothes, that is up to you. And this message has to be sent all over the world to all the communes. It will be more beautiful to have all the colours. I had always dreamed of seeing you in all the colours of the rainbow.

Today we claim the rainbow to be our colours.

The second thing: you return your malas – unless you wish otherwise. That is your choice, but it is not a necessity anymore. You return your malas to President Hasya. But if you want to keep it, it is up to you.

The third thing: from now onwards, anybody who wants initiation into sannyas will not be given a mala and will not be told to change to red clothes – so we can take over the world more easily!

Osho, From Bondage to Freedom, Ch. 12

The rest of the clothes in my suitcase were red and, in a synchronicity which happens only in families, all of us five sisters were portrayed at Xmas sitting on the family sofa wearing red (the following year it would be black and gold). Despite my red clothes and eating no meat, my stepmother still considered me the most 'normal' of all: she had to struggle with one sister's dog who was biting the private parts of my little nephews and with the other sister having a nervous breakdown. As usual, talking about Osho or the Ranch was taboo. This saved me from giving explanations about how and why the Ranch closed.

Thanks to the economic boom in Switzerland, I found a job over the phone the day I arrived, although it was right before Christmas and I was now 42, an age which made it difficult for companies to employ people because of a new pension law. But there was no extra cost for them if it were a temporary job, and temporary was fine with me. It was a bit of a shock to be suddenly confronted with the fact that age mattered. In the commune one was just a person, irrespective of age, sex, nationality or race. For sure our bodies had aged during these years but that had not affected our jobs or friendships.

If I had almost died at age 35 (5 x 7) I was certainly going to die on the next Saturn transit ($6 \times 7 = 42$) which was the current year. I was not scared or worried, just on the lookout for when it might happen. At the end of the year, while talking to a friend, I realised I had not died but had completed many old wishes and desires. I had gone by train up to the Jungfraujoch (also called the 'top of Europe'), visited Russia (USSR at the time) where one of my great-grandfathers had come from (or at least I liked to think so), bought myself a good camera and picked up photography again (a series of albums about Moscow and Leningrad are proof of that), taken Modern Dance classes and gone mountain climbing with the fittest body ever. (Waking up one morning with the sound of cowbells was the highlight of one of those excursions.)

One night I came home from work at the advertising agency and popped in for a visit at one of the flats in our Höngg settlement. Old friend Atiti had brought the news that Osho was in Greece and that he was giving discourses. I was excited to finally know his where-abouts and to hear that we could go and see him. Atiti came up with the idea of renting a jet and flying over that very night. He might have actually been able to afford the jet – I think he was already driving his red Ferrari – but he was the only one in the group, apart from me, to jump up and want to take immediate action. Why I did not follow him and book a flight the next day (it didn't necessarily have to be a jet) is still not clear to me. Did I want to learn to be more patient, less in a rush to always be at the master's feet? I decided to book a regular flight – not for the coming weekend but in two weeks' time when I could add a few extra days and have a proper holiday, as was suggested to me by Passiko and Martina. They would join me on the trip. This was much more rational, I told myself. I could learn from my Swiss friends to act in a more 'civilised' manner.

But to postpone the journey was a very bad idea: the same day the flight tickets arrived by post we heard that Osho had been arrested and deported from Greece (he could not refrain from jokes about Orthodox priests). Those who were going to travel with me took it light-heartedly the moment it was confirmed that we could return the tickets. I was devastated and was haunted by nightmares for the rest of the year. I promised myself to remain true to my rushed ways of acting whatever others might say.

The crazy way works better for me.

The whereabouts of Osho faded into mystery again. Rumours were that he was in Portugal, Ireland, Sweden, the UK... I remember hearing names of countries but could not say in which sequence. The Italian sannyasins had collected signatures from influential people and applied for a visa to their country for Osho.

The United States had given out a warning to all countries that Osho was not to be given a permit to enter – as though he were a dangerous man. He was even refused entry into Switzerland, backed by a decision taken by our socialist mayor, Ursula Koch – if I remember rightly. Was Switzerland so dependent upon the United States that it had to follow that behemoth's orders? Only later did I get to hear about the odyssey Osho had to go through with some of his closer disciples – when I saw his video discourses from Uruguay and Nepal. For us in Switzerland, in the meantime, it was 'no news is good news'.

Tanmaya, my no longer yellow friend from the hepatitis ward, had stayed behind at the Ranch as a caretaker and had invited me to visit her and go for a trip around California in her VW van. I met up with her at the Ranch where, together with a dozen sannyasins, she was keeping everything in good order while waiting for any sales deals to come along. The group was living in Sheela's Jesus Grove house, which was strategically well situated on the county road and in the centre of the Ranch. It was funny to live in the very house where all the scamming and bugging had taken place.

The stainless steel bowls reminded me so much of Magdalena cafeteria that I hated to help out in the kitchen – maybe I was not as happy there as I had thought – and I preferred to help with the cleaning. Tanmaya's bathroom needed a good scrub. She had the bad habit of taking off her glasses when relaxing in her room...

I was given the keys to Osho's house, an unexpected treat, and was going to visit it. On Nirvana road I met my willow tree but the feel of the grandmother was no longer there. Maybe she had moved elsewhere. Further down the road near the creek were the white marble pyramids which had hosted the ashes of Dadaji, Osho's father, and of Vimalkirti and Asanga. I am not sure if during that visit the ashes were still there or if they had been removed already. My perception was very confused: whatever I saw did not correspond to what I felt. Although I knew that everyone, except for the few caretakers, had left the Ranch over nine months ago there was a feeling in the air as if all 5,000 inhabitants were still present. Maybe there was a general meeting in the Mandir and this was the reason why I did not see anyone on the roads? I looked over to the car park near the hall but there were no yellow buses waiting.

Following the directions I had received I found Osho's room, next to the swimming pool, and then I suddenly remembered that I had seen it before, during its construction. At the time it had struck me that the parquet tiles were being laid not only on the floor but all the way up the four walls. I respectfully took off my trainers and sat for a while in the empty room. Through the window I saw my hill, the hill I had admired from my room – it was a perfect cone – but I saw it now from the other side. His eyes must have also rested on it and enjoyed its perfect form.

I remembered the day I was going to move out of the room in that townhouse and move in with Tanmaya – but eventually cancelled the move. I was packed, clothes in a couple of pillow covers and my plant ready to go, happy to be able to decide about my fate after Sheela had left the Ranch, but I was sitting on the floor, sobbing and looking at the hill until I decided to stay where I was. Tanmaya was upset that I had changed my plans, mainly because I could not give her a plausible reason. Can you say that you cannot move because of a hill? We had so many of them around. Now I understood that it was a very, very special hill.

Tanmaya's van, an old yellow and orange VW, was soon ready for the trip. She showed me a greasy 'How to fix your VW van' book and I believed her when she told me that she had done most of the fixing herself. She was a girl of many talents. In that small community, apart from learning how to fix cars, many were into things esoteric, a subject which was taboo during our hands-on years on the Ranch. Someone had given me a booklet on visualization which I read with great interest. Before I had left, my gynaecologist in Zurich diagnosed a cyst on my remaining ovary – I had seen it myself on the ultrasound monitor – and I was meant to go back to see him in two months time. I would certainly need an operation, he told me. So desperate was I to avoid any further scalpel cuts on my belly (and going on hormone replacement therapy at this early age) that I religiously started practising the exercises from the book, imagining my cyst becoming smaller and smaller by the day.

Also the fractured meniscus in my knee which had caused a lot of disturbance during the excursions on Mount Rigi with Passiko found a cure during my short stay on the Ranch. I had a dream of my left leg missing from the knee down and, looking at it, I heard myself say, "No need to be so drastic." The message was so clear that the following morning I made a call all the way to Switzerland to cancel the surgery appointment I had made before I left. That meniscus never misbehaved ever again.

Soon the time had come to load our belongings into Tanmaya's van. Her big German shepherd required so much space that some of my luggage had to be left behind. He was one of our sniffer dogs. She had got him when the Ranch closed down and the dogs which we kept for checking visitors and luggage for drugs and firearms were no longer needed. He still behaved strangely at times, but was on his way to becoming a friendly pet dog, the second pet dog on the Ranch. There had been another dog which belonged to a girl. I remember seeing them, when I was a bus driver, walking together on the side of the roads and wondered each time why that dog was allowed to be on the Ranch. There was a total ban on pets but I liked the fact that there were exceptions to the rules. Pets (as well as children) are not the best companions for vagabonds and travellers like us. It is true that Tanmaya never travelled to see Osho again 'because of the dog'. When the dog finally died, Osho was no longer in his body.

Still in the state of Oregon, in a town called Sisters, I bought my sexy red western boots and in North California's Eureka we took photographs of splendid, intricately-carved Victorian houses. At the sight of magnificent Mt. Shasta I indeed heard some voices, as advertised. We camped at the lake which reflected the majestic snow peak surrounded by pink clouds.

I was amazed that I could have lived for so long without ever hearing about the redwoods. They were more of a miracle than the Taj Mahal and I gathered literature and photographs about them. I even brought home a seed in the hope my father could add a sequoia to his great collection of fir trees at the top of his garden. In awe we looked up at their tips, bathing in the dim light filtered through the branches. We both felt the silent presence of these old trees. As an explanation I came to the conclusion that one of the trees had become enlightened and that all redwoods remembered that.

On the way back to Switzerland I made a stopover in New England to visit my old friend, Big Prem, where I learned a few things about life in America. Philippe, her Swiss-French partner, said that I should never go for a walk without taking their dog with me lest their neighbours become suspicious (only tramps walk – proper people drive) and from his son I learned the rules of American baseball. He was probably tired of being interrupted with stupid questions while he followed his favourite team on TV. On an excursion to Montana, in search of a school for Philippe's daughter, we drove through the golden autumn leaves of the maples. Although I had to wear my sunglasses to bear the glare, they told me, "The colours of the leaves this year are not as spectacular as last year."

On the last day of my visit, Big Prem apologised for being such a nag while we worked in the bakery. She said that she was just following orders: Chandrika had asked her to keep an eye on me. I was amazed at this revelation, but it explained the sudden and disharmonious move from the Zarathustra plastics storage to the bread and buns in the bakery. I was such a small fish, how could I be regarded as a threat? Why was Chandrika involved in the kitchens? What was the relationship between Chandrika and Sheela? Was this her revenge that, while I lived in her centre many years ago, I had organised Chaitanya's concert in Zurich without asking her permission?

The flight from Boston took me back to Zurich and I returned to the flat Passiko and I had been sharing. After the Ranch had closed, the commune in Zurich also had to close because of huge debts and was declared bankrupt. I would never have expected that from the Swiss. Individual sannyasins took on leases for various flats on Geeringstrasse, and Passiko and I had chosen the poshest one: it was on the top floor and had a big living room with a fireplace, a balcony for sun bathing and the occasional night under the stars. On a *Föhn* day, when the warm and dry winds from the south cleared the sky, we could even see the snow peaks of the Alps. The flat had three bedrooms. The third one saw various occupants over the eighteen months, coming and going, adapting more or less to our harmonious household.

Mr. Abächerli was happy to have me back, again for a voting campaign. His advertising agency was now reduced to fewer staff and he had also changed location. My travel to work was now by tram. This gave me the opportunity to join Passiko on her morning fitness walk through the woods – be it sun, rain or snow – to catch the No. 14 at the Polytechnic. She was a skinny, athletic girl with healthy eating habits and was a welcome influence on my phlegmatic nature. I did not need much persuasion to follow her on a Sunday excursion onto Mount Rigi, but did require convincing to try the brown rice and tofu diet. On the other hand she might have profited from me when I lured her to a good movie followed by – oh terrible – a huge ice-cream sundae.

With some trepidation I turned up for my second check-up with the gynaecologist, but this showed a sonar scan clear of any cyst, validated by a manual check to make sure we were not seeing things. "How unbelievable," he exclaimed, running around his office like a headless chicken, "I was just going to fix a date for the operation on the cyst." But when I mentioned the visualizations, he immediately replied: "These things can happen naturally; cysts do shrink sometimes."

For a while I stood outside the surgery, motionless, staring at the bleak, grey, heavy stone buildings around the square. What I had wished so badly had really happened: my visualization had worked. I had done it! The shock was such that I did not feel any exhilaration, just a dispassionate "Aha, OK."

By November we heard that Osho was giving discourses in Mumbai. I immediately got hold of the address, booked a return ticket and packed my red Samsonite for a three-week holiday. "Even if I might only see him once, it is worth it," I said to Passiko who looked at me in astonishment. She had decided to avoid India at all costs because of all the parasites she used to catch and there was no chance of her joining me in the venture.

Osho was the guest of a sannyasin who owned a beautiful house in a residential area in a suburb of Mumbai called Juhu Beach, and the multi-tiered living room was the perfect setting for his discourses. As there were more people wanting to see him than seats available, it was possible to attend the discourses only once a week. I therefore had to wait a few days before I could see Osho.

In the meantime I had settled in a room at the Iskcon Hotel, the Hare Krishna lodge. Like all Indian guest houses it had clean grey stone floors, hard beds and hard pillows which I liked. The only downfall was the early morning *puja* chants with cymbals which interrupted the sleep of innocents. Others lived in fancy hotels with swimming pools or in hotels with red wall-to-wall carpeting which had functioned as brothels before the sannyasin rush.

There was plenty of time to catch up with old friends and make new friends out of old faces. I met Yoga Puja, my best friend from the early Pune days, whom I had not seen since 1974 or '75. I spent many evenings with her and Bhaven chit-chatting in an outdoor chai shack, sitting on a wobbly wooden bench under a rusty lantern, while memories and gossip were drowned by the traffic of scooters and rickshaws on the road. There I heard for the first time that people thought I was rich, in times when I did not even have a penny to my name. I must have a wealthy aura, I thought.

With Puja I attended the Kundalini which was held daily in a nearby hall. We had not done any active meditations for years. We had thought we had grown out of them, our work being our meditation all that time. The meditation made me feel sick in the beginning and I had to keep my eyes open while dancing. But it was great to do this meditation again, and with a fresh mind.

One evening, on the stairs of Iskcon lodge, I bumped into Madhuri, Sarita's sister, with whom I had not had the chance to speak since the darshan we had had together, following my three weeks in silence and isolation. She offered me a psychic body reading to which I agreed with enthusiasm. I had to lie on my bed with eyes closed and she spoke in pictures and waved her hands over my body. I vaguely remember the picture of a tiger. It was not a tiger in action, rather one asleep under a tree on a hot day.

Madhuri told me she had just given a session to her mother back in the States which had lasted five hours (with a break in the middle). I would have liked to have such an open relationship with my own mother as well. (She accepted the fact that I was abroad most of the time and she was happy that I was wearing orange – and not black – which she dreaded I would wear when she first heard I was on a spiritual path. But I could not really share with her what Osho meant for me and why meditation was the most important thing in my life.) As you see, esoteric stuff was now definitely 'in'.

It came to my ears that Maneesha was looking for someone to type the manuscript of a book she was writing. I had plenty of time to spare after sunbathing as a visitor in the Holiday Inn and needed something to do when the sun became too hot. I remember re-typing the corrected manuscripts on a black portable typewriter on a cold black marble countertop in a kitchen. It was about Osho's arrest, later published under the title, *Bhagwan: Twelve Days that Shook the World*. In the darkness of the kitchen I could just make out a few scattered books and research notes and, closer to the window, Amrito, Osho's physician, who was also writing a book. While working there I overheard Maneesha say that Osho had suggested she omit all references to relationships and that kind of everyday trouble and rather write about her meditation, her growth and how she felt Osho was working with her. I took this suggestion on board while writing this book even if it was not given to me directly.

Finally the day on my discourse ticket approached. I bought myself a ready-made silk outfit in a fancy shop inside the Holiday Inn. It was pink and had a small mango pattern and borders around the bottom of the *kurta*, the sleeves and the pyjamas, worthy of a darshan with the master. In the late afternoon I joined the people who were already sitting on the bare concrete floor of the car porch below the house, forming a typical English zig-zag queue. I was soon going to see my master, after more than a year! My heart rate increased and my awareness got sharper. Manu came to pick us up. Winding steps brought us up to the hall and I was assigned a seat. In silence we waited for the magical stroke of 7pm. Osho greeted us as he walked along the corridor. He held onto Neelam's hand when he came down the few wooden steps, still with one hand in *namaste*. He joined his hands again when he reached the chair. I wondered if he noticed when old faces reappeared in his audience. Was I one of his old faces? But I knew that I was thrilled to see him alive and kicking, to see him so close that I could hear the rustling of his robes.

As soon as Osho was seated in his chair, Ashok Bharti, a small-boned Indian sannyasin, grabbed his hand drum and accompanied his song with a clicking snap of his middle finger. I was told that he was singing his own songs and that every night he came to discourse with a new devotional song. One part of me must have heard the words Osho was speaking but I could not remember a single word afterwards. It was more of an imbibing of his presence rather than a listening to his words. The discourse ended; *namaste* to all of us and *namaste* back to him. I wanted to lean over and crane my neck like a child and see Osho disappear along the corridor, to see him for as long as I could, but I refrained from doing so and told myself that I would see him again and that I did not need to be so rude. I regretted not having followed my spontaneous, childish impulse as indeed it was the last time I saw Osho in Mumbai. He came down with a cold and all further discourses were cancelled. I had said to Passiko, 'even if I should see him only once...', and only once it was!

Back home in Zurich I found my room occupied by a whole family. Majida, with whom I had chopped vegetables in Vrindavan canteen way back in Pune, had left Seattle to return to Switzerland. With her were her husband, Vedam, an exquisite flute-player from New York, and their little chocolate-coloured son, Shanti. After listening to a pleading speech about the importance for a child of having a steady place, I accepted an offer to house-sit a nearby studio flat until they had found permanent accommodation; but I would come back to the old place for dinners. I loved that little kid with his huge diapers and did not mind living out of my suitcase for a while just for him. When Vedam eventually found a job as a flute teacher and Majida as an elementary school teacher, and a flat in the same compound came their way, I moved back into my former space.

With Passiko I resumed the early morning power walks through the woods to catch the tram on the other side and we both admired the patterns of the snow resting on the pine branches. Then, in spring, we rejoiced at the soft, light green shoots at the tips of the branches. As they looked like little paws we took them between our fingers and pretended to shake hands with them – something I still do to this day. This was a way to welcome the spring and the beginning of more trekking days on weekends. Mount Rigi was explored via different routes, but the boat ride on Lake Lucerne on the journey home was always a 'must'.

9

Yaa-Hoo!

Poison

Six months later, out of the blue, I was sacked from my new job. It was the first time in my life that I had been fired – usually it was I who resigned. It had not been easy to work there: my predecessor had taken with her all contact details of clients and suppliers which made work very difficult; the apprentice was becoming more know-ledgeable by the day because of his evening classes, and the copywriter had so much to brag about that I was left numbed and speechless (the creativity of her job, the amount of money she earned and could spend on clothes and jewellery, the admirers who sent her bouquets!). Somehow, I did not fit into the team and some of the clients had nothing better to do than to shout at me over the phone. My ego was hurt and I ended up crying the whole morning.

Only after lunch did it cross my mind that instead of going to visit Osho for my four-week summer holiday, I could now go for an indefinite time. Being fired became a blessing and I started to smile – to the bewilderment of my boss and my colleagues. In January Osho had moved from Mumbai to Pune – this being 1987 – to our old property in Koregaon Park. There was no reason why I should not be there as well.

After almost six years of Indian weather and low maintenance the commune buildings were in a pretty derelict state and the gardens had become a jungle. We jokingly commented that wherever Osho sets his foot down there would be a construction site. The noise of hammering and drilling came from all corners of the compound. It was impossible to walk from A to B without coming across an obstacle: the paths were being laid out in white marble from the front gate to Lao Tzu and in flagstones towards the back gate. The electricians, plumbers and A/C engineers, trained on big projects on the Ranch, were back with their tools and technical knowledge. So much noise, so much dust.

Many of the trees around Buddha Hall had to be cut down as, in search of light, they had grown at dangerous slanting angles and were leaning into the hall space. The concrete floor was being covered in white marble and I heard that we were waiting for a temporary plastic roof to arrive. It would be supported by a steel structure. A building permit for a permanent roof had still not been granted.

In the meantime, discourses were held in Chuang Tzu Auditorium, the roofed hall attached to Lao Tzu, where we had experienced so many darshans in the past. Because of its small size, we could attend the discourses only every other day. As part of the security measures we introduced frisking, which was similar to techniques being used at airports. I became part of the security crew and was allowed to have a seat behind the musicians, to the side of Osho's chair – a wonderful opportunity for me to sit as close to Osho as possible.

The roof for Gautama the Buddha Auditorium was eventually delivered, but the mounting of the plastic sheet required the intervention of a computer in Germany to calculate the angles and tensions for it to be tight enough so that it did not sag. The hall was going to be surrounded by mosquito netting and people were stitching together – in situ – miles of fabric on old pedal Singer sewing machines. People murmured that Osho was disappointed that the roof was not ready for his Birthday Celebration as planned. On the Ranch we would have been much better with deadlines...

I had found a flat in the newly-constructed Popular Heights complex, about ten minutes on foot from the commune. Because it was new it was fairly clean, but it had a downside. Right next to the compound there was a shanty village where the residents would gather to watch movies on the one TV set which was placed in the middle of the courtyard. Of course it ran for hours at ear-splitting volume and on into the middle of the night. One would then be woken up by noisy, guttural retching cleansing yoga practices at dawn. Haridevi, the fearsome vegetable lady from Vrindavan, was one of my neighbours. She was renting a few flats in my building and then subletting them to new arrivals.

My first job was taking care of the stationery store and the safety deposit. There were two of us, Anatta and me. We had two rooms in what were originally the servants' quarters of Krishna House – one room for stationery and one for passports and valuables. Each had its window from where we could serve our customers.

As a child I had wanted to own a stationery shop and here I had the chance to live out my dream, although the quality of our goods was not that outstanding. In those days, paper in India was never white – it always had a purple tinge. Cardboard was yellow and very rough and never flat. Glue was so liquid the paper rippled. The pencils had broken leads and the rubbers smeared. Such a difference from the fancy coloured cardboards and self-sealing envelopes we had in Switzerland.

The next room housed metal cabinets where we stored the numbered black plastic envelopes containing the passports and air tickets of our visitors. I invented an In and Out signing procedure and a way to keep track of the monthly contributions. To fulfil the demands of customers whose emotions were so close to the surface because of Dynamic and therapy groups, was not an easy task – especially if they had to wait in a queue. Not being centred and relaxed ourselves did not help much either and there were often tantrums on both sides of the windows. At night we could see our workspace lit from the inside through heavy metal shutters and, under the constant vigilance of the guard at Lao Tzu gate close by; we were certain that all the valuables were safe indeed.

Anatta became a good companion despite the confined space we had to share. But I could not relate to her in my usual way. One day she confided in me that she had difficulty in dealing with people and understanding their emotions. Maybe this was her first incarnation as a human being; maybe she came from the innocent world of plants and flowers? I do not know, but I liked to think of her like that.

One morning I was called to Neelam's office in Krishna House, the same office in which Laxmi used to sit. On the Ranch I had admired how Neelam managed to run the tea room in our garage with such grace, never getting upset with the mechanics, their greasy boots and rough manners. Neelam was now Osho's secretary for India, as well as the head of the commune. Her words began: "Osho is concerned about the health of his people." I supposed (correctly) that what she meant was that I should take care of the cleaning in the kitchen. And this starting today. 'Not the kitchen again!' I howled inside. But if Osho was worried about our health, how could I say no?

Latifa was in charge of the kitchen. It was in the same place as the old Vrindavan but was now called Zorba the Buddha. I had seen Latifa on the Ranch wearing the blue outfit, heavy gloves and boots of the welders. She was tall and strong, full of energy and fun. As old buddies from Deeksha's canteen, we spoke the same kitchen language and a good co-operation began. Every few days we met the head of the new hygiene department. This was Amiten, a ginger-bearded man from the North of England whose accent was so thick that Latifa and I often looked at each other to see if maybe the other had understood his instructions. (Only fifteen years later, when I was introduced to his parents in Newcastle, did I get to know that this speech is called 'Geordie'. His mother is still the only person in his family I can understand without a translator!)

Amiten later told me that he used to meet our doctors who kept him informed of any outbreaks. His department tested water and food and he often came to the kitchen to observe the way things were done. His colleague even sat there for hours in the middle of the night to try and solve a certain mystery: Why did the yogurt keep going off? Then one early morning she came across a couple who were innocently drinking warm milk from their private not-very-clean cups – before the kitchen was open. They'd dipped the cups in the yogurt drum – and this was enough to spoil the whole 60 litres of milk. And after observing how the cleaners swept up clouds of dust –

full of contaminated particles – which then engulfed the eating area of the canteen, Amiten suggested the area be paved. It was difficult to relate to him as he was solely concerned with his mission: to keep sannyasins healthy. He was not interested in any personal interaction.

The cleaning of the kitchen depended mostly on my own efforts. The vegetable cutters were all Indians, people who had grown up with many servants around them, and for them to bend down and pick up the debris of their chopping was not part of their mindset. I felt very frustrated as I had a mission and a goal – sparkling cleanliness – which I was unable to implement.

My personal frustration and exhaustion were soon put into perspective when we heard that Osho was not coming to give discourses – not because of a cold, but because of an infection in his ear. He was no longer able to use his earplugs for his naps so the kitchen had to stop its activity during certain hours in order not to disturb him with the clatter and banging of pots and pans. We first tried to work without using this drastic measure but we were not aware enough to work in silence. It reminded me of the time when Deeksha used to give us fifty rupee fines when we dropped a lid during darshan. Why should a noisy kitchen be so close to Lao Tzu Auditorium and so close to Osho's bedroom in the first place? After a few days Neelam started to think that we might need to close the kitchen altogether. With my narrow mind I was unable to cope with such an idea as I was unaware of what was really happening with Osho.

With a very soft voice he spoke to us after a long absence and revealed facts none of us had ever suspected:

My beloved ones,
I have been away from you much too long. It has been a very painful absence for me. For seven weeks continuously I have been only filled with your love, your patience, your thirst, your longing.
These days were remarkable in many ways. Seven weeks before, I was infected in the ear. It was a simple thing; according to the best expert

available here, Dr. Jog, it cures in four days at the most – but it continued for seven weeks. He has never come across such a case in his life. He could not believe it, because no medicine was working. He tried all kinds of medicines, all kinds of ointments. Finally he had to do an operation, but then the wound of the operation was not healing. Dr. Devageet thought perhaps it was something to do with my teeth – he is my dental surgeon – but nothing was found.

My personal physician, Dr. Amrito, immediately informed all sannyasin doctors around the world and asked them to contact the best experts about poisoning, because his own analysis was that unless I have been poisoned there is no possibility to explain why my body has lost all resistance.

And as this idea became stronger in his mind, step by step he started searching into the matter and he found all the symptoms that can happen only if some kind of poison has been given to me.

I myself had been suspicious about it, but I have never mentioned the fact to anybody. The day I was arrested in America for no valid or even invalid reason, they refused to bail me out – although the United States attorney argued for three days and concluded in the end by saying, "I have not been able to prove anything against him, but neither has the other party been able to prove anything."

It was hilarious, because the innocent cannot prove his innocence by any means, and no law in the whole world requires that an innocent person should prove his innocence. The burden was on the government of America, which had arrested me, to prove the reason for my arrest.

And even though the United States attorney himself accepted the defeat, still the magistrate denied me bail. I had immediately an intuitive flash – what could be the reason? We offered to the government our own jet plane so that their pilot, their officers, could take me to Oregon because that was where the court had to take the case. The journey was only five or six hours at the most, but the government refused that offer. They said, "Only our airplane will take you." And their airplane took me to Oregon – a six-hour flight was completed in twelve days.

I was taken from one jail to another jail. In twelve days I had to pass through six jails, all over America.

In Oklahoma my suspicion became a certainty, because I landed in the middle of the night at a silent airport, and the U.S. Marshal himself was there to take charge of me. He himself was driving the car, I was sitting behind him. The man who was giving the charge to him whispered in his ear – which I could hear without any effort, I was just behind him. He said, "This guy is world-famous and all the world news media is focused on him, so don't do anything directly. Be very careful."

I started thinking, What is their intention? What do they want to do indirectly? And as I reached the jail their intention became very clear to me.

The U.S. Marshal asked me not to fill in the form with my own name. I should write instead, 'David Washington' as my name. I said, "According to what law or constitution are you asking me to do such a stupid thing? I simply refuse, because I am not David Washington."

He insisted, and he said, "If you don't sign the name 'Washington' you will have to sit in this cold night on this hard steel bench."

I asked him, "You are a reasonable man, well educated; can't you see that it is a stupid thing you are asking me to do?"

He said, "I cannot answer anything. I'm simply fulfilling the orders from above." And 'above' certainly means Washington, the White House, Ronald Reagan. Seeing the situation – I was tired – I told him, "Let us compromise. You fill in the form, you write whatever name you want to write. I will sign it."

He filled in the form. David Washington was my name, and I signed my own signature in Hindi. He asked me, "What have you signed?"

I said, "It must be David Washington." I said, "This will be a reminder to you that anything that you want to do – directly or indirectly – you will be caught. It is with your handwriting that you have written David Washington and it is my signature, which is world-famous and can be recognised without any difficulty. Your whole conspiracy has failed. I can see it clearly in your eyes, in your nervousness, in your trembling hands."

The idea was that if I write David Washington and sign David Washington, I can be killed, poisoned, shot and there will be no proof that I ever entered the jail. I was brought from the back door of the airport, I entered the jail also from the back door, in the middle of the night so that nobody can be ever aware – and only the U.S. Marshal was present in the office, nobody else.

He took me to the cell and told me to take one of the mattresses, utterly dirty, full of cockroaches. I said to him, "I am not a prisoner. You should behave a little more humanly. And I will need a blanket and a pillow."

And he simply refused: "No blanket, no pillow. This is all you will get." And he locked the door of that small, dirty cabin.

Strangely enough, in the early morning at five o'clock he opened the door and he was a completely changed man. I could not believe my eyes, because he had brought a new mattress, a blanket, a pillow. I said, "But in the night you were behaving in such a primitive way. Suddenly you have become so civilised."

And he offered me breakfast early in the morning – five o'clock. In no other jail I was offered breakfast before nine o'clock. I said, "It is too early – and why are you paying so much attention?"

But he said, "You have to eat it quick, because within five minutes we have to leave for the airport."

I said, "Then what is the purpose of the mattress and the blanket and the pillow?"

He said nothing and simply closed the door. The breakfast was not much: just two slices of bread soaked in a certain sauce – I could not figure out what it was – tasteless, odourless.

Now, Dr. Amrito feels I was poisoned. Perhaps they poisoned me in all the six jails; that was the purpose of not giving me bail and that was the purpose in taking twelve days to complete a journey of six hours. A slow poisoning which will not kill me immediately, but in the long run it will make me weak – and it has made me weak. [...]

Later Osho continued:

The European experts in England and Germany have suggested a name of a certain poison, thallium. It is a poison of a family of poisons of heavy metals. It disappears from the body in eight weeks' time, but leaves its effects and destroys the body's resistance against diseases. And all the symptoms [...] are part of thallium poisoning.

The American experts have suggested a different poison which they think has been used by governments against rebellious individuals. The name of *the poison is synthetic heroin. It is one thousand times more dangerous than ordinary heroin. All the symptoms are the same as with thallium, but the poison is more dangerous and after two years there is no possibility to find any trace of it in the body.*

The Japanese experts, who have been working in Hiroshima and Nagasaki on atomic radioactivity, have suggested that these symptoms can also be created in a more sophisticated way by radioactive exposure – either while I was asleep, or food can be exposed to radioactivity and there is no way to find any trace of it. [...]

In the same discourse he reveals to us:

Dr. Amrito's own research... and he is a genius as far as medical science is concerned. He is a fellow of the Royal Society of Physicians in England, and he is a rare individual in the sense that he is the youngest man ever accepted by the Royal Society of Physicians as a member. He has all the highest qualifications. His own research is about a fourth, very uncommonly used poison. The name of the poison is fluorocarbon. This poison disappears immediately. Even within minutes, you cannot find any trace in the blood, in the urine, but all these symptoms indicate towards it.

It does not matter which poison has been given to me, but it is certain that I have been poisoned by Ronald Reagan's American government.

There is other circumstantial evidence for it. Because they had no evidence against me – I have not committed any crime – they blackmailed my attorneys, the best in America. The United States attorneys told my attorneys, "If you are interested in Bhagwan's life, it is better not to go for trial, because you know and we know that he has not committed anything, that all thirty-four charges are false. But in no case will the government of America be willing to be defeated in the court by a single individual."

They had named the case United States of America versus Bhagwan Shree Rajneesh. Now the greatest nation in the world, the greatest power in history, naturally would not like to be defeated in the court by a powerless individual. My attorneys came to me with tears in their eyes. They said, "We are here to protect you, but it seems impossible. We cannot take the risk to go for trial, because we have been told very directly that your life is at risk. So we have agreed on your behalf to accept two nominal charges, just to give the American government a face-saving device, so that they can fine you and deport you."

This was just ten minutes before the court was to start, and in the Federal Court, Judge Leavy asked me just about those two charges that had been chosen by my attorneys to be accepted because they were just formalities. It was strange that out of thirty-four charges, Judge Leavy immediately asked me only about those two: "Are you guilty of those two crimes or not?" It is clear that Judge Leavy was also part of the whole conspiracy.

But I am a crazy man of my own type. I simply said, "I am." And my attorney, Jack Ransom, immediately added – he was standing by my side – "guilty." So on the court record it has become the full sentence, "I am guilty." I have not said that at all. I would rather be crucified than to accept a false charge.

Outside of the court Jack Ransom told me, "You created such a strange situation. It is good that Judge Leavy has not taken note of it."

He immediately pronounced his judgment. That too is a strange thing. The judgment has to be written after my acceptance or denial, but the judgment was ready-made. It was there on the table, he simply read it out. Perhaps the judgment was not even written by him. Perhaps it was just given to him.

The judgment was that I was to be fined four hundred thousand dollars. My attorneys were shocked; they could not believe that for those two formal charges, which are false, more than half a crore rupees are fined; deportation from America, for five years no entry, and if I should enter then ten years suspended jail sentence would have to be served. And I was told that I had to take my clothes from the jail immediately and my plane is waiting at the airport. I have to leave America immediately, so that I cannot appeal in a higher court.

I was taken to the jail. The Portland jail is the most sophisticated kind of jail facility. It was recently built; only three months before it had been opened. It is very sophisticated, with all the latest security measures. As I entered the jail, the ground floor was absolutely empty. There were all kinds of offices but there was nobody in those offices.

I asked the man who had taken me to the jail, "What is the reason why the whole ground floor is empty?"

He said, "I don't know."

But I looked into his eyes and I could see – he knows.

As I was taken inside there was only one man in one room. The other man immediately left and the man in the room told me to sit on a particular chair. That was also strange because there were so many chairs; I could have chosen any. But he indicated to me that I had to sit on this chair. And he said, "I have to go to get the signature of my boss, so you will have to wait for at least ten, fifteen minutes."

Later on I came to know that there was no need of any signature of any boss. I myself could see on the form, and I asked the man, "Where is the signature of your boss? There is no need; the only need is my signature that I have received my clothes. No other boss is needed to sign it."

He was so nervous he was perspiring – in an air-conditioned room. And because he was holding the form in his hand… the form was trembling, the hand was trembling. As I reached the airport the rumour reached immediately to me that a bomb had been found underneath my chair where I was sitting for fifteen minutes. Perhaps this was the arrangement, that if I insist for trial and don't accept that I have committed two crimes then it is better to finish me by exploding the bomb. That's why the whole ground floor was empty. And even the man in the room who was to give me my clothes disappeared in the name of taking the signature of his boss, and locked the room from outside. But because I had accepted the guilt and I had been fined, I had been told to leave America immediately, the bomb was not exploded. He must have gone to enquire what he was supposed to do, because he was not aware what had happened in the court.

One of my attorneys – and also my sannyasin – Swami Prem Niren is present here. I had left him two years before in tears in America, and he is still in tears – tears of love and trust and immense helplessness against the primitive, brutal, and violent heritage of man.

Only such tears give a hope that one day man will be out of the clutches of animality. Niren knows the inside story of what happened to me and my beautiful commune, how brutally they were destroyed because of religious persecution by the fundamentalist, fanatic and bigoted Christians and politicians just because they could not tolerate a beautiful thing happening. They were aware that this was the beginning of the new man and the end of the old, of which they are the representatives. These parasites of the society completely forgot all democratic values and humanitarian concepts when it was a question of their own vested interests being in danger. The commune in Rancho Rajneesh of five thousand sannyasins had exposed the priests and politicians and their conspiracy against humanity as such.

Another one of my attorneys – Bob McCrea, a beautiful man with some understanding of what was happening – told Vivek [later called Nirvano, ed.], my caretaker, after my last appearance in court, "It seems and feels to me that they have done it again. They have crucified Jesus again. I'm sorry and I feel so helpless."

It is absolutely certain that I had been poisoned, and these seven weeks I have been in an immense struggle.

I don't have any reason to live in the world. I have experienced, I have realised the very essence of eternal life, but something else forces me to linger on a little more on this shore before leaving for the further shore beyond.

It is you, it is your love.

It is your eyes, it is your hearts.

And when I say 'you' I don't mean only those who are present here; I also mean all those who are spread all over the earth – my people.

I would like these small sprouts to become trees. I would like to see the spring come to you all, the flowering of your ultimate being, the blissfulness and the ecstasy of enlightenment, the taste of the beyond.

These seven weeks you were not aware… you were simply thinking I was sick. Doctor Premda, my eye surgeon, had immediately rushed from Germany with the recent most medications, but nothing helped against the poisons except my meditations – the only medicine that can transcend all that belongs to matter.

These seven weeks I have been lying in darkness almost the whole day and night, silently witnessing the body and keeping my consciousness unshadowed by anything.

I was struggling with death. It was a fight between death and your love.

And you should celebrate that your love has been victorious. [...]

And finally:

Remember it: I am here for you.

That remembrance will help you not to go astray. That remembrance will help you to be aware of the uncivilised world in which we are living, in this madhouse that we call humanity. It will go on reminding you that we have to give birth to a new man and to a new humanity.

This is the tremendous challenge. Those who have guts and intelligence and a desire and a longing to touch the farthest stars... only those very few people have been able to understand me, have been able to become my fellow travellers. I don't have any followers – I have only lovers and friends and fellow travellers.

I would like you all to reach to the same beatitude, to the same bliss-fulness, to the same ecstasy that has become my very heartbeat. It is also the heartbeat of the whole universe.

Okay, Vimal?

Yes, Osho.

Osho, *Jesus Crucified Again, This Time in Ronald Reagan's America,*
Ch. 1

It was a short discourse, almost like an announcement. His voice had been scarily transparent. I stayed behind in the cool dark hall whilst others slowly made their way to the exits. The news was such a shock that no thought, no feelings of anger stirred within. But I felt embarrassed that I had not sensed what was happening across the garden and why we might have needed to close the kitchen. I judged myself for being a small housewife more concerned with her day-to-day life than with the bigger events around her. And a sentence like "Remember: I am here for you" was very difficult to take.

Today Ojas called musicians and drummers together from various departments to revive the 'Oshoba', which was the famous Samba music Nivedano and his band used to play in the lead-up to the silent part of the meditation in White Robe – just before Osho left his body. (I heard from a reliable source that Osho thought this to be the best music for this meditation.) We are now trying to be as good as the musicians who were trained daily by 'capitano' Nivedano ten years ago.

Ojas is standing at the ready behind his snare drum; the shaker, *agogo* and *tambourim* are on my left in front of the keyboard. With my left hand placed on the skin of a gigantic *surdo* I hold with my right a huge mallet. Yoko on the flute has a position way in front so that she does not get overwhelmed by the sound wall. My partner in action is Amlas, an outstanding bass player, who is going to play the slightly smaller *surdo*. We have previously tuned them carefully so that the gap between them has a harmonious interval. The first piece we play has a slow rhythm where the lower drum is calling for an answer from the higher. It sounds as if two drummers are slowly approaching town, walking down the main street at dusk, the sound coming closer and closer. As they are Brazilians – in our imagination – they would be moving their hips sensuously in rhythm. We cannot walk because the drums are securely hung on a metal structure but we can certainly move our hips while playing. We both enjoy the sensuousness of the rhythm interspersed with the more ethereal notes of the flute and the string pads of the keyboard.

Ten minutes before 7pm we stop. From the musicians' stage I can see the floor of the hall from above with all the white robed meditators sitting in concentric half-circles around Osho's illuminated podium. The light spreads over the people in the first few rows and fades off towards the back, but because of the white marble and the white robes I can see most details all the way to the edges of the hall. The lights at the entrance are now switched off which means it is time for us to start with Oshoba proper. Ojas gives the beat by hitting his drumsticks together and off we fly. It is easy to fly off too quickly, to run off too fast and I often see him leaning back as if pulling back some horses to remind me to stay steady. There will be enough time to speed up and come to a crescendo for the 'Osho!' shouts. We are barely aware of the melody of the flute, being so concerned with holding the rhythm tight. But finally it is time for the 'Osho!'s and they come almost by themselves, so loud that they can be heard for miles. Finally we sit down.

Yoko moves to a small area in front of the stage where Arpita already has her *tamboura* (in G today) placed by her side and the *tabla* player lifts little cushion-like pads off the skins of his drums which have kept them in tune, or so he hopes. An eight-inch video screen at the front of our stage flickers and a video tape starts playing. Osho directs the rhythm for the meditation and the timing for the silent phase with his hands.

When he gets up from his chair it is time to play the three beats which signals the end of the meditation. I swing the mallet over my head and give my drum a good whack, three times, at equal intervals and equal strength. It seems such an easy thing to do but it gives me a flutter each time.

We step down from the musicians' stage, sit on our cushions and enjoy tonight's video discourse on the big screen in front of the podium.

One night during discourse, Maneesha read a question from Jivan Mada to Osho. She asked if he could explain the sentence he had uttered in a previous discourse: "Let-go is the most fundamental principle of religiousness." After he had answered her question with the help of anecdotes and jokes, he told us that we would practise 'let-go' together. We should then not bother if our bodies ended up lying on top of those behind us, and that we should just relax and enjoy the 'let-go'.

Osho had a particular fondness for our German cameraman, Niskriya, so he asked him then and there to fall backwards and remain lying for a while. Finally, at the end of the discourse – to everybody's surprise – Osho asked him to stand up and shout "Yaa-hoo!" as an order for all of us to fall back in 'let-go'.

We all toppled backwards on top of each other and when we had sunk deep enough into 'let-go' Osho asked us to sit up with a very loving "Come back…"

That Osho had chosen the shout 'Yaa-hoo!' to give an instruction was particularly hilarious because it came from a joke he had just told us:

A pretty girl is driving through the American West when her car runs out of gas. An Indian comes past and gives her a ride to a gas station, sitting behind him on his pony. Every few minutes as they ride along, he lets out a wild whooping yell that echoes around the hills. Finally, he drops her off with a last, "Yaa-Hoo!"

"My god," says the gas station owner, "what were you doing to that Indian to make him shout like that?"

"Nothing," says the girl, "I just sat behind him with my arms around his sides, holding onto his saddle horn."

"Miss," says the man, "Indians don't use saddles."

Osho, *Yaa-hoo! The Mystic Rose*, Ch. 6

The following morning Sarita asked me to join her in the Press Office. She badly needed someone with an 'office mind' to send out press releases. They were ready to be typed and sent out by post and were entitled 'Bhagwan Shree Rajneesh leading meditations' and the text read something like this: 'For the first time in more than thirteen years, disciples and seekers have the opportunity to experience a meditation process in Bhagwan's presence, under His guidance.' I had never thought about the historical implication of our new let-go meditation; I was just living my life in day-to-day wonder.

The first journalists from abroad were from *Die Bunte*, a slander gossip magazine from Germany. Sarita and Shanta had taken them around the commune during the day and at night accompanied them to the discourse. They were sitting quite close to the front and Osho probably knew who they were. I was expecting any minute to hear some provocative comment thrown in the direction of the journalists but, curiously, they did not get any. But when the discourse was over, instead of greeting us with the traditional *namaste*, he raised one arm which clearly looked like a Nazi salute.

The salute had repercussions not only with the journalists, who cut their visit short, but also with the sannyasins in the hall. Some were old enough to have seen German soldiers march into their homeland and felt traumatised by it.

What was the trouble with her [the journalist]? It is not only with her; it is with all of my German sannyasins, more or less. But it is natural. Under Adolf Hitler, Germany has made such wounds in the heart of humanity that every German – even if he was not a participant in it, perhaps he was not even born at the time of the second world war – still, just being German, something inside hurts that "my country, my people have been so nasty, so destructive, so inhuman." They have destroyed forever a healthy heart without any guilt.

My effort was simply to help you to laugh at the point, because what is past is past. And what Adolf Hitler did, you are not responsible for. If you can laugh, the wounds can be healed, the guilt can disappear.

Osho, *Yaa-hoo! The Mystic Rose*, Ch. 4

Osho's idea was that we should salute each other, even on the streets, with the new salute, shouting 'Yaa-hoo!' at the same time. When he heard that the salute was outlawed in Germany and could not be used there, he suggested we salute with both arms raised. Journalists, of course, started immediately asking about the meaning of the shout 'Yaa-hoo!'.

"Yaa-Hoo!" means nothing, but it has tremendous significance. It somehow vibrates you without saying anything; just say, "Yaa-Hoo!" and something in your belly…

Osho, *Yaa-hoo! The Mystic Rose*, Ch. 8

The discourses were full of laughter and practical pranks and there were moments when there was so much laughter in the hall that we could not hear a word of what Osho was saying. Sometimes he himself was unable to speak, laughing and chuckling over our questions which were being read out to him; we could then see the ridiculousness of our questions which we thought were so profound and important. I felt Osho very close in these discourses. He was more of a fellow companion with pranks and laughter – no longer playing the part of a master, aloof and distant, giving discourses from the height of a podium. But unfortunately we were unable to cope with such intimacy.

As with children who do not know their boundaries, many of us did not know when boisterous behaviour was appropriate and when silence was the correct discipline. I was particularly disturbed when at the end of the discourses, after the beautiful silence in the let-go meditation, people started laughing hysterically. A few times I approached the offenders hoping to make them understand that silence was more appropriate at that particular time, but always found vacant, if not hostile, looks. I also felt foolish because I was the only person giving suggestions like this. Maybe the times of reproach, law and order were over. Was I not in step with the times? Moreover, I was a middle-aged woman and probably looked like their mother!

The noise in the hall climaxed on a stormy and windy evening when the rain had torn part of the mosquito net and flooded the left side of the hall, close to Osho's podium. Despite being drenched, most people remained unmoving and meditative, but in the back one person started to laugh loudly, hysterically, completely out of control. It was so out of place that Osho stopped speaking, got up and walked out of the hall saying to those close by: "Don't wait for me to come back tomorrow night."

When this sentence was made known to all and I realised that we might neither see nor hear Osho ever again, I blamed myself for not getting up in the middle of the discourse and taking the hysterical person out of the hall. It showed Osho's compassion that, with the insistence of his secretaries, he let himself be persuaded to come back.

The following evening, when the roof and the netting of the hall were again battered by winds and rains, Osho read the first 'question'.

It was actually an apology from Zareen for our misbehaviour of the previous night. Only then did I become aware that the whole night I had felt angry at Osho because he wanted to punish us with his absence – I hadn't felt like apologising at all!

As far as I am concerned, just as the storm has come again, I have come again. I was not going to come; it is the storm that persuaded me: "I am going again – you will be missed."

We had taken him for granted again: we were not aware that these were rare moments. To be in the presence of a living master had become so habitual to us. And we certainly did not hear the following words which were also uttered in the same discourse:

I am holding myself together with difficulty.
I can disappear any moment.

Osho, *Yaa-hoo! The Mystic Rose*, Ch. 21

The same series of discourses brought us another meditation, called 'The Mystic Rose'. It was first tested in the hall at the end of a discourse and consisted of three five-minute stages of laughing, crying and sitting silently.

Leela, a therapist from South Africa, was appointed to create a three-week group process. The sessions were in the morning and lasted three hours. In the first week we had to laugh. I remembered how, as children, my sisters and I often laughed together, without reason, just enjoying the laughter and the buzz we got from it. We started with little helps like: "You know, some men laugh like this: ho ho ho," and we could go on laughing for quite some time until, after a while – inevitably – Mother interfered and made us stop. This time we were allowed to laugh stupidly for a full three hours. I found a few companions who were good at laughing and we made a trio. If one of us stopped laughing, the others could infect the group again. To laugh for a full three hours was easy, though at times a bit exhausting, but it generally gave me a lot of energy for the rest of the day.

For the following week, the crying phase, the facilitators had arranged a darkened room with languid Western classical music. There were mattresses on the floor and spare sheets to cover ourselves. The mantra which was called out was: "Yaa-boooo..." If I remember well, there were also a few drum strokes from time to time to deepen and sadden the atmosphere. It was easy for me to find scenarios in my memory which made me cry. After going through sadness and despair about boyfriends who had left me, I eventually saw mothers and wives saying goodbye to their sons and husbands. In the black and white visions in my mind they were departing as soldiers to one of the many wars. Then I saw sons and husbands on their deathbeds, saw loss and despair, not from my own life, but from lives of women in the past, of womanhood as a whole. I had the impression I was crying for the whole world, as if my meditation was deeply cleansing the collective unconscious.

Towards the end of the week, when it became difficult to find something to cry about, I usually thought of a *dacha*. In my imagination I saw a house in a forest, its walls made of rough wood. The sunrays falling onto its patio, into the garden and onto the trees of the thick forest behind created such a longing in me that tears came to my eyes each time. I had no idea why this picture had such an effect on me. I had never seen a *dacha* in real life, not even when I had visited Russia. I had just read about them in Russian novels. The main thing was, it worked – it made me cry!

The final week was called 'The Watcher on the Hill'. We sat on meditation stools, watching what movies the mind had in store for us that day. There were periods where we could get up and walk around and stretch our legs. Whatever was being presented to us by our minds was just to be watched, as if we were standing on a hill looking into a valley. We were meant to be unaffected by all the mental traffic. I do not remember if it was easy or difficult for me.

In the afternoons after the morning meditation session, I typed, copied and sent out the press releases and prepared the press kits, as I used to do on the Ranch. The world had become aware that Osho had not disappeared from the face of the earth, and more and more journalists were arriving at the gates.

The Press Office was in the hall of the ground floor of the ly acquired Mirdad House, across the road from the back gate. A German architect, whom I had known as a bus driver on the Ranch, was restoring some of the exquisite Art Nouveau features like the wall lamps and the wood railing to the first floor. Haysa, who was now Osho's international secretary, had her office just next to us. She was one of the few who were allowed to smoke, not only in her room in Lao Tzu House, but also in her office. It was not very pleasant when we had business to do with her, especially for ex-smokers like me, but her charm made everything acceptable.

Mirdad House was now separated from its garden by a tall bamboo fence. We could just make out the movements of the diggers which were preparing the ground for new buildings (at different levels apparently as there was a deep hollow in the middle). We did not see much but we certainly heard the constant roar.

Rumour was that there would be new houses with pyramid roofs and, as so often before, I did not believe in such outlandish rumours. I heard that a renowned architect from Delhi was appointed to do the design and the project was in the hands of a contractor. We certainly did not have the manpower to construct buildings ourselves anymore.

Jokes were still a vital part in the discourses and there was now a team – Vimal, Satyadharma and Chetan – who were in charge of collecting new jokes and re-writing old ones. One day I found an abandoned book – a collection of jokes – on a window ledge. They were in Italian. Every day I came in early to work and took the time to translate a few of them on my electric typewriter. To hear a joke being read by Osho where my phrasing had been left unaltered was such an energy boost! It was if he were reading out a question of mine.

Many press releases went out concerning the 1988 World Academy of Science and Creativity. As far as I understood, Osho was trying to gather intelligentsia, scientists and creative people from all over the world, to form an Academy which was independent from politics, nations and religions. It was a tremendous vision, but somehow it did not take off and after a few months the message came that the project had come to a halt.

You can be a scientist and a meditator. In fact, the more you go deeper into meditation, the more clarity, the more intelligence, the more genius you will find flowering in you which can create a totally new science.

The old science was created as a reaction against religion. The new science I'm talking about is not a reaction against anything, but an overflowing energy, intelligence, creativity. Politics corrupted science because its own interest was only war. Religions could not accept science because they were all superstitious and science was going to demolish all their gods and all their superstitions.

Science has passed these three hundred years in a very difficult situation, fighting on the one hand with religion and on the other hand, unconsciously becoming a slave to the politicians. [...]

There is an immense vacuum which I want to fill by creating a world academy absolutely devoted to life, love, laughter – absolutely devoted to creating a better humanity, a better and more pure healthy atmosphere, and to restoring the disturbed ecology.

Osho, *Om Mani Padme Hum*, Ch. 30

Here in Pune, 2001, my emotional stability is being tested again: I am in the graphic department of the Multiversity. Sharing the office is Asmita, a girl from Chile, who is coordinating Osho's meditative therapies like the Mystic Rose and Born Again. She is not in most of the time so I have the office practically to myself. We often have a cup of Chilean coffee together which she brews in a cafetière she has brought with her all the way from the West. But she is not the problem...

As in the bookshop, the results of my endeavours are on show to everyone who cares to see. I now prepare the announcements for therapy groups and sessions as well as the advertisements for the demos, which are mostly given in the Plaza at lunchtime. (Details for these last often change for logistical reasons or because the facilitator or coordinator gives me wrong data. This creates a lot of extra running around as the flyers are posted in different locations: in neat plastic stands in the Plaza itself; in sealed plastic pockets at the back gate and in Meera near the Post Office.)

To create the flyers, Chetna had shown me how to use Word (the computer is not strong enough to use Photoshop) and in which folders she had stored the images. She had also shown me how to print, glue and cut the displays to be stuck with magnets on a half-dozen metal panels along the entrance wall of the Multiversity in the Plaza. It is such a complicated and labour-intensive procedure that it takes me half an hour to explain it to Amiten when I first learn it. In the meantime the supplier of the PVC sheet does some of the gluing and cutting for a small extra cost. Many times I wonder if there is not an easier way to get the message across. I already have a few scars on my thumb from the Stanley knife! Needless to say, it is again I who has asked for the black metal panels to be repainted and the halogen lights checked weekly. The electricians and painters already know me from the bookshop – and they laugh.

The Multiversity is run by a down-to-earth Australian girl whom I did not know before. This astonishes me because in the past there was always one of the 'important' people in charge. However, Anando, who used to run the Multiversity, still feels at home here and comes into my office, uses my cutting pad for her things when I am out for a coffee, or removes the advertisements just half an hour after the group has started, maybe out of good-will, but to me it always looks like a reproach that I have not been quick enough to remove them on the dot. So many things are welling up. Poor me! I even take a session to help me dig deeper into my past to discover the thought patterns which make these incidents happen to me in the first place (as if my mind is asking people to do this to me – but then, I am doing exactly the same thing to them…).

The secretary of my boss, a Japanese girl, cringes each time I call her. She says the way I say her name reminds her of her grandmother. So I have stopped talking to her. It seems we are a bunch of lunatics! Then a therapist comes in, big in size and voice. He comes to Pune just for a couple of weeks, gives his NLP group and then goes back to the West. He throws the announcement of his group with a loud thud onto my glass desk. "Shit picture!" he says. I wish it would not affect me the way it does and that I could just reply in a very British voice, "You certainly have bad manners!"

To make the display always varied and interesting, I research and print out new images, mostly at night after the White Robe Meditation when Amiten is on guard duty. I love images! I even find some treasures in the many boxes from the old archives of the photo department which is now being dismantled. Most of the time I manage to match the picture with the group – sometimes in a humorous way – and the therapists are happy with my choice, but if they prefer a picture they have used in the past, I am happy to accommodate them (very much one of my characteristics).

The newcomers are now more attracted to Osho's active meditations instead of therapy groups. These have gone out of fashion, even worldwide, and no longer have the appeal they used to have in the eighties and nineties. But not long ago the therapists were the gods in the commune. They generated a lot of cash and I think that many of the buildings could be built thanks to their groups. Now most therapists have moved to their own countries and run their own schools there; only a few of them come to Pune in winter for the high season and offer their groups as a voluntary contribution.

To compensate, 2-3 day processes have been designed which are run monthly by members of staff who have not been trained as therapists, but as lawyers, accountants and nurses. There is no longer the glamour of doing a group with, say, Aneesha, or Leela. Those times are gone. When I gave the Reiki training my helpers thought I was exaggerating when I wanted to help with the cleaning as I used to do in my cottage in Yetholm, but they remembered group leaders coming into the group room a few minutes before the group shouting "Oh no!" and demanding that the whole decoration be taken down and redone according to new instructions. Real prima donnas!

Luckily things have changed. But a few other things I would rather have as they were in the past. You keep comparing constantly. Was it better then? Should the new people learn how to work from us 'old' ones? I guess that for the people running the place it is easier to have new people around who have no reference to the past rather than 'oldies' like me who might object to this and that. Our commune has gone through many changes in the past, but when Osho was in his body we accepted the changes more easily. Also names changed and we got used to them after a while. Even God was discarded! I am also aware that – and this is just my understanding – Osho played out the role of the guru just to tempt us into meditation – and spoke about God because if we were interested in spirituality, his using the concept of God would attract us to listening to his talks.

Then came the therapies which, thanks to the high quality of courses we offered, brought many newcomers here. Now maybe we want to attract people to a spa, a resort, a place where they can feel good in their bodies and then dip their toes into meditation out of curiosity. I must admit that I also taught Reiki for five years as a means to give the participants a taste of meditation – which indeed many got. Most of them would not have booked a meditation weekend – meditation not being part of our culture in the West.

Today is Wednesday and I am meeting my musicians in the music room to rehearse for the Sun and Moon Dance (previously called Heart Dance and before that, Sufi Dance – many names for practically the same thing). To rejuvenate the repertoire, I make it a point to introduce a new song each week and this time it will be one from Israel. Last week a young chap came up to us after the dances and said that he had a song he would like to teach us. He came on Monday with his flute and we wrote down the chords. No words really so we are just singing: *Tininay nananay nay nananay…* and together we made up and rehearsed a dance for this three-quarter beat. For each musician I am now quickly printing out sheets with the lyrics and chords of the songs we have chosen for today.

A few months ago I was asked to run these dances, as a singer and leader, on a regular basis, and I am lucky to have found some musicians who are happy to participate each time (now all musicians and therapists have to be workers in the commune). It is a pleasant round-up and I must confess that I seem to be quite good at running it. I must have learned a lot just from sitting in at the rehearsals and doing sound-checks with the great musicians of the time. Unfortunately none of these musicians come to Pune anymore and it is sad because I miss their music and their talent. I guess this now very well-organised place is not attracting the creative and crazy ones any longer.

Whenever we have a singer visiting, I ask if they want to contribute and mostly I get a "Yes, of course!" This week it is Disha. I need to come to terms with this change as well: she is now a grown woman. I had seen her grow up as a kid here in Pune, then on the Ranch as a teenager, then I heard her as a young woman sing, together with Milarepa, for Osho. She now lives in Australia with Bhakta, another musician, and they have produced a few CDs with her songs. Very graciously she told me on Monday that she is happy that I do the leading and that we will sing the songs together. I am so much looking forward to this!

We will fill the hall with invisible heart-shaped flowers and lift the roof off!

An Enlightened Drum

When I was working in Zurich and living in Vedam and Majida's flat together with their now walking and running Shanti, Vedam presented me with a tambourine and a wooden *guiro* in the form of a fish, presents I cherish to this day. I bought a pair of blue *maracas*, a triangle and again a set of *claves*. From then on I would never travel back and forth without having these in my red suitcase. In the beginning I did not feel confident enough to play them in public, so I practised on them in my room and slowly, slowly brought them out into the open when I thought I was good enough. There were birthday parties in Pune where I discreetly pulled out the tambourine from my bag and played along. Then came semi-official music sessions for Amiyo's dance workshops or Meera's painting group.

Most often I played in the Heart Dance which was run by Savita and Ramananda, or by Svarup from Italy. The conga player was Satprem from Japan and the bass player Pramod from Germany. We had all, more or less, just started playing and had the opportunity to practise our steadily improving skills in a band. It was a joy to be playing for people to dance and sing in Buddha Hall.

I played for Osho just once, when Nivedano asked me to play the *maracas* before and after evening discourse. I was so excited that not only did I not hear a single word of Osho's discourse, but almost had to hold myself back, afraid I would start playing in the middle of the discourse! This was an incredible treat.

Kaveesha's Mystery School was in full swing and the musicians were invited to play at different events, in groups, and in the evenings. I remember sitting on the marble wall in the Plaza next to Kaveesha after one of these musical outings (we'd gone to play around a fire in the back near the Nalla), when she put her hand on my knee and said: "If we did not have the musicians, what would we do?"

For these events I started turning up with a drum. It was a

wooden drum, a *surdo* from Brazil. It was not too big to carry about and still had a lovely deep sound with a particular ring which probably came from the wood. I took care of it, cleaned and waxed it every so often, as if it were mine. It lived in the music room and I had permission to use it. Satprem had shown me how Brazilian drums were played and I soon got the swing of it.

The drums became famous, and this one in particular, while Osho was commenting on the following Zen story:

Kasan said, "Learning by study is called hearing; learning no more is called nearness; transcending these two is true passing."

A monk asked, "What is true passing?"

Kasan said, "Beating the drum."

The monk asked again, "What is the true teaching of the Buddha?"

Kasan said, "Beating the drum."

The monk asked once more, "I would not ask you about 'this very mind is the Buddha', but what is no mind, no Buddha?"

Kasan said, "Beating the drum."

The monk still continued to ask: "When an enlightened one comes, how do you treat him?"

Kasan said, "Beating the drum."

Nivedano had to illustrate a few times how a drum beat sounded and Osho's comment was:

This anecdote about Kasan's beating the drum looks so simple from the outside, but from the inside it has tremendous meaning and is multi-dimensional.

First, you have to understand what a drum is.

A drum is emptiness enclosed.

There is nothing inside the drum. That is our actual state. We are just an outside cover, inside is emptiness. And just as the drum can speak out of emptiness, you are doing everything out of emptiness. This is one dimension of the meaning of Kasan's beating the drum.

The other dimension is that whatever question is asked of him, he goes on saying in answer, "Beating the drum." It does not matter what question you are asking – there must be millions of questions but there is only one answer – and the answer cannot be verbalised. That's why Kasan used to keep a drum by his side. You ask him anything – it does not matter what you are asking, he will simply beat the drum. That was his answer.

Reduced to your understanding, it means, "Be nothing just like the drum and you will find the answer. I cannot give it to you; it is your own emptiness. At the most I can hit you from the outside, but the sound comes from within you."

Then Osho asked:

Have you got the feel of beating the drum?
There is nothing inside, still... it makes so much noise. Just look within yourself. What is there? A heartbeat, breathing coming in and going out... and what else? When you are utterly silent you are pure emptiness. Emptiness breathing... Emptiness full of the dance of the heartbeat...

After all the many beats which were illustrating the point, Osho said:

Yes, it hits well – many people seem to realise the emptiness!
Even if nobody else becomes enlightened, Nivedano's drum is going to become enlightened. That is not a small matter.

Osho, *Live Zen*, Ch. 14

The discourse ended, as usual, with a few questions from Maneesha, the jokes (*"I would like your silence to be deeper and the only way to make it deeper is to have a good laugh."*), a period of silence and then the let-go, where everybody falls back and rests in silence. Osho would then ask us sit up again with a soft: "Okay, come back!"

Nivedano told me later that the following day, while preparing his instruments for discourse, he had the impression that the wooden *surdo* was laughing at him, as if saying: "I am now enlightened!" He had to quickly fetch another drum as this one was not willing to cooperate. In the book with this discourse there is a photo next to it showing Nivedano beating a drum, but it is not the 'enlightened' one.

Not long after the discourse on Kasan's beating the drum Osho added another feature to the closing meditation: gibberish. These were a few minutes where we could speak in tongues and throw our arms about. These stages were also introduced with a drum beat. It was enough for Osho to call: "Nivedano!" for the drum beat to come. Even if by chance Nivedano was absent and another drummer was standing in for him, the command was: "Nivedano!" Just as the wording "OK, Maneesha" was a signal for the end of discourse, so other names became like signals.

Gibberish simply means throwing out your craziness, which is already there in the mind, piled up for centuries. As you throw it out you will find yourself becoming light, becoming more alive, just within two minutes.

You will be surprised that when Nivedano gives his second beat, to enter into silence, you enter into silence as deeply as you have never done before. Just those two minutes have cleaned the way.

In fact in those two minutes, if you put your total energy… the more you put into it, the deeper will be the following silence. So don't be partial, don't be middle-class. Just be a first-rate crazy man!
Osho, *Zen: The Solitary Bird, Cuckoo of the Forest*, Ch. 12

Nivedano had to keep his eyes open and look at Osho's hand for the signal to stop the gibberish. It was so noisy. If you were sick and were at home during discourse, you could hear the noise from afar.

Today is Sunday, the day visitors are allowed to enter the construction site of the new pyramid which will replace Buddha Hall. As I understand, it is built according to how Osho wanted it to be. The temporary plastic roof of our old Buddha Hall is quite a few years past its sell-by date (unfortunately we were never granted permission to build a permanent structure) and it is time we get a place where we can play music and do Dynamic Meditation loudly without disturbing the neighbours. Although

I have participated in so many discourses and celebrations and seen Osho speak from this podium, I have no particular attachment to Buddha Hall and welcome the move – but some of my old friends are shedding tears over it.

We meet Mukto at the construction office in Meera. When the ten or so people who have booked their visit have all arrived we are shown into the new compound. Mukto waves with big gestures and explains: "This will be the pond." And: "The roof is now finished." We look up and see that the black tiles on the pyramid roof have all been placed already.

Amiten helps me climb the uneven steps within the construction site and we are first shown a room in the guest house. This one has been decorated and furnished for us to see what all the rooms will look like. It is a bit small, but then for a short stay this should be big enough. But what a luxury it would be to just take the elevator down to the auditorium, do my loud Dynamic first thing in the morning, come back up for a shower in my own room and go back down for breakfast! Mukto shows us how close the auditorium is: "Just one flight of stairs down." And here we are with our necks tilted backwards trying to get a glimpse of the highest point of the pyramid. Most of the scaffolding has come down now that the insulation and the outer layer of sheetrock are up. Our jaws are hanging, speechless. "So big!" we hear whispered. Then Mukto interrupts the silence with an, "And here will be the musicians' area!" looking at me in particular.

The steps outside the building take us along the concrete slabs back to the exit of the construction site. We can hardly manage to say a thank you for the guided tour. Amiten and I give each other support as we feel our knees giving way. My head is light and I feel as if thousands of bees are roaming around my brain. My friend Jeevan, an elderly lady from the US who has made India her home and is my faithful lunch companion (we usually talk about computer programs), intercepts me while Amiten starts walking back to his painting crew. "What happened to you?"

she asks. "We went to visit the pyramid, I think Osho has moved in there already. I feel like I am coming out of an energy darshan!" She hooks her arm with mine and we slowly walk to Mirdad, to the Multimedia department where I now also work.

After one and a half years of continuous play/work I took a week's holiday in Goa. On my return I had applied to work in this department. It was the first time in my commune life that I had 'applied' for a job. They are usually 'given'. As a graphic designer I would have enjoyed creating the covers for new editions of Osho's books or to work for the Osho Times, but they needed someone in the audio department. "I see you are a musician and you are now a mixer, so your hearing must be good," were the reasons Yogendra put forward when I started with some 'buts...'

Within two hours I was shown how to use the application to turn a .wav file into an .mpg and .rm file and how to take out the noise of the air conditioning from Osho's discourses. I also managed to send the webmaster a large amount of jokes read and commented on by Osho and I am now working on re-mastering some discourses for the bookshop. When plugging in leads and cables from the PC to the amplifier and then to the data-recorder as if this has always been my job, I sometimes wonder where all this is coming from and say to myself: "I cannot believe I am doing this." Maybe it is in my genes but is only becoming apparent now. My sister Kätti is a great electrician. She used to fix the telephones in all the offices she worked in and has re-wired all her houses by herself. I am also becoming bold in using the computer and have overcome my technophobia thanks to the benevolence of Neelamber, our IT-administrator, who does not scold me even when I crash the system.

But still, so many questions: would I need a proper sound card on my computer? Are these the best quality tapes in India? Do we need to have a better supplier to do the audio work? When I was in the bookshop many visitors looked at me in disbelief that we were still selling audio cassettes. Where are the CDs and the mini-disks? Why don't we offer discourses on CDs, at least a selection?

My mind is overwhelmed with all these questions I do not have an answer for and to compensate I am writing a manual for the mixing desk to help me grasp what at least I *do* know.

When Deekshant left with Yoko to go back to Japan he taught me the essentials of mixing the live music for White Robe Meditation, and I learned further tricks from visiting DJs, but now that we have to repair our good old 32-channel mixer and temporarily move to a mixer half that size, I had better be acquainted with the ins and outs of our set-up. Luckily, I have also found a willing student to give me some evenings off: it is Alok, a young designer and friend of Ojas. He would probably be happy to have a manual in case he forgets what I have told him, but at least all will be clear in my mind when I have to explain 'the art of mixing' to him tonight.

Someone knocks at the glass door of our office. It is Vishva and she brings the mangoes I have ordered. A whole box full! Her husband is in the trade and these are the very best ones: Alfonso mangoes from Goa. She lifts the lid and I see she has arranged twelve neatly packed yellow fruits like little babies in coloured silk paper. She also brings a book in her native German for me to read and I return the one I have just finished.

My colleagues turn around at the whiff of mango. There are just two of them despite the vastness of this room: Anupradha who is editing a book and Nirav, the video-technician who prepares the video for us to see each night. As many discourses are very long, he cuts them in half at the most appropriate spot, then adds a joke and the let-go meditation at the end. He usually manages to make a good blend and we have got used to these doctored video discourses.

I gently wedge the lid back into place and, nonchalantly looking out of the window into the greenery beyond the mosquito netting, I give Vishva a hug and a kiss and wave her goodbye. Tomorrow I am going to have these mangoes for breakfast, lunch and dinner and am going to share them with Amiten only!

After another four months of secretarial work in Zurich I returned with a suitcase full of even more percussion instruments – as well as a new visa and a few traveller's cheques which were the main reasons for leaving Pune in the first place. A drum shop in the Stauffenbachstrasse, called Latin Music, was a treasure trove. They had just received a shipment of *shekeres* from Africa. I loved the shape of the natural gourds with their long necks. The beads were made from greyish-blue seeds held together in a net wrapped around the gourd. The rattling sound was music to my ears and one of them was going to be mine.

Then Vedam, whose family I had lived with again in our old housing estate in Höngg, taught me the three-two beat of the *claves.* He also introduced me to his salsa band with whom I was allowed to participate in summer competitions and street concerts. For one gig I even got 10 franks! – my first money earned from playing music.

The job I was given on my return to Pune really suited my music involvement: kitchen storeroom early shift. Sharp at 12 noon I exchanged the down jacket and gloves I used in the walk-in fridge for my jingling bag and rushed to Buddha Hall. This time I also had the courage to participate in the African Dance. In previous years, because the musicians were all men, I was too scared to go up and ask them if I could play. Soon they enjoyed my small, high-frequency sounds which enhanced the low beats of the congas and electric bass, sometimes so much so that they dipped into my music bag, leaving me with nothing to play with.

It must have looked funny, for anyone who did not know me, to see this middle-aged woman approach the musicians, who were already set up in the middle of the hall, with her flower-patterned bag slung over her shoulder. If I were a young black man I would have had a much easier life! But there was a huge amount of encouragement coming my way which I need to acknowledge to the reader and above all to myself: from Teertha, Kamal and Anugama and later Rishi, Joshua, Chinmaya, Miten and Milarepa.

Despite all the insecurities of a musician taking her first steps, it was worth the hassle. While playing I would sink into a soundless, velvety dark abyss, where all beats had their right place, where everything was in order and harmony. My old friends could not understand why I was suddenly besotted by music until they saw me playing. They saw the relaxation and meditation in my face and some even saw me as a big black woman rattling her shaker with the rhythm in her bum.

One day the energy between the musicians and the dancers built up to such high intensity that the African Dance drew in everybody around. Even workers from offices in Krishna House came running into the Hall. In the afternoon, though, unable to think or walk, all we could do was sit on the Zen wall and watch the comings and goings of people – as if from an Italian roadside café. We were so stunned by the energy which had gone through our bodies – the closest resemblance to which, for me, was an orgasm.

It was not unusual to see Milarepa there on a Sunday afternoon, smiling sheepishly and unable to do much else other than sit and wait for the normal functioning of the body to catch up. He knew that I would understand why he was there. I was lucky to be often invited to the sannyas initiation ceremony to play my small bells. Avirbhava, the organiser of the celebration, commented regularly that Milarepa was very much in tune with those taking the initiation because he always chose the most suitable song for the person on the hot seat without knowing anything about them. I had also noticed that when I did not let my mind come in the way, my hands knew what instrument to play and at what moment. Sometimes my little *caixixis* had a visible effect on the people being initiated, as if I were a shamanic witch doctor.

The room I had found to live in this time was very conveniently located. Across from the main gate where in the old days we used to sit and smoke our *beedies* (with a wall we could sit on called the 'beedie wall') was the entrance to Nanu's place. His brother was now standing guard in the guise of a cigarette vendor so that he could give the alert – because Nanu was a not-strictly-legal money changer. He provided the foreign currency which Indian citizens needed if they wanted to open a bank account abroad. The barren compound had a few trees, housing nests of eagles, and a big barn. It was big enough to house a herd of water buffaloes which I could just see through the open door. The shiny black hides in the dark barn barely reflected the light from the few small windows on the roof, but I could hear their shuffling. Nanu's modest house was in the back, behind the barn. It looked rather like servants' quarters. In the front room stood the dark grey steel cupboard and the flower-patterned sofa we all knew well from our transactions.

My way home was past the cigarette vendor and the barn, past Nanu's door – with a "Hello, Punya" from within – over a six-foot wall and up two flights of stairs in a newly-built apartment block. The passage over the wall was easy even with a bag, as long as one hand was free for the difficult bit on top. It was certainly Nanu's escape route, but he did not mind me using it as well. My room came with a wonderful plant which loved the light from the two windows so much that in a short time it reached the height of the loft where I kept my suitcase and covered part of the clothes-hanging space below. I had a wooden bed, made to measure, and bought a wicker chair for the balcony.

I see myself walking up and down the room practising the triangle on the off-beat. It also had to have that particular 'ing' sound when the hand closed onto one of the sides. I could hear it in the lesson on the tape and wanted to get the same effect. I had brought with me also an extensive collection of learning material as well as tapes from Vedam's hero, Tito Puente, and Santana. I was so besotted with music that I could hardly think of anything else. The few times I was asked for a date I weighed up in my mind a choice between going out or going home and practising music before replying.

In the morning I was woken by the sun shining straight onto my face and by the smoke of the fire which Nanu's father lit every morning. His loud prayer to God in a fervent chant must have helped the business to thrive, but the old man kept living in rather primitive conditions. And at night, if the moon was up, it kept me awake with its bright light and I felt as if it were checking me out.

From the balcony I could see onto the arched roof of Buddha Hall, partially covered by stately fronds of poincianas, and behind it, Manu's slender eucalyptus tree towering over the gardens. In the distance was the top of the ancient peepal tree which I had so much admired when living in Jesus House. This magnificent specimen was now going to be incorporated into the new campus with the pyramids and become the focal point of many night painting sessions.

It was as if I were again living in the ashram. When I heard the drummers already tuning their congas, I could dash over Nanu's wall with my jingling bag and still start the dances on time. No need for a clock either: from the music played in Buddha Hall I could tell exactly what time it was. If it was the first stage of Kundalini, then it was after a quarter past four.

This was particularly useful when I worked from home on a compilation I had started.

One day while walking to the commune the long way round I had the idea of making a compilation of Osho's words when he spoke about art, when he touched the sensitivity of our artists and gave them advice. I wanted to collect what he had said about beauty, the Buddha statues, objective vs. subjective art and the marble hills near Jabalpur he had visited on full-moon nights. I also remembered what Osho had said in a darshan to a friend of mine, an artist, when he first arrived from Italy. Darshans in those days were not yet recorded so I would not be able to include this, but I did remember what he had said to Alok: whenever he had finished a painting he should meditate while sitting in front of it, and only if the painting was good enough to meditate on, should he sell it or give it away.

I asked Osho's secretary, Anando, if Osho would agree to such a project. The answer was, "Great idea," but that I should look for a publisher myself. Osho had also suggested the title: *Art Expressed through Meditation*.

From a rolodex, similar to the one on which Margaret had filed the press clippings on the Ranch, and from a typed book which good old Ashok had compiled in the early days, I found the passages I was interested in. From the books in the research library I made photocopies and to organise the wealth of texts, I made two cards with the content; one I clipped onto the photocopies, the other was kept loose. This was long before the time when the discourses were scanned and could be searched by queries on a database. The research library was in Jesus House across from Mariam Canteen. It was a small room with all the walls lined with books. On the round porch in front of it, enshrined by a mosquito net and by a sculpted door, small white custom-made formica desks were available for those working on projects. But the desks were way too small to display the number of cards I had gathered and so I moved the project to my room.

On the double bed I could spread out the reference cards and sort out a sequence to present this valuable material. I found darshans where Osho was talking directly to creative artists from different fields – musicians, dancers, sculptors, painters, cinematographers – and where he compared a poem written by an ordinary poet and one written by an enlightened master. I was warned that one of the greatest difficulties of preparing a compilation was deciding which texts to eliminate. There was always something special in each piece even if the concept was repeated in another one. Which one to choose? Which one to put aside?

In the evenings the sound check of the musicians and singers in the hall was my signal to get ready for the evening discourse: a shower and a change of clothes. Then through the metal detector, the friskers and the sniffers... I liked to sit right behind the musicians, about six or seven rows from the podium. It was an energetic spot and it also gave me the opportunity to check out how Nivedano produced that lovely sound with the *ghungroo* ankle bells which Gayan had stitched onto a stick for him. The discourses were on various Zen masters and I loved to hear their stories which, I have to admit, I would not have understood if Osho had not given his commentary.

Osho had started wearing sunglasses. His eyes must have been hurting, I thought, but I missed not seeing his eyes and missed not knowing where he was looking. Maybe he was looking at me? I felt him to be more distant and paid more attention to his words. Also his gestures, which had been as expressive as his face, had become minimal because a bone in his hand was hurting and impeded movement. He had even stopped crossing his legs after sitting down, something we had seen him do for so many years. All the robes he wore now were black with tiny decorations in gold. These fitted well with the Zen discourses.

Then, again there was another period when Osho did not come out for the discourses. We gathered in Buddha Hall as usual and watched a discourse on video instead. We saw for the first time the discourses which had been recorded in Uruguay during the so-called 'World Tour', which took place after Osho was thrown out of Crete. We later also saw the discourses from Nepal where he had been before visiting Greece.

Then one day Osho was ready to come back. He looked very different, changed, as if glowing from within – as if shining in a light blue light. Before he sat down, he took off his glasses and gave them to Avirbhava. She was one of the women who opened the door to the car for him and was famous for screaming when, most unexpectedly, Osho pretended to poke her in the belly when he walked past her to the podium. We could finally see his eyes again.

Maneesha, this time has been of historical importance.

For seven weeks I was fighting with the poison day and night. One night, even my physician, Amrito, became suspicious that perhaps I cannot survive. He was taking my pulse rate and heartbeats on his cardiogram. Seven times I missed one heartbeat.

The seventh time I missed a heartbeat, it was natural for his scientific mind to think, "Now we are fighting a battle that is almost lost." But I said to him, "Don't be worried. Your cardiogram can go wrong; it is just a mechanical device. Trust in my witnessing. Don't bother about my heartbeats."

On the last day of the seven weeks' struggle when all the pain from my body disappeared, Amrito could not believe it. It was happening almost like a miracle. Where has all the pain disappeared?

The last night, in the middle of the night I heard somebody knocking on the door. It is rare; nobody knocks on my door. I had to open my eyes. There was absolute darkness in the room, but I saw suddenly, with the door closed, a human being made of pure light entering. For a moment there was silence, and I heard from nowhere, "Can I come in?" The guest was so pure, so fragrant. I had simply to take him into the silences of my heart.

This body of pure light was nobody but Gautam the Buddha.

You can still see in my eyes the flame that I have absorbed into myself, a flame that has been for twenty-five centuries wandering around the earth to find a shelter. I am immensely blessed that Gautam the Buddha knocked on my doors.

Osho, No Mind: The Flowers of Eternity, Ch. 4

I now understood why I felt that Buddha Hall was more crowded than before, not just with the 10,000 disciples Osho used to mention, but more like with 100,000. I even had the impression that some people were sitting inside me, maybe Buddha's old disciples who wanted to participate in the discourses. I wrote a note to Osho asking him if I was hallucinating – he had always made fun about people believing in ghosts – but I had to risk it. The reply came within a sentence and with a nanosecond glance in my direction as I heard: "…and ghosts do exist."

He was fulfilling Buddha's prophecy that he would come back as Maitreya the Buddha after twenty-five centuries. If more confirmation was needed, even a Japanese seeress and prophetess of an ancient Shinto shrine, Katsue Ishida, recognised Osho as Maitreya Buddha.

Osho had given a warning two days earlier…

I have accepted Gautam Buddha's soul as a guest, reminding him that I am a non-compromising person, and if any argument arises between us, "I am the host, and you are the guest – you can pack your suitcases!"

Osho, No Mind: The Flowers of Eternity, Ch. 2

…and indeed, the honeymoon between the two, Osho and

Maitreya, did not last long. Apparently Gautama the Buddha had preconceived ideas how things had to be and was unable to adjust to the 20th century. He was asked to leave. This is how Osho explained the event:

My Beloved Ones,

These four days have been of immense difficulty to me. I had thought that Gautam Buddha would be understanding of the change of times, but it was impossible. I tried my hardest, but he is so much disciplined in his own way – twenty-five centuries back – he has become a hard bone.

He used to sleep only on the right side. He did not use a pillow; he used his hand as a pillow. The pillow was, for him, a luxury.

I told him, "The poor pillow is not a luxury, and it is sheer torture to keep your hand the whole night under your head. And do you think to lie down on the right side is right, and the left is wrong? As far as I am concerned, this is my basic fundamental, that I synthesize both the sides."

He was eating only one time per day and he wanted, without saying a word, that I should do it also. He used to beg his food. He asked me, "Where is my begging bowl?"

This evening exactly at six o'clock when I was taking my Jacuzzi, he became very much disturbed – "Jacuzzi?" Taking a bath twice a day was again a luxury.

"You have fulfilled your prophecy that you will be coming back. Four days are enough – I say goodbye to you! And now you need not wander around the earth; you just disappear in the ultimate blue sky. You have seen for four days that I am doing the work that you wanted to do, and I am doing it according to the times and the needs. I am not in any way ready to be dictated to. I am a free individual. Out of my freedom and love I have received you as a guest, but don't try to become a host."

These four days I have been having a headache. I had not known it for thirty years; I had completely forgotten what it means to have a headache. Everything was impossible. He is so accustomed to his way, and that way is no longer relevant.

So now I make a far greater historical statement, that I am just myself.

Osho, *No Mind: The Flowers of Eternity*, Ch. 5

With Maitreya gone, Osho was again himself, with his usual golden glow, and Buddha Hall had emptied itself of the guests, and the ghosts had left me as well. We were again family. Back to business, back to ordinary life. I felt it as a relief.

The hosting of the Maitreya produced many angry statements from Buddhist groups; even United Press International sent in a question asking if Osho had now become a Buddhist. The discourses started with news topics he wanted to discuss. This was then followed by a Zen story, a question by Maneesha, the jokes and the let-go meditation. In the beginning I was not particularly interested in the news. I would rather hear Zen stories and did not want to be reminded of the outside world, although from time to time I read *Newsweek* over a cup of coffee at the Blue Diamond hotel. But then, these answers to politicians and heads of religious groups were wake-up calls, not only for the recipients of the tirade but also for us. As far as I understood, the video recording of the discourses were then sent to the persons concerned.

The previous year Osho had spoken on the Zen Master Ta Hui. The first sayings Osho commented upon were from the time Ta Hui was still a teacher, according to Osho. He hammered the poor fellow, until one day we heard a poem which had a totally different sound. It was written after Ta Hui's enlightenment: the words were falling into place in an organic way, like leaves strewn on a lawn by the wind. It was beautiful for me to learn to feel when something rings true or not. Now with the media, I could learn to see behind the façade of politics, learn how to discern truth from untruth.

The name 'Bhagwan' which Osho had adopted thirty or so years earlier – to spite the Hindus who give this title to Gods, as to 'Lord Krishna' – was dropped the day Maitreya had come. Maneesha had to adapt her script from moment to moment to address him correctly as Beloved Buddha, then Zorba the Buddha when the Maitreya left, then Beloved Master and later Osho. In the past we had been curious to see what colour robe he was wearing for discourse; now we were curious about what name Maneesha was going address him with.

We were acquainted with the expression 'Osho' as many of the

Zen masters, whose stories we heard in discourse, were addressed in this manner. It could well have been that one of the sannyasins suggested the name to him and that he adopted it. In some of his books on my bookshelf there is a sticker stating that the new name of the author is Osho.

It adds: 'O' means 'with great respect, love and gratitude' as well as 'synchronicity' and 'harmony'. 'Sho' means 'multidimensional expansion of consciousness' and 'existence showering from all directions'. It also sounds like 'oceanic' which must have inspired Osho.

The graphic designers were at a loss with all these changes as they had corrected the jackets for the new books a few times already and were not sure at what stage the final layout could be sent to the printer lest there was a change again. As an exception, the name Osho Rajneesh was kept for the Italian book market as Videha had managed to bring Osho's books under the name Rajneesh high up in the charts and it would have been a shame to spoil all those marketing efforts.

And the shouted greeting at the beginning and end of the discourses changed from 'Yaa-hoo!' to 'Osho!', reverberating around the dark neighbourhood for a mile at least.

10

The Gateless Gate

The Song of the Waterfall

I remember the visit of an enlightened Japanese woman to our commune. She was a small, frail and unassuming lady (I later heard she was in her mid eighties!). She was called Tamo-san (Ryoju Kikuchi was her legal name). She was a priestess in a Shinto temple in Japan. One evening after discourse our Japanese friends organised an unofficial gathering in Buddha Hall to which I was invited. I sat down near the entrance, just inside the hall, on the cool marble in the dark. Thanks to the street lights streaming in through the mosquito net I could make out that a few dozen people had gathered already. I did not really know what was going to happen as they were all talking in Japanese. Tamo-san walked in, knelt down gracefully in Japanese style and one of the girls announced that she was going to sing for us and that the poem was about a waterfall.

I closed my eyes so that my ears could take in all the details of these unusual sounds; they were low and powerful but still conveyed the glittering lightness of water falling. At a certain point I opened them again to see if they were really coming from the small, white-haired and wrinkly lady I had seen before. They were!

Tamo-san was enlightened and Osho had acknowledged this in the discourse earlier by showering petals of red roses on her. Apparently the message he sent to her was that she had now to take the next step: she had to learn to go beyond enlightenment. For us unenlightened beings it is difficult to understand what he meant by 'going beyond'. Maybe coming back to this world as an ordinary human being, like the tenth picture of the story of the Ox?

In ancient China, there used to be ten cards, ten beautiful pictures about ox-herding, mastering the ox.

In the first picture, the ox has escaped from its owner into the deep forest. The owner is looking all around, but he can see only trees and trees and trees, and no ox.

In the second picture, he finds the footprints of the ox. Now there is some hope he may find the ox – he follows the footprints. In the third picture, he finds that the ox is hiding behind a bush; just his tail and the backside he can see. But he is immediately happy – "He is trying to deceive me!"

In the fourth picture he has seen the whole ox. In the fifth picture, he takes hold of the ox by the horns. It is a difficult struggle; the ox is far more powerful an animal than man. With difficulty he manages. In the sixth picture, he is riding on the ox. In the seventh he is moving towards home. In the eighth, he has put the ox in its stable. In the ninth picture, he is sitting before his cottage, playing a flute.

When these pictures came to Japan, the tenth picture was dropped out, thinking that it might be dangerous, particularly for people who are very new and don't know the whole world of Zen. The tenth picture shows that the man is so happy... he takes a bottle of wine and rushes towards the marketplace, perhaps towards the pub, to enjoy with his friends. He has found his ox – now this is a celebration.

Being afraid that this will mean that you can drink wine – and this will go against Buddha – they dropped the tenth picture.

But I love the tenth picture, because it does not represent wine; wine is only a symbol of being drunk with the divine. Wine is only a symbol of being utterly at ease with existence – relaxed, in tune, in harmony, in accord. And his rushing towards the pub is also symbolic. It is rushing towards your own juices of life, to the very centre of your being, where you will get drunk.

This kind of getting drunk is unending. Once you have tasted it, you have tasted it; it is not going to fade away. It is going to overwhelm your whole life. Your whole life will become a festival of lights; your whole life will become a ceremony of laughter, of dance, of song, of music.

Osho, Communism and Zen Fire, Zen Wind, Ch. 1

The walk along the waterfront of the Tyne in the evening is always spectacular, whatever the weather has been during the day. The sky lights up in golden orange colours, creating a wonderful backdrop for the black silhouettes of the many bridges in front of me. When we first moved to Newcastle six months ago – after our two-year stay in Pune – I was amazed at seeing pedestrian, road, metro and train bridges high up in the sky, 100 feet above the river, and could not understand that along the water one found towering flour mills, oil storage containers, gravel plants and ammunition factories instead of stately homes as we have in Paris, Rome, Vienna or Geneva. Then I learned that the bridges needed to be so high to let tall ships sail beneath and, as I later discovered in other towns in the UK, the industrial parts of the cities needed to be built along the rivers for easier transport.

I am walking towards town and will meet Amiten near the Millennium Bridge, the newest of the bridges and the prettiest. On Sundays we often walk over its raised arch toward the Baltic (a mill recently converted into an art museum) and stop in the middle watching the cormorants dry their wings in the sun. Now the water is dark with glitters of orange reflecting the evening sun. The tide is in. It is the time when the river flows in the wrong direction, back towards the hills. Isn't this mind-blowing? Rivers changing course four times a day?

Amiten works as a dishwasher in a department store and his shift ends at 7pm every night. He had painted more paintings in a small but airy studio close to home, but when he felt that it was too stressful for him to 'come out' as an artist (in the sense of networking and finding an art gallery in which to show his paintings), he decided to get a job – whatever would come his way. He remembered the dishwashing spree he had in Pune when we first met but working here is not as much fun.

When we meet at the bridge I turn around and we walk back to our small rented cottage. He is quite grumpy, feeling sweaty and sticky from work and does not say much. As I love him and know that he loves me, I do not take it personally. He is wearing his red neck warmer and has pulled it up high, even over his mouth. The winds love this valley where they can speed up and chill everyone in their way. I chat away, praising my ankle which has finally healed from the fall I had in Pune shortly before we left. I tell him that I have discovered a quicker route to drive to work – although still in the dark before our start at 7am – and that I have found a new dry cleaner now that my shopping habits have changed again since our office moved to a new location.

I am working in a call centre in Gateshead, supporting an IT application in English, Italian and French. I must admit that I had never thought that I would find a sitting-down job when coming back from Pune. Before I left, Vishva gave me a hypnosis session because I was so scared I would end up in the gutter once back in the West. If I wasn't in the gutter, I thought, I might be lucky enough to find a job in a corner shop selling cigarettes and magazines.

During lunch-break I am having a discussion with a Swedish colleague who intends to move to Barcelona. I say that her future knowledge of Catalan would not be a great asset on her CV because it is a language not spoken by many, just as my Swiss-German would not be either. Another colleague refutes this opinion by saying that on the internet she had just found that a call centre in Scotland was looking for someone who spoke Swiss-German. I tell Amiten about the incident and he simply replies, "I would not mind moving back to Scotland."

When Osho spoke the word 'sammasati' – Buddha's last word meaning 'right remembrance' – at the conclusion of a few discourses, we did not imagine that these were going to be also Osho's last words he would say to us.

Gautam Buddha's last words on the earth have to be remembered: sammasati. Sammasati means right remembrance. His whole life is condensed into a single word, remembrance, as if on dying, he is condensing all his teachings, all his scriptures into a single word. Nobody has uttered a more significant word when dying. His last message, his whole message: sammasati, remember. And when you remember, there is no way to throw your consciousness away.

Zen is not a meditation. Zen is exactly sammasati – remembrance of your ultimateness, remembrance of your immortality, remembrance of your divineness, of your sacredness. Remembering it, and rejoicing it, and dancing out of joy that you are rooted, so deeply rooted, in existence that there is no way for you to be worried, to be concerned.

Existence is within you and without you – it is one whole.

Osho, *The Zen Manifesto: Freedom From Oneself,* Ch. 4

I had heard him talk earlier on awareness:

Buddha uses the word 'mindfulness', sammasati, but he means the same, awareness.

Watch each act, watch each thought, watch each feeling. The awareness has to be three-dimensional: action, thought, feeling. This is our inner triangle, and if you can watch all the three you will find the centre. When you stand exactly in the middle of the triangle you have arrived.

Osho, *Don't Let Yourself Be Upset by the Sutra, rather Upset the Sutra Yourself,* Ch. 31

I had made awareness my constant meditation from the very start, while driving, eating, walking; in particular while washing the dishes – that was the easiest for me. But often I also forgot. I did, however, have the discipline to at least acknowledge the times I had forgotten.

These discourses were followed by quite a few months when Osho was unable to leave his room. For us, the days ended the same: with high-energy music and the 'Osho!'s, a video discourse, gibberish and let-go meditation. Looking back, there was hardly a difference between Osho being physically present in the hall and not; my meditation could go as deep as when he was present.

The only difference I remember is that I now had the opportunity to play in the discourses because many of the musicians were not interested in attending if Osho was not physically present. Nivedano was travelling up north in Rajasthan to find marble blocks for the waterfall he was building outside Osho's bedroom. I was allowed to use his percussion collection which gave me a big boost of confidence. I never went to the rehearsals but turned up for the sound check where, according to the style and pitch of the music, I spread out the most befitting instruments on my black velvet cloth in front of me. I learned to improvise, to go with the flow and to trust my hands.

This delight came to an end after a few weeks when I became ill. It felt like dengue fever (very high temperature with excruciating aches in the bones) and I reckoned that it would last a couple of days as it had each time I had come down with it before. But when after a week the fever was still there, my flatmate, Vishnu, urged me to go to the hospital. I didn't go because I was being well looked after by Kairava, a friend from Switzerland, who brought me food twice a day – swinging the tiffin over Nanu's wall – and who cooled my fever with wet towels over my feet as my mother used to do.

Finally after two weeks of fever I gave up and turned myself in. The hospital was just down the road in a brand new building. Although I was treated with quinine against malarial fever, the temperature did not subside as expected, and I was examined by a number of specialists, including a dentist and a gynaecologist. Nothing was found and the doctors had to admit that they did not know what was causing the fever.

A therapist friend thought this fever had something to do with my mother's death. Six months earlier this friend had come up to me in the garden at the very moment I had received a fax announcing my mother's death. I had told her that I had visited my mother just before coming to Pune, as I always used to do. Grandfather had died the previous year, also while I was abroad, and mother had just received her inheritance with which she had bought herself – among other desired objects like a Rolex watch, a leather coat and a trip to Paris – new book shelves in Palisander wood. They were already standing in her living room but in the wrong place. We pulled our sleeves back, piled the books on the floor, moved the heavy shelves and neatly stacked the books back in. It was lovely to do something active together, even if sweating, instead of just sitting on the sofa and talking. Mother had recently stopped smoking and complained that because of a sprained ankle she now had to wear 'old ladies' shoes'. She was sixty-seven and dreaded becoming old. When I left, she kept saying: "Only with you could I have had a day like this!" and gave me a red jacket as a token of my endeavours, adding: "You can use it where you are going; it is too light for me now that winter is coming."

My friend consoled me by making me aware that my mother must have died at the right time as she had fulfilled all her wishes and did not want to become an old lady anyway. That the fax had arrived too late for me to book a flight to get there in time for the funeral she dismissed with a: "Don't worry! As they say: Let the dead bury the dead…" So I had not really had the chance to mourn the death of my mother.

When the fevers had started, my thoughts went back to Mother. She had died from what seemed to be flu. I pinched one of my arms and said to myself: "Her body was only twenty-three years older than mine and this body of mine could decide to die now." During the periods of fever I felt high and enjoyed the buzz but when the heat finally subsided I was afraid to fall asleep in case I died during the night. Many times during meditation I had reached a space where, if death had knocked at my door and told me to go with her, I would have followed without fear, but now I was terrified. I felt bad and thought that my meditation had not grown much if I was so terrified of dying. Maybe the mourning of my mother's death did not happen through emotions and tears but through my body by getting sick. In hindsight, maybe it was also a mourning for Osho's body: we all knew he was not at all well.

I am sitting at my desk in Greenock entering orders for laptops and peripherals, checking their prices, and if these don't fit, writing e-mails or making calls to Germany or Switzerland to discuss the matter. The customers are companies who give IT support but also do the shopping for their clients and I know them all by name. Sometimes they ask me about the weather because they know that we work out of Scotland. Today I can report that it is a sunny day here as well and that, yes, the flock of sheep are grazing again on the hill in front of me. Earlier, when it was drizzling, we even had a very bright rainbow, so bright we wanted to leave our desks and dig for the treasure. From my seat I can also see, through the upper part of the glass partition, my two colleagues on the team: Daniela on the left and Sabine on the right. Although we are entering the orders of the same customers and share the work more or less equally, they have not spoken to me in months. When they need to communicate between each other to make arrangements to go for a smoke or a coffee break they use the messenger on their computers.

When IBM sold their laptop business to a company in China (from this very same computer I have now done three different jobs in less than three years) the move created a lot of disruption. I often made a big fuss if the new problems were not quickly dealt with by the management and tried to come forward with my ideas how to solve them – and this probably put the girls off.

Was I trying to be more pro-active than what was expected? Was I showing off? As sannyasins we had learned to go to the root of things and fix them ourselves, and not just wait for the team leaders to do it for us. We have learned to take responsibility for what is happening around us, in whatever hierachical position we find ourselves.

I felt isolated and considered asking for another job but, in meditation, I always got the message to keep hanging in there. Slowly, slowly I started to work in silence, concentrating on what I had to do, and could remain unconcerned about what was happening around me. One day while meditating I realised that I was now able to find that point deep in the belly – 'two inches below the navel' – of which Osho had spoken so often. I had been able to meditate and expand into far-reaching spaces, but never managed to go inside to that spot so clearly and neatly as I can do now.

I am closing my computer and locking up my desk. My little car which has been taking me around since the days in Newcastle is waiting almost alone in the huge car park. This shows clearly that this place, once a beehive of activity, is slowly shrinking. All my previous jobs have gone to the new East-European countries and I know it will not be long before this happens to my present job too. Instead of going straight home I take a detour and stop at the beach. It is a small beach and at this time there is hardly anyone around so I have it all to myself. In the distance I see the steep and jagged mountains of the Isle of Arran through the evening mist and hear the engine of a small yacht returning to the marina. The tide is too high right now for me to find the beautiful green shells I like, but I can check on the blackberries at the edge of the sand. I know each single bush – I even made jam out of the berries – and I call Amiten on my mobile phone to tell him that I am on my way home; he likes to know where I am when I use the car. So unlike the way I have been brought up, where it was not customary to keep each other informed about our whereabouts.

We live in Gourock on Victoria Road which runs on the hillside parallel to the main street along the water. The flat is twice the size of the one we had in Newcastle, but we are now well accustomed to the high ceilings and to the multitude of drawers and cupboards that can store practically all our belongings including Amiten's many paintings.

The best part of this flat is its view. We can see over the Clyde estuary which at this point is certainly five miles wide, the low hills on the other side of the water and, on a clear day, the rounded shapes of the Trossachs behind. In the beginning I had the feeling that I did not deserve so much beauty but then, after a visit to Purnam and Deva Dhyan in Germany where I was initiated into giving 'light circles' I learned that I was indeed worthy of beautiful gifts.

I can now say that I deserve all this, that 'I am worth it' as the ad says.

As soon as I was well enough to travel I flew back to Switzerland to again work for a few months. Mountain climbing was out of the question for a while and Passiko had to wait until my health caught up after being so depleted by the fever. This stay was not as smooth as it had been on other occasions. The jobs I found were not satisfactory and I had to leave Vedam and Majida's flat after a short while because the janitor had started following my footsteps despite the fact that I was entering via a route through the cellars. Paying guests were no longer allowed in the flats and we feared Vedam and Majida would lose their lease. We were as afraid of this Mr. Gross as if he were part of the KGB! This was not far from the truth: shortly afterwards it was made public that there was a file on every sannyasin who had lived in the commune in Höngg – as if we were criminals. And certainly Mr. Gross had been a great contributor with his information.

Within three months of my arrival, an old friend, Satlok, called up quite unexpectedly. He had returned from Pune to sort out some of his affairs and wanted to talk to me. The best place to meet was a vegetarian restaurant in Zurich, the famous 'Veggy'. After catching up on each others' lives, he said he had some important things to tell me. Satlok started by informing me that for the evening discourses everybody was now wearing white robes and that Osho had given a new name to the event: 'Meeting of the White Robe Brotherhood'. He told me that Osho would come to the hall to meditate in silence with us but then leave after the ten-minute meditation and that the discourses (and the let-go with the gibberish) were video tapes and no longer live.

And what a show it was when Osho entered and left the hall! He would move his arms in an up and down motion faster and faster, raising them high above his head and then suddenly stop. At that point the frantic music also stopped and everybody shouted "Osho!" He would stay in that position, unmoving, for what seemed like eternity. Everybody remained silent, with arms raised, looking at him, ready to detect the first movement of his hands, a signal for the drummer to start the music again. This interaction took so long that it exhausted both the audience and musicians but at the same time filled them with energy. What about Osho? Satlok had the impression that Osho was putting out all the life force he had left in his body – and urged me to go back immediately. According to him, Osho did not have long to live. I did not waver for a second and took his advice, applied for a visa, booked a ticket and within a week I was in Pune.

The music to accompany the play between Osho and his disciples was something I had never heard before: the low beats on the drums and the fast rhythms played on the *agogos*, *tambourims* and shakers reminded me of a samba, but it was backed by a layer of ethereal sounds from the keyboard and highlighted by vivid, almost crazy, melodies on flute or electric guitar. The speed of the rhythms slowly grew, like the engine of a Ferrari, climaxing in shouts of 'Osho!' And Osho was always the director of the timing. Then Osho sat down and we closed our eyes.

The meditation, after all that frantic activity, the shouts and the deafening music, took me very deep inside myself. I felt like I was falling into a dark tranquil hole from where it was difficult to come back. The meditation was loosely structured with three parts of wild music and three parts of silence. My favourite instrument was Amareesh's *bansuri*, the Indian bamboo flute, accompanied by *tamboura* and *tablas*. It took me a while to understand that Osho was also leading the timing of this meditation with movements of his hands, because my eyes were always closed.

To my regret I had not found my way into the troupe of musicians, but soon surrendered, thinking that maybe I had to experience the meditations from the audience's side, at least for some time. There should have been space for one of my little instruments in the whole mosquito buzz, I thought, behind Nivedano on the snare and Milarepa and Marco on the *surdos*; in fact, my African gourd had already found its place, but in someone else's hands. I made a few attempts to join but the message from friends in the band and from Nivedano himself was a clear "keep off." Maybe Nivedano was getting tired of teaching new people to achieve the subtleties he demanded. ("You should have been more assertive!" was all he told me later – and he had a point.)

During my stay in Switzerland, Osho had also introduced a new rule: maroon robes should be worn for all daytime activities in the commune. For the first few days I felt reluctant to follow this rule (hadn't I been wearing orange and red for twelve years already?) and walked around the commune in my panther patterned trousers and black top (because of the fever I had lost a lot of weight and my figure was good for once – so why should I hide it now?) It did not take long before I became aware of the harmony the new rule created in the meditation hall and on the paths: black buildings, white marble, green foliage and maroon people. The people were one collective, one mass, one yearning: that of learning how to meditate. I could also see how the men slowly got accustomed to the freedom which the robes gave to their legs and how their way of walking changed into a naturally elegant gait.

To facilitate the change from street clothes to maroon robes and then to the white robes in the evening, the commune had installed lockers (black!) which we could rent on a weekly basis. People always said that they felt 'stoned' when entering the 'Gateless Gate', as our main gate was called, and this was even before they had done their first meditation! And now for me, even after my very short stay in the West, it took a while to get accustomed again to the high energy in the commune. Just to remember where I had put the keys to my lockers required a lot of effort and after a few embarrassing incidents I hid a set of keys in my instrument bag which was easily accessible in the music room. Another test of groundedness was to be able to put together maroon robe with maroon shawl or, at night, white robe with white socks and white shawl!

I was given a job at the Welcome Centre and it was a delight to have Lani, my old roommate from the Alan Watts quadruplex, as my boss. They liked me there as I spoke a few languages – the Italians still had not started learning foreign languages, as they do now, and needed a hand with the registration. I checked passports, AIDS tests and gave them a short introduction to the voucher system, where to get food and where to find a hotel. The job was not tied to a desk nor to set shift times so I had ample time to steal off to play music in Buddha Hall and in painting and dance groups. And whenever I had an innovative idea and got the go-ahead from the main office, I could disappear from the Welcome Centre until it was done. One of these projects was to supervise the accounts for a new garden being made in a compound we had recently bought down the road. It was already housing group rooms and even a boutique. I had never experienced such a restless time, feeling like a butterfly, unable to remain more than half an hour in one place. It was beautiful that I was given the chance to live it out until it naturally eased off.

In the Depth of Meditation

Osho had recently been complaining that during the White Robe Meditations he heard disturbing noises from a certain direction. The following night a section of the hall was emptied to see if the noise came from electrical cables or other devices. During the meditation I was so keen to detect this sound that, through this intensive listening, my thoughts had vanished. It was the first time that I had fallen so deep into meditation.

Then on one of the following evenings it was announced that Osho was not going to join us but that he would meditate with us from his room. I could feel his presence as if he were right there sitting in front of us, his energy enveloping the whole hall. There was such an urgency to it that I felt I was meditating at the point of a sword – and this made me fall even deeper.

The following evening Amrito came with an announcement before the gathering. He was just holding himself together, reading from a piece of paper which was shaking wildly in his hands. Barely able to hold back his tears he came with the news which everybody dreaded, but which everybody knew would come sometime: Osho had left his body.

Amrito briefly described his last few moments with Osho:

"We asked him how we should celebrate his death and he said, 'You just take me to Buddha Hall for ten minutes and then take me off to the burning ghats.'

"He said that his *samadhi* will be in Chuang Tzu. [...] Let me just say to you that in death he was just as you would have expected: incredible! And when I started crying, he looked at me and said, 'No, no, that's not the way.' Then he looked into Jayesh's eyes and said, 'I leave you my dream.'

"So let's give our beloved master the send-off in death that is appropriate for someone who has lived his life as fully as any man ever has."

In the hall wailing sounds started in the back, people 'freaking out' and crying out loudly. I remembered Osho saying that we needed to 'freak in' and not 'freak out', so I sat motionless and dived deep into myself, letting the screaming and the music, which had picked up, take me even deeper into myself. Then Osho's body was brought in and the stretcher was laid on top of the podium. I asked myself what I was doing the moment Osho had left his body and I remembered that I was learning how to play the *agogo* in the back gardens with Tathagat, our Brazilian rhythm teacher. I was glad of that as music means so much to me. I suddenly jumped up and joined the musicians: I felt like expressing my gratitude and joy with music.

When the stretcher left the hall by one of the side doors the musicians grabbed drums and mallets and I reached for the tambourine and together with them I followed Osho's body out of the main gate. Many times before I had been in a procession down this road, shaking my shaker or swinging my tambourine for the death celebration of a sannyasin. But now it was for the farewell of my beloved master. While walking and playing behind the stretcher I could see Osho's head in his black cap studded with beautiful natural black and white pearls. His head was slightly moving from side to side with the rhythm of the steps of those carrying the stretcher and from time to time I could also see his cheeks. They were glowing with light. I could not believe that this was a dead body. His face was more filled with light than that of any one of those walking in front, on the side or behind him!

Down at the burning ghats on the riverbank the stretcher was laid across a shallow pit in the ground and logs of wood were carefully placed around and then on top of his body. One of Osho's brothers, according to Indian tradition, sprinkled ghee over the logs, then lit the fire. The ghee, together with the resin in the wood, produced a beautiful white cloud studded with tiny pieces of red amber which danced in the air. As the wood pile became smaller and smaller we played on our instruments and sang all the songs we knew, crying, laughing, dancing – feeling sad, exhilarated, joyful, in despair, silent and expressive, all at the same time. I took these feelings home and was quickly knocked out by a deep and relaxed sleep.

The previous week I had booked a group with Sagarpriya, totally out of the blue. I was not much of a 'groupie' and this was one of the few groups I had ever participated in. It was planned for the following morning. We gathered in one of the therapy rooms in Meera; it was a small room and there were only about a dozen participants. It was interesting to see that everybody who had booked was present; so disciplined had we become that not even the master's death could upset our commitments. But there was indeed no better place to be than right there: we were allowed to give in to our emotions and it was a relief to be able to cry for our loss, in a group and not alone in one's room. Part of me was almost relieved that Osho had left his body; it had become so painful to see him walk from the car to his seat on the podium. There was obviously a lot of pain in his body. This pain was now gone. He was free from his body, no more pain and restrictions. But it hurt to know that from now on I would not see his beautiful face and his radiant smile anymore. It also crossed my mind that now that he had left his physical form his presence was no longer tied to any location. He could be everywhere – he could even be inside me! It also meant that I was now on my own, that it was time to learn how to follow my own inner light: Osho must have been confident that the time was ripe and that I would be able to do that now. I had heard him say:

I am preparing my people to live joyously, ecstatically.
So when I am not in my body, it won't make any difference to them.
They will still live the same way – and maybe my death will bring them more intensity.
I will dissolve into my people.

Osho, The Goose is Out, Ch. 10

That evening, before the White Robe Meditation, Amrito stepped in front of the gathering again and with more sheets in hand told us in detail about the events of the last few days. I was touched to hear that Osho had given precise instructions about how his room was meant to be left – in a matter-of-fact way as if he were leaving for a weekend – to whom the stereo was to be given; and that the room should be re-marbled. Osho had mentioned again that the deterioration of his body was thanks to the "Christian fundamentalists in the United States government" and that he had kept his pain to himself, but "living in this body has become a hell."

"Never speak of me in the past tense," Osho had said. "My presence here will be many times greater without the burden of my tortured body. Remind my people that they will feel much more and they will know immediately."

Amrito then also said, "About nine months ago Osho formed The Inner Circle, a group of sannyasins now numbering twenty. Osho said he would have no successor. The Inner Circle would be his successor. The function of the Inner Circle is, in Osho's words, to reach unanimous decisions about the continued functioning and expansion of the commune and Osho's work."

The months which followed were, for me, as if someone had suddenly opened a box. It sometimes felt like a Pandora's box. A simple straightforward astrology session made me burst out into sweat (and it was still winter): my body started feeling hotter and hotter as I sat across from Kabir. His loving smile helped me relax into it and see that, although it might be uncomfortable at the moment, what was coming up was going to be a gift. The following week, during a past life event with Wadud, I was confronted with that part in me which we call 'the witch'. So many women had been punished by the Church in the past and ended up on the stake that it is understandable that the word 'witchy' had a dangerous connotation. To top it all and to move headlong into the scary abyss of all 'forbidden things', I booked Madhuri's three-week, aptly named 'Mouth of the Dragon' workshop after a friend, who had learned palmreading from her, had given me a captivating session. The training was intensive and had gathered many of my girlfriends (at least all the ones from France) under one roof. Some of the days even ended late at night with various colourful and surprising experiential sessions. On the last day we were given the opportunity to give a reading to a guest, a person we'd not met before. At first I was nervous but the moment I closed my eyes and bathed in the energy of the person in front of me I felt confident and comfortable, as if I was being held in their arms. Pictures came up which I described as well as I could; sometimes I asked if it all made sense. I do not remember who my first 'client' was, but I think that she was happy with my work. Anyway, I felt that I was now ready to go out into the world and have fun giving readings.

After the course we practised on each other on the benches in the gardens. The part I liked the most was that I would see how very different we were from each other; I learned that something may be valid for me, but still of no concern to another. With respect, I observed and described the various flavours I felt whilst in their presence. I could see the truth of what I was saying reflected in the expression on the other's face. It was definitely time to understand that judging another person was a matter of impossibility, but then... old habits die hard.

My days back in the world, or 'in the West' (as we used to say), began at my father's house where I innocently talked about the readings and the hands-on healing technique called Reiki that I had just learned. Father's wife Ambra, an Italian beauty just a couple of years older than me, was thrilled by the news of a 'white witch' in the family; but she was soon silenced by my father. On my next visit she told me that he did not want us to mention any of that 'stuff' anymore. This showed me clearly that what I had sensed as 'forbidden things' were not only forbidden in the past, during the Inquisition, in some 'past life', but that they were meant to remain unspoken in the present, and in my own family.

Instead of going straight into one of the office jobs as I used to do in the past, I wanted to see if one of my recently learned skills – playing percussion and giving psychic readings – would bring in enough income to survive.

Miasto, the Osho Centre in Tuscany, was staging a summer music festival. It was organised to attract as many visitors as possible from all over Italy and from abroad. The aim was to find people who would be interested in participating in an association which would buy the property from the previous owners (who wanted to sell it and move away) and keep the centre running. It was a very successful venture as the centre is still thriving to this day!

As a musician I was now earning my lodging and the delicious Tuscan food of the canteen. There were concerts in the open, Heart Dances on the lawn, live meditations, jugglers and mime. The musicians and artists were given a large meditation room as a dormitory space which was soon filled to the brim. In the afternoons I gave readings in the Psychic Tent and also in the woods, which added a shamanic feel.

Before leaving Pune, I had already been asked to give sessions in a Zen garden café at the seaside in Viareggio. Amongst tables and chairs, but under a tree, there was an aluminium pyramid and that was the perfect spot for the sessions. I was booked out every evening. It was interesting work and I was learning more and more about people. I was later told that some clients travelled to Pune after my sessions. Once all those in the neighbourhood who wanted a session of this kind had come, the bookings petered out and I understood that I had to move on.

I travelled to Munich having only a few pennies in my pocket but bags heavy with musical instruments. At the Tao Osho Meditation Centre I was granted lodging in exchange for a shift at the reception desk, and dinner in exchange for playing at the evening discourse. And to get my free meal at lunchtime I used to give out leaflets on the streets for a vegetarian restaurant. Music was my real interest and the reason why I was there. We had guest musicians who were making their names through their CD releases: musicians like Anugama, Karunesh, Sanjiva and Joshua. The centre also organised live satsangs and with Pratibha I even went to play in nearby Prague which was now reachable without a visa. My playing in supportive company and on a daily basis improved my skills and gave me the confidence to become more creative and adventurous. I also want to mention that the 'enlightened drum' which had been accompanying me everywhere was the one giving the beats for the gibberish meditation at the end of the videos.

I looked for indications to find in what direction my life should go. A life in a centre, and above all in Germany, was not really enriching my aura. One picture had come up in a reading from a channeller with whom I had traded a session: it was filled with mountains and lakes. When on my way to my temporary base at my father's house I stepped off the train, I became aware of the mountains and the deep blue lake glistening in the sun just below. Was this maybe the place for me to be? I had always associated Lugano with holidays and family visits and never thought of putting down roots there.

I first tried to find a job in a bank, as this small town was not likely to offer an opportunity to work in advertising but, to my astonishment, I found a job in my trade: I was going to supervise the production of catalogues for art galleries. The job brought me back into the midst of the art world with its gallery openings and offerings of glasses of white wine and finger-food that I remembered so well from my student years. Now, however, the artists who were avant-garde in my day were considered part of the classical world. I certainly had a lot of catching up to do.

The rhythmical suction noise of the printing presses on the run and the smell of ink in a dark hall had always created exhilarating impressions on my senses and now they were engulfing me again. The linotype machines with their clattering noise had been replaced by computers which produced texts on acetate directly, but the human mistakes and the proofreading symbols had remained the same, as was the frustration of those who had to correct them! I was amazed to see that the almost unbelievable, cutting-edge innovations I used to write about for the 'Il Poligrafico Italiano' twenty years before had indeed been implemented and even surpassed.

In addition, I was now learning to see books as a progression in time of right and left pages; and our long-haired graphic designer taught me how to appreciate the different qualities of printing paper. How to deal with very temperamental Italian artists and critics was a new lesson, but I was well acquainted with working to tight deadlines. We once published a multi-lingual catalogue within three weeks! But once the catalogue was printed I was always afraid to open the first copy. There was always a mistake in it – that appeared to be the rule of existence. I would just hope that it was a small one which no one else would notice.

One of the sannyasins who lived in Lugano, Berta (mother of Divyo and old friend Krishna), kindly left me her Nissan car while she was visiting Pune. This gave me the opportunity to book a series of lessons with a drummer who lived in a small village too difficult to reach by public transport. I was determined to learn how to play using drumsticks with both hands. As the lessons were just across the valley from my father's house I visited him every Wednesday, after the lesson, for a cup of tea with biscuits. This was our very private time, because his wife, Ambra, was giving a language lesson on that day. Father never expressed it but I think he liked these few hours together – at least the cups and the biscuits were always ready when I came.

Also on a Wednesday we had a video evening and the local sannyasins would come over to my place, all wearing white. I was renting a beautiful flat, costing way over my limit, but I wanted to have a living room big enough to meet in for meditation and big enough for Grandfather's colourful 'flying' carpet. The flat had its own little balcony for my lunch-breaks in the sun with a beautiful view of Mount Generoso – and it was just a few minutes walk to work. For the meditations I had specially bought a TV with a large screen and a video set, a cassette player for the meditation music and lots of coloured silk pillows to sit on. (I had a big collection of VHS tapes of Osho's discourses which I got together over the years. I used to order them individually the day after I had heard a discourse I particularly liked.) Our gathering usually ended with dinner: a quick wok dish in which I fried ingredients I had prepared earlier.

After two years of travelling back and forth between Lugano and Milan – to meet artists, typesetters and printers – it was time to pay a visit to Pune again. Even if it was going to be just for a short period of three months. Colleagues and friends tried to dissuade me from giving up my job, being scared about the recession which had started to hit Switzerland. Our region, Ticino, was the most vulnerable, they said. I decided to risk it, also because I was convinced that on my return I would have a job: I wanted to help Father, who was less convinced, to install a computer to make his accounting work faster and more efficient.

After a few weeks in Pune I had the intuition that I had to close my flat at home. I wrote to my father and asked him to send on my behalf a registered letter to my building society to cancel my lease. I had to give a full three months' notice. He could not understand why I should do that, "It is such a lovely flat." On my return, it happened that my father's faithful secretary had twisted her ankle and I had to take over her job. To work as an accountant and, on top of that, for my own father, was the last thing I would ever have imagined doing, but there I was. The computer project was not going to be followed through, though.

Soon the end of the three months' notice approached. Books, tapes, pictures, clothes and kitchen utensils, neatly packed in cardboard boxes, were sitting on the barren parquet floor, waiting to find their next destination. Maybe I was going to find a flat to share with another sannyasin? All the contacts I had made in this direction did not work out. I waited and trusted that some idea would pop up, hopefully sometime soon. One evening, out of the blue, I got a phone call from America. It was my musician friend, Navyo. He asked me if I could come and play percussion for his new CD. When did he need me? Was middle of next week soon enough? "Yes."

The boxes went into my father's cellar, nicely marked with a 'P' in red, and the mattress and grandfather's carpet, both wrapped in plastic, were stored in the spare garage. The next day Father took me – with my trusty red Samsonite – to the train station and we both waited on the windy platform for the train to arrive. He stared at the grey asphalt in his usual body posture: slightly bent over at the neck, proof of the many years he had spent at a desk stooped over papers. (He stood up straight only when he was being photographed and was told to by his wife.) Seeing him with that sad face made me angry. I was now almost fifty years old and I could certainly decide how to lead my life. Or was he concerned about me? He knew that I barely had five hundred dollars in my purse but he also knew that I had a return ticket!

Not Returning to Marin County

I felt welcome in Mill Valley, California. There was a room ready for me in a sannyasin house on the very top of one of the surrounding hills. With the room in California Avenue also came a station wagon. Bharti from Australia, with his bass and *dilruba*, and Gyandip, a drummer I had met in Munich, had also just arrived. The project we were working on had the working title: 'Circle of Light'. We met in Navyo's tiny bedroom which was used during the day as a music studio where we recorded the demo tracks straight onto his Korg keyboard. Between sessions we treated ourselves to tea and cake in the sun on the pedestrian square in front of the Depot Bookstore and Café (I had never seen a café that was also a bookstore…) or to a very strong cup of coffee at the Bonavita across the street.

Highlights were the weekly satsang meditations which were held on a Sunday morning, each time in a different house. Even after the project was finished, I drove Navyo with his keyboard and myself with my instrument bag to these sannyasin houses. Sometimes we even managed to reach an 'Osho!' climax with just his keyboard and my tambourine!

In San Francisco I bought myself a *kalimba* (it was in G). To take away the stress of learning how to play it in the 'proper way' I used to take it with me on my walks over the hills. I would let my thumbs play on it almost absentmindedly, just the fingers playing the rhythms. Sometimes this was the instrument we chose for the evening meditation before the video. The hills were covered in tall sunburnt grass and even before the Pacific Ocean came into view there was a salty taste in the air. It was now autumn and the sun shone warmly every day, a relief after the cold and misty summer caused by the fogs, like tongues, rushing inland at visible speeds.

Once the music project reached the stage where all the tracks were recorded and Navyo needed to contact the record companies, I was ready to look for a job.

A post as an archivist for a company manager became available so I took it. The job was to be done in her home. My desk on the lower ground floor had a wonderful view of the moored yachts and house-boats in Sausalito Bay and of a huge agave in her garden. Once I was through with all the boxes of office papers, I was going to tackle an abandoned box of photographs. It looked as if Linda's whole life since she was a child, through her first marriage and the birth of her son, and her present second marriage, was contained in that small plastic box with its red plastic lid. I came up with an idea: the photo album would be three dimensional, using Fabriano pastel paper as a base and colourful Japanese tissue paper between the pages. On the path in my garden I had admired the shape and colour of the dried eucalyptus leaves: they echoed the sepia photos of her many aunts. I made a few trials, she liked it and I got the commission.

I later collected more leaves and barks from various trees when I took three weeks off for a retreat in a Zen monastery. The idea for the retreat came when I noticed that I was totally besotted with everything Japanese. Below my office in Sausalito there was a sushi bar, something totally new for me coming from Europe. (This being California they even served vegetarian options.) My obsession was such that in that bar I spent all my money I had earned the previous day... And if I saw an object decorated with Japanese calligraphy my heart would jump, and I had to buy it. While talking to a friend about this craving, she suggested that it might not have so much to do with the desire to visit Japan as with the need to meditate.

Through friends I found the Sonoma Mountain Zen Center in Santa Rosa, not far from us. The temple was a beauty and it was not difficult to imagine I was in Japan. It was built entirely in redwood and it had a huge cast-iron bell at its entrance, just visible in the early morning light. This bell called out in different rhythms, one to wake us up, one to say that it was now time to walk to the temple; and the more urgent strokes were for the immediate start of the sitting.

Rupda, my new landlady in Mill Valley, had lent me a black jersey dress which I wore for the meditations. It matched the Zen robes all the others were wearing fairly well and the Japanese 'feel' was secured. We meditated with half-open eyes in front of a wall. As it was a tradition to meditate in the same place every day, it did not take me very long to learn by heart the vein patterns of the panel in front of me.

My little cabin was made entirely from recycled wood and I quickly became fond of it. After a few days I also got accustomed to the noises in the night. They were amplified in the cabin which acted as a resonant box. After dark the deer used to make themselves comfortable underneath the cabin where they chewed their food with big crunching noises, and squirrels used the roof to chase each other around with loud shrieks.

Before the morning meditation at 5am I did my Japanese bio-spark exercises. These slow stretches and breathing exercises helped me to not feel restless during the sitting, and in the afternoon I took a walk in the surrounding woods, followed by good old Kundalini before the night session. I stayed silent during the whole period, with a few exceptions, but did not take the retreat as seriously as I had in Lonavala. I looked around, enjoyed the trees in the woods – and collected more leaves for Linda's photo albums. On Sundays I had to meditate alone in the temple as everybody had a day off. This was strange. Osho had never taken a day off from giving his discourses just because it was Sunday!

Over one of the weekends there was a three-day retreat for which many people had arrived. The sittings were now also in mid-morning and in the afternoons. The dinners were served in the temple; I liked to eat slowly and with attention but could not stomach it when at the end of the meal we had to rinse out the bowl and then drink the water. It was also a good awareness training to sing the name of the masters during the invocation as they were so many and it was easy to get them mixed up despite the fact that we could read them from a sheet. The funny thing was that all masters were addressed with 'Osho', which meant 'respected master'. It was as if Osho had come into the temple by the back door.

After the first week of meditation, the pain in my right shoulder had subsided and I could really enjoy all the sitting sessions of the *seshin*. I also welcomed the moment when the abbot came behind me and hit me hard with his wooden Zen stick (the strength of the hit was agreed upon beforehand and then it was given on both shoulders). Unexpectedly I was asked to go for an interview with the abbess. She asked how I was doing with the sittings. I had started to feel that relaxation and alertness were pulling me in different directions, one upwards and the other downwards, and this tension was not yet familiar to me. She must have been happy with my comment as she sent me back to the temple with a big smile. When a cicada which had found its way into the temple and was singing along at high volume 'disturbed' one of our sessions, my meditation went deeper and deeper into an almost soundless space. Almost everybody else later complained about the poor cicada.

On the last day every participant had the chance to ask questions of the abbot or merely share what had happened to them since their last visit. From what they said, I was reminded of how lucky I was to have met Osho and to have done – and to be still doing – his active meditations. The people present had been sitting for fifteen years and still had a very hard time sitting silently. With frustrated looks they spoke of heat in their body and emotions disturbing their silence. I remember Osho saying that we are all sitting on a volcano.

The following day, on my regular morning walk, I fell into a space where there were no boundaries with nature, even thoughts were not available to think. It was as if the path, the bushes and the sunny sky were within me and I was within them. A bunny rabbit, when we suddenly met around the corner of the path, ran towards me rather than away. No separation at all. This feeling reminded me of the months after my first retreat in Lonavala. Then it had lasted for months; this time only a few days.

Returning from the retreat I found a new room in Larkfield with a sannyasin family and moved in with my few belongings. While queuing to pay for my first big shopping at the Mill Valley health food store – a big store, as big as a supermarket in Scotland – I met Aria from the house in California Ave. where I had first stayed. She asked me if I had received the message from my sisters. A fax had arrived saying that my father was going to die and that he had been given only another ten days to live. "What, already?" I shouted and, looking at the shopping which would have lasted for the coming week, just said, "Well, I will not need all this then."

A few months previously I had had an astrology session with Antar, memorable in the way that, instead of his pointing out the difficulties created by the many oppositions in my chart – which others usually did – he said: "These are great challenges. A lot of energy!" He then also added that – in the next few months – a big burden, jealousy, would drop once my father was gone. "Or when his influence on you is no longer so strong," he corrected himself when he saw the shock in my face at the mention of my father's death. My father had just turned seventy-five in May and we had celebrated his birthday in style, all his daughters attending. He looked healthy, had lost some weight on Ambra's insistence and the idea of his death was far away. And what jealousy had to do with my father was very curious indeed.

I immediately booked an air ticket and called my sister, Kätti. She told me that doctors thought metastases had reached his liver and that they were counting his days. I knew that what she was saying was true because while in isolation I had had excruciating pains in the liver, mainly while relaxing at night. It had been a mystery to me at the time because I was eating very healthy food. I packed my suitcase, watched by the little boy in the flat whose friendship I would have liked to explore. He asked me: "How is it you come one day and the next day you leave?"

At the hospital my father had probably been wondering if I would make it in time because the first thing he said, "Was just thinking if 'that one' has received the fax and now in she walks." His wife Ambra, his secretary Pia, and my sister Kätti were there. He looked quite perky from his pillow and I thought the doctors were wrong about the short prediction. He started talking about going mountaineering again.

Ambra told me that his energy had suddenly picked up but that he had been so poorly that the priest had already given him his last rites (together with the Catholic marriage sacrament now that my mother was dead).

On the next visit I brought him my Walkman with the few tapes of classical music I owned. He loved music and he was so pleased to listen to it that I wondered why nobody else had thought of it. Later I came with my travelling *tamboura*. The five notes played with their overtones helped relax not only my father but also those who came to visit him. Between visits I re-arranged my belongings so that they could be transported to my uncle and aunt in Rohr, who were willing to keep them again in their loft, and wrote for my visa to India. I knew that, before going back to California, I needed meditation and some sessions to overcome the loss of my father.

The business people with their phoney "Sir, when will we see you again?" had stopped visiting – it was now only family: his wife, my sisters, a cousin, and me. One night I stayed until dark and held his hand without speaking. It appeared as if he were giving all his life energy to me, all the healing love which he had always denied he and I had. When I left the hospital I ran to the train station to return to the place where I lived. The energy was so strong I would not have been able to walk – I had to run.

I had painstakingly arranged with the nurses that they would call me as soon as Father was passing away so that I could come to the hospital immediately, but that one morning I leisurely went to town to send away my visa application and organise my ticket for Pune, and so missed the call. The sun was shining brightly onto the lake and I was talking to Father, telling him how beautiful it was out here. I felt him very present and alive in me. But when I arrived at the hospital his room was already in the process of being cleaned out. He had died that morning while Ambra and her niece were with him. I blamed myself for not being present at his death the way I thought I had to be and it took me quite some time to understand that it was probably best that things had happened as they did.

During the funeral ceremony I had an unexpected experience: I felt as if my father's energy filled the little church like a big warm wave. I let it fill my body and I relished the sensation. But to my astonishment I saw, between tears, that the other members of my family were not aware of it. They sat crouched in sadness on the benches in front of me. I wished they knew how to partake of this glorious moment and realised that I must have learned from Osho how to let energy flow into me and to connect with people in other than merely physical ways! With gratitude I 'talked' to him lying in the shiny wooden coffin in front of the altar and felt that he was aware of the light in the church – and of his cold body.

His body was buried next to his brother's in front of the little church in the village where he had lived for the past twenty years. To see his name on the temporary tombstone in the same embossed capital black letters he forever had on his stationery was still frightening: they spoke of authority, of stability, of how things must be and should be done – or at least this is what I projected onto them. Suddenly it dawned on me that things had changed and I told myself almost aloud: "This man's body is now in the ground and he has no influence over me anymore. I am free!"

A few days later I went to visit the grave with my little step-sister, Lucia. I always had a soft spot for her. When she was only four she asked me why, although I was a grown up, I still needed a master. When I replied that Osho was my meditation master she asked me what meditation was, to which I replied: "When there are no thoughts in the head." Returning from a stroll up the hill behind Father's house, the winter sun setting behind the twin mountains we knew so well because of seeing them every day from our windows, we stood still and watched the huge red globe slowly disappear below the dark grey silhouettes of the hills. After it disappeared the little girl, holding my hand, said with a big smile: "I had no thoughts in my head when I was watching the sun – this must be meditation!" After dinner that winter evening, when we went to the graveyard, we both – independently – felt that Father was hovering above his grave like a pink cloud or twirl of energy. But when we returned the evening before my departure to India to say good-bye to him, we both knew he had moved on.

During one of the first video discourses I watched in Buddha Hall

I felt that same energy twirl above my head, but it was golden this time. I felt that it was my father and I started to 'talk' to him with words like: "This is Pune, the place I have been visiting all these years." "Aha, I understand now. Well done, OK." I had finally received the so-much-longed-for approval from him, approval for what was the most important part of my life – even if I had to wait for his death to get it!

I am looking down onto the Kelvin, craning over the broad sandstone balustrade of this stately bridge in the most beautiful park of Glasgow. The river is meandering through willow and yellow ash trees, jumping over rocks, forming grassy sandbanks in its bends and, this morning, carrying topsoil after the overnight rains. Fishermen, unemployed men in the prime of their lives, tell me that the trout and salmon are back. I believe them as I always see a heron when I walk upstream towards the botanical garden. From the bridge I just see a corner of the children's playground where I stopped earlier to watch the skaters and boarders practise their tricks on the graffitied concrete curves – no need to visit the circus: it is free entertainment each time. But the Kelvingrove Museum with its red sandstone turrets is hidden behind the trees. I could easily imagine I am somewhere in the country were it not for the noise of traffic in the distance. We are between the West End of Glasgow and the borough of Partick – where we have been living for the last year or so.

We have chosen to live in this part of town because of the park which I visit every day, not just to get fresh air and exercise which I so badly need, but because of the park itself. Even after a holiday in the countryside I have to come and visit the park as if to con-firm that I have come back home, as if home were in the middle of the river. I often walk through the park as if it belonged to me. In a way it does, because I love each single tree, but I am happy to share it with the students who gather in summer on the lawn with their stereos, the elderly cyclists in full attire on their healthy excursions, the dog owners playing with their dogs on the lawns and the chatty nursery girls pushing prams which accommodate three toddlers abreast. In the mornings I walk past office girls in high heels and colourful dresses, youngsters in dark office clothes, jacket and tie, and students with faces from all over the world – each encapsulated in their own world: the enveloping music from their iPods.

From the bushes on my right, I hear the call of a robin. Last spring, from this same place, I heard the song thrush. When I had stopped two Chinese students in their path to also listen to the astonishing variety of melodies (one of them apparently knew everything about birds because the other nudged her forward to answer my question), they were able to point out the bird to me. Well camouflaged with its specks in the thick of the bush, it confirmed with its song that it was indeed the song thrush.

Now on my left is one of the benches where I sometimes sit to read a book in the sunshine or to sketch the design of a new website. Here I made the plan for the remake of our website advertising Osho's meditations held in the UK. When Veena had started writing articles about news, people and places the website grew out of all proportion and had to have a major overhaul. That was within the first year. I work on it over the weekends to keep it up-to-date and interesting. This is now my sitting-down way of contributing to Osho's work.

My gaze goes back to the river and I lose myself following the moving reflection of the bright morning sky. The water caresses the roots of the deciduous trees whose leaves have been scorched by the recent frosty nights. I feel a little nip of cold moisture in the air. This river is reflecting my life, I ponder, happily meandering along, bubbling with excitement at small encounters with rocks and branches of fallen trees. Then it suddenly drops over a weir – once built for one of the many mills along the Kelvin – and finally, just a mile down, disappears into the Clyde. The end of an identity while it merges with a bigger river; but after a few miles also the Clyde will need to disappear: into the salty waters of the Atlantic.

The full sound of the bells in the University tower striking the hour bring me back to my bodily presence, time of day and place in space: it is time to go back and finish writing this last chapter.

Painting came into my life the moment Linda's photographs arrived in Pune by DHL, packed in a huge box. She wanted me to finish her photo albums and she thought that it did not matter if they were made in California or in India. I could return the finished products by courier and bill her by the hour the way I had done before. As Fabriano papers were out of reach in India, I had to decorate and paint colourful backgrounds onto the hand-made papers that I got straight from the factory. Inks, acrylics and tempera bottles, brushes, rulers and knives soon scattered my bedroom/studio floor.

Peter Mandel had been coming to the commune for a few years after being personally invited by Osho to teach us his revolutionary coloured light therapy. He had evolved his techniques together with sannyasins who offered training courses in the commune. I was going to be a 'trial client' for one of the trainees who turned out to be a young, intelligent girl from Germany. She used to write her notes in a tiny curly handwriting, as curly as her short black hair. Before the start of the two- or three-month process I had to sign a form vowing that I would be doing Dynamic and Kundalini every day.

The treatment series ended for me in a rather unpleasant way when one of the course leaders, Devageet, told me in his undip-lomatic manner (which is worse than mine) that I was not ready for the final session. The positive side of it was that I was going to receive a private session from Sarita, my old Twinkie friend and colleague from the Press Office, who was now part of the team of teachers. With her torch she swept the side of my torso and asked me if some insights were coming up. All I could say was: "Paint the leaves."

During this heavy-duty Transmitter Relay Programme I had also done a course given by the Chinese calligraphy master, Qui Zheng Ping, the one who illustrated Osho's last book of discourses: *The Zen Manifesto*. He had been invited to come to the commune by Osho himself and the book had been illustrated by him at Osho's specific request. I learned from Mr. Qui how to hold the brush and how to rotate the wrist while painting the characters. He gave us many demonstrations through which emerged not only his skill but also a raw energy. I became more and more aware of the energy behind the strokes rather than the harmony and the beauty of the painting alone. During this course I researched, for the benefit of the whole training class, the audio tape where Osho explained at length the meaning of calligraphy in old China. I was astonished to see that the discourse was from 1974 but that I still remembered it word for word even after twenty years – it must have been a subject close to my heart already back then! And this is how I met Amiten again, the hygiene technician who made Latifa and me sweat when we worked in the kitchen. I liked the way he kept the research room light and tidy and the very down-to-earth way in which he explained how to copy the discourse from the master tape.

I also participated in one of Meera's classes. We all knew her art from the jackets of Osho's books and from the many paintings hanging around in the commune. (Some I salvaged when I found them abandoned, without frame or glass, in storage cupboards. She was happy about this.) I had also played drums in many of her workshops as she liked to use movement and dance with painting. A speciality of hers was that from the beginning of the course to the end, which could be more than a month, we had to paint on the same piece of paper. We could observe life emerging and death taking it away again. Very often we regretted painting over something we thought looked great, but this was the rule. I learned many techniques with acrylic paint which she shared with us, and learned also to have courage in just 'going-for-it!' and 'going-with-the-flow', which created many coloured puddles on the floor.

To 'paint the leaves' started when Upadhi, an old friend from Magdalena Cafeteria, asked me if I wanted to use her flat while she was gone to Italy over the summer. It had a bedroom, living-room-kitchen and bathroom. I could even use her stereo. And it had a small private garden! Before my move, I cleaned out some books which I returned to our free library. This was a steel cupboard on the first floor in Mirdad. When I walked past the research library I felt a cord in my belly reaching into that room and this sentence rang in my ears: 'go and give him a hug in there'. So I did. Amiten was taken aback and I felt stupid, but the hug felt beautiful and fulfilling.

The garden was tiny but full of interesting plants. I knew by name the banana plant, which was stealing the show; then there were various kinds of hibiscuses, some with small red curled-up flowers and some with flowers as big as a plate. One had to catch them (and paint them) the same day, as the flowers were sadly gone by the evening. There were also roses and a pomegranate bush, but there were many others which I could not name. They were all waiting to be painted.

I had the impression that the moment I walked onto the porch in the morning they called for my attention. Not all at the same time, but individually on various days. Perhaps this coincided with their prime time in that season? So it happened that I started my day walking through the tiny garden asking who wanted to be painted. That plant would then be the background for the next page of the photo album. It reminded me of the story Nivedano told me when he went to Rajasthan to collect marble blocks to build the fountain outside Osho's *samadhi*. He had to buy more stones than were actually needed, just because "so many stones wanted to come."

On the walls in my living room/studio I pinned up one of Master Qui's calligraphies and a signature of Osho against which I could judge if my paintings were of any worth: to see if they had the strength of a calligrapher or just that of a painter. When Alok, who was now the translator in the classes, met Master Qui in China and showed him a signature of Osho, he had apparently exclaimed "But this is a great calligrapher." The two great calligraphers were now the judges of my paintings!

I was happy to live like an artist. It was a dream I had had for so long and it had finally come true, all by itself. I had my own space, I was doing something I loved doing and I was free to plan the day the way I wanted. At night, I used to go to the White Robe Meditation in the commune but did not feel too guilty if I skipped it for one reason or another. In that case, I would cook a vegetable soup with ginger or go to Prem's Restaurant, which was just around the corner. On one of those nights, Prem's was full to the brim and my only option was to share a table with Amiten. He had finished his dinner but stayed on until I was finished with mine. With no frills and with the elegance of a 'Geordie' he asked me if I wanted to spend the night with him. He must have remembered the hug in the research library, I thought. However, when I wanted to postpone this very rushed date he just said: "If it is not tonight then it will never happen." We stopped at my little garden flat to switch off the lights, but did not get much further than that. From that night on he became part of the garden flat and of all the flats and houses I have lived in since.

While I was painting on the porch, which was just big enough for myself and a sheet of handmade paper, someone shouted from a window across the garden. I recognised him – Nandano from Japan. He was also a musician and I had heard him practising on his guitar. I invited him over for a cup of tea with biscuits and he said he would come immediately. He asked me about Osho, and I started telling him anecdotes of my life in the communes. There were quite a few and the next time he came over he brought along his housemate. When they left I thought that I should write down all these lovely stories. So blame it all on Nandano and his friend – but if you have read until here you must have enjoyed them as well.

Thank you, Osho.

Acknowledgments

My thanks go to Pat Mosel and Audrey Jenkinson who read my first drafts. Their comments and questions helped me describe things in such a way that those not acquainted with the world of Osho could understand and follow my story. Audrey (who later became Ikkyu) insisted I should expand the section where I talk about my past as a child and young woman in order to give a better picture of where I come from.

Thanks to Bhagawati who suggested I re-write the first three chapters which had been drafted years before. It was a blessing to look again at those events with new eyes and new understanding. Thanks to Roshani for correcting and completing many details about the Ranch in Oregon, a very big thank you to Veena who has painstakingly gone through the manuscript with a tight comb for style, grammar and spelling, and to Madhuri and Kaiyum who deftly administered the final manicure.

A lot of encouragement to keep working on the book came from Veena, from Bhagawati and from Amiten, my partner of 20 years, who has been supporting me with this, as with many other crazy projects. And were it not for Osho, the life story of this ordinary girl would not have been inspiring enough to write about.

Yoga Punya

Biography of Osho

OSHO

Never born
Never died
Only visited this
Planet Earth between

Dec 11, 1931 – Jan 19, 1990

Osho was born Rajneesh Chandra Mohan on 11th December 1931 in Kuchwada, a small village in Madhya Pradesh, India. He became enlightened at age 21, studied Philosophy and became a lecturer and professor at Jabalpur University. Osho began speaking in public in 1958 and for years travelled throughout India until he settled in Mumbai in 1970 when he started initiating seekers into 'neo-sannyas' and adopted the name Bhagwan Shree Rajneesh.

His teachings and meditation techniques attracted more and more seekers from the West and his move to Pune gave the spark to a large international commune which offered meditations, therapy workshops and work-as-meditation. Osho moved to the USA in 1981, where his commune became a thriving town in the Oregon desert.

In 1985 Osho was unlawfully arrested and expelled from the USA. In order to find another suitable place to gather seekers around him he travelled for months being denied entry to various countries, until, in early 1987, Osho returned to Pune. He died on 19th January 1990 shortly after adopting his new name 'Osho'. The cause of his ill health was that he'd been poisoned by the authorities during his stay in an American jail. The commune in Pune, now called Osho International Meditation Resort, continues to attract visitors as do many of the Osho Meditation Centres all over the globe.

One of Osho's greatest contributions are his Active Meditations which he devised specifically for the modern (busy-minded) man. His discourses and individual interviews, transcribed in over 650 volumes and translated into 55 languages, are a source of inspiration and help in understanding our day-to-day lives. He called his vision of bridging materialism and spirituality with meditation 'Zorba the Buddha'. Osho is generally considered to be one of the most controversial spiritual leaders of this age and the greatest spiritual master since Buddha.

Biography of Punya

Punya spent her formative years in Italy and Switzerland and met the Indian mystic Osho (then known as Bhagwan Shree Rajneesh) in 1974. She lived for many years in his communes – Pune, India; Oregon, USA; and then again in Pune.

Punya was also involved in Osho's meditation centres in Milan, Geneva, Zurich, and Edinburgh. Her work 'in the world' has mostly involved design, publishing, languages (she speaks four) and advertising.

She now runs the successful online magazine Osho News and lives on the island of Corfu, Greece.

Made in the USA
Middletown, DE
22 July 2021